BULLETPROOF

BULLETPROOF

AFTERLIVES OF ANTICOLONIAL PROPHECY IN
SOUTH AFRICA AND BEYOND

JENNIFER WENZEL

THE UNIVERSITY OF CHICAGO PRESS • CHICAGO AND LONDON

JENNIFER WENZEL is associate professor of English at the University of Michigan.

The University of Chicago Press, Chicago 60637
The University of Chicago Press, Ltd., London
University of KwaZulu-Natal Press
© 2009 by The University of Chicago
All rights reserved. Published 2009
Printed in the United States of America
18 17 16 15 14 13 12 11 10 09   1 2 3 4 5

ISBN-13: 978-0-226-89347-1 (cloth)
ISBN-13: 978-0-226-89348-8 (paper)
ISBN-10: 0-226-89347-2 (cloth)
ISBN-10: 0-226-89348-0 (paper)

Library of Congress Cataloging-in-Publication Data

Wenzel, Jennifer.
  Bulletproof : afterlives of anticolonial prophecy in South Africa and
beyond / Jennifer Wenzel.
     p. cm.
  Includes bibliographical references and index.
  ISBN-13: 978-0-226-89347-1 (cloth : alk. paper)
  ISBN-13: 978-0-226-89348-8 (pbk. : alk. paper)
  ISBN-10: 0-226-89347-2 (cloth : alk. paper)
  ISBN-10: 0-226-89348-0 (pbk. : alk. paper)
  1. South Africa—History—Xhosa Cattle-Killing, 1856-1857. 2. South Africa—Politics and govern-ment—1836-1909. 3. South Africa—Politics and government—20th century. I. Title.
  DT1863.W46 2009
  968.04′5—dc22
                                    2009003740

CONTENTS

ILLUSTRATIONS

ACKNOWLEDGMENTS

This book has enjoyed the support of numerous friends, colleagues, and institutions. I gratefully acknowledge permission to include here previously published material: "Refashioning Sub-national Pasts for Post-national Futures: The Xhosa Cattle Killing in Recent South African Literature," *History, Nationalism, and the (Re)Construction of Nations*, edited by Susana Carvalho and Francois Gemenne (Palgrave, 2008); "The Problem of Metaphor: Tropic Logic in Cattle-Killing Prophecies and Their Afterlives," *African Studies* 67, no. 2 (2008): 143–58; "Voices of Textual and Spectral Ancestors: Reading Tiyo Soga alongside H. I. E. Dhlomo's *The Girl Who Killed to Save*," *Research in African Literatures* 36, no. 1 (2005): 51–73 (with the permission of Indiana University Press). I wish to thank Jane Alexander and the South African National Gallery, David Goldblatt and Michael Stevenson, Elsabe van Tonder, and the University of Cape Town Libraries for permission to use their art and photographs. Special thanks are due to Reverend Bongani Ntisana for permission to use material from the Lovedale Press Collection.

I could not have written *Bulletproof* without the financial support of an American Council of Learned Societies (ACLS) yearlong fellowship, a National Endowment for the Humanities (NEH) summer stipend, a summer grant from Stonehill College, and a yearlong fellowship at Princeton University's Shelby Cullom Davis Center for Historical Studies. Moreover, Katie Conboy and Barbara Estrin at Stonehill College were instrumental in making the ACLS and NEH grants possible; Gyan Prakash and Jennifer Houle at Princeton's Davis Center ensured that my time there was productive—and enjoyable—beyond all imagining. Support from the Davis Center, as well as the University of Michigan's Office of the Vice President for Research and Humanities Block Funding Initiative, facilitated research trips to London and South Africa. Jane Johnson and Donna Johnston at the University of Michigan smoothed the logistical details of leaves and research trips. Numerous librarians assisted with archival materials, among them Regina Egan at Stonehill College; Lesley Hart and Andre Landman at the University of Cape Town; Ebrahim Kenny at the Western Cape Archives; Shirley Stewart, V. V. Gacula, and the irrepressible and irreplaceable Zweli Vena at the Cory Library at Rhodes University in Grahamstown; and the accommodating and patient staff at the British Film Institute's National Archive.

Opportunities to present this material to several audiences have been indispensable to making the book what it is. First among these was Tim Brennan's suggestion that I focus on questions of nostalgia for a Modern Language Association panel, "Who Needs the Third World," which spurred the thinking on time, memory, and anticolonialism that became central to *Bulletproof.* Carol Daeley's invitation to participate in the Austin College Symposium on Southern Africa allowed me to visit old friends (including the late Jim Knowlton) and to make new ones, among them Laura Mitchell and Zolani Ngwane. Additional talks at Boston University, Syracuse University, Princeton University's African Studies Seminar, the New School for Social Research, and the Wits Institute for Social and Economic Research at the University of the Witwatersrand (with an invitation from Sarah Nuttall, Rita Barnard, and Mark Sanders) helped me to think through my ideas about afterlives. Thanks to the hospitality of Tobin and Jill Siebers in Ann Arbor, I shared this work in lively conversation with David Halperin, Susan Najita, Ziv Neeman, Maria Sanchez, Xiomara Santamarina, Sarita See, Viv Soni, and Andrea Zemgulys.

The manuscript benefited from the incisive comments of many generous readers, including Michigan colleagues Sara Blair, Patsy Yaeger, Ifeoma Nwankwo, David Porter, and Elisha Renne, who read early drafts in their entirety, and the anonymous readers for Duke University Press and the

University of Chicago Press. A summer writing group with Cathy Sanok and Meg Sweeney inspired and guided my revisions. Help with individual chapters came from Sandra Gunning, Christi Merrill, Josh Miller, and John Whittier-Ferguson at Michigan, as well as David Alvarez, Sheila Boniface Davies, Joanna Brooks, John Comaroff, Jeff Peires, and Dave Petrak. In addition, conversations with colleagues have been instructive in more ways than I can describe or even remember: at Michigan, this work has particularly benefited from the wisdom of Lorna Goodison, Danny Herwitz, Arlene Keizer, Anita Norich, Scotti Parrish, and Adela Pinch. While at Princeton, I was fortunate to share the intellectual company of Helen Tilley, Dave Anderson, Ben Baer, Laurie Benton, Emmanuel Kreike, Ishita Pande, Jackie Stewart, Kamala Visweswaran, and most especially my comrades Susanna Hecht and Elen Deming. Adam Ashforth, Ian Gabriel, Simon Gikandi, Isabel Hofmeyr, and Terence Ranger have helped me to see my work in new ways; I am particularly indebted to Rita Barnard and Crystal Bartolovich for their generosity at crucial moments. Graduate students in two seminars—Meg Ahern, Nasia Anam, Sayan Bhattacharya, Suphak Chawla, Mandy Davis, Roxana Galusca, Tiana Kahakauwila, Chung-ho Ku, Joanie Lipson, Navaneetha Mokkil-Maruthur, Preeta Samarasan, and Corine Tachtiris—as well as Pavitra Sundar, Manan Desai, Laura Murphy, and Andrew Offenburger—have been inspiring interlocutors.

For their invaluable guidance through the treacherous waters of publishing a first book, I cannot thank enough Sara Blair, Jonathan Freedman, Gaurav Desai, Simon Gikandi, Sandra Gunning, Yopie Prins, Sid Smith, Helen Tartar, and Patsy Yaeger. David Brent at the University of Chicago Press understood from the beginning what I was trying to do and stuck with the project to this happy end. Laura Avey's steady hand has made the production process nearly painless; likewise with Maia Rigas and copyediting. Clifton Crais, Miki Flockemann, Barbara Mather, and Tim Stapleton provided timely assistance with photographs, and Karl Longstreth introduced me to the world of mapmaking.

I owe deep gratitude to Barbara Harlow, Ben Lindfors, and Mia Carter, as well as Carol Daeley, Peter Lucchesi, and Bill Moore—all of whom recognized and helped to shape the scholar in their student. Christi Merrill, Alisse Portnoy, Meg Sweeney, and Andrea Zemgulys have laughed with me through the absurdities of this process. I am awed by the unflagging support of my parents, Karen and Richard Wenzel, as well as of others I am so lucky to call my family—Amy Boling, Amy Slaughter, Kathleen

McKenzie and David Laffitte, Bill and Jeanie Slaughter, Von and George Simon, Louise Bell, and my grandfather, Bernard Petrak, whose persistent questions about when I would finish my book motivated me more than he will ever know. This book is for him.

Finally, Joey Slaughter knew before I did that my tangle of ideas was a book; he knew when to tell me that it wasn't good enough and when to assure me that it was. He has, at every step, paved my way; although this road has been longer and harder than we could have imagined, I wish no other life more than to travel it with him.

A NOTE ON TERMINOLOGY

My central focus in *Bulletproof* is on the Xhosa people, who for centuries have inhabited the eastern Cape of southern Africa, now demarcated as the Eastern Cape province of the Republic of South Africa. In referring to different aspects of Xhosa society, I borrow basic elements of the prefix system in the Xhosa language: the Xhosa language is referred to as *isi-Xhosa*, the Xhosa people collectively are *amaXhosa*, and Xhosa territory is *kwaXhosa*.

My concern is to examine how the Xhosa past has been revived over the past 150 years, and my use of sources ranging from the early nineteenth century to the present reflects sometimes confusing shifts in orthography and terminology. I have chosen to retain the terminology and spelling used in these sources, while using currently accepted forms in my own sentences. Thus the young woman prophet Nongqawuse is sometimes referred to as Nongqause or Nonqause; her father Mhlakaza is referred to as Umlakasa; the Gcaleka Xhosa chief Sarhili as Kreli or Krili; the warrior-prophet Nxele as Lynx or Makana; and the prophet Mlanjeni as Umlangeni. The Tyhume River and the mission station named for it may appear as Chumie. Nineteenth-century colonial discourse referred to black inhabitants of southern Africa, and specifically the amaXhosa, as Kaffirs (from the Arabic for infidel): thus the western part of kwaXhosa, adjacent to the Cape Colony, was demarcated as British Kaffraria. *Kaffir* is now regarded as a term of abuse. It appears in my study only in citations from nineteenth-century documents.

INTRODUCTION

Each generation must discover its mission, fulfill it or betray it, in relative opacity. In the underdeveloped countries preceding generations have simultaneously resisted the insidious agenda of colonialism and paved the way for the emergence of the current struggles. Now that we are in the heat of combat, we must shed the habit of decrying the efforts of our forefathers or feigning incomprehension at their silence or passiveness. They fought as best they could with the weapons they possessed at the time, and if their struggle did not reverberate throughout the international arena, the reason should be attributed not so much to a lack of heroism but to a fundamentally different international situation. More than one colonized subject had to say, "We've had enough," more than one tribe had to rebel, more than one peasant revolt had to be quelled, more than one demonstration to be repressed, for us today to stand firm, certain of our victory. For us who are determined to break the back of colonialism, our historic mission is to authorize every revolt, every desperate act, every attack aborted or drowned in blood.

FRANTZ FANON, *THE WRETCHED OF THE EARTH*

Our country is in that period of time which the seTswana-speaking people of Southern Africa graphically describe as "mahube a naka tsa kgomo"—the dawning of the dawn, when only the tips of the horn of the cattle can be seen etched against the morning sky.

THABO MBEKI, SPEECH AT HIS INAUGURATION AS PRESIDENT OF SOUTH AFRICA, 1999[1]

I did not begin with the desire to speak with the dead. I began with what seemed a remarkable coincidence: the nineteenth-century emergence of anticolonial millenarian movements in Asia, Africa, and the Americas, in which indigenous peoples on colonial frontiers responded to the alienation of land and vital resources. They heard, and heeded, a prophet's vision of a new era: the dead shall rise, the bounty of the land will return, and invaders and unbelievers will be swept away when the people purify their tradition and undertake new ritual practice. Such practices will protect them until the new order is established, for the invaders' guns will shoot only hot water. The people will become bulletproof.

My initial curiosity about such movements—why and how does the image of bullets turned to water emerge around the globe?—has led to a broader concern with their afterlives, the uses to which these movements are put after their spectacular, seeming failures. How do apocalyptic visions survive an apocalypse to evoke future transformation? In other words, how do such visions *become* "bulletproof"—surviving their apparent failures to become repositories of aspirations for later movements? What are the mechanisms of iteration, accumulation, or momentum in the "more than one" anticolonial impulse Frantz Fanon sees as necessary for victory? Emphasizing previous generations' efforts, Fanon traces continuities and acknowledges differences between primary resistance to conquest and twentieth-century anticolonial nationalism. We must ask similar questions about the legacy of those decolonization movements now, in a postcolonial, post–cold war, post-9/11 moment. What do the answers to these questions tell us about the world today, in an era of resurgent imperialism?

Bulletproof traces the afterlives of anticolonial millenarian movements—movements driven by collective expectations for imminent, total transformations of the world to be accomplished (at least in part) by supernatural means[2]—as they are revived and revised in later nationalist struggles. Retrospective invocations of past insurgencies call our attention to how understandings of nationalism and the nation vary across time and space. I examine the role of literary and other cultural production in these fractured histories of resistance: how does aesthetic experience offer a site of connection between past and present, dead and living? How can the dynamics of prophecy help us to understand literary questions of authorship, intertextuality, and reception? In colonial contexts, millennial visions promised to restore life as it was (imagined to be) before the conquest, albeit through unprecedented, innovative means. Such visions are not merely anticolonial but also *acolonial*—impossibly, simultaneously, pre- and postcolonial. This radical temporality pushes cultural representations of these visions beyond the formal constraints of linear narrative: recuperations of millenarian movements measure contemporary oppression against their visions of liberation. Afterlives are about unfinished business, incomplete projects, and the ways in which quelled revolts and failed resistance in the past can inspire—and constrain—movements for justice in the present. My study of the afterlives of millenarian movements engages broader questions of time, narrative, and nation: how the past is put to use in the present, the complex temporalities and narrative strategies of such appropriations, and their role in various modes of nationalist (and postnationalist) imagining.

The Xhosa cattle killing in the eastern Cape of southern Africa (1856–57) serves as my central example. The prophecies that drove this movement demanded that the Xhosa people, whose livelihood and identity were bound up with cattle, should kill their cattle and destroy their grain in order to catalyze the return of ancestors and cattle, the renovation of the world, and the expulsion of European invaders. The immediate failure of cattle-killing prophecies meant the beginning of the end of the Xhosa nation. A few decades after the cattle killing, the eastern Cape became the cradle of a black nationalism that imagined a multiethnic South African polity. In tracing the cattle killing's role in successive incarnations of nationalist resistance to colonial domination (and within that domination), I tease out a seeming paradox: how does *Xhosa* prophecy enter a *South African*—and indeed *global*—imaginary? I am interested not only in the spectacular failure of the cattle killing's aftermath but also in its prophetic vision, which was always already global, its transnational anti-imperialist solidarity imagining a "black race" united against British incursions in Africa, as well as in the Crimea, India, and China. The global thinking at work in cattle-killing prophecies charts an imaginary, even magical map in which black becomes the color of resistance to empire.

Bulletproof excavates the role of the Xhosa cattle killing and its afterlives in imagining national communities and transnational networks of affiliation, but I must emphasize that this example is one among many. One could undertake similar projects for other prophet-led movements, including the Taiping Rebellion in China (1843–64), the Pai Marire movement in New Zealand (1862–72), the Ghost Dance movement in North America (1870 and 1888–96), the Birsa Munda uprising in India (1895–1900), the (first) Chimurenga among the Shona and Ndebele in Rhodesia/Zimbabwe

(1896–97), the Canudos movement led by Antonio Conselheiro in Brazil (1896–97), the Maji-Maji Rebellion against German colonial rule in Tanganyika (1905–7), the series of movements associated with Simon Kimbangu in the Belgian Congo (1921–60), and many others.[3] While differing in many respects, all these movements featured charismatic, messianic leaders whose messages were either Christian-missionary inspired (Hong Xiuquan of the Taiping Rebellion, Te Ua Haumene of Pai Marire, Birsa Munda, and Simon Kimbangu) or conveyed to them from spirits (Wovoka of the Ghost Dance, Nehanda of the Chimurenga, and Bokero of Maji-Maji). The Christian-inspired prophets experienced dreams or visions that led them to turn away from mission orthodoxy; they proclaimed themselves (or were taken to be) brothers or envoys to Jesus as they inserted their people's history into the Christian story. Both Christian and indigenous millenarian prophets understood natural disasters like drought, crop blight, and epidemic disease as signs of impending apocalypse (Antonio Conselheiro), catalyzed by the presence of European invaders (Mlimo of the Chimurenga). They urged social and spiritual reform and promised to relieve economic suffering caused by taxation, forced cultivation, or loss of access to land or forests. Followers flocked to leaders like Birsa Munda and Kimbangu as their reputation as healers spread. Such leaders inspired their followers to defy the military force of European colonial armies or of the state (Taiping, Canudos)—most of them making bulletproof claims. Even after imprisonment or death, their visions continued to inspire followers with visions of an autonomous future in a renovated world: twentieth-century nationalists and revolutionaries from China to the Congo invoked the memory and claimed the mantle of their struggles. Millenarian rebellions continue into the present: the Lord's Resistance Army has fought in northern Uganda for more than two decades, and Muqtada al-Sadr's Mahdi army is a force to be reckoned with in Baghdad.[4]

Not only were anticolonial millenarian movements a global phenomenon in the nineteenth century, but, like the Xhosa cattle killing, some of them made explicit connections to movements and histories elsewhere, and they sometimes posed near-simultaneous challenges to British imperial administration. The immediate aftermath of the Xhosa cattle killing overlapped with the Sepoy Rebellion in India, and Sir George Grey, governor of the British Cape Colony in the late 1850s, soon faced (and perhaps provoked) another anticolonial prophet-led movement (Pai Marire and its militant sect, Hauhau) after he began his second gubernatorial stint in New Zealand in 1861. These transnational imbrications merit further study, as part of an effort to deprovincialize postcolonial studies: critiques of anticolonial nationalism as a derivative discourse, or postcolonial studies as Eurocentric, are necessary but insufficient. What remains to be done is to remap anti-imperialism in order to take account of connections among colonized peoples, rather than merely tracing unidirectional lines of influence between Europe and its colonies. In order to suggest the global reach and explanatory power of afterlives, I draw on other examples before returning to the Xhosa cattle killing.

RETHINKING FAILURE

In considering the afterlives of anticolonial millenarian movements, I aim beyond conventional tropes of individual literary immortality and beyond "the desire to speak with the dead" that imagines literary experience as a kind of necromancy in which texts allow readers to commune, if not communicate, with the past.[5] I examine literary and cultural texts as sites where unrealized visions of anticolonial projects continue to assert their power. *Bulletproof* aims not to revive dead voices but to trace continuing resonances of failed social movements and the dreams that drove them. I use *afterlife* in a worldly, nontheological sense, to denote relationships of people to time that produce multilayered dynamics of presence and absence, anticipation and retrospection. This radical reimagination of time juxtaposes questions of historical process and narrative structure. How do the formal capacities of narrative approximate a layered experience of time that understands past hopes and failures as alive in the present?

The possibilities for literary engagements with historical, worldly afterlives are suggested in Mahasweta Devi's *Chotti Munda and His Arrow*, a novel that traces the ambivalent legacy of the tribal movement led by Birsa Munda in central India in the final years of the nineteenth century. Birsa Munda imagined the liberation of the Munda people from the stranglehold of moneylenders, landlords, forest officials, and other *diku* (nontribal outsiders). His life spanning most of the twentieth century, the novel's protagonist, Chotti Munda, struggles as much to help his fellow Mundas eke out a bare life as to manage the memory of Birsa's unrealized vision. Having come to the town of Ranchi to free his son from prison, he stops to rest under a statue. Because he is illiterate, Chotti fails to recognize this "man of copper and iron" as a monument to Birsa Munda.[6] This failure of recognition demonstrates the gap between subaltern attempts to reckon with the unfulfilled promise of Birsa's vision and hegemonic postindependence appropriations of the leader regarded by the colonial state as a tribal terrorist.[7]

Afterlives are sites of persistent or renewed contests among domination, resistance, and interstitial negotiation; the unwitting collision between the keeper of Birsa's memory and his monument is, in effect, a clash between afterlives. Questions of representation and interpretation become particularly vexing when the meaning—and even the manifestation—of a revolutionary hero exceeds a single human lifespan. Multiple personifications play an important role in *Almanac of the Dead*, Leslie Marmon Silko's epic novel depicting the five-hundred-year history of the postcontact Americas as a palimpsest of prophecy. The Apache warrior known as Geronimo, we read, was actually three, four, or more men whom whites couldn't distinguish once they pinned a name on an Indian fugitive.[8] Neither could the whites' cameras render the men's features: the image of a single, unknown Apache warrior "appeared in every photograph taken of the other Geronimos."[9]

Silko slyly revises clichéd notions of indigenous peoples' anxiety about photography capturing the soul: cameras condense the multiplicity of Apache warriors into a single Geronimo, but "the real Geronimo got away" (224). The nexus of filmic representation, death, and protean anticolonial heroes also is at stake in recent films like Raoul Peck's *Lumumba* or Jonathan Demme's *The Agronomist*, in which the technology of cinematography enables assassinated anti-imperialist leaders Patrice Lumumba (Congolese prime minister) and Jean Dominique (Haitian resistance radio broadcaster) to elude hegemonic distortions of their images and even death itself. Not merely the existence of these films but, more specifically, their narrative structures generate afterlives for Lumumba and Dominique: the films effect a double resurrection when their protagonists reappear even after the films depict their deaths. Both films link the mediated survivals of their heroes to legends of magical or trickster figures who cheat death. Likewise, the opening montage of *When We Were Kings*, a documentary about the 1974 Rumble in the Jungle boxing match and music festival in Zaire, implies a serial personification of pan-African heroes: an image of Lumumba just before his death (on January 17, 1961) is followed by an interview with Muhammad Ali on his birthday, January 17. "No one knows the name of the next Lumumba," wrote Fanon.[10]

These geographically and generically disparate texts all demonstrate how narrative form can accommodate the presence of the dead and the haunting absence of their collective dreams: what survives anticolonial movements is an imagined but as yet unrealized future, not merely memories of fallen heroes or of some primordial past. In *Chotti Munda and His Arrow*, Birsa Munda is repeatedly remembered as having "shown the way"—that is, as having opened a possible future and identified a trajectory or strategy leading to it. But these moments are caught between retrospection and anticipation in their confrontations with rupture and failure: Birsa and other characters who are remembered as having "shown the way" could not themselves follow it to freedom.

Mahasweta Devi's novel about Birsa Munda's legacy fictionally enacts Fanon's valorization of previous generations' struggles: even if "forefathers" like Birsa Munda failed in their day, their example is indispensable for later generations. Fanon and Devi confront the difficulty of tracing noncontinuous traditions of resistance, where past failures take on new significance for present struggles. Elsewhere in *The Wretched of the Earth*, Fanon acknowledges the pitfalls of looking to the past to inspire an emergent national culture. This tension between the necessity of historical understanding and the difficulty of claiming the past also informs Karl Marx's ambivalence about revolutionary traditions in *The Eighteenth Brumaire of Napoleon Bonaparte*, in which Marx disavows the "tradition of all the dead generations [that] weighs like a nightmare on the brains of the living."[11] While Fanon's recovery of the forefathers' efforts seems a rejoinder to Marx's call to "let the dead bury their dead," Marx—like Fanon—recognizes that the past can either inspire or distract. Marx depicts both alternatives when he writes that some revolutionaries productively "conjured up the spirits of the past" from previous revolutions, so that the "awakening of the dead in those revolutions served the purpose of glorifying the new struggles, not of parodying the old; of magnifying the given task in the imagination, not recoiling from its solution in reality; of finding once more the spirit of revolution, not making its ghost walk again" (322). After publishing *The Eighteenth Brumaire* in 1852, Marx wrote for the *New York Daily Tribune* from 1853 to 1861 about the Taiping Rebellion in China and the Sepoy Rebellion in India, as well as other imperial conflicts in Turkey, Persia, Morocco, Ireland, and the Crimea: he wrote, in other words, about and in the midst of anticolonial struggles that Fanon would urge his contemporaries to remember a century later.

As tangles of time bound up with the potential promise that remains in failure, afterlives are about practices of reading, questions of interpretation, and the exigencies of disparate historical contexts. Echoing Marx's ambivalence about the circumstances under which "men make their own history" (320), Fanon's paradoxical insistence on accretive traditions of resistance assumes that texts (and historical practices) signify differently over time, resonating more or less strongly in different "international situations." And for us, Fanon's certainty of victory signifies differently than when *Les damnés de la terre* was published in 1961. Luminous dreams of liberation have given way to the disillusionments of postcoloniality, themselves both tragic and farcical realizations of Fanon's prophecies of the half measures and foreclosures of self-interested bourgeois nationalism and unrepentant European imperialism.

And yet, in the face of such melancholy, *Bulletproof* is centrally concerned with rethinking failure. "Colonialism triumphs . . . in its moments of failure," Simon Gikandi writes in his discussion of the unpredictable, reflexive ways in which colonial encounters generate metropolitan and colonial identities;[12] there is, I argue, similar fecundity in the seeming failures of anticolonialism. Attending to alternative historical logics and fluid temporalities allows us to perceive in failure not finality but incompletion. To imagine the past as incomplete requires rejecting not only narratives of historical progress (as Gikandi does in inverting the teleology of imperialism) but also conceptions of time as unitary, linear, and unidirectional. Here again Silko's *Almanac of the Dead* suggests how the afterlives of failure generate new conditions of possibility. Her late twentieth-century character Wilson Weasel Tail rejects the idea that the millenarian Ghost Dance met failure in the 1890 massacre of Lakota Sioux by US troops at Wounded Knee, North Dakota.[13] It was the whites, he says, who expected ghost shirts to repel bullets and the ghost dance to make Europeans disappear overnight; the Ghost Dance—an effort to "reunite living people with the spirits of beloved ancestors lost in the five-hundred-year war" of European invasion—"has never ended, it has continued, and the people have never stopped dancing. . . . Throughout the Americas, from Chile to Canada, the people have never stopped dancing; as the living dance, they are joined again with all our ancestors before them, who cry out, who demand justice, and who call the people to take back the Americas!" (722, 724). Far from ending in military repression, the Ghost Dance expands into a transcontinental, transgenerational quest for justice. Wilson Weasel Tail evinces what David Attwell calls, in the South African context, "an optimism of the long term."[14]

In reframing the trajectories of decolonization and its contemporary legacies, I am arguing for renewed attention in postcolonial studies to the unrealized aspirations of anticolonialism, as opposed to celebrations of the hybridity of elite migrants in the first world or Afro-pessimistic melancholia about the sham of independence. By rethinking "failed resistance" and by elucidating relationships between retrospection and anticipation, or between memory and prophecy, postcolonial studies could attend just as seriously to the utopian potential of dreams of liberation as to the reasons why they have not been realized.

MAGICAL HISTORIES: MILLENARIANISM AND MODERNITY

In addition to reclaiming insurgent, transnational pasts for postcolonial studies and demonstrating how imaginative narratives can reanimate visions of liberation, *Bulletproof* aims to resituate our understanding of anticolonial nationalism within an epistemological context shaped by Enlightenment rationality, secularism, and modernization. One of the challenges in tracing fractured histories of anticolonialism is the conventional historiographical distinction between nineteenth-century primary resistance, often expressed in nonmodern idioms, and twentieth-century mass nationalism. The putative modernity of twentieth-century anticolonial nationalism derives from its perceived departure from earlier modes of resistance: an urbanizing proletariat or literate elite replaces illiterate peasant rebels; new, multiethnic institutions like trade unions, political parties, and welfare associations replace primordial communities led by charismatic chiefs or prophets; and the desire for modernization replaces retrograde movements to restore a lost golden age, through divine or magical intervention. Christianity (in its temperate, respectable varieties) replaces indigenous spiritual traditions.[15]

This progress narrative is untenable for many reasons. Rather than seeking to turn the clock back, millenarian visions convey a sense of rupture and demand new beliefs and behaviors. In this sense, millenarian movements share the predicament of other responses to colonialism, caught between the desire to restore a precolonial past and the necessity to forge new cultures within colonial modernity: the tension, in other words, between cultural nationalism as revival and national culture as forged in anticolonial struggle.[16] What makes millenarian movements a special and particularly instructive case is their imbrication of magic and modernity—the ways in which, for example, religious concepts and technological artifacts of the colonial encounter are incorporated into prophetic visions in ways that colonizers could not have anticipated.

The global dissemination of Christianity by European missionaries catalyzed the proliferation of anticolonial millenarian movements, whose visions were often shaped by Christian notions of resurrection and eschatology.[17] Of course, millenarian movements predated and existed independently of Christian evangelism, and millenarianism was usually articulated *in opposition to* mission Christianity, even while drawing on its imagery. Similar complexities hold for technology in colonial contexts; far from rejecting the artifacts of modernity, "cargo cults" and other movements embraced European objects and technologies (clothing, weapons, photography, "aeroplanes," books, etc.) as objects of desire or modes of deliverance. Even when unfamiliar technologies like European weaponry inspired fear, claims of invulnerability to bullets often evolved from earlier traditions of war doctoring that promised protection from enemies' weapons and magic.[18] Guns did not necessarily effect asymmetrical warfare: given their limitations before the invention and widespread dissemination of technologies like rifle boring, percussion caps, and rapid reloading, firearms did not always guarantee military advantage. Bulletproof claims were not the only adaptations to the introduction of European weaponry: in Melanesia, invaded peoples soon learned that diving underwater or making guns wet could neutralize bullets without resorting to alchemies that promised to turn them *into* water.[19]

Resistance to European imperialism cannot be traced solely through modernizing elites who internalized European discourses and turned them against the colonizers. Anticolonial nationalist movements of the twentieth century succeeded in mass mobilization when they drew on methods and memories of millenarian and other revitalization movements.[20] If modern nationalism is the afterlife of primary resistance, what links them is not only shared goals, strategies, and organizations but also the memory of these things as mediated through songs, stories, and other cultural forms. "They may call it by other names," Wilson Weasel Tail says of the Ghost Dance, but the people keep dancing.[21] Silko's novel posits continuity across historical rupture in a way that conventional historical discourse could not, but its delineation of this counterimaginary space also participates in keeping the dance alive.

In order to understand the relationship between primary resistance and later nationalist movements, we cannot merely challenge progress narratives that chart a turn from one to the other; we also must confront the epistemological reasons why even Fanon, despite his interest in earlier generations' resistance, constructs a "transition narrative" of anticolonial nationalism in which superstitious tradition is superseded by robust modernity.[22] Before the emergence of modern nationalism, according to Fanon, the colonized are mystified by a "magical superstructure" of taboos and practices that displace colonial distress onto a "phantasmic plane." Colonialism actively maintains the people's "petrification" by "marabouts, witch doctors, and customary chieftains." However, when people "formerly lost in an imaginary maze" confront the colonial enemy directly, they become "alienat[ed]" from such beliefs.[23] This form of alienation—unlike psychic or economic alienation—is salutary, in Fanon's view. Because Fanon associates the supernatural with self-destructive violence through which anticolonial impulses are "canalized," he does not recognize that the memories of primary resistance that "spring again to life with peculiar intensity in the period which comes directly before action" might feature magically inspired heroes, nor that the forefathers' weapons may have been supernatural ones (69).

At stake in Fanon's contradictory account is the tension between modernity and millennialism in anticolonial discourse, itself a local example of the broader epistemological tension between the secular (if also normatively Christian) rationality assumed by scholarly discourse in the wake of the Enlightenment and the stubborn "presence of the divine or the supernatural."[24] Dipesh Chakrabarty's critique of the developmentalist assumptions of historicism is important to my aim to reframe the conventional divide between "irrational" primary resistance and "modern" anticolonial nationalism. Even if we understand "gods and spirits to be existentially coeval with the human," rather than anachronistic remnants of the premodern, the challenge remains to "render this enchanted world into our disenchanted prose" (16). This challenge, however, involves not merely accommodating the supernatural (which literature may accomplish more easily than historiography) but also imagining time outside the uniform linearity of a progress narrative. Chakrabarty grasps only part of the situation when he observes that "third-world nationalisms, as modernizing ideologies par excellence, have been equal partners" in ascribing modernity to Europe (43); as I have suggested, modernization coexists uneasily with millennial visions and magical thinking in anticolonial discourse. The contradiction between Fanon's valorization of previous generations and his disavowal of nonmodern practices is only tenuously resolved when he posits the people as *metaphorical* messiah: "the demiurge is the people themselves and the magic hands are finally only the hands of the people."[25] Fanon cannot do without magic, even if it manifests primarily in the vivid figurative language that is indispensable to the rhetorical appeal of *The Wretched of the Earth*.

This kind of metaphorization recurs throughout *Bulletproof*, as writers revive millennial visions and transform them into figures that express contemporary desires. I should stress that I use notions of "magic" not in derisive opposition to modernity (to denote "primitive" or "superstitious" belief outside of the European, hegemonic, or mainstream), but rather as an expansive term for the supernatural, mysterious, or wondrous that crosses temporal, colonial, and theological divides. *Bulletproof* traces complex interrelationships among four key terms—magic, metaphor, materiality, and modernity—in which the lines that distinguish each domain are in flux and thus difficult to draw. In her challenge to received notions of secularism, Gauri Viswanathan has suggested that we understand secularization not as a rupture "between reason and religion, but, rather, between belief and imagination."[26] The tension between belief and imagination aptly describes the process of metaphorization we have already seen in Fanon; throughout *Bulletproof*, I show how authors engage the imaginative energies associated with cattle-killing prophecies by contemplating the relationship between literary or figurative imagining, on the one hand, and spiritual or cosmological thinking (or belief), on the other. Some authors reduce the "magical" aspects of the prophecies—those elements that elicited missionary/colonial charges of "superstition" perhaps because of their uncanny resemblance to mainstream Christian ideas, but that also challenged the conventional assumptions of Xhosa cosmology—into metaphors for more mundane processes. Some authors explore experiences of wonder shared by the literary and the prophetic. The dissemination of millennial prophecies of all kinds (Christian and otherwise) relies upon figurative imaginings and comparisons with the familiar as it seeks to compel belief in transformations of the world that are so radical as to seem otherwise incredible.

It should come as no surprise, then, that the modernizing project of twentieth-century anticolonial nationalism is shot through with millennial imagery. The language of Christian eschatology pervades *The Wretched of the Earth*, which describes decolonization as an attempt to "set afoot a new man" and create a world in which "'The last shall be first and the first last,'" at the same time that Fanon insists that "this creation owes nothing of its legitimacy to any supernatural power" (316, 36–37). Fanon's contradictory embrace of Christian imagery is all the more strange when we remember that the national liberation struggle in Algeria was his immediate context. Millennial language also appears in Chinua Achebe's recent recollection of Nigeria's independence struggle in the 1950s: "There was a feeling in the air that we were new people, that we were going to create a new heaven and a new earth. Something was in the air that made this possible, almost inevitable. We were responding to something inside us, but also to the atmosphere of freedom. . . . You see, this freedom was going to happen, it was already ordained."[27] Although Fanon and Achebe (son of a Church Missionary Society catechist) both describe decolonization as a new millennium, the sources of these images are likely different. The uneasy coexistence of modernization and millennialism in decolonization discourse is a legacy not only of the role of evangelical Christianity in European imperialism but also the secularization of millenarianism in Marxian thought, which influenced many twentieth-century nationalist leaders.[28] Locally derived millenarian images also recur throughout anticolonial struggles; the desire to "drive whites into the sea," for example, emerges in early nineteenth-century Xhosa prophecies, decades before the cattle killing, and recurs throughout twentieth-century struggles against segregation and apartheid.

Millennial imagery not only recovers a sense of improbable continuity but also reflects ruptured traditions of resistance. Achebe remembered the sense of preordained liberation from a vantage point on the other side of Nigeria's independence movement, after four decades of civil war, dictatorship, and reckless economic policies exacerbated by the structural inequalities of international capital. Achebe's invocation of the language of Biblical authority gives way to reminiscence about what now seems to have been a false prophecy. This memory of preordained liberation that has yet to arrive ironizes the relationship between independence and liberation articulated by Amílcar Cabral, leader and theorist of Guinea-Bissau's anti-imperialist struggle. Cabral spoke of economic liberation as a task that would follow (rather than enable) political autonomy.[29] Yet the decades since Nigeria's independence in 1960 seem qualitatively different than the time lag that Cabral imagined as the condition of possibility for true national liberation.

Although situated within discrete local histories, all these figures confront the difficulty of constructing traditions of resistance amidst the spatial, temporal, and epistemological ruptures engendered by imperialism. In the early twenty-first century, we can hardly understand challenges to contemporary neoimperialism—whether under the motley banners of antiglobalization protest coalitions or those of al-Qaeda and its allies— without grasping earlier trajectories of imperial expansion and decolonization, as well as their enduring legacies.[30] What gaps remain between the formal achievement of flag independence and the economic, cultural, and psychological autonomy envisioned in movements for national liberation? If decolonization is a story of failure, for what contemporary or future projects might its continuing promise be mobilized?

For decades, South Africa has been the quintessential site where unrealized hopes of mid-twentieth-century liberation struggles might be realized, a charged site for the afterlives of hopes and fears that drove decolonization. "'It is imperative for us that you succeed!'" one European participant implored at a 1998 conference at the University of the Witwatersrand.[31] Neil Lazarus recently recalled reading *The Beautyful Ones Are Not Yet Born* (Ayi Kwei Armah's 1968 novel of postindependence disillusion in Ghana) in 1976, when the uprising of students in Soweto sparked a new insurgency in the antiapartheid struggle. Lazarus noticed then that "in *Beautyful Ones*, time has ceased to be the repository of political hope," while "inside the anti-apartheid movement, by contrast, time was decidedly on the side of 'the people.'"[32] Disturbed by the "disjuncture between the politics of time in South Africa and the continent at large," Lazarus recognized that conventional wisdom assumed that

> *our* decolonization, when it came, would not prove to be the neocolonization that it had been elsewhere; *our* nationalism really *would* correspond to the "all-embracing crystallization of the innermost hopes of the whole people"; it would not decompose, as it had elsewhere on the continent, into ethnic chauvinism or class rule; *our* national liberation front would not serve, once it became the party in power after decolonization, to cover over its traces and disavow both its heritage and its historic responsibility; *our* leaders, our "men of the people" (and "women of the people") would not become, as elsewhere on the continent, the puppets of international capital. (611, emphases in the original)

Looking ahead to a prospective postapartheid era, these hopes of the 1970s keep alive dreams of a liberated future—a future in which *postcolonial* signifies the end of colonialism rather than its onset. Formulations of post-coloniality as the ambivalent condition *created by* the colonial encounter bear the marks of late twentieth-century disillusion,[33] particularly in comparison with the inevitable liberation Achebe remembers in 1950s Nigeria. We can hear in Lazarus's recollected hopes for South African decolonization a repetition, rather than repudiation, of the trajectory of decolonization elsewhere on the continent. South Africans shared the *same* hopes that other Africans had, daring still to dream of their realization. In this sense, South Africa is typical, rather than exceptional, in the history of modern Africa. Indeed, Lazarus finds that the neoliberalism of South Africa's postapartheid decade, which has revealed the enormity of the task of economic redistribution necessary for true liberation, has somewhat dashed hopes that South Africa's decolonization would be different.

In a similar vein, philosopher Ato Sekyi-Otu wondered about Nelson Mandela's election in 1994: was it

> the iridescent light that truly relieves the oppressive monotony of the encircling African gloom? Or is it but another cruel prelude to what Armah, threnodist of the postcolonial condition, saw as the ineluctable miscarriage of "the beauty of the first days"? . . .
>
> Are we not . . . condemned to be always furtively looking over our shoulders in order to check the bitter fruition of a macabre possibility—the emergence of reincarnations of Amin, Mobutu, Bokassa, even the great and tragically flawed Kwame Nkrumah and their retainers out of the ashes of Anglo-Boer domination?[34]

If South Africa offers a chance to get decolonization right, it also is haunted by the possible return of postcolonial Africa's dictatorial "big men." This spectral temporality—in which South Africa is haunted by the ghosts of decolonization past—invites us to consider South African nationalisms from a continental (rather than exceptionalist) perspective, with a view toward synchronic relations between South Africa and other sites, as well as the powerful, yet problematic notion of South Africa as the afterlife of African decolonization.

The global hopes invested in South Africa as a second chance to redeem the failures of African decolonization die rather hard; outside observers can be loathe to give up the notion of a harmonious transition to a Rainbow Nation. De Kock notes the "palpable . . . dismay" of international participants at the 1998 Witwatersrand conference, who regarded criticisms of the new South Africa "as misstruck, mistimed notes in that otherwise euphonious symphony of the democratic 'miracle.'"[35] To dispel the myth of the miracle is not to minimize the achievements of the antiapartheid struggle and the first decade of democracy. These ambivalences emerge in the documentary film *Amandla!: A Revolution in Four Part Harmony.* Comparing archival footage of masses *toyi-toyi*-ing shoulder to shoulder in the townships[36] with contemporary shots of smaller groups reprising freedom songs at the filmmakers' request, one notices telling changes: locally printed struggle t-shirts of the 1980s give way to transnational corporate-logo tees of the 1990s. Nonetheless, the postapartheid HIV/AIDS Treatment Action Campaign has borrowed t-shirts, mass marches, and many other tactics from the antiapartheid struggle in order to claim its promise of democracy and human rights. In order to recognize how improbable even the partial victories of the struggle may once have seemed, one need only look to the curious references in Silko's *Almanac of the Dead* to "the terrible bloodbath in South Africa" through which "the African people had retaken Africa" (616) that serve as an omen that the natives of the Americas also are rising up to reclaim their land.[37] Just as Ayi Kwei Armah's *The Beautyful Ones* could serve as a warning for the South African struggle, the counterfactual South African bloodbath recurs in the near-future projections of *Almanac of the Dead* as a sign of both the possibility of success for native struggles and their potential cost in human lives. Silko's novel "authorize[s]"—albeit ambivalently—what Fanon termed revolts "drowned in blood."

THE AFTERLIVES OF ANTI-IMPERIALISM AND THE XHOSA CATTLE KILLING

South Africa is a compelling site for considering intertemporal questions about the afterlives of anti-imperialism, although its history complicates attempts to synchronize the temporality of postapartheid with that of postcoloniality. Unlike much of Africa, South Africa was "post–colonial" (in the literal, historical sense) for most of the twentieth century: British colonies joined Boer republics in the 1910 Act of Union. The postcolonial era that began in 1910 inaugurated decades of segregation and apartheid, so that meaningful decolonization could not begin until the 1994 election. The 1910 and 1994 events demonstrate the gap between *independence* and *liberation* observed by Cabral. At stake in hopes for South Africa is a desire for a difference between apartheid and postapartheid that has not been possible for colonialism and postcoloniality. To what extent, however, has contemporary South Africa been able to realize these dreams of liberation? My examination of the afterlives of the 1856–57 Xhosa cattle killing seeks to answer this question by considering issues of national imagining, narrative desire, temporalities of resistance, and the intersections of modernity, magic, and metaphor that are central to African and postcolonial studies.

The cattle killing was the climax of nearly a decade of millenarian prophecies among the Xhosa people, or amaXhosa, who inhabited a region of the eastern Cape spanning from the coast of the Indian Ocean to the south and beyond the Amatola Mountains to the north. They had been repeatedly dislocated for more than a half century as the border of the British Cape Colony pushed eastward in a series of nine frontier wars, eight of which were fought between 1779 and 1853. The eastern Cape frontier was extraordinarily violent; even in peacetime, stock thefts and other conflicts with British and Boer settlers kept tensions high.

British policy toward the amaXhosa and their system of chiefdom shifted along with the colonial boundary; the arrival of Sir George Grey, governor of the Cape Colony from 1854 to 1861, marked an unprecedented assault on the authority of the chiefs, whom Grey aimed to co-opt as paid employees of the colonial state. Grey's attempts to "civilize" the amaXhosa through mission-sponsored education, colonial jurisprudence, European medicine (and suppression of indigenous healing practices), and wage labor (sometimes forced) were frustrated not least by the overlapping political geographies of British colonial territory and the Xhosa kingdom. In the mid-1850s, Grey ruled directly, and under martial law, the territory known as British Kaffraria, between the Cape Colony to the west and independent Xhosa territory to the northeast (separated by the Kei River). The Ngqika and Ndlambe Xhosa clans lived in British Kaffraria; the Gcaleka clan lived northeast of the Kei, autonomous of British rule (see fig. 1). All the clans recognized the authority of the Gcaleka Xhosa king, Sarhili. This complex political geography constrained the colonial response to the cattle killing.

The prophecy originated just east of the Kei but found adherents on both sides of the river. The land across the Kei—the Transkei—has continued to accrete layers of political significance. In the apartheid era, Transkei became a designated "homeland" for Xhosa language (isiXhosa) speakers, enjoying the dubious distinction of becoming the first Bantustan that the

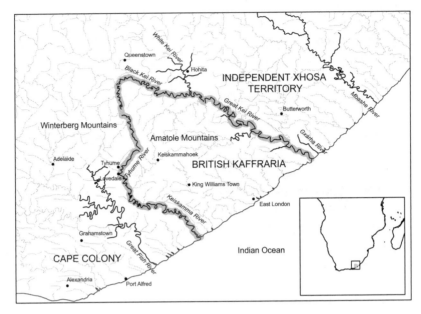

1. The eastern Cape, 1856.

South African state proclaimed to be independent, in 1976; residents of the "independent" puppet state lost their South African citizenship.[38] The ideology and institutions of black South African nationalism emerged in the Transkei in the late nineteenth century; yet, in democratic South Africa, the former Transkei homeland, which is now part of Eastern Cape Province, remains among the poorest regions of the country.

Although one of my aims in *Bulletproof* is to trouble the desire for a single, definitive history of the cattle killing "the way it actually happened," a brief description of the event seems necessary.[39] In addition to colonial challenges to their culture and political structure and the devastations of the 1850–53 frontier war, the amaXhosa faced drought, floods, crop blight, and land and cattle shortages in the 1850s. In early 1856, a prophecy was delivered to a young Xhosa woman near the Gxarha River, just east of the Kei, by strange men who identified themselves as ancestors. Their message was disseminated by the young woman, Nongqawuse, and her uncle (in some versions, her father), Mhlakaza, who reported the prophecy to Sarhili.[40] The prophecy promised the ancestors' return if the amaXhosa killed their cattle, abstained from agriculture, and destroyed their grain. The return of ancestors among the living would have been a new departure in Xhosa cosmology, which understood ancestors to be watching over the living and sometimes intervening in their lives. The amaXhosa were to prepare new grain pits, strengthen their houses, refrain from witchcraft and incest, and await the return of the ancestors, who would bring with them herds of new cattle and piles of grain. The world would be renewed, with Europeans and unbelievers driven into the sea. This vision drew on earlier anticolonial Xhosa prophecies—articulated by Mlanjeni and others in the early 1850s and by Nxele and Ntsikana in the 1810s—that included promises of invulnerability to bullets, driving whites into the sea, and the return of fallen warriors, to be achieved by limited sacrifices of cattle, noncultivation, and the cessation of witchcraft.

The prophecy divided the amaXhosa into believers and unbelievers—the *amathamba*, who were "soft" or "submissive" to the prophecy, and the "hard" or "unyielding" *amagogotya*.[41] Several dates for resurrection were set; the prophecy was refined, and additional prophets emerged as Xhosa chiefs took differing stances and the colonial administration looked on warily, fearing that the chiefs' underlying motive was to drive their desperate people to war against the colony. Approximately 400,000 cattle were killed in 1856–57 in compliance with the prophecy; as many as 150,000 cattle had already died or been culled during an epizootic of bovine pleuripneumonia (lung sickness) that arrived in the Cape in 1853. After the ancestors and cattle failed to return on the final announced date in February 1857, the human toll was devastating: approximately 40,000 people died of starvation, and 50,000 left their land in kwaXhosa to become laborers in the Cape Colony.

For the amaXhosa, the cattle killing was the beginning of the end of their autonomy from British colonial power. Throughout *Bulletproof,* I address suspicions (recorded in Xhosa oral tradition in the mid-twentieth century) that the British were behind the cattle-killing prophecy. In a 1975 narration, for example, storyteller Nongenile Masithatu Zenani describes a young girl paid by white people to disguise herself and hide in a riverside thicket; she was to tell the people that she had been sent by the Creator, who wanted them to destroy their food and livestock and await the resurrection of the dead.[42] Regardless of whether Sir George Grey had any hand in what Nongqawuse saw and heard, he took maximum advantage of the movement's aftermath. Grey's policies tied famine relief to labor contracts that pulled the amaXhosa away from their lands and chiefs, and he oversaw the passage of legislation that required "passes" to enter the Cape Colony for some Africans but not others, on the basis of ethnicity. The cattle killing was not only a devastating event in the history of the amaXhosa but also a seminal moment in the history of colonialism, segregation, and apartheid in southern Africa. This foundational importance of British colonial policy for later South African history undermines nostalgic recollections of nineteenth-century British rule as liberal and enlightened, compared with the excesses of twentieth-century Afrikaner segregationism. Grey did not invent the pass laws that beleaguered Africans for nearly two centuries, but he used and modified them in ways that rivaled the labor canalization efforts of later architects of apartheid.[43]

Moreover, the colonial response to the cattle killing represents an early example of the global dynamic that Mike Davis identifies in *Late Victorian Holocausts*: "colonial expansion uncannily syncopated the rhythms of natural disaster and epidemic disease" because colonial responses to drought and famine in Africa, Brazil, China, and India intensified, rather than ameliorated, the market logic of commodity extraction.[44] Like these later colonial administrators, Sir George Grey tied famine relief to the capture of labor and tightened the screws of empire in the aftermath of disaster; Grey's strategy of forced villagization as a mode of controlling insurgency anticipated the British use of this tactic a century later, in Malaya in 1950 and Kenya in 1952.[45] In our own era, we can recognize in Grey's opportunistic response to the cattle killing the lineaments of what Naomi Klein dubs "disaster capitalism"—the predatory "reconstruction industry" that "uses the desperation and fear created by catastrophe to engage in radical social and economic engineering" in the wake of disasters like Hurricane Mitch, the 2004 tsunami in southeast Asia, Iraq and Afghanistan, and Hurricane Katrina.[46] "Disaster is the new *terra nullius*," Klein writes—the form that colonial impulses take in the twenty-first century. Sir George Grey understood very well that the disaster of the cattle killing could only mean good things for his Cape Colony. "All Kaffirland is now at your feet—now is your time," a Wesleyan missionary wrote to Grey's British Kaffrarian commissioner.[47]

We also can understand the cattle killing within the global context of resistance to British imperialism. The cattle killing occurred just after the 1854–56 Crimean War and just before the shock of the 1857–58 Sepoy Rebellion in India, to which Grey had to dispatch troops while he worried about the threat posed by masses of Xhosa survivors on the colonial frontier. From 1856 to 1860, the British fought the Arrow War in China to break resistance to the opium trade. British imperialism also would be challenged by a series of wars in the 1860s in New Zealand and the 1865 Morant Bay rebellion in Jamaica.[48]

The global imbrications of the cattle killing undermine conventional historiographical characterizations of primary resistance as aberrational, "backward," and intensely local—bounded by village and cosmos and unaware of any spatial scales in between. Adherents of cattle-killing prophecies were cognizant of other anti-imperial struggles, which they understood to be parallel and allied movements of black peoples against British rule. In Xhosa prophecies of the mid-1850s, Russians, who were battling the British in the Crimea (and had killed former Cape governor Sir George Cathcart), were understood to be black men, or even Xhosa ancestors, who would come to the Cape to help defeat the British there. News of the Sepoy Rebellion in India renewed hopes among the famished amaXhosa that Indians (another "black race") would help deliver them. Millenarian hopes revived briefly in 1860, when some Xhosa survivors understood the British war in China as a war of black peoples against British domination.[49] Thus, some nineteenth-century believers understood themselves to be participants in global anti-imperial resistance. In the 1920s, millenarianism was revived in the eastern Cape with expectations of deliverance by African Americans in "aeroplanes": inspired by ideas of deliverance associated with Marcus Garvey, some believers understood African Americans to be not only a "black race," as with the Russians, Indians, and Chinese of the previous century, but also the dominant force in the United States.

The geopolitical awareness shaping millenarian movements in the eastern Cape puts into broader historical perspective the expectations of external deliverance characteristic of cargo cults: far from being mystified by the unprecedented appearance of powerful strangers and wondrous machines on their shores, the amaXhosa considered how faraway events and people they had never (yet) seen figured into their own history. In other words, the amaXhosa had a nascent understanding of empire "as a space . . . of multinational 'blackness,' with multiple national communities defined in the British empire as native or black, stretching across Asia, Africa, America, and the islands of the sea."[50] I borrow this notion of "multinational blackness" from Michelle Stephens's account of twentieth-century African American and Caribbean intellectuals. Where Marcus Garvey provides the impetus for Stephens's inter-American narrative, early twentieth-century Garveyism *revives* an earlier black global imaginary at work in the eastern Cape in the 1850s and 1860s: *Bulletproof* shifts our understanding of black anti-imperialist transnationalism back by nearly a century. From the perspective of the eastern Cape, this transnational imagining limns not a "black Atlantic" but, rather, a rounding of the Cape that joins Atlantic and Pacific, the Americas and Asia. The perceived transnational struggle of the amaXhosa also unsettles the orthodoxy that imperialism worked unidirectionally as the penetration of a globalizing Europe into discrete, local spaces. No matter how idiosyncratic or illogical the cattle killing and its Xhosa adherents' millenarian (mis)readings of mid-nineteenth-century geopolitics may seem, we can see in their incorporation of Russian, Indian, and Chinese militants into cattle-killing prophecies a nascent anti-imperialist imagined community. The notion of deliverance by Russians took on another layer of significance during the cold war, given Soviet and Cuban support for the antiapartheid struggle.

These echoes between the role of Russians in nineteenth- and twentieth-century South African struggles demonstrate one of the ways that the unrealized hopes articulated in cattle-killing prophecies inform later nationalist movements. The most compelling retrospective narratives of the cattle killing imagine, however briefly or cynically, what it would be to believe that the dead would rise, temporarily suspending the burden (or relief) of the historical knowledge that they did not. It is the doubled perspective of this moment of hope held against the knowledge of the aftermath that makes the cattle killing such a compelling repository of images for articulating later desires, generating laminate temporalities in which past hopes reemerge to pressure the present. Tracing the cattle killing's afterlives into the post–Truth and Reconciliation Commission (TRC) era requires confronting tensions among luminous visions of liberation, their devastating aftermaths, and the quandaries of partial victories: of what use to the present are the unrealized hopes of the past?

In the first few years of South African democracy, the TRC undertook public memory work that resonates with questions I raise in *Bulletproof.* By providing a sanctioned (perhaps even sanctified) forum for harrowing testimony about human rights violations from perpetrators, victims, and their survivors, the TRC demonstrated that these events do not belong only to the past: they have afterlives. The TRC report acknowledges both its limited historical scope and its broader geographic implications:

The purpose was to place in historical context what happened in Southern Africa in the period 1960–94. In a continental context, this represented the last great chapter in the struggle for African decolonization. In a South Africa–specific context, it was the climactic phase of a conflict that dated back to the mid-seventeenth century, when European settlers first sought to establish a permanent presence on the subcontinent.[51]

The historical mandate of the TRC was to consider acts committed between the Sharpeville massacre on March 21, 1960—when police killed 69 unarmed demonstrators (and injured at least 180) at a protest against pass laws—and the election on April 27, 1994; the TRC report recognizes this period as the "climactic phase" of a centuries-long struggle. The TRC report also contextualizes the antiapartheid struggle as "the last great chapter in the struggle for African decolonization." Echoing in an official document the expansive, metonymic trope that we have seen earlier—the antiapartheid struggle as a chance to close the book on empire, to rewrite the story of African decolonization—the TRC report also acknowledges its limited mandate in the context of South African history. It names earlier "violations" left unaddressed: slavery, wars of dispossession (including those against the amaXhosa), systematic exterminations, mass casualties in twentieth-century wars, and massacres of demonstrators before Sharpeville (1:25–26). My inquiry into the afterlives of the cattle killing complements the project of the TRC and exceeds its mandate in at least three ways: by examining visions of hope rather than acts of atrocity; by taking a broader view of relationships among past, present, and future; and by considering the extent to which contemporary South Africa has realized the global hopes invested in it, not least in the TRC itself. The TRC was, on the one hand, modeled on truth commissions of the 1970s and '80s; yet, a number of subsequent truth commissions have (at least rhetorically) taken the TRC as their model for addressing systematic injustice, both historical and new. Such an ambivalent legacy suggests that we view South Africa's transition to democracy not as the *completion* of the "struggle for African decolonization" but, rather, as the revival and partial deferment of its hopes.

PROPHECY AND POSSIBILITY

"Africa is a land of prophets and prophetesses," the journalist, novelist, translator, and activist Solomon T. Plaatje wrote in *Native Life in South Africa* (1916).[52] I am interested in what happens when we take prophetic visions of renovation seriously as frames for understanding South African cultural history, not least in Plaatje's own work, as I discuss in chapter 3. If prophecy is endemic to Africa, as Plaatje suggests, what motivates my focus on the cattle killing in particular are its consequences for the history of the amaXhosa and the broader trajectory of colonialism and anticolonial nationalism in southern Africa, as well as the singular status of its prophet. Nongqawuse tends to be remembered as a dupe or liar, rather than as a fallen or frustrated hero, and her association with what has been deemed a shameful episode in Xhosa history cannot be separated from the fact that she was a young woman, approximately 15 years old; her gender and age also elicited skepticism from those who rejected the prophecy in the 1850s.[53] The fact that a "female" claimed to speak with the ancestors "itself was a sham, / A curse to the land of the Xhosa," the *imbongi* (oral praise poet) David Livingstone Phakamile Yali-Manisi intoned in the early 1970s.[54] Strong feelings about Nongqawuse derive from the scale of the devastation associated with her: it is hardly surprising that Dr. Manto Tshabalala-Msimang, the former South African minister of health who questioned the safety and efficacy of antiretroviral treatments for AIDS and advocated dietary changes instead, has been described as a reincarnation of Nongqawuse. The cattle killing's immediate and enduring costs in human lives and livelihoods and in sociopolitical and cultural autonomy have been profound—"*sisimbonono kwizizukulwana*," "a perpetual lament to generations," in Yali-Manisi's words (200). I acknowledge these losses in *Bulletproof*, at the same time that I examine what meanings have been made of them.

Such meaning making has generated a rich historical and literary archive that compels sustained attention. As I discuss in chapter 1, European Christian missionary endeavor and the introduction of literacy began among the amaXhosa shortly before the cattle killing and gained considerable momentum in its aftermath. Thus the cattle killing is not only coincident with but also wrapped up in the emergence and development of a black South African literary (as opposed to oral) tradition, as we will see with figures like Tiyo Soga, the first ordained Xhosa minister, and W. W. Gqoba, one of the first black South African newspaper editors.

This meaning making continues. The cattle killing's significance remains a contested question, as is evident in two recent essays that posit Nongqawuse as an emblem for the present. Meg Samuelson associates Nongqawuse (as recuperated in Zakes Mda's novel *The Heart of Redness* [2000]) with post-TRC triumphalism, in which the democratic transition fulfills a teleology of inevitable liberation. This narrative of "sacrifice and redemption

... threatens to silence those who trace continuities between the apartheid past and the postapartheid present and to foreclose past loss in favour of present unity."[55] Diametrically opposed to this view is Achille Mbembe's diagnosis of a "Nongqawuse syndrome," a suicidal impulse threatening a post-Mbeki South Africa: this dangerous mix of populism, nativism, and millenarianism emerges from the betrayal millions of South Africans feel more than a decade after a "liberation" that brought pandemic disease, violence, and deepening inequality.[56] Moreover, Mbembe argued in the *Sunday Times*, this "Nongqawuse syndrome" repeatedly emerges in times of instability in southern Africa, and it also explains postcolonial tragedies elsewhere (for example, in Rwanda, Liberia, Congo, and Sudan).

Mbembe's conception of the "Nongqawuse syndrome" as susceptibility to a false prophecy that "advocates, uses, and legitimises self-destruction, or national suicide, as a means of salvation" represents an important aspect of the cattle killing's afterlife. Since the 1850s, the cattle killing has often been described as the "Xhosa national suicide." This epithet, however, is potentially misleading in conflating the movement's outcome with its motivation: among the range of causes identified by colonial and modern historians, no one suggests that the Xhosa nation *intended* to destroy itself. Mbembe's diagnosis reflects longstanding invocations of the cattle killing as a symbol for spectacular self-destruction (as I discuss in chaps. 2 and 4), but I also excavate a broader range of interpretations that see the cattle killing as something other than atavistic, irrational self-destruction. The desires expressed in Nongqawuse's unfulfilled prophecy also have been reimagined as a utopian surplus, capable of not only "generat[ing] an alternative meaning of what our world might be," as Mbembe fears South Africa can no longer do, but also addressing continuities between the apartheid era and the present that Samuelson fears are obscured by Nongqawuse as redemptive figure.[57] The incompatibility of Samuelson's and Mbembe's arguments about Nongqawuse's contemporary significance, both published in 2006, demonstrates the continuing currency and dynamic richness of the Xhosa cattle killing's protean afterlives.[58]

Conceived most broadly, my interest in prophecy and its afterlives is about understanding the relationships among temporality, historicity, and narrative form, a concern I share with David Attwell, who advocates a shift in South African literary historiography "from an emphasis on how to write about sameness and difference, to writing about *temporality*, which is to say, writing about one's place in history or one's place in the present and future."[59] My genealogical inquiry into cattle-killing discourse traces the ways in which intertextual, intertemporal relations exceed and trouble linear certainties, in order to grasp the transformative potential inherent in bringing past and present into communication so that they distort and remake one another. This approach is particularly resonant in reading texts that attempt to come to terms with speaking with the dead (or having believed one was speaking with the dead) and the death and devastation that followed. The Xhosa notion of a parallel existence of vigilant ancestors, who watch over and actively intervene in the world of the living, implies a concept of social time in which the past is never fully complete. The time of expectation opened up by a prophecy and the relationship between prophet and people are figures for understanding the complex dynamic of reception and revision involved in cultural production as the afterlife of historical movements. "One of the essential features of prophecy is the extended conversation between prophets and their audiences down through the generations": this historical insight has important implications for the discipline of literature, which also can be understood as transgenerational conversation, "the unfinished home of planetary time, the unfinished home of the living and the dead" because "words spread out, spill over into unexpected historical periods, unexpectable human communities: the bidirectional flow of time is such as to fill any given text with recesses of antecedence and stretches of afterlife."[60] *Bulletproof* identifies narrative strategies that emerge from imaginative engagements with histories of resistance, and it articulates reading practices that can attend to such layered, transhistorical experiences of memory and desire. The afterlives of anti-imperialism demand that we think about nation, time, and narrative in new ways, in order to grasp and move beyond the contradictions of the "post-" in both "postcolonial" and "postapartheid."

Perhaps appropriately for a book that ranges from the historical conjuncture between mission-mediated literacy and millennial dreaming on the mid-nineteenth-century eastern Cape frontier to the postmodern aporias of African American novelist John Edgar Wideman's depiction of a transhistorical black diaspora, the figure who most informs my conceptual frameworks is Walter Benjamin. Benjamin's work defies systematization but circles around questions of temporality, memory, history, interpretation, and the relationship between oppression and cultural production.[61] Zygmunt Bauman proposes that we understand Benjamin "as the philosopher and practitioner of *possibility*," moved "by the spirit of rebellion against

history as a graveyard of possibilities" yet nonetheless aware of the vulnerability of possibilities that "do not know of themselves as possibilities as
long as they stay alive."[62] Like Fanon and Marx, Benjamin attends to the
ambivalent intersections of magic, messianism, and modernity. Despite
obvious differences between the nineteenth-century eastern Cape and
interwar Germany, Benjamin's concern with problems of historiography
in times of crisis, and with the necessity of grasping relationships between
moments in time without the mystification of a progress narrative, makes
his work indispensable for theorizing afterlives.

My use of the term *afterlives* derives less from Benjamin's early, explicit
account of translation as the "unmetaphorical" afterlife of a literary work
than from his later historical reflections.[63] Benjamin's sense of "a revolutionary chance in the fight for the oppressed past" in which *"even the dead
will not be safe from the enemy if he wins"* raises the crucial question of
whether the subaltern dead can speak or be heard.[64] In *The Arcades Project*,
Benjamin explains his idea of the dialectical image:

> It's not that what is past casts its light on what is present, or what is pres-
> ent its light on what is past; rather, image is that wherein what has been
> comes together in a flash with the now to form a constellation. In other
> words, image is dialectics at a standstill. For while the relation of the
> present to the past is a purely temporal, continuous one, the relationship
> of what-has-been to the now is dialectical: is not progression but image,
> suddenly emergent.[65]

This radical—if oracular—notion is both a description of temporality and a
statement of historical method,[66] and this duality is crucial for understanding how the cultural afterlives of the cattle killing ask us to imagine the
past as incomplete and time as multiple and recursive. Benjamin's "weak
Messianic" notion of *Jetztzeit*—the pregnant time of the now that is the antithesis of what Benjamin famously called "homogeneous, empty time"—is
instructive both for its sense of the *historical* potential of unrealized hopes
in the past and for its relevance to the idea of afterlives as an *interpretive*
practice.[67] Benjamin insists not only that dialectical images "belong to
a particular time . . . but above all, that they attain to legibility only at a
particular time. . . . [E]ach 'now' is the now of a particular recognizability."[68]
The stakes of such recognizability are high for the living and the dead: those
who misread the forefathers' actions as passivity or complicity, in Fanon's

account, would accede to the colonizer's version of history and thereby impede anticolonial action in the present. To read afterlives is to attend to the ways in which pasts haunt each present moment differently.

Benjamin's friend and rival Ernst Bloch also appears repeatedly in *Bulletproof*. Like Benjamin, Bloch is concerned with the potential of the incomplete, the unfinished, the unrealized—what he calls the utopian surplus. Bloch insists on the possibilities of an open, undetermined, "real future," as opposed to an "unreal future" legible through extrapolation from the present; he writes about the role of art and literature in confronting the alienation of modernity and anticipating the new.[69] Together, Benjamin and Bloch help me to confront the knife edge of utopian thinking, attending to its openness toward the new and mindfulness of the unfinished, as well as to the devastation of its disappointments and the losses that it attempts to justify.[70] Bloch's notion of a real future is particularly important as I examine 150 years of colonialism, segregation, and apartheid from a vantage point on the other side of the antiapartheid struggle: in writing about the uses of the cattle-killing prophecy's failure, I actively work against teleological assumptions of the antiapartheid movement's inevitable success. Reading the afterlives of anticolonialism retrospectively, while holding a sense of inevitability in abeyance—either inevitable devastation or inevitable liberation—might recover modes of dreaming difference that would transform remembered prophecies of acolonial restoration into prophetic memories of postcolonial justice.

What follows is not a history of representations of the cattle killing but, rather, a meditation on how history works: how change is imagined and then reimagined in the face of change other than what was envisioned, and how imaginations borrowed from the past enable and constrain visions of the future.[71] The amaXhosa who killed their cattle and forsook their grain did so in expectation of "new people," new cattle and grain, and a renewed social and natural order of harmony and plenty. Life for the amaXhosa changed irrevocably after 1857, but the complex relationship between the active anticipation and (re)creation of *newness*, and *difference* experienced as devastation, offers a way of thinking through the intersections of cultural production and political strategy, imagined possibility, and historical constraint. Narrative revisions of the cattle killing are bound by their own historical contexts as they measure the promise and costs of Nongqawuse's prophecy against the urgencies of the present.

This is true even and especially in the case of narratives whose form is not textual nor even primarily verbal, as in the monumental tapestry (modeled after the Bayeaux tapestry) created by women from the Keiskamma region of the Eastern Cape. The Keiskamma Tapestry "narrates" the history of the Eastern Cape, with 120 meters of panels ranging from the San people to long lines of South African citizens waiting to vote in 1994. The upper and lower borders of the tapestry are a continuous series of images of cattle, and a long panel depicts both Nongqawuse's vision and the horror of its aftermath. The tapestry now hangs at the Parliament building in Cape Town. At the opening of an exhibition of the tapestry at the 2004 National Arts Festival in Grahamstown, speakers invoked Thabo Mbeki's characterization of the South African present as the early dawn moment when the tips of the horns of cattle are just becoming visible; they spoke movingly of the "resurrection" achieved by these women who had "dreamed the dream of cattle" and thereby recovered a historical memory so that they could show their children where they came from. This project of historical recovery is also decidedly an intervention into the urgencies of the present, as the Keiskamma Trust seeks to build skills, foster livelihoods, and provide health and education services for this impoverished Eastern Cape community.[72]

Bulletproof makes important conceptual and methodological contributions to the study of nationalism and its relationship to cultural production. I consider the crucial role that the Xhosa cattle killing has played in intersections between literary and cultural history and in broader efforts to define a Xhosa, black South African, or nonracial nation in the century and a half after the event. Reading conventional literary genres such as fiction, poetry, and drama alongside newspaper editorials, convention speeches, missionary memoirs, biographies, colonial correspondence, and documentary exposés, I show how authors manipulate recurring images of the cattle-killing prophecy and its aftermath—harvesting, sacrifice, rebirth, devastation—to speak to successive contemporary predicaments of cultural alienation, segregation, repression, and unrealized dreams of liberation and economic justice. Yet the fiercely contested interpretations of the cattle killing's motivation and meaning, as well as institutional inequalities in publishing, distribution, and literary education in South Africa, obviate any sense of a shared national tradition. While I do not claim to narrate an exhaustive history of South African literature traced through the cattle killing, *Bulletproof* contemplates the problems of writing literary histories for a "new South Africa." I engage difficult questions about language, literacy, audience, genre, connections to European and African traditions, relationships between formal strategies and political engagements, and competing regimes of value. In the early 1980s, Nadine Gordimer observed that "literary standards and standards of human justice are hopelessly confused" in late-apartheid South Africa; nearly three decades later, this tension continues to vex debates about literary value and canon formation even though (or perhaps precisely because) the urgencies of the struggle have passed.[73] In keeping with my broader argument, I suggest that we can find value in "failed" texts and be troubled by the currency of "successful" ones—currency which may vary over time or between South African and other audiences.[74] Beyond the South African context, my theorization of the narrative strategies and interpretive practices of afterlives offers a framework for understanding what happens to time and history, memory and desire when visionary pasts erupt in disenchanted presents.

The five chapters of *Bulletproof* trace an overlapping and recursive trajectory from the 1850s to the post-TRC era. The logic of the argument proceeds less in terms of chronology than in terms of a series of concepts that constellate the afterlives of failed prophecy: literacy (chap. 1), intertextuality and reading alongside (chap. 2), remembered prophecy and prophetic memory (chap. 3), heterotemporality and unfailure (chap. 4), and affiliation, the otherwhile, and internarrativity (chap. 5). In juxtaposing different kinds of texts and asking different questions of them, the chapters emerge from different methodologies. Chapter 1 traces the cattle killing's emergence amidst colonial efforts to subjugate and "civilize" the amaXhosa; my readings of late nineteenth-century historical accounts of the cattle killing show how the technology of literacy mediates these competing millennial dreams. Drawing an analogy between the rhetorical structure of prophecy and the polyphony of intertextuality, chapter 2 untangles intertextual webs involving H. I. E. Dhlomo's *The Girl Who Killed to Save (Nongqause the Liberator)* (1936), a play that reflects the ambivalence of elite, mission-educated New Africans in the segregationist era. In chapter 3, I consider what I call *remembered prophecy* and *prophetic memory* in Sol Plaatje's protest against racialist legislation, *Native Life in South Africa* (1916), and I measure Plaatje's early twentieth-century sense of broken time against two iconic moments in late-apartheid cultural politics: Njabulo Ndebele's notion of the "rediscovery of the ordinary" and Mtutuzeli Matshoba's post-Soweto narratives, one of which reimagines the cattle killing. Chapter 4 shows how invocations of the cattle killing in two postapartheid novels,

Sindiwe Magona's *Mother to Mother* (1998) and Zakes Mda's *The Heart of Redness* (2000), evoke questions about how to read the end of the apartheid era; ideas of heterotemporality and unfailure can work against viewing the transition as an inevitable fulfillment of prophecy. In chapter 5, I examine the cattle-killing prophecy and its afterlives in terms of transnational, transgenerational networks of affiliation; John Edgar Wideman's novel *The Cattle Killing* (1996) and Brett Bailey's play *The Prophet* (1999) stage the cattle killing as a global reimaginary, refusing to forget what has never been and revealing a radically different map of what the world might be.

CHAPTER ONE

WRITING RESURRECTION AND REVERSAL

The Cattle Killing and Other Nineteenth-Century

Millennial Dreams

> By listening to the Word a struggle commenced within me, and I felt as if I had two hearts, the one loving the Word, and the other hating it.
>
> CHARLES HENRY MATSHAYA, CONVERT AT LOVEDALE MISSION, 1842

> Words do not perish.
>
> MHALA, CHIEF OF THE NDLAMBE XHOSA, 1857

> We must die to continue living.
>
> WALTER J. ONG, 1982[1]

"In the year 1856, two girls went out to the lands to keep the birds away from the corn": so we read in a rare account written by a Xhosa witness to the events of 1856–57. It narrates a strange encounter between one of the young women, Nongqawuse, and men claiming to be "people who . . . died long ago."[2] Her people initially thought she was "'telling stories'" when she returned home and claimed that the "whole community" would "rise from the dead," bringing with them stores of grain and herds of cattle (71). But her message was embraced with tragic conviction when her father, Mhlakaza (most sources say he was her uncle), and the chiefs and councilors accepted that Nongqawuse had been chosen as a medium. Having complied with demands to kill their cattle, abstain from agriculture, and refrain from witchcraft, "the people died of hunger and disease in large numbers" when the returned people, cattle, and grain failed to appear. The story concludes, "Thus it was said that whenever a person said an unbelievable thing, those who heard him, said: 'You are telling a Nongqawuse tale'" (75). This pithy moral closes the narrative, like an etiologic folktale that explains natural phenomena or social customs. In this case, however, the narrative explains a historical event in which at least 40,000 people and 400,000 cattle died and approximately 50,000 survivors left their devastated homesteads to seek work and food in the Cape Colony. Those who remained were forced into villages, and the amaXhosa lost more than 600,000 acres of land.[3]

This narrative was written by William Wellington Gqoba, who was sixteen years old during what he called the "Nongqawuse period"—approximately the same age as the young woman who shares a name with the catastrophic events of 1856–57.[4] Gqoba wrote his account three decades later, across a cultural divide separating him from Nongqawuse and her followers. He had become a preacher, poet, and journalist, a member of the mission-educated elite beginning to emerge when millenarian prophecies spread among the amaXhosa in the 1850s. From 1885 until his death in 1888, Gqoba edited *Isigidimi samaXhosa* (Xhosa Messenger), a newspaper published in isiXhosa by the Lovedale mission press. He printed his cattle-killing account in *Isigidimi* in 1888.

Although Gqoba was affiliated with institutional mission Christianity, his narrative challenged colonial understandings of the cattle killing. Most accounts by nineteenth-century administrators, missionaries, and historians held that the cattle killing originated as a conspiracy among Xhosa chiefs to starve their people, thereby driving them to war against the Colony. Gqoba rejects this colonial consensus about a Xhosa "chiefs' plot," a consensus he fears is generating confusion among the amaXhosa about their ancestors' actions in the 1850s. Dismissing the idea of a chiefs' plot, Gqoba explains that the amaXhosa were faced with two choices: accepting the strangers' miraculous promise or "becom[ing] the subjects of the chief named Satan . . . mounted on a grey horse," Sir George Grey, governor of the Cape Colony from 1854 to 1861 (73). The Xhosa predicament is figured as a choice between subjugation to demonic colonial forces and obedience to ancestors making compelling and timely but ultimately impossible promises. In Gqoba's version, the cattle killing was an anticolonial movement, but in the sense of sidestepping colonial domination rather than fomenting a frontal attack. Furthermore, in keeping with his depiction of Grey as Satan, Gqoba described Nongqawuse's followers as *amagqoboka*, the term for Christian converts: remarkably, given his attachment to mission institutions, his account posits the cattle killing as what Helen Bradford calls an "Africanised Christianity" with an "anti-imperialist theology."[5]

Gqoba's narrative also diverges from the causal logic in Xhosa understandings of the episode. Xhosa oral tradition, as recorded in the twentieth century, maintains that the Nongqawuse (the event, as it is known in isiXhosa) was in effect a *European* chiefs' plot, a hoax perpetrated by Grey to destroy Xhosa autonomy and seize their land.[6] Positing the cattle killing as an *alternative* to subjugation to the "chief named Satan," Gqoba's account differs significantly from Xhosa interpretations of the Nongqawuse as a deceitful *mode* of conquest orchestrated by Sir George Grey.

I begin with Gqoba's account not to posit it as authoritative but, rather, because it unsettles these standard interpretations of the events of 1856–57. Indeed, contingent notions of authority and obscured networks of interest that "authorize" cattle-killing narratives are my concern in this chapter as I map intersections between the cattle killing and the technology of literacy. The dissemination of literacy began among the amaXhosa not long before the cattle killing and accelerated as starving survivors sought relief at Christian missions. Gqoba and his newspaper *Isigidimi samaXhosa* were fruits of this effort. Gqoba's narrative—and its complex textual history—offers an instructive and cautionary example of the transformations and distortions to which texts about the cattle killing have been subject, raising a number of issues at stake in this chapter.

Gqoba published his narrative in two installments of *Isigidimi* shortly before his death in 1888; an abridged version appeared in *Zemk'inkomo magwalandini* (There go your cattle, you cowards), a 1906 anthology edited by W. B. Rubusana that reprinted oral praise poetry (*izibongo*) and prose and poetry from isiXhosa newspapers like *Isigidimi*. It was this abridged version of Gqoba's narrative that isiXhosa novelist and critic A. C. Jordan translated into English and published as "The Tale of Nongqawuse." Jordan's translation of Rubusana's abridgment of Gqoba's narrative is the only published translation, and this chain of transmission has shaped our understanding of what Gqoba wrote about what he saw in the 1850s.

Rubusana's abridgment omitted much of Gqoba's second installment, and the pithy moral that concludes the story in English does not appear in the original *Isigidimi* version.[7] Another important omission is the role of sexuality in Nongqawuse's prophecy. In Gqoba's original, Nongqawuse says that the strangers demanded not only slaughter, noncultivation, and the abjuring of witchcraft but also the cessation of illicit sexual practices— forms of pollution that necessitated the destruction of resources "reared with defiled hands."[8] The young female prophet's injunctions against a range of male sexual behaviors addressed links between women and cattle in Xhosa sociosexual economies—an issue long underexplored in cattle- killing scholarship. The exchange, gift, or loan of cattle was necessary for contracting marriages among the amaXhosa; unmarried girls and young women were "'*inkomo zomzi*' (the cattle of the family) . . . through which wealth in cattle comes to the home."[9] Chiefs and senior men controlled access to cattle, which became a site of intergenerational conflict if elders were unwilling or unable to release them for young men to pledge as *lobola* (bridewealth).[10] Cattle were in short supply in the 1850s, after losses during war, drought, famine, and a lung-sickness epizootic that claimed at least 100,000 cattle by 1856. Chiefs in British Kaffraria lost an important source of cattle when Grey proscribed their authority to levy judicial fines. Cattle shortages—and the consequent difficulty in contracting marriages—had led to a proliferation of illicit sexual relationships, premarital pregnancies, and abortions by the 1850s.[11]

The lung-sickness epizootic provoked a crisis for a people whose iden- tity, social relations, and survival were invested in cattle: this is the lesson of modern cattle-killing historiography.[12] Although many writers address questions of gender in debating whether a young Xhosa woman—or a "cra- zy-headed girl," as the Xhosa Christian Nkohla Falati dubbed Nongqawuse in 1895[13]—could claim the authority to speak publicly, the role of sexuality in Nongqawuse's prophecy has been obscured. This silence derives partly from the form in which Gqoba's narrative circulates in isiXhosa reprint and English translations. Rubusana's abridgment of Gqoba's account—and thus Jordan's influential translation—omitted any reference to illicit sexuality. In the most widely available version of Gqoba's account, subtitled "The Cause of the Cattle-Killing at the Nongqawuse Period," this cause of the cattle killing remains obscure.

Rubusana abridged Gqoba's text after his death; likewise, Jordan's translation appeared after his death in 1968, in *Lotus: Afro-Asian Writ- ings,* a quarterly published in Cairo by the Permanent Bureau of Afro-

Asian Writers.[14] The text that appeared in the April 1972 edition of *Lotus* represents another transmogrification of Gqoba's account: *Lotus* attributed this narrative, entitled "FOLKTALE: The Cause of the Cattle-Killing at the Nongqause Period," not to Gqoba but to Jordan himself. It was neither Jordan's nor a folktale; like Nongqawuse, its author was not merely "telling stories." The *Lotus* "folktale" elides not only Gqoba's authorship but also the rich history of nineteenth-century isiXhosa newspapers. As the editor of *Isigidimi*, Gqoba filled its pages with "articles on customs, traditions, and proverbs"; transcriptions of *izibongo*; and isiXhosa poetry modeled after English versification.[15] *Isigidimi* ceased publication with Gqoba's death in 1888; it was succeeded by *Imvo zabantsundu* (Native Opinion) and *Izwi labantu* (The Voice of the People), which, unlike the Lovedale-published *Isigidimi*, were autonomous from the mission presses. Amidst late nineteenth-century consolidation of British colonial power, these newspapers provided a forum that could "mobilise African public opinion and bring pressure to bear on both colonial and imperial authorities."[16] The construal in *Lotus* of this cattle-killing text as nontextual—that is, as Jordan's folktale—all but obscures its original status as an interventionist historical document. Gqoba's narrative itself becomes a "Nongqawuse tale"—a thing not to be believed.[17]

The confusion in *Lotus* over Jordan and Gqoba, or the elision of sexuality in Rubusana's abridgment, may seem to be minor philological details. Yet the issues that they raise—orality and literacy, as mediated by the Lovedale mission press; voices from beyond the grave, whether heroic ancestors' or published authors'; narrative authority, inflected by competing gender ideologies; translation and the scholarly hegemony of English; international anti-imperialist movements and their limitations; the tension between literature and history, or between explaining a proverb and accounting for the death and dislocation of thousands of people—are central to my consideration of the immediate aftermath and continuing afterlife of the cattle killing. I read the cattle killing in terms of the literary, ideological, and material consequences of the dissemination of literacy in southern Africa in order to ask, what difference does literacy make in telling cattle-killing stories? That Nongqawuse has been both scapegoated within and erased from the historical record suggests the epistemological conundrums at the intersection of textual transmission and ideological interpretation.[18] That an 1888 isiXhosa newspaper article appears in 1972 as a folktale told by a dead man illustrates how speaking and writing the words of others, whether one calls this prophecy, ventriloquism, plagiarism, citation, or translation, constrain the uses to which the cattle killing has been put since "Nongqawuse" returned with her tale in 1856.[19] However much one might want to counter versions of the past accreted in the colonial archive with oral and/or indigenous understandings, the examples of the isiXhosa anthology *Zemk'inkomo magwalandini* and the anti-imperialist journal *Lotus* signal the difficulty of establishing impermeable distinctions between indigenous and colonial, literary and historical, oral and written.

Literacy was a crucial engine of the civilizing mission, a project undertaken by missionaries and colonial administrators to make of the amaXhosa a new people. I argue that we must understand Nongqawuse's millennial vision within the context of this competing millennial dream. The structure of prophecy can illuminate the import of literacy in the colonial encounter; the narrative plots and rhetorical figures through which the cattle killing was written into the archive reveal tensions between these competing dreams of the future at work in the eastern Cape. Authors treat the prophecy's magical aspects in metaphorical terms that expose their own implication in the material predicament of the decimated Xhosa.

I bring the tools of literary analysis to readings of historical documents in order to understand how stories written about the cattle killing are imbricated within the broader trajectory of Xhosa subjugation. The texts I examine in this chapter are nineteenth-century accounts written by colonial administrators, European missionaries, and Tiyo Soga, the first ordained Xhosa Christian minister. Reversing the logic of Nongqawuse's prophecy, Tiyo Soga describes literacy not as a challenge to Xhosa tradition but, rather, as its transmediating sustenance. Tiyo Soga's metaphorical recuperation of the cattle killing contrasts with accounts by European missionaries and administrators, in which the literary trope of peripety, or reversal, figures the Europeans' presence among the famished amaXhosa as providential. Eliding the technology of literacy on which they depend, these accounts are framed as *stories* that lavish figurative detail on anticipated visions in which their authors could not have believed. In a context where the dissemination of literacy was a key modality of colonial conquest—what Adam Ashforth has called "both a product of domination and form of domination"[20]—these texts' engagements with questions of representation, narrative structure, and metaphor invite us to rethink the relationship between literacy and the cattle killing's aftermath.

NEW PEOPLE: XHOSA AND EUROPEAN VISIONS OF
CHANGE IN THE EASTERN CAPE

Nongqawuse's followers were not the only people dreaming of different futures in the 1850s. Cattle-killing prophecies divided the Xhosa community in two, but both "submissive" believers and "unyielding" unbelievers were looking for change: the believers were "hoping for the regeneration of an old world, and the [unbelievers] grasping eagerly at the new."[21] That is, believers awaited the restoration of autonomy, resources, land, and loved ones lost in nearly a century of colonial encroachment and armed conflict, while unbelievers saw future possibility in a nascent mercantile economy where cattle and grain were commodities rather than communal resources to be shared out by chiefs.[22] Although believers and unbelievers disagreed most urgently over whether to kill cattle, their divergent visions of the future involved deeper questions. The unbelievers' embrace of innovation, as opposed to the believers' desire for renovation, was informed by (although not identical with) the hopes of Christian missionaries and colonial administrators to make of the amaXhosa a new people.

These competing dreams of newness differed in their understandings of historical change: Nongqawuse's prophecy promised *renewal* in which ancestors would return as "new people,"[23] while the colonial vision imagined a world and people *transformed.* The project of religious conversion was the most obvious of these transformations, part of the nineteenth-century global dispersal of European and American Christian evangelicals who intended their work to redeem the sin of slavery, create a kingdom of God on earth, and even hasten the fulfillment of Biblical prophecies of the millennium.[24] For this reason, I refer to the European civilizing mission as a millennial dream: missionaries saw their work of spreading the gospel to all nations within the framework of Christian eschatology, while colonial administrators imagined a wholesale transformation of people and land, the creation of "new men."[25] As early as 1827, missionary and government agent William Ritchie Thomson described changes underway at the Glasgow Missionary Society's (GMS) Tyhume station, at that time near the colonial frontier:

> Where formerly a wilderness of long grass was, and the soil never turned up since the Flood, we have now growing many of the necessaries, and even some of the luxuries of life. A neat little village has been formed,

inhabited by those who a little while ago roamed the world at large, as wild and savage as their old neighbors, the lions and tigers of the forest. They imitate us in all things—even in their dress; and now beads and baubles have fallen in the market, and old clothes are in demand. . . . If you except the black faces, a stranger would almost think he had dropped into a little Scotch village.[26]

This account overstates the eagerness of the amaXhosa to take up a new economy, new clothes, new houses, and a new god.[27] Thomson's magisterial claim also misses less-predictable ways in which prospective converts responded to the Christian story—including millenarian movements that missionaries dismissed as "superstition," as we saw in Gqoba's recounting of the Nongqawuse in an Africanized Christian idiom.[28]

Colonel John Maclean, chief commissioner of British Kaffraria, described a more wary, selective appropriation:

The Kaffir, contented like the North American Indian with his barbarous state, and apathetic as to improvement, has in addition to these other characteristics, that he clings tenaciously to his old customs and habits, is proud of his race, which he considers pure and superior to others, is therefore eminently national, is suspicious, and holds aloof from others; and while considering the white man as a means of obtaining certain articles which the despised industry of the latter supplies, would yet prefer their absence. . . . They cling to the native chieftainship as to a power which . . . represents them and their race.[29]

Maclean describes the situation facing Cape governor George Grey. A series of frontier wars beginning in 1779 had pushed the colonial frontier eastward, resulting in successive evictions of the amaXhosa from lands where generations of ancestors were buried. By the mid-1850s, the amaXhosa inhabited territory on both sides of the Kei River, the eastern boundary of British Kaffraria, a military colony established in 1847 east of the Cape Colony. Grey ruled British Kaffraria under martial law through a network of military commissioners and magistrates settled with Ngqika and Ndlambe Xhosa chiefs (Maclean's remarks about Xhosa autonomy were a warning against Grey's proposal for this magistrate system). East of the Kei River, the Gcaleka Xhosa chief Sarhili ruled independent Xhosaland; his authority as king of the amaXhosa was recognized by chiefs under British military occupation as well as by those in unconquered territory. This political geography complicated the colonial response to Nongqawuse's prophecy, which emerged in Sarhili's territory just across the Kei from British Kaffraria but spread on both sides of the river.[30] Magistrates could exert pressure over the chiefs with whom they were resident, but they had almost no influence, save the (not insignificant) threat of invasion, over chiefs in the Transkei.

Even before the cattle killing, Grey's project amounted to an antinational colonialism, a challenge to the stubborn independence of the "eminently national" amaXhosa. Grey was "full of the spirit of improvement," to borrow from John Stuart Mill's apologia for coercive methods appropriate for ruling barbarians but not civilized nations. Mill's *On Liberty*, written between 1855 and 1859, offers contemporary justification for Grey's approach to the amaXhosa: "Despotism is a legitimate mode of government in dealing with barbarians, provided the end be their improvement, and the means justified by actually effecting that end."[31] Grey transformed chiefs into paid agents of the colonial administration; he sought to replace the Xhosa pastoral economy with wage labor on European farms and public works. To consolidate his control, he looked forward to the arrival of "new people" in British Kaffraria: not the ancestors expected by Xhosa believers but, rather, British settlers who would "civilize" the amaXhosa by capturing their labor.[32] "If we leave the natives beyond our border ignorant barbarians," Grey told the Cape Parliament, "they must always remain a race of troublesome marauders."[33] In stirring rhetoric that camouflaged the brutality of his policies, Grey urged instead that the Colony "use our time of strength . . . to instruct and civilize—to change inveterate enemies into friends . . . destroyers of our stock into consumers of our goods and producers for our markets" (58). The role of missionaries was to "help build up a whole system of new ideas, new needs and desires, new allegiances, new authorities, and a new morality, all leading to an *acceptance* of the new civilization by the Africans," wrote a twentieth-century critic of missionaries' colonial complicity.[34] More than one millennial dream was at work in the eastern Cape in the 1850s: Grey described the Xhosa prophecy as envisioning "a kind of Kaffir paradise," but he had his own vision for British Kaffraria.[35] For those who embraced the civilizing mission, according to Grey, "a day of hope had already dawned."[36]

The catastrophic end of Nongqawuse's dream, in 1857, only furthered Grey's vision: "I think . . . that I see my way clearly out of all this trouble, and that instead of nothing but dangers resulting from the Kaffirs having during the excitement killed their cattle and made away with their food, we can draw very great permanent advantages from the circumstance, which may be made a stepping stone for the future [European] settlement of the country."[37] Grey's labor and resettlement policies made good his words: famine drew survivors to the missions, which succored them until they could be sent into the Colony under labor contracts.

For those who joined mission communities and willingly embraced at least some aspects of the colonial dream of civilization, disillusionment would come a half century later with the foundation of South Africa as a segregationist state:

> The African elite who readily assimilated missionary education in the hope of joining the millenarian society implicit in the promise of civilisation and Christianity, and who looked eagerly to the fulfillment of grand humanitarian ideals associated with the name of Victoria and formulated in the face of settler colonialism and Boer hostility, were ultimately betrayed as the "liberal" Cape Colony was drawn in to the first version of South Africa in 1910.[38]

Believers and unbelievers in the cattle killing can both be seen as adherents of prophecies unrealized. "Loners and prophets, filled with delusions, fantasies, ambiguities, and otherworldliness" because they ignored the stark realities around them: so historian David Chanaiwa describes *not* Nongqawuse's followers but, rather, the mission-educated elite, producers and consumers of newspapers like Gqoba's *Isigidimi.*[39]

Nongqawuse's prophecy and the colonial project of civilization were competing visions of a world remade. The conventional names in English—the cattle killing, the Xhosa national suicide—for what is known in isi-Xhosa as the "Nongqawuse" emphasize destruction and thereby obscure believers' expectant preparations. The prophecy called for actions that were *rejuvenating*: preparing new cattle kraals, grain pits, and homesteads and abjuring witchcraft and illicit sexuality would make way for the emergence of ancestors, cattle, and grain from underground riverine caverns, in a reenactment of the creation. The amaXhosa had long believed that if they could find uHlanga, the site of the original emergence, they could obtain new cattle; Nongqawuse claimed to have access to the site and the waiting herds and armies, ready to expel invaders and restore the land.[40] In this aspect, then, the prophecy envisioned an iteration of the original creation. The colonial dream, on the other hand, emphasized innovative, unprecedented aspects of millennialism. In other words, the temporalities of the Xhosa prophecy and the European civilizing mission can be roughly distinguished—a recursive vision of renewal as compared with a unidirectional, linear vision of progress. But it would be a mistake to interpret the cattle killing as a reactionary movement, imagined in some putative premodern, non-Western oceanic time. The prophecy contained elements without precedent before the 1850s (most significantly, a black/ Russian army): realization of the prophecy would have meant a radically new departure in the history of the amaXhosa, not turning back the clock. Xhosa cosmology assumed the vigilant presence of ancestors intervening in the world of the living, but the whole community returning from this parallel existence would have been something utterly new.[41]

The appeal of the new was crucial to the European millennial dream in the eastern Cape. The civilizing project worked through technologies of transformation: guns that gave lethal motion to bits of lead, turning people into corpses; scripts and printing presses that gave visual, permanent, and reproducible form to spoken words; and ploughs and irrigation furrows that turned agricultural surplus into money. Missionaries offered literacy and new agricultural methods; "the construction of the irrigation furrow became the *sine qua non* of mission stations, for very good agricultural and evangelical reasons."[42] Literacy and irrigated agriculture extended agency spatially and temporally in ways that could seem magical to the uninitiated. Using water to draw people to the Word, missionaries also depended on the weapons of colonial armies.[43]

The printing press, which reproduced grammars and dictionaries of African languages and translations of religious texts, was a technology of transformation particularly important to missionaries. Carrying a press with him from Scotland, John Ross arrived at the Tyhume mission station on December 16, 1823, and joined his new colleague, John Bennie. Bennie soon wrote to GMS secretary John Love, "On the 17th, we got our Press in order; on the 18th the alphabet was set up; and yesterday we threw off 50 copies. . . . Through your instrumentality a new era has commenced in the history of the Kaffer nation. . . . The day dawns. The star of hope is above the horizon. May its cheering light usher in the rays of our better sun."[44] Bennie described his enumeration of an isiXhosa vocabulary as "reducing to form and rule this language which hitherto floated in the wind."[45] (A suggestive typographical error describes isiXhosa as that which "hitherto floated in the mind."[46]) The Lovedale mission press, among the oldest and most prolific mission presses in southern Africa, traces its origins to those four days in 1823. Scholars cite Bennie's words almost ritualistically, but none comment upon how he marks this "new era" of print evangelism by describing its day-by-day creation in terms that echo Genesis, the emergence of human order from divine (or savage) chaos.[47]

For the missionaries' immediate audience, the relationships among these technologies of transformation and the logic of Christian resurrection or of the colonial economy were no more or less self-evident than was Nongqawuse's idea of destroying wealth to renew the land.[48] One of the earliest Christian converts, Ntsikana, was an early nineteenth-century prophet-poet remembered as urging his followers to embrace the Bible brought by the "nation who comes from overseas" but to reject its "round button with no holes" (money), otherwise "you will be scattered like a flock of sheep and lose your nation."[49] Several of Ntsikana's followers joined missions; one of them, Soga (a councilor of chief Ngqika), was the first to adopt ploughing and irrigation at Tyhume in the 1830s.[50] Yet, as Soga discovered, the Bible and the button without holes were not easily separated.

Missionaries among the amaXhosa understood Christianity in broadly civilizational, rather than narrowly doctrinal, terms: conversion was as much about practices of everyday life as about matters of theological belief. GMS missionary Robert Niven reveals the agricultural idiom underlying mission endeavor: "'the gospel plough will speed the faster that it is accompanied by the *school* plough and the *land* plough.'"[51] Soga asked C. L. Stretch, military officer and Ngqika resident agent, for cattle to replace those lost in the 1834–35 frontier war. Stretch told Soga, "You have both oxen and cows in your beautiful Chumie land, and if you will take the trouble to dig them out of the field you will be relieved from begging." Soga no more believed that herds of cattle waited under his fields than he would believe Nongqawuse's similar claim two decades later, but Stretch explained to him that, by growing and selling vegetables, Soga could earn money to buy cattle.[52]

Commodity logic could seem as magical as a resurrection; Ntsikana rightly regarded money as a black magic that would break the nation. For the amaXhosa, cattle were a special kind of commodity, a singular locus of value: their ownership rested with chiefs and elders (and ultimately with the ancestors), and their circulation created networks of patronage and filiation that made social relationships visible, rather than obscuring them.[53]

Cattle resist commodity fetishization, while their auratic aspect—"beyond the purview of the coin"—exceeds secular calculations of value; the use and exchange of cattle link people with ancestors.[54] The commodity, Marx tells us, is a "very strange thing," with its "metaphysical subtleties and theological niceties."[55] Some prospective converts found the value of literacy even more mysterious than the value of cattle may seem in Marxian analysis. Since literacy "'does not literally make cows,'" missionary Niven wrote, "'so the wanting it, [the amaXhosa] conclude, cannot be any great loss.'"[56] Finding apprentices for the Lovedale mission press was particularly difficult, principal James Stewart observed: "Every native can understand the value of being able to make a table, or a chair, or to repair a waggon. With printing, however, it was a different matter,—Kaffir experience not showing how a man could make a living by arranging small bits of lead in rows. By patience and much persuasion one apprentice was got."[57]

Stewart's agricultural image of typesetting, the orderly planting of lead yielding life, reverses more-common associations between lead type and lead bullets, the "ink as well as blood" that established in the eastern Cape a "powerful new order of representation . . . backed by greater military and social power."[58] The interchangeability of these forms of lead is evident in an oft-cited anecdote: during the war of 1846–47, when Lovedale was abandoned and its denizens had retreated to the safety of military forts, "the types of the printing-press were converted into bullets, and pages of the sacred books into wadding, for the guns of the Dutch Boers."[59] Guns and books—particularly the Bible—have been yoked in the Xhosa imaginary. The contemporary *imbongi* (oral praise poet) David Livingstone Phakamile Yali-Manisi draws upon a centuries-old trope of books turning into guns:

> the day that the missionaries arrived
> They carried a Bible in front,
> But they had a breechloader slung behind.[60]

Opland speculates that longstanding Xhosa suspicion of the "technology of writing" might have facilitated the survival of oral poetry as a living tradition.[61]

The first ordained Xhosa minister was Tiyo Soga, son of "old" Soga, the follower of Ntsikana and skeptic of Stretch's claims. Tiyo Soga returned to Africa from his ordination in Scotland in July 1857, a few months after cattle and ancestors failed to emerge as prophesied. During an 1866 visit to Sarhili's territory across the Kei River, Tiyo Soga encountered an uneasy understanding of the transformative and pacifying effect (in the notorious colonial sense) of "*the Word*," as Sarhili's people called it:

> Missionaries are the emissaries of Government, to act upon the minds and feelings of the people, with an instrument which they call 'the Word,' and . . . those who become affected by the Word, and exchange Kafir customs for those of the white men, become subjects of the English Government. Thus white men plan to get a footing in their country, which they afterwards take altogether. These are the views of not a few of Kreli's people.[62]

This interpretation of the power of literacy appears in Tiyo Soga's 1877 biography, composed by fellow GMS missionary John Aitken Chalmers.[63] Although Chalmers might have wished to challenge this belief in the complicity between Christianity and conquest, he unwittingly shared with Sarhili's people a belief in the transformative, perhaps even "miraculous," potential of texts to "seize and convert those they encounter," as Isabel Hofmeyr writes.[64] He describes religious conversion as a process of textual transformation and, in exemplary cases, transformative textualization: he titled his biography *Tiyo Soga: A Page of South African Mission Work*. Tiyo Soga's tenuous position is evident in the pages of Chalmers's biography: the conviction of Sarhili's people that missionaries acted as colonial agents (which had actually been colonial policy until 1830) implicates Tiyo Soga's vocation,[65] while his fellow missionary labels him a "Model Kafir," evidence of the beneficent success of missionary endeavor (see fig. 2).[66] Negotiating this liminal position, Tiyo Soga drew on the power associated with writing when, at the laying of the foundation stone for his church, he solemnly "read out, and held up for the people to see, two inscriptions . . . one in English and the other in Caffre" that were buried in a lead box under the foundation stone.[67]

Tiyo Soga's burial of text in the foundation of his church, like the association of books and guns in the Xhosa imaginary, reconfigures the relationship between literacy and death as theorized by Walter Ong. Imagining the ambivalence of "persons rooted in primary orality," who desire the "vast complex of powers" associated with literacy yet fear to lose what is "deeply loved in the earlier oral world," Ong concludes, "We have to die to continue living."[68] Figuring the transition to literate consciousness in terms of death,

2. Missionary and chief, c. 1871: Tiyo Soga (back, second from right) and Sarhili (front, center). Also pictured: W. W. Fynn and W. R. D. Fynn (back); other chiefs and councilors, possibly Mhala (back left), Fadana (front, second from left), Sandile (front, second from right). BC293 Sir W. E. M. Stanford Papers, University of Cape Town Libraries.

Ong also invokes the Christian resurrection in theorizing textuality. The written or printed word is a dead thing available to "being resurrected into limitless living contexts by a potentially infinite number of living readers" (81). Tiyo Soga literalizes this notion when he buries texts to inaugurate the life of his church. Dead men cannot speak (except through prophets); in literate cultures, however, their words can rise again.

Literacy can be imagined as the *afterlife* of orality. The transition to literacy marks a rupture—a figurative death, in Ong's terms; yet that rupture enables continuity, an afterlife. If reading reanimates dead text, so too must inscribing old texts in "limitless living contexts"—through citation, allusion, and other modes of appropriation—make the past live within the present. In this infinite potential for reanimation, textuality is intertextuality. This notion of afterlife connotes the ineffable commingling of essential continuity, substantial transformation, and spatiotemporal displacement and return that are implicit in a resurrection. Textual afterlives are wildly unpredictable, as we have seen with Gqoba's cattle-killing narrative. The links between mission-sponsored literacy and British military supremacy make clear that the sense of loss or rupture in the transition to literacy that Ong figures as death occurs within a context of coercion, if not quite at gunpoint. Furthermore, the traffic between orality and literacy is more multivalent than Ong's eschatological imagery implies: dead texts remain available to reanimation and transfiguration in oral modes, and, as Isabel Hofmeyr demonstrates, African converts (even those not themselves literate) incorporate the "technology of print" into "existing understandings of the sacred . . . to speak to existing spiritual and ancestral worlds."[69] The relationship between orality and literacy in colonial contexts is not a zero-sum game in which literacy makes steady advances over orality. Given the missionary conjunction of education and proselytization, it is important to remember that *oral* transmission of Christian ideas and images was equally as important as the printing of African language dictionaries, grammars, and Biblical translations.[70] In other words, although Ong's evocative figurations of the transition from orality to literacy are compelling and uniquely apposite to the cattle killing, I want to set his metaphors in motion against the historical context of British colonial conquest, in which the technology of literacy was a crucial modality and the conquest of orality by literacy was never fully complete.[71]

Mhala, the only chief charged with treason after the cattle killing, invoked the transfigurational quality and historical implications of writing in testimony at his court-martial: "'I have nothing further to say but *I wish this recorded* and await what is in the heart of the court and beg them to remember that words do not perish, that though I may die [you had better judge me truly] that nothing hereafter may arise to disturb you. People die of sickness, and are killed in war; my words seem few but they are long enough.'"[72] Not literate, but conscious of speaking into the juridical record, Mhala seizes upon writing's capacity to enable posthumous speech as his only recourse against the representational machinery of the colonial state. Mhala warns that textuality can effect a haunting; for Chalmers, the living after enabled by print was instead a blessing. In his obituary for Tiyo Soga, Chalmers urges that his sermons be printed "so that even though dead, his voice would still be heard."[73] Chalmers played a crucial role in both amplifying and muffling Tiyo Soga's voice after his death, as I discuss below.

Ong labels print's capacity to preserve and reanimate speech its "vatic quality": "Like the oracle or the prophet, the book relays an utterance from a source, the one who really 'said' or wrote the book" (78–79). This anthropomorphic trope of the book as secondhand speech blurs the distinction between orality and literacy, enabling a comparison between the mobility of words in each mode that requires thinking about authorship in terms of prophecy. Just as the prophet is an inspired medium for suprahuman utterance, the book is a medium that "speaks" another's words. In contemporary literary theory, the author is figured more as dead (and without hope of resurrection) than divine. Nonetheless, theorizing literacy in terms of prophecy and the afterlives of textuality is particularly evocative in the context of the cattle killing: the dissemination of textuality, and the textualization of the colonized other, advanced the project of colonial transformation against which Xhosa prophecies were articulated.

THE RESURRECTIONS OF TIYO SOGA

Tiyo Soga, Chalmers's "page" of mission work, made his own connection between prophecy and print. Tiyo Soga believed that Nongqawuse's words emerged from the sinister potential of prophetic language—the prophet's manipulation of, or by, spurious authority. Yet he also believed that the sociality of print could protect the amaXhosa from future deceptions. In the inaugural, August 1862 issue of the Lovedale newspaper *Indaba* (The News), Tiyo Soga's article "A National Newspaper" (*Ipepa le-Ndaba Zasekaya*) urged readers to consider the newspaper a "national corn-pit," "a beautiful vessel for preserving the stories, fables, legends, customs, anecdotes and history of the tribes."[74] If writers "disgorge all they know" and "unearth . . . from the graves" the histories of earlier eras and chiefs, they will "revive and bring to light all this great wealth of information" and "resurrect our ancestral forebears" (152–53). The newspaper could reanimate the buried Xhosa past, so that literacy creates an afterlife for orality. This exhortation to fill the "national corn-pit" effects an ancestral return different from that promised by Nongqawuse: Tiyo Soga reverses the causal logic of Nongqawuse's claim six years earlier, that by *emptying* grain pits, believers would prepare the way for ancestors who would return to fill them.

Tiyo Soga directly confronts Nongqawuse's prophecy and its costs. Addressing *Indaba*'s editor (Bryce Ross) and speaking for the amaXhosa, he admits, "As people who are always hungry for news often we find ourselves dupes of deceivers under the guise of relating genuine facts" (151–52). He recalls the disturbance caused by a recent partial solar eclipse when some took this "'unexplainable thing'" (153) as fulfillment of Nongqawuse's prophecies;[75] she was said to predict that the resurrection would be marked by a red sun, double sun, or sun that would reverse course at noon.[76] Soga speculates that a total eclipse might have sparked another tragedy among the Xhosa nation (*umzi*). However, the partial eclipse had been predicted through scientific "knowledge and wisdom"; since it could warn about phenomena that might otherwise "come upon us suddenly and unexpectedly, . . . now the newspaper will make our minds and hearts be at peace" (153). Literacy, then, offers access to reliable, reassuring information about the future, for people weary and wary of millennial dreaming.

Tiyo Soga's privileging of European meteorology over Xhosa prophecy in the same article that exhorts *Indaba*'s readers to fill the national corn pit and thereby revive the ancestors indicates the ambivalence of his position. Meteorological ambivalence also runs through Soga's writing about rainmaking. Describing in an 1860 letter an "inhuman foolish . . . sad expedient for obtaining Rain," Tiyo Soga laments the persistence of that "hedeous [*sic*] hateful monster," superstition (24, 59). Elsewhere he is encouraged by the fact that "those natives who Know something of the gospel . . . believe that if Rain will fall at all during drought it will be on the Sabbath" (58). Facing a drought in 1862 that threatened "famine worse than that of Umlakasa" (Nongqawuse's uncle), Soga notes that his church has been crowded with worshippers: "The object was to humble ourselves before God, confess our sins, and beseech him to remove his hand from us, and to grant rain. We got rain. Indeed, we have been one of the few favoured spots" (92).[77] These scattered passages in his letters and journal suggest the challenges Tiyo Soga faced as a Xhosa Christian missionary: how could he distinguish heritage from superstition, superstition from Christianity, and the promise of Christianity from the coercive propagation of European power?[78] Karin Barber dubs this process "cultural editing"—new elites created by colonial literacy "refashioning and sanitizing their oral traditions from within, but as if from outside."[79]

Competing modes of interpretation and overlapping scissions of power and authority shaped Tiyo Soga's reception among those he called "fellow countrymen." Although his gender-exclusive term was likely incidental, European missionary presence among the amaXhosa evoked questions about masculinity that became urgent in Tiyo Soga's case. Some early missionaries were likened to charismatic male figures of Xhosa prophetic tradition, and missionaries' ability to provide water gave them authority that rivaled (and threatened) the power of chiefs.[80] Chiefs were anxious to assert their authority over missionaries: the Ngqika chief Sandile referred to missionaries as "my wives," among whom he had favorites.[81] Categoriz-

ing male European missionaries as wives—who should not intervene in
such matters as war—was a strategy to reassert masculinity at a time when
drought, land pressures, and cattle shortages (which led some men into the
mostly female domain of agriculture), as well as British Kaffrarian chiefs'
transformation into colonial employees unable to adjudicate cases and col-
lect fines, had severely undermined Xhosa masculinity, particularly that of
chiefs.[82] Amidst these competing masculinities, the fact that Tiyo Soga had
not been initiated into Xhosa manhood undermined his authority among
"fellow countrymen" as much as his lifelong campaign against circumci-
sion raised him in the estimation of fellow missionaries.[83] Tiyo Soga could
not be ideologically subordinated as a missionary "wife," but his not being
a Xhosa "man" either was, for some, an untenable anomaly.

Such contradictions are evident in Tiyo Soga's consideration of relationships between orality and literacy in *Indaba*: he imagines the newspaper's
production and circulation in terms of its editor visiting homes where
people share food, news, and conversation. The article opens by initiating
a dialogue: "Greetings Mr. Editor! We hear that you will be reporting and
publishing events. Is it true?" (151). Writing about this article, Leon de Kock
notes "the contradiction of seeming to celebrate a pristine oral culture in
an orthodox missionary publication whose existence denies such a state
of innocence."[84] If colonialism obviates the possibility of orality in a "state
of innocence," what Tiyo Soga posits, then, is the afterlife of orality in the
age of literacy, orality extant though transmediated. Homestead sociality
can, through the medium of the newspaper, be developed on a national
scale: "Everything must be imparted to the nation as a whole," he urges.[85]
This nexus of orality and literacy can recover what threatens to be, or has
already been, lost to the grave.

The Lovedale mission press launched *Isigidimi* (where Gqoba's cattle-
killing narrative appeared) in 1876 as the successor to *Indaba*; Soga's
vision of the cooperation of orality and literacy in the 1862 inaugural
issue of *Indaba* contrasts starkly with the editorial rationale provided
for its successor: "Our aim is to scatter ideas in the moral wastes, and
desert places of heathen ignorance. . . . Without printing, the mass of
the people must remain barbarous."[86] Against Tiyo Soga's conviction
that newspapers could facilitate a transmediated cultural continuity, the
later editorial posits a rupture wherein *Isidigimi* can bring civilization
to the wilderness. For Tiyo Soga, Xhosa oral tradition is not a wasteland
awaiting the "instrumentality" of Christian conversion; rather, literacy

can salvage a tradition threatened by the colonial encounter. His concern about Xhosa susceptibility to "superstition" emerges from deep sadness about the cattle killing, as opposed to the civilizational superiority assumed in the editorial statement about *Isigidimi*. Tiyo Soga envisions Xhosa culture renewed through literacy; the Lovedale publishers envision the transformation of savagery into civilization.

What is most remarkable about Soga's *Indaba* article is that, just as he describes literacy using metaphors of convivial orality (the itinerant editor sharing conversation in Xhosa homes), Soga uses metaphors of resurrection to exhort *Indaba* readers to reap and winnow oral tradition for preservation in the national corn pit. He urges *metaphorical* resurrection of the ancestors at the same time that he disavows Nongqawuse's prophecy of their *literal* resurrection. These tropes of resurrection operate within an integral Xhosa worldview: Tiyo Soga urges a project of cultural retrieval and revival, not one of religious conversion or syncretism. Despite his own vocation, Tiyo Soga's *Indaba* article juxtaposes not the "truth" of Christian resurrection with the disillusionments of Nongqawuse's failed prophecy but, rather, figurative hopes of bringing back the Xhosa ancestors with literal ones.

In embracing cultural renewal through memory and narrative rather than the destruction of material resources, Tiyo Soga redeems the desires expressed in the cattle killing by transforming them into metaphor. Metaphor functions as a technology of temporality, an aid in imagining links among past, present, and future. Tiyo Soga's figuration of the newspaper as national corn pit is more powerful for the ways in which it is constrained by its invocation of the cattle killing, while also reimagining that historical trajectory. His metaphors undo the reversal of expectations in the cattle killing by reversing its resurrectional logic: the amaXhosa must fill, not empty, the corn pits to bring back the ancestors. What is significant here is not that Tiyo Soga uses a familiar trope of immortality-through-print but, rather, that he appropriates specific images from cattle-killing prophecies: the restoration of plenty, the unity of the nation, and the presence of ancestors whose memory threatens to evaporate amidst rapid change. He reconfigures the causal relationships among these elements so that Nongqawuse's vision of renewal survives its immediate failure by means of revision in metaphor. I am not arguing that Tiyo Soga sought to redeem Nongqawuse's prophecy but, rather, that his endorsement of literacy reshapes the dynamic of cultural renewal she had promised and thus offers an alternative to the dangers of "superstition" that had so recently decimated the Xhosa nation.

The singular image of the newspaper as national corn pit reflects Tiyo Soga's commitment to stewarding (or editing) the Xhosa past through a critical, paradoxical moment: the technology of literacy facilitated such archival impulses, yet the ideology of literacy, as part of a civilizing project, threatened to sweep away the culture constituted in orality. Tiyo Soga contributed several articles to *Indaba*; he urged subscribers to preserve their copies as a "precious inheritance for generations of growing children"; and he sent his sons off to school with a booklet of history and lore he titled "The Inheritance of My Children."[87] Chalmers relates that Tiyo Soga was often to be seen "long past midnight sitting in a Kafir hut, note-book in hand, jotting down some incident or tale or bloody fight as described by an old wrinkled countryman of his own."[88] Yet Tiyo Soga recognized that literacy was not the only way to keep the past alive. He was moved by his congregation's response to singing a hymn composed by Ntsikana, who had urged Tiyo Soga's father to the mission: "It . . . awakened in their minds the memories of the past. . . . I saw many an eye bathed in tears, and many a strong frame shaking and trembling, from the intensity of mental emotion."[89] Those who could not read *Indaba* could reanimate the past by singing Ntsikana's hymns.

Ntsikana's hymns provide a useful counterpoint to Tiyo Soga's thinking about the Xhosa past and future. Ntsikana was among the earliest Xhosa converts; he claimed to be "renewed" by God even before Joseph Williams of the London Missionary Society began work among the amaXhosa in 1816.[90] After his conversion experience, Ntsikana urged, "'The thing that has entered within me directs that all should pray.'"[91] Unlike Tiyo Soga, Ntsikana never learned to write, but he was clearly impressed by the technology of literacy: he often "read" out the words to his hymns, having found them "written" on his cloak and on the tail of his favorite ox, Hulushe.[92] He composed four hymns in the 1810s, drawing on the formal conventions of isiXhosa oral poetry and song; they remained enduring favorites because they cast Christian ideas in Xhosa imagery, much as Tiyo Soga recast the imagery of Nongqawuse's prophecy. Unlike the stories that Tiyo Soga posits as belonging to the nation as a whole, Ntsikana's hymns were transmitted *as his*, not as transcriptions of anonymous tradition; these individual compositions function, according to Jordan, as a "bridge between the traditional and the post-traditional" in Xhosa cultural history.[93] Beyond his claim of metaphorical, mimetic, or magical literacy in "reading" his hymns, Ntsikana asserted that his hymns could protect the living. In conflicts between

Xhosa clans that climaxed in the 1818 battle of Amalinde, Ntsikana told his followers to discard their assegais and take up the "assegai of God": if they sang his "poll-headed" hymn (named for the defenselessness of cattle without horns), they would be protected from the enemy.[94] This claim was more than metaphorical. Claims of magical literacy are not unique to Ntsikana or the amaXhosa; as Hofmeyr argues, "shared ideas of literacy as a miraculous agent and books as magical objects" fostered encounters between missionaries and prospective African converts.[95]

Ntsikana asserted the talismanic power of song; Tiyo Soga argued that preserving cultural traditions, rather than destroying material wealth, would bring back the ancestors. These shifts away from armed confrontation and physical violence resonate with the innovation of cattle-killing prophecies as responses to colonial encroachment and military occupation. British Kaffraria was under martial law and awash in rumors of war and colonial threats of invading independent kwaXhosa; unprecedented numbers of troops were stationed on the frontier in 1856—twice the number present at the beginning of the 1850–53 war and four times as many as in 1846–47.[96] The cattle-killing prophecy offered alternatives to a direct offensive against the British, at a time when British attack seemed imminent.

Nongqawuse's prophecy replotted wartime devastations that were familiar to the amaXhosa, offering the act of destruction as a prelude to renewal and autonomy rather than defeat and desperation. The destructive actions the prophecy demanded—razing huts, gardens, fields, and grain pits and eliminating cattle—were tactics used by British forces against the ama-Xhosa since 1811, although cattle were seized rather than slaughtered.[97] The prophecy promised to reverse the valence of chronic losses of cattle and other wealth to colonial forces: to put it crudely, by inflicting on themselves the equivalent of the scorched-earth policy that the British had imposed on them, the amaXhosa hoped to recover wealth and eject the invaders. We also can read this decision strategically: without vital resources like crops, grain pits, or herds in need of protection, the amaXhosa could devote more military attention to thwarting what seemed an imminent colonial attack.[98] Bradford calls our attention to versions of the prophecy that envisioned the return not of all Xhosa ancestors but, rather, of an army variously composed of Xhosa warriors of old, a new brave black race, or Russians (imagined to be black) rumored to have defeated the British in the Crimean war.[99] Compliance with the prophecy would bring victory over Europeans in an apocalyptic war that the living would not have to fight.

Yet, just as it is too reductive to say that the amaXhosa killed their cattle because they might have died anyway of lung sickness,[100] we fail to understand the cattle killing by concluding that it simply made good military sense. In suggesting that the prescribed acts of destruction rearranged the familiar plot of frontier war, I do not want to lose sight of the ways in which the cattle killing, as a kind of ancestral stock exchange,[101] eludes explanation through cost-benefit analysis, however culturally sensitive that analysis might be. The prophecies predicated the arrival of new and beautiful cattle on the destruction of potentially contaminated ones, but that contamination was overdetermined by a range of economic, political, social, sexual, and spiritual factors, all of which would be undone in a millennial renovation. Cattle-killing prophecies, I argue, were inextricably material and metaphorical, demanding a destruction of resources that would realize their visions through tropic logic, a metaphor on which a people staked their survival. But skeptics also invoked tropic logic: "'Cattle are the race, they being dead the race dies,'" warned the Bomvana chief Moni when he advised Sarhili against killing cattle.[102]

Writing at a moment when Moni's warning about the metonymic link between cattle and people seemed to have been realized, Tiyo Soga undertook his dual project of Christian evangelism and cultural retrieval in the aftermath of national catastrophe. His vision of Xhosa survival refigured Nongqawuse's prophecy (as it, in turn, rearranged the plot of war), but Tiyo Soga turned decisively away from imagining a wholesale eradication of the colonial order. In confronting colonialism, segregation, and apartheid, subsequent writers and activists also negotiated the alternatives of armed resistance, working through state institutions and mobilizing memory and metaphor. As I discuss in chapter 2, the late nineteenth- and early twentieth-century "New African" elite confronted the dislocations of colonial subjugation and postcolonial segregation not through physical resistance but through written articulation of present grievances and oppositional recuperation of the past.

But if Tiyo Soga shows that Nongqawuse's vision could survive the horrors of its aftermath, the fate of his own writing illustrates a recurrent necessity to recover what has been lost. Much of Tiyo Soga's writing about the Xhosa past was lost, according to Chalmers, who claimed that what survived was largely illegible.[103] Tiyo Soga's literary reputation rests instead on his isiXhosa translation of the first part of Bunyan's *Pilgrim's Progress*; he also served on a committee that translated the gospels, and he wrote and collected isiXhosa hymns. While Tiyo Soga embraced these literary-evangelical translation projects, he rejected overtures from both chief Maqoma and colonial officials to interpret for them during the 1850–53 war (58, 68). In his work as a translator, Tiyo Soga embraced the Book over the gun.

Although written words might be infinitely available for reanimation, they remain dead if they are lost or forgotten; their transfigured afterlives are shaped by the concerns of those who reanimate them.[104] The loss of Tiyo Soga's writing is compounded by the biases of his first biographer, who took his subject as an exemplary "page" of mission work and constructed his portrait accordingly. The relationship between Tiyo Soga and Chalmers, dating back to student days at Lovedale, was complex. An 1865 exchange in the *King William's Town Gazette and Kaffrarian Banner* reveals a deep rift between the men, then colleagues at Mgwali mission. Lamenting their intractability to "civilization," Chalmers predicted the extinction of the amaXhosa. Tiyo Soga's pseudonymous response (as "Defensor") is crucial to understanding his significance as an African intellectual—not only because it reveals ugly tensions between biographer and "Model Kafir" subject but also because it outlines a global vision of "Negro" survival despite "all these disasters" of recent centuries.[105] Looking to the continent as a whole, Tiyo Soga grounds the future of this broader "Kaffir race" in Biblical prophecy, the "glowing prediction . . . [that] 'Ethiopia shall soon stretch her hands to God'. . . . I for one shall adhere to the declaration of the 'old book' before I accept the theories of men" (181). The exemplary convert's deployment of Biblical authority in denouncing Chalmers' contemptuous evangelical despair epitomizes what De Kock calls Tiyo Soga's "agonistic," triangulated relationships to the Xhosa nation and European civilization.[106] Tiyo Soga appropriates the civilizing mission's philosophical foundations in order to reveal its failures, anticipating similar strategies (both secular and religious) in elite anticolonial nationalist movements in South Africa and beyond, in the era of high imperialism.[107] The Ethiopian "rallying cry" of African and diasporic nationalists "invokes and adapts a religious trope to a secular imagining of an Africa lifted up onto the world stage otherwise denied it."[108] Tiyo Soga's glimpse of global black community led his second biographer, Donovan Williams, to identify him as a precursor of "Black Consciousness" in South Africa and "negritude" on a continental and pan-African scale.[109]

Setting Williams's overstated claims for Tiyo Soga as a precursor for twentieth-century black (trans)nationalism against Chalmers's construction of him as "Model Kafir," David Attwell considers "how the man could play

these apparently diametrically opposed roles at the same time; that is to say,
... how Soga's nationalism involves both a claim to participate in a universal
history and an affirmation of his Africanness."[110] Attwell writes incisively
about Tiyo Soga negotiating contradictions between Enlightenment ideals
and the racial realities of the Cape frontier: "Soga's moment is that of the
transformative paradox" that generates a "transculturated" or "homemade"
enlightenment (565, 563). To Attwell's articulation of these synchronic
contradictions, I would add a diachronic caveat that, as historical figure,
Soga has not been seen to play these roles *at the same time*, even if his own
experience was thoroughly conflicted. As with Tiyo Soga's refiguration of
Nongqawuse's prophecy (itself drawing on earlier prophecies), Williams's
"resurrection" of Tiyo Soga is a transformative recuperation, a reappraisal
that bears the imprint of its "living context."[111] Tiyo Soga's achievement
survives today in *partial* (both fragmentary and interested) accounts of his
work available in written records. The resurrected Soga might not recognize himself, an inversion of the ironic possibilities driving plays such as
Woza Albert! in South Africa or *Godspell* in the United States: in the late
twentieth century, what would we do with Jesus?

THE PERIPETIES OF THE CATTLE KILLING

Chalmers interrupts his biography of Tiyo Soga with a chapter-long interlude, "The Cattle Killing Delusion," in which Tiyo Soga appears only in the
final paragraph. He was in Scotland completing his studies and returned
to Africa, newly ordained, in July 1857, a few months after the failure of the
cattle-killing prophecy. In this digressive chapter, Chalmers describes the articulation of the prophecy by Mhlakaza, Nongqawuse's uncle, who "preached
to the Kafirs a *new gospel*, which was none other than a resurrection from
the dead."[112] We read of the anticipated transformations, the prophecy's
unsteady dissemination in British Kaffraria and the Transkei, the perplexed
colonial machinations to stop it, and the disappointment and desperation
of a starving people nobly relieved through Christian charity.

Not content with the implicit rejoinder of the "injunction of Scripture"
to the catastrophe of the Xhosa "new gospel," Chalmers's final paragraph
narrates Tiyo Soga's return to African shores and his discovery that "those
to whom he had come to preach the Gospel were a dispersed nation, utterly
destroyed by their own folly" (129).[113] However devastated Tiyo Soga was to
find his people in such a state, Chalmers identifies as good news the prospect

that "the nation that clung with such tenacity to a lie, and demolished its dearest idols in that belief, and so readily yielded up present possessions in the hope of future good, has surely the capacity of being taught to trust in Him who is the resurrection and the life. Tiyo Soga resolved . . . to teach his countrymen that there is a resurrection, in which all will participate, who look to Jesus" (129). Chalmers finds hope for Christian missions in the Xhosa capacity for faith and susceptibility to sacrificial logic.[114] Tiyo Soga juxtaposed literal and figurative modes of resurrecting Xhosa ancestors; Chalmers contrasts resurrections heralded by false and true Xhosa evangelists, the exceptionally deluded Mhlakaza and the exceptionally pious Tiyo Soga.[115] Christianity is the corrective to Xhosa "gospel"; people easily converted to error should be even more amenable to Truth delivered by a prophet in his own land.

The arrival of Tiyo Soga, bearing another gospel to the Xhosa, resumes the central narrative thread of Chalmers's interrupted biography. The neatness of the chapter's structure, however, points to a broader issue in cattle-killing discourse: how colonial sources make sense of the movement's ends by constructing the endings of their narratives, or how narrative structure expresses historical teleology. The uneven parallelism of Mhlakaza and Tiyo Soga in Chalmers's biography implies that the civilizing mission might turn the cattle killing's apparent historical tragedy into another narrative mode, with Tiyo Soga as the hero. I invoke the crucial insight of Hayden White— that the narrative impulse of historiography constructs particular kinds of plots familiar to readers of literature[116]—because Chalmers's framing of his narrative is only one example of the extravagantly literary aspects of early cattle-killing accounts.

Hayden White demonstrates how history written as narrative emanates a sense of naturalness, as if "the world [could] speak itself and speak itself as a story."[117] If literacy is the afterlife of orality, written narratives mask and naturalize this transposition by projecting a speaking, storytelling world. In nineteenth-century cattle-killing narratives written by missionaries, colonial administrators, and early historians, what is remarkable is not their naturalness, however, but the insistence with which they call attention to their literariness. Although variously plotted, many of these narratives open with some variation on *once upon a time*. This temptation to construe the cattle killing as story (and as story heard, rather than read) is particularly striking when cattle-killing accounts are embedded within broader discussions of missionary endeavor or Cape history.

The best example of this tendency to narrate the cattle killing as literary set piece is in the oeuvre of George McCall Theal, whose voluminous output on southern African historiography began while he was a teacher and printer at Lovedale.[118] The cattle-killing account in Theal's *Compendium of the History and Geography of South Africa* (first published in 1874) begins, "One morning in May, 1856, a girl named NONGQAUSE, daughter of a councillor of SARILI, went to draw water from a little stream that flowed past her home."[119] This early work is structured around a moral theme of progress against "ignorance, superstition, and indolence" among each chief (49); its subjective narrative perspective is that of a Christian colonial observer in the Cape Colony. In later writing, Theal takes a more (ostensibly) objective approach to political history organized chronologically. His account of the cattle killing appears nearly unchanged throughout his work, however, save for some factual corrections and different terminological choices, like substituting *people* or *tribe* for *nation* and *Xosa* for *Kaffir*.[120] Theal's fabulous narration of the cattle killing is even more striking when it appears in the more sober, monumental *History of South Africa, from 1795 to 1872*.

Theal's account is not unique in its figurative language or the descriptive energy devoted to the prophecy's anticipated transformations. Theal borrows Biblical similes to describe the projected appearance of cattle "like stars of the sky in multitude. Enormous skin sacks were being made ready to contain the milk shortly to be like water in plenty."[121] Beyond sketching anticipated wonders, other sources enumerate, with remarkable sympathy, strange perceptions already afoot:

Wonderful reports were constantly in circulation. Armies were seen reviewing on the sea, others sailing in umbrellas; thousands of cattle were heard knocking their horns together and bellowing in caverns, impatient to rise, only waiting until all their fellows who still walked the earth were slain; dead men, years in the grave, had been seen, who sent pathetic appeals to their kindred not to delay their coming back to life by refusing to obey the prophet.[122]

This passage appears in Chalmers's biography of Tiyo Soga, but it was written by Frances Brownlee, wife of Charles Pacalt Brownlee, the commissioner of the Ngqika Xhosa in British Kaffraria in 1856–57.[123] The passive voice of Frances Brownlee's verbs heightens the impression of wondrous portents seen and heard, while making her own sense of their credibility grammatically irrelevant and thus ideologically invisible.

These sympathetic depictions of expected transformations and won-derful phenomena that bolstered believers' faith are remarkable precisely because their authors could not have credited them, not least because they were written after the prophecy's failure. They differ substantially from the account of Wesleyan missionary William C. Holden in *The Past and Future of the Kaffir Races* (1866). Holden devotes almost no descriptive attention to the prophecy, a "gigantic piece of jugglery" orchestrated by chiefs who manipulated "the deluded superstitious masses [who] believed these wild unnatural announcements."[124] Holden would have had to sup-press his contempt in order to show readers how the prophecy appealed to the imagination.[125]

In their descriptions of the promised resurrection, Theal and Frances Brownlee also are more exuberant than Xhosa writers. The son of Tiyo Soga, J. Henderson Soga, spares only four sentences in *The Ama-Xosa: Life and Customs* (1932) to describe the prophecy. The relative asceticism of J. H. Soga's account matches his abrupt treatment of the aftermath: "Needless to say none of these wonders came to pass" (121). Likewise, the abridged version of W. W. Gqoba's narrative tells us simply, "Nothing happened. The sun did not set, no dead person came back to life, and not one of the things that had been predicted came to pass."[126] Although this version of Gqoba's narrative allots more attention than Soga's to phenomena that the "deluded" chiefs "seemed" to see and hear, it is devoid of figurative language.[127] These matter-of-fact narrations of expectations and actualities help to explain, I think, Theal's and Frances Brownlee's lavish descriptions of wonders promised to the Xhosa, which transfix readers with visions of the anticipated transformations. J. H. Soga actively undercuts readers' potential enchantment by the prophecy, while writers like Theal, Frances Brownlee, and Chalmers build up descriptions of expectations in order to heighten the effect of disappointment.

The differences among the accounts are evident in their treatment of portentous movements of the sun and moon. Holden explains why a full red moon failed to rise in January 1857 as a sign of imminent resurrection: "the God who made the moon, had given no direction to the pale lamp of night to bestow her sanction on this gross superstition; and, therefore, she neither rose blood red, nor, when she changed, exhibited any extraordinary phenomena." Holden assumes that heavenly bodies manifest signs of the divine will of the Christian god, rather than of Xhosa "spirits" (294). Chalmers, by contrast, notes that "the full moon rose blood-red," an encouraging sign that spurred believers' final acts of destruction.[128] What is more significant than the factual discrepancy between the missionaries' statements is the vehemence with which Holden rejects any connection between Xhosa prophecy and natural phenomena, compared to the causal logic in Chalmers's narrative, in which fulfillment of minor predictions reinforced faith in the ultimate "marvellous transformation" (120). Holden implies that the deluded erred not in looking to the sky but in failing to recognize it as a creation of *his* god. In contrast to Holden, Theal and Frances Brownlee read the sky as a mirror of human consciousness; the constancy of its diurnal rhythms offers an ironic foil for human error. After depicting anticipated wonders on which Xhosa believers staked their future, Theal writes, "the dawn of doubt had never entered their thoughts till the dawn of the fatal day."[129] Frances Brownlee links the "usual darkness" of an ordinary sunset with "the black darkness of a bitter disappointment in the hearts of thousands."[130] This pathetic rendering imbues the sky with meaning within the terms of Xhosa prophecy, even while registering its failure.

Another aspect of the prophecy that receives tropological attention is the anticipated return of the dead ancestors. They do not appear, and yet they do, when the aftermath is figured as a reversal of the prophecy. The spectacle of widespread famine includes "emaciated living skeletons passing from house to house," as Dr. John FitzGerald of the King William's Town Native Hospital wrote to Commissioner Maclean.[131] "Living skeleton" recurs almost as a clinical diagnosis throughout FitzGerald's mid-1857 correspondence. Frances Brownlee makes the reversal of expectations even more explicit, and the pathos of her account derives from connections she draws among anticipated, actual, and figural appearances of the dead. She links proleptically the innumerable, uneaten carcasses of slain cattle to a later moment when "it was the carcases of men and women, young men and maidens, children and infants, that strewed the wayside" (144). She describes starving masses in search of relief as a reversal of the promise that the dead would rise: "as these spectres came in crowds and crawled along, one might have imagined that the prophet's prediction had come to pass, and that the dead had indeed risen from their graves" (148). Mrs. Brownlee captures the reader's imagination by framing the cattle killing as dependent on, and productive of, human imaginings.

This investment in imagination conveys the enormity of physical suffering; Frances Brownlee allows readers to sympathize with expectant believers in order to heighten the affective response when the prophecy is fulfilled figurally—through reversal—in the appearance of the living dead rather than resurrected ancestors. In other words, the extravagance of Frances Brownlee's metaphors communicates the stark reality of material devastation.[132] In contrast to J. H. Soga, many colonial writers deem it *not* "needless to say" that the expectations were not fulfilled. Having framed the anticipated wonders as fairy tales that occurred once upon a time, the authors must jolt enchanted readers into a generic recognition that history is not a fairy tale. The obsessive numeracy characteristic of descriptions of the aftermath—so many thousand cattle killed, so many thousand people dead—seems an ironic, empiricist rejoinder to Xhosa visions of *innumerable*, fat, beautiful cattle, "like stars of the sky in multitude."[133]

These accounts depend on the shock of reversal after readers temporarily suspend their disbelief in the prophecy, and whatever meaning is to be found in the cattle killing in these accounts is to be found in peripety, in ironic pairings of before and after, imagination and actuality.[134] For Frances Brownlee, "sad horror" is the explicit effect of this reversal (148); in recollecting memories of two decades earlier, she relives the pity and fear that Aristotle saw as precipitates of tragic plots structured around *anagnorisis* (recognition) and *peripeteia* (reversal). In classical Greek tragedy, the protagonist's misinterpretation of prophecy drives the plot and generates dramatic irony: spectators know more than characters. Although writers like Theal and Chalmers inscribe the cattle killing into plots of redemption rather than tragedy, the effect of peripety depends on an analogy between a reader's seduction and disillusion and that of Xhosa believers; readers know objectively that the cattle-killing prophecy will not succeed, but the pathos of these narratives works toward the suspension of this historical knowledge. What is so remarkable about these accounts, in other words, is that they generate some measure of narrative surprise about the failure of a prophecy that their readers would not have expected to succeed.

The significance of reversal in these cattle-killing narratives explains why Holden devotes almost no attention to the prophecy itself; he assumes that readers *cannot* be seduced because "enlightened Christian nations" have left witchcraft behind, if only recently.[135] Now their duty is to free others from its thrall: the cattle killing epitomizes the pervasive "vile superstition" among "Kaffir races" and thus "make[s] a loud and long appeal, not only to Missionary and philanthropic societies . . . but also to *humanity*, to colonial governors and governments and magistrates . . . that these enthralled nations may soon be liberated, and the privileges of civil and religious liberty succeed the reign of terror and death" (160, 295–96). Holden misses or ignores the fact that the cattle-killing movement was directed *against* witchcraft. He posits the expansion of colonial control as an act of liberation by figuring Xhosa witchcraft as a tool used to "enchain the national mind, and establish . . . undisputed empire over their souls" (286). The stakes of the contest between the empire of witchcraft and the "liberating" colonial government are so high that Holden seems immune to the prophecy's appeal to the imagination. If only in this aspect, Holden's account is surprisingly similar to J. H. Soga's: people whose ancestors suffered in the aftermath of the prophecy's failure and whose subjugation was thereby consolidated hardly need be told that the expected phenomena did not occur.

The gravity I read in Holden's account should not imply a corresponding levity in accounts of the cattle killing that offer more protracted expositions of what Aristotle called a plot's "tying" and "untying"; I do not mean to imply that Frances Brownlee, Chalmers, and Theal are merely spinning good yarns, "telling stories," as her people initially understood Nongqawuse to be doing. The dynamism of peripety in their accounts implicates their sustained interest in elements of the prophecy involving Europeans. The resurrection would inaugurate a "golden era of liberty," because whites would meet a variety of catastrophic fates: metamorphosis into "frogs, mice and ants," the sky falling and crushing them, and, most spectacularly, being "driven into the sea" (together with Xhosa unbelievers) by either a "mighty wind" or armies of returned Xhosa ancestors.[136] Contemporary Europeans who recorded their thoughts seemed to have little doubt about the motive behind the movement.[137] Amidst convoluted articulations of the prophecy that varied in space and time, the singular image of being driven into the sea captured the imagination of anxious settlers. The consensus in these accounts is that the cattle killing was, at least in part, anticolonial, directed at the destruction of whites and colonial rule.

The chiefs' plot thesis—articulated in Grey's official dispatches during the events of 1856–57 and long dominating colonial accounts—held that the cattle killing was a scheme by Xhosa chiefs to drive their desperate people to war against the colony.[138] Both Grey and Charles Brownlee recognized the obvious logical problem with the chiefs' plot thesis: "a starving people are not in a position to undertake an aggressive warfare," Brownlee wrote in August 1856.[139] Although Grey's official dispatches repeatedly report that believers were amassing weapons as enthusiastically as they were killing cattle, other reports describe believers "destroying their guns, assegais & ammunition."[140] No recent historians credit the chiefs' plot thesis, but they have disagreed significantly about the extent to which this millenarian movement was anticolonial, directed not merely against *effects* of colonial presence but against colonists themselves. Bradford describes compellingly the events of 1856–57 as war by supernatural proxy: in the context of British war fever and Grey's relentless threats of invasion, Xhosa chiefs who followed Sarhili's commands to stop cultivation and slaughter cattle did so for strategic reasons, the better to defend against the seemingly imminent colonial attack and to catalyze a military offensive against British rule to be undertaken by an army of Xhosa (or, more broadly, "black") warriors returned from the dead.[141] Peires, by contrast, reminds us of moments when at least some Xhosa informants saw European participation as integral to the prophecy. After the first date for the resurrection passed in August 1856, Mhlakaza encouraged Europeans to kill their own cattle because "'the people that have come have not come to make war but to bring about a better state of things for all.'"[142] Magistrate John Gawler reported in September 1856, "I understand the word to kill [cattle] is for all people; Kaffirs, English, and Dutch": this at the very moment that the chiefs' plot thesis congeals in Grey's official dispatches.[143] Sarhili apparently spoke the truth when he insisted, "I have done nothing against the British government."[144]

Theal takes the chiefs' plot thesis so completely for granted that he cannot recognize it as hypothesis rather than fact; he judges the seeming failure of the amaXhosa to storm the colony after the ancestors did not return to be a tactical "blunder, such as a child would hardly have made," rather than considering that this fact undermines the chiefs' plot thesis itself.[145] The tenacity of the chiefs' plot thesis in Theal's successive historiographical endeavors reveals another reversal at work in juxtaposing spectacular expectations with spectacular suffering. Europeans would not have expected Xhosa ancestors to appear bearing cattle and grain, but they probably feared being "driven into the sea," whether literally or metaphorically; this much-feared war against the Colony, a war that never happened, would seem a "rational" explanation for Xhosa motivations, however ill advised as military strategy. Far from being driven into the sea, however, Europeans remained to write these accounts; it is the amaXhosa who died, were starving, and were driven out of British Kaffraria and into the Cape Colony as laborers.[146] Yet the permanence of European presence means that being "driven into the sea" survives into the apartheid era as a quintessential image of white anxiety in South Africa.

The narrative closure of these accounts belies an ideological thrust that, despite hiding in plain sight, is no less powerful than Holden's polemic. Chalmers shifts from Frances Brownlee's scenes of suffering to his own depiction of acts of charity, through which "the very nation, whose destruction was secretly sought by this perfidious tragedy, became the savior of many thousands of Kafirs."[147] According to Chalmers, the epitome of this selflessness is Frances Brownlee, "a Christian lady" who not only worked alongside her husband at famine relief despite having lost several family members to Xhosa "butcher[y]" but also took up a "graphic pen [and] narrated this tale of sorrow" (129). Chalmers lays bare the narrative perspective that constitutes the peripeties of the cattle killing in colonial historiography: the European survivor of an anticolonial plot, surrounded by a sea of dying Xhosa people, responds with not only acts of compassion but also compassionate acts of textual composition. Chalmers's praise for Frances Brownlee is followed by his narration of the return of Tiyo Soga, his "page" of South African mission work.[148] Later writers, who did not participate in relief work, nonetheless stress the selflessness of those who aided the famished amaXhosa so soon after fearing an imminent attack on the colony.[149] After the cattle killing, colonial individuals and institutions remained to give succor. Implicit in this narrative topos is the glimmer of a possibility, from a colonial perspective, that the teleological end of the cattle killing was this opportunity to demonstrate the necessity of European presence: the amaXhosa had been devastated so that they could be relieved of their suffering (not to mention their autonomy and their land).[150] Colonial writers reap where they did not sow, gleaning scenes of Xhosa suffering in order to fill a "national" corn pit with providential narratives: "the country is almost empty.... Our mission chapel is well filled," wrote Anglican missionary H. T. Waters in a pithy example of this reversal.[151] Having detailed the demise of the chiefs' authority and the capture of land and labor, Grey remarked, "However much Her Majesty's Government may deplore the sufferings which necessarily attend the crisis through which this country is passing, they may rest assured that ultimately the most beneficial consequences will follow from what is now taking place. All that is necessary is, that every exertion should be made to improve, to the utmost, the present occasion."[152]

As Grey's remarks imply, however, this topos of providential suffering and relief is precisely that—a rhetorical figure, whose relationship to colonial policy is inverted, even perverted. Although authors lavished detail on European charitable endeavors, they did so in English (or German) and often decades after the fact. During the famine, Commissioner Maclean was concerned not to publicize among the amaXhosa these European relief efforts, particularly those incompatible with his stringent Victorian understanding of "true charity," namely, relief only for those who indentured themselves in the Colony: "if the idea once gain ground that Relief is afforded in King W[illiam's] Town to the starving who seek it—no amount of accommodation or funds will be sufficient for those who crowd in for Relief."[153] The spectacle of European charity to the formerly hostile Xhosa nation has radically different valences, depending on the projected audience for such images.

Brushed against the grain in this way, to invoke Walter Benjamin, the most sympathetic narration of the cattle killing also is an act of domination that is all the more insidious for being bathed in the warm light of compassion.[154] The sympathetic accounts are not so different from Holden's Manichean argument for European colonial liberation of the "Kaffir race" from the empire of evil. I do not mean to assert an ideological uniformity among these authors but, rather, to call attention to their texts as documents produced within a history of conquest and conversion.[155] My concern is not so much with genetic aspects of their composition by writers who can be counted among the victors but, rather, with what Benjamin describes as their modes of cultural transmission: the technologies of representation at stake in competing millennial dreams in the nineteenth-century eastern Cape. The narratives that I have been calling "sympathetic" are extravagantly literary, in the sense that they intimate, however paradoxically, a desire to create the illusion of storytelling, of orality in its textual afterlife.

At the level of form, these accounts foster presumed identification with the subjects of the story as members of an oral culture, at the same time that they assume the inherent superiority of literacy. Theal concludes the opening of his description of the prophecy by writing, "Such is the tale which the Kaffirs told each other, of the manner in which MHLAKAZA and NON-GQAUSE became acquainted with the secrets of the spirit world."[156] Theal takes his fabrication of the illusion of storytelling so far as to put his own narrative into the mouths of Xhosa survivors as "the tale [they] told each other." This invented scenario inverts Tiyo Soga's image of the newspaper as the social itinerary of its gregarious editor: both scenes dramatize transmediations across the oral/literate divide, yet Theal's scene paradoxically buttresses the authority and hegemony of his colonial historiography by describing it as a Xhosa tale, by cloaking colonial literacy in the mantle of indigenous orality. It is no wonder, then, that Gqoba published his account in *Isigidimi* to dispel confusion about the Xhosa past among the amaXhosa themselves. Both Gqoba and Theal, however, ultimately privilege the truth claims of written history over the wild and dangerous imaginings of oral "tales": it is Nongqawuse's prophecy that Theal frames as a fantastic "tale [the amaXhosa] told each other," set within his authoritative, written narrative of the event and its all-too-real aftermath.

Tiyo Soga turned to the Bible to discern portents of the future survival of the amaXhosa. These colonial authors, conversely, found in Xhosa prophecy and its aftermath signs of the rightness of their own presence and endeavor. The cattle killing departed from previous Xhosa responses to colonialism by not immediately engaging guns and assegais; technologies of the book were a crucial means by which missionaries, administrators, and historians managed the immediate afterlife of the event, framing its meaning within a teleological narrative of colonial beneficence. The passage from orality to literacy was an important part of this teleology, yet orality retains a complex and contradictory appeal within these narratives, not merely in their textual form but also in the content of the form, following Hayden White. Authors like Chalmers, Frances Brownlee, and Theal inhabit literate traditions with particular conventions for structuring narrative and dramatic plots. By imagining the cattle killing as a story of recognition and reversal, colonial authors append a redemptive denouement to the "tragedy" of the cattle killing: they link the prophecy's failure to the enduring necessity of colonial presence, and they inscribe their narratives within the enduring medium of print. These accounts thus manifest an effect of history constructed as narrative, "a coherence that allows us to see 'the end' in every beginning."[157] This perspicacity of narrative is analogous to a capacity to read the future: "All plots have something in common with prophecy, for they must appear to educe from the prime matter of the situation the forms of a future," writes Frank Kermode.[158] Kermode reminds us of the importance of *peripeteia* for Aristotle; he argues that the "more daring the peripeteia," the more a fiction, "by upsetting the ordinary balance of our naive expectations, is finding something out for us, something *real*" (18).

The relationship between structures of narrative fiction and the "*real*" in Kermode's examination of apocalyptic thinking characterizes the fundamental tension in the reversals of the cattle killing: any epistemological work of "finding out" that the cattle killing might be made to do is undermined by the extremity of its adherents' disappointment. This extremity of suffering—measured in the deaths of tens of thousands of people, the dislocation of many more, the loss of land and livelihood, crumbling autonomy, and persistent conditions of colonial subjugation and postcolonial poverty—is too easily contained in narrative, evacuated of its materiality when it is opposed and equated to the fantastic excesses of the anticipated transformations. This tension not only impels my consideration of the cattle killing; it also implicates my project within the epistemological and technological legacies of the intersections between literacy and this event in Xhosa history. My challenge is to understand recurrent fascinations with the cattle killing's spectacles of hope and failure and the uses to which such fascinations have been put—a task that involves analyzing and deploying within my argument the visions' imaginative appeal, as well as confronting the terrible price that they exacted.

Yet there is no simple line to be drawn between metaphor and materiality, between the figuration of a thing and the thing itself. When missionaries see the hand of God in starving masses and colonial governors invoke divine Providence in promoting their own designs, we see that metaphors and plot structures can often have material effects. Jean and John Comaroff identify, as one of the misprisions of colonial encounters, the "misreading of mission metaphors" by Africans who "interpreted the admonitions and promises of the mission in highly literal, immediate terms."[159] Tiyo Soga's response to the cattle killing implies that Xhosa believers misread Nongqawuse's prophecy by acting upon their literal interpretation of a highly suggestive vision of cultural and cosmic renewal, which itself seemed to rearrange the plot of recent Xhosa confrontations with Europeans. But Europeans also misapprehended the cattle killing when they embraced the trope of reversal in order to project a linear progress narrative for which so little evidence of progress was to be found in a half century of mission endeavor.

A remarkable scene in a little-cited account of British Kaffraria in July and August 1857 offers a final angle from which to consider competing millennial dreams on the colonial frontier. *Recollections of a Visit to British Kaffraria* (1866) performs the eclipse of Xhosa millennial dreams by Christian ones: in the simplified argot of cross-cultural conversation, the anonymous English woman author[160] tells an inquisitive Xhosa man that she "had come to see the Kafirs because I believe in a resurrection from the dead, though not in that of which Umklakasi [*sic*] tells them; but I believe that we shall all rise and live together in a very happy and beautiful country. That as I hope to meet the Kafirs then, I like to know something of them now."[161] She speculates about the role of the amaXhosa (as possible Ishmaelites)[162] in Christian eschatology; understanding missionary endeavor in Africa as the unfolding of prophecy, she admits that Xhosa resistance to civilization may be foreordained. Yet the role of European believers is to "help [them] to be ready for the coming of the Lord" (83–84). She plays her own part in this design, and the narrative shifts markedly, recounting the failure of Xhosa visions of renovation not within the elevated register of Christian apocalypse but, rather, in the quiet register of female domesticity.

This account also reflects the fault lines of gender ideologies on the colonial frontier and the marginalization of Nongqawuse within the historiographical record. The author embeds her most extensive narrative of the cattle killing in a scene set in the housekeeper's room of the Anglican St. Luke's mission. She sits with Mrs. S—, the matron, both women sewing while Mrs. S— recounts the tale to her. This scene, already charged in terms of orality and literacy because "there seems to be among [the amaXhosa] a longing to dive into the past, and no records to aid them in their search," is still more significant because the women are sewing frocks for Xhosa girls to wear, without which (despite the author's protests) they are not allowed to set foot in the mission (118–20, 115). The Xhosa girls seem eager to enter—perhaps because of the excitement of the lady visitor, perhaps because of famine and dislocation, perhaps because they are fleeing marriages or coerced extramarital sexual relations at the behest of chiefs, headmen, or frustrated young men, perhaps despite their families' fears about the difficulty of contracting marriages for mission-educated women.[163] Stitch by stitch, these European women labor, in a quasi-domestic setting at once far from home and on the front lines of the civilizing mission, in order to enable Xhosa girls to enter their domain.[164] Yet, at the same time, the traveling author laments Mrs. S—'s tale of the cattle killing and the suffering that continues months afterward. How remarkable, then, that in this narrative set in an overdetermined space of extroverted female domesticity—a narrative that borrows the discreet naming conventions of the nineteenth-century novel—Nongqawuse has no place in its cattle-killing story.

CHAPTER TWO

SPECTRAL AND TEXTUAL ANCESTORS

New African Intermediation and the

Politics of Intertextuality

[T]he man's heart is renewed, . . . he has become an entirely different person to
what he was before, seeing with different eyes, and hearing with different ears; . . .
he now holds communion and intercourse with the invisible world.

J. C. WARNER, REPORT TO JOHN MACLEAN, CA. 1857

"Old things are passed away" with them, and "all things are become new." Their
present environment, their outlook on the future, has, under the influence of
new laws and customs, focussed their attention on matters of life and conduct
unknown to their fathers.

J. H. SOGA, *THE SOUTH-EASTERN BANTU*, 1930

He had read history, and although he believed himself to be in communion with
God, he could find no warrant for a belief in the non-penetration of rifle bullets.

G. HEATON NICHOLLS, *BAYETE! "HAIL TO THE KING!"* 1923[1]

The account of the cattle killing in both Chalmers's *Tiyo Soga: A Page of
South African Mission Work* and Charles Pacalt Brownlee's *Reminiscences
of Kaffir Life and History* was written by Brownlee's wife, Frances. Her
narrative begins:

In March 1856, the most renowned of Kaffir seers arose, Mhlakaza by name, assisted by his daughter Nongqause, a prophesying medium (Mr. Brownlee thinks she may have been a ventriloquist). He preached to the Kaffirs a new gospel, which was none other than a resurrection from the dead. She professed to have held converse with the spirits of the old Kaffir heroes.[2]

These sentences record an interpretive dispute between the Brownlees: Frances reports that Nongqawuse was *spoken through* as a "medium," but she adds that Charles wondered whether Nongqawuse *projected* her voice outside herself. (This parenthetical interjection resembles one spouse interrupting the other in conversation.) The split between what Mhlakaza "preached" and Nongqawuse "professed" brings the number of voices in the passage to four, not including the spirits. Nongqawuse's voice resurfaces so strangely that it almost seems as if "He preached" or "She professed" contains a typographical error; in any case, Mhlakaza dominates the account as the figure who interprets and disseminates the prophecy. This competition between Nongqawuse's and Mhlakaza's voices reflects the marginalization of Nongqawuse within cattle-killing historiography.

Like that of Nongqawuse, Frances Brownlee's voice is obscured even as it resurfaces in the afterlives of the cattle killing. Her authorship is not credited in bibliographic records, yet her account appears not only in books by Charles Brownlee and Chalmers[3] but also in texts whose authors attribute it to Chalmers, Charles Brownlee, or (by omission) themselves. The recurrent appearance of her narrative imbues it with the aura of a revealed text, a prophecy in its own right, when identical words speak through so many accounts. Voices split and merge in the transmission of Frances Brownlee's cattle-killing narrative, just as the voices of the Brownlees, Mhlakaza, and Nongqawuse jostle in its opening passage. Such polyphonic accounts are not merely *about* prophecy but also approximate the structure of prophecy: the text becomes a *medium* that conveys words autonomously from their author's presence. The identity of the voice speaking through a medium— whether prophetic or textual—is open to contest. If words are dead things awaiting resurrection, they might not rise wrapped in the cloths of their authors' names. If prophecy and citation are vatic modes of communication, marking the gap between the medium of words and their source, then perhaps ventriloquism and plagiarism are its spurious, cynical, or even secular modes. The "zone of occult instability" that is intertextuality is the subject of this chapter.[4]

The proliferation and elision of voices in Mrs. Brownlee's account and its transmission serve as an emblem for my consideration of the intertextual imbrications of *The Girl Who Killed to Save* (*Nongqause the Liberator*), a play written by Zulu journalist, playwright, and poet H. I. E. Dhlomo and published by Lovedale Press in 1936. We do not hear ancestors' voices in this play, but, instead, Nongqause's reenactment of the moment they spoke to her. Her performance of the prophecy's transmission serves as a figure for the many voices in Dhlomo's play—not only his characters but also his textual predecessors, the authorial voices that he engages. Dhlomo's characters and his textual interlocutors are often the same people. Mrs. Brownlee's account is excerpted in a historical preface to the play; as I argue, however, the process by which her own words came to appear in Dhlomo's play (as distinct from the dialogue he writes for her character) reveals much about the politics of intertextuality and the power dynamics between African authors and mission presses. Tiyo Soga appears as a silent character in *The Girl Who Killed to Save*, yet his voice is nonetheless present, as I will show. Just as Dhlomo stages Nongqause repeating the ancestors' words and struggling to understand their meaning, the intertextual imbrications of Dhlomo's play generate dissonant echoes between the voices of his characters and their own writing. This mediated intertextuality is even more complex when, as with Mrs. Brownlee, authorship has been confused or obscured. What kind of interpretive practice can orchestrate these audible and inaudible voices?

My meditations on intertextuality consider conjunctures and tensions among three historical moments: Xhosa believers in the 1850s expected *new people*; in the early twentieth century, ideas of a *new Africa* and *New Africans* mobilized elite political and cultural nationalism; and the challenges of recent decades have been imagining, realizing, and resisting the foreclosures of a *new South Africa*. This recurrent, transmodernist imperative to "make it new" suggests a series of ruptures, losses, and transformative recoveries—a kind of punctuated disequilibrium in the history of southern Africa. How do texts that revive the cattle killing contribute to the postapartheid project of constructing a South African literary and cultural history that confronts infrastructural and ideological legacies of colonialism, segregation, and apartheid?[5] The central images of the cattle killing—harvesting, destruction, resurrection, bringing back the ancestors—are uniquely resonant with the dynamic of retrieval, loss, and recovery common to Tiyo Soga and H. I. E. Dhlomo, and this predicament is hardly unique to those writers. In postapartheid debates about whether and how a new national literary history might be constructed out of traditions divided by language, race, class, audience, censorship, and access to the state and to cultural institutions, the question of how to theorize potential relationships among texts becomes urgent. I examine the role of intertextuality in these debates and then turn to the politics of intertextuality in Dhlomo's play and its critical reception.

Dhlomo's work has been situated in terms of the New Africans, an emergent mission-educated, petit bourgeois intelligentsia. My goal is not to retrace the critical path blazed by Tim Couzens in reading Dhlomo's life and work through the New African lens but, rather, to consider how such literary recuperations open possibilities and pose obstacles for a contemporary literary historiography committed to historicizing and overcoming institutional, linguistic, and ideological divisions of the past.[6] Using archival evidence establishing Tiyo Soga's authorship of a hymn in Dhlomo's play, I read *The Girl Who Killed to Save* as an expression of ambivalence about the prospect of assimilation and the necessity of a new kind of nationalism. This reading confronts the difficulties of drawing conclusions through and about intertextuality by situating Dhlomo's play within a constellation of texts by Frances Brownlee, J. H. Soga, Mary Waters, R. H. W. Shepherd, and Thomas Pringle. Examining the play's engagement with cattle-killing historiography, I articulate a reading practice that can untangle the relationships among these voices.

While intervening in recent debates about South African literary history, I imagine broader applications for these intertextual reading practices that listen for occluded voices. In tracing intricate connections among texts constellated around Dhlomo's play, I draw on unpublished materials held in archives, as well as obscure published texts that constitute the figurative literary "archive." As Joanna Brooks insists, "It is not enough to recover texts from the archival tomb. We must also be willing to believe in and search out their meaningfulness, even if that search entails a reformulation of our assumptions about literature, history, race, and religion."[7] Such recovery projects, if undertaken with "intelligent receptivity," contribute to "the regeneration of memory and thus the raising of the dead" (19, 14). My consideration of intertextuality unfolds around the idea of hearing voices—both textual and spectral—as I trace how they become, fail to become, or cease to be meaningful, when writers borrow (wittingly or unwittingly) the voices of their predecessors. Citing or ventriloquizing *textual* ancestors is as precarious and productive a process for writers as claiming to hear the voices of *literal* ancestors is for prophets like Nongqawuse. I theorize the politics of intertextuality as a recursive, nonlinear practice of reading and writing that can attend to ambivalences and aporias of both explicit citation and more veiled textual intersections. Mr. Brownlee (Mrs. Brownlee tells us) thought that Nongqawuse may have been a ventriloquist; I seek to understand the complexities of speaking and writing the words of others, not only in terms of dystopian deception, co-optation, and containment but also in terms of a meliorative recovery (or even projection) of voices that might otherwise not be heard.

A NEW LITERARY HISTORY FOR SOUTH AFRICA?

Examining possible connections between Tiyo Soga and H. I. E. Dhlomo, David Attwell finds "no ready-made continuity between Soga and intellectuals like Dhlomo or leaders like Mandela who follow him in the history of African nationalist resistance in South Africa. That tradition has had to reconstruct itself in the event, in each encounter that shaped its formation."[8] In the absence of a continuous tradition, constructing this series of figures— Soga, Dhlomo, Mandela—assumes that some meaningful relationship can be asserted among their respective historical moments. In the 1980s, South African revisionist scholarship posited such relationships in recovering the work of Dhlomo and Tiyo Soga.[9] These recuperative projects confronted state pressures of censorship, inferior education, and co-optation that enforced the isolation or forgetting of discrete figures in suppressed traditions of resistance. Mandela's release from prison in 1990—a return from literal obscurity to public visibility—functions as another formative event for this historiography.

One institutional manifestation of this process was the founding of the Centre for the Study of Southern African Literature and Languages at the University of Durban-Westville. Founded the year that Mandela was elected, the Centre aimed to "align critical practice with the more radical potentialities of the larger democratic transitions occurring in the present."[10] It held a colloquium in 1995 examining the necessity and pitfalls of forging an "integrated" study of literature. Under apartheid, a genuinely representative literary history was just as impossible as a genuinely democratic government: the practice of literary scholarship was fragmented into "ethno-linguistic *bantustans* of English, Zulu, Afrikaans, Xhosa, etc."[11] Some critics, however, doubted that a new *national* literary history was the most effective way to realize the transition's "more radical potentialities." The foreclosures inherent in the nation form threatened to reduce multiple linguistic and generic traditions into a single, teleological narrative.

The debates in this watershed of political transition continued earlier conversations about whether literary history in southern Africa was best approached from a centrifugal perspective of fragmentation or a centripetal perspective of integration. In 1989, Stephen Gray advocated interrogating the fault lines that obviate a unified cultural field; writers were isolated not only by differences in the institutional, literary, and social status of South Africa's languages but also by the exigencies of censorship and exile.[12] Focusing on commonality rather than division, Michael Chapman asserted in 1993 that "despite racial and linguistic division, we have all been part of the same South African story"—a shared narrative nascent even before the formation of South Africa as a political entity in 1910.[13] For Chapman, integrating literary history would foster national reconciliation: literary criticism is "a social activity concerned with justice."[14] The centripetal impulse in such literary historiography sets itself against two ideologically opposed centrifugal forces: on the one hand, apartheid's atomizing pressures and, on the other, epistemological suspicions of synthetic projects, often informed by poststructuralism or Marxism.

At the 1995 colloquium, one centrifugal skeptic was Malvern van Wyk Smith, who questioned the assumption that "if we look hard enough we shall find that southern African writers have really been talking to one another all these years." In other words, the centripetal impulse assumes a "rockbed of infinitely complex intertextuality and commonality of purpose" obscured by the overwhelming centrifugal forces of the predemocratic era.[15] Instead,

> [w]hat needs to be demonstrated, by scholarly archival research and close textual analysis, is whether our writers have actually listened and talked to one another across the cultural and linguistic rifts and abysses which till recently defined our socio-political landscape. What is required is the evidence of genuine intertextuality, of texts resonating intentionally to one another, and not merely exploring the same subject matter because they happen to have been written in the same part of the world. (75)

Van Wyk Smith adapts his concept of "genuine intertextuality" from Harold Bloom, an influence reflected in his determinant emphasis on exchanges between writers; even when he uses the poststructuralist formulation, "texts resonating," the issue is the "intentional[ity]" of that resonance.

At first glance, Van Wyk Smith's use of Bloom seems inappropriate to the South African context, because Bloom's notion of authorial influence as "misreading" assumes cultural homogeneity and equality of access to a shared tradition (in terms of class, if not also of gender, race, language, or national origin) that are precisely the issues at stake in postapartheid debates about literary history.[16] In other words, South Africa lacks the kind of literary social formation that Bloom takes for granted, which suggests not only Bloom's elitism but also the challenge of forging and understanding intertextual relationships in an uneven, multilayered cultural landscape. More diffuse versions of intertextuality might be better suited to reading South African literary history, particularly the webs of texts about the Xhosa cattle killing. For example, Julia Kristeva's coding of intertextuality as permutation and transposition, "the passage from one signifying system to another," could illuminate Tiyo Soga's transmediation of orality or Dhlomo's deployment of vernacular oral conventions in modern drama.[17] Roland Barthes's conception of "the intertextual in which every text is held"—"woven entirely with citations, references, echoes, cultural languages . . . antecedent or contemporary, which cut across it through and through in a vast stereophony"—seems to realize the most radical implications of Walter Ong's notion of texts as infinitely capable of resurrection. Compared with Bloom's author-focused anxieties of influence, these protean models of intertextuality dispense with authorial agency and even the unitary work. Barthes disavows any old-fashioned attention to the "'sources,' the 'influences' of a work" as vestiges of "the myth of filiation."[18] The cultural afterlife of the cattle killing, however, reveals the implications of this dissolution of authorship: as we consider structural similarities between prophecy and writing, or material action as the consequence of inspired utterance, it seems not entirely immaterial who is speaking, who is speaking through whom, and how and why.[19]

Thus Van Wyk Smith's emphasis upon authorial agency is helpful, not least because questions of authorial commitment and complicity have been so important in South African cultural politics. Although I do not accept his narrow definition as the only model for "genuine intertextuality," Van Wyk Smith's insistence that authors bear the onus of intertextual agency clarifies the range of possible connections among authors, texts, and discourses. If literary historians are to reconstruct a shared cultural field "wilfully obscured by South Africa's political masters and cultural institutions," Van Wyk Smith urges that it be constructed not merely out of scholars' desires but with archival evidence of intertextual conversations (72). This empirical demand grounds my discussions not as an absolute imperative but, rather, as a productive problem, a reminder of the "abysses" across which authors would converse. In my reading of *The Girl Who Killed to Save*, Tiyo Soga is far from silent, but it remains difficult to say precisely how Dhlomo and Tiyo Soga have "actually listened and talked to one another across the cultural and linguistic rifts," as well as those of time. I extend the parameters of intertextual inquiry in another direction, heeding Edward Said's once-polemical observation that "political, institutional, and ideological constraints act in the same manner on the individual author" as the pressures of a more narrowly defined *literary* intertextuality.[20] Dhlomo's predicament was shared by the New Africans, caught in the transition from promised assimilation to enforced segregation; his syncretic dramatic practice also must be read against those worldly constraints that Said brought within the purview of literary criticism.

"TAKE UP THE PEN": NEW AFRICANS AND THE REDEFINITION OF RESISTANCE

For nearly a half century, Dhlomo's reputation as a dramatist rested mostly on his sole published play, *The Girl Who Killed to Save*. The 1985 publication of his *Collected Works* (including eight unpublished plays) and Tim Couzens's scholarly biography facilitated a reappraisal in which critics tend to read Dhlomo's work through the lens of the "New Africans," a mission-educated, petit-bourgeois intelligentsia.[21] In the early twentieth century, New Africans confronted the emptiness or obsolescence of promises of assimilation into a "universal," egalitarian civilization. The beginning of the end of this dream was the 1910 Act of Union, which created a South African state from British colonies and Boer republics. The promise of assimilation was replaced by segregation and the erasure of limited rights that propertied Native men in the Cape Colony had secured, rights the New Africans had hoped would be extended across the Union.

Several things were new about the New Africans. First, with each segregationist law, they faced a political situation for which an ideology of assimilation and an attitude of patience were increasingly inappropriate. Second, as they recognized the necessity of protest against their deteriorating situation, New Africans turned to new weapons: pens and petitions rather than the guns and assegais with which their ancestors waged primary resistance to conquest. Third, they took a new look at the African past, understanding it not as a long night of savagery from which Europeans had awoken them (to paraphrase Chinua Achebe) but, rather, as a resource for contemporary struggles. Finally, the polity for which this struggle was waged was imagined in a new way, not in terms of disparate conflicts of amaXhosa, amaZulu, Basotho, Batswana, or other discrete tribal nations against Europeans but, rather, in terms of a broader black nation.[22]

The contradictions that Tiyo Soga had faced reached a crisis point for New Africans, constituted by Xhosa "school people," Zulu *kholwa*, and other mission-educated groups who began to coalesce into a national social and political force. Newspapers helped forge these communities, as Tiyo Soga had hoped; increasingly, however, they became an important forum for protest against government policy. In 1882, an essay in *Isigidimi samaXhosa* (Xhosa Messenger)[23] promoting a petition to release incarcerated Xhosa regents concluded with a poem, whose first line echoed a traditional call to arms, "*Zimkile!*":

> Your cattle are plundered, compatriot!
> After them! After them!
> Lay down the musket,
> Take up the pen,
> Seize paper and ink:
> That's your shield.
>
> Your rights are plundered!
> Grab a pen,
> Load, load it with ink;
> Sit in your chair,
> Don't head for Hoho:[24]
> Fire with your pen.
>
> Put pressure,
> Engage your mind;
> Focus on facts,

And speak loud and clear;
Don't rush into battle:
Anger stutters.[25]

The essay and poem were signed by I. W. W. Citashe (Isaac Wauchope); the essay is mostly forgotten, but the poem has become an emblem for the emergent cultural and political situation of the New Africans.[26] In imagining survival by means other than armed resistance and advocating forms of leadership other than that of chiefs, Wauchope's "Zimkile!" is a war cry that calls for new kinds of weapons. Wauchope wrote in the wake of widespread rebellion and warfare, sparked by colonial attempts to limit African access to firearms and to complete the task of conquest through wars against the amaXhosa in 1877–78 (the last frontier war), the amaZulu in 1878–79, and the Basotho in 1880–81.[27] In subsequent years, New Africans took up the new weapons of pen and petition, the convention, and (for men, on a limited basis in the Cape until 1936) the vote. In 1884, J. T. Jabavu, former editor of *Isidigimi*, founded *Imvo zabantsundu* (African Opinion), the first black newspaper that was autonomous from the missions.[28] In an editorial, Jabavu criticized legislative efforts to limit the African franchise as attempts to "disarm Africans 'even of constitutional weapons' after the Africans themselves had turned to 'Pen and Speech as the new and effective weapons.'"[29]

The enthusiasm with which New Africans created a newspaper culture and the vehemence with which they protested the constriction of their political rights illustrate their contradictory position, "straddling the frontline of the European-African colonial encounters," as Korang writes of the Gold Coast.[30] Like similar communities elsewhere in colonial Africa, New Africans were self-conscious about their intermediary role, as "the only ones who can bridge the gulf between the old culture and the new technological civilization."[31] Their relationships on both sides of this gulf were fraught, given the growing stratifications among the black peasantry and urbanizing proletariat and the ambivalence of the colonial encounter in which they were "simultaneously affirming—saying an intimate 'yes' to—an alien dominant even as they mobilize its categories to say 'no' in revolt against it."[32] New Africans played not only a social mediatory role between their African and European contemporaries but also a cultural one in which they engaged in a high-stakes debate about the African past. Although colonial literacies often catalyzed such "cultural editing,"[33] forging a useable past became particularly urgent in South Africa when segregationists articulated reductive, atomizing versions of discrete "tribal" pasts and offered them as the only future for Africans, thereby reversing the New Africans' political, social, and economic gains.

New Africans recuperated a heroic African past from the distortions of colonial historiography, and the Xhosa prophetic tradition of the nineteenth century played an important role in this effort. The redefinition of resistance to colonial encroachment had a history that predated Wauchope's call to fight with the pen. Tiyo Soga hoped that literacy might replace armed resistance and "superstition"; two generations earlier, the prophet-poet Ntsikana urged his followers to put down their assegais and take up his talismanic hymn. At odds with this turn away from military confrontation were promises of war doctors (*itola*) like Ntsikana's rival, Nxele, who claimed to be able to make warriors bulletproof. Like Nxele, the prophet Mlanjeni urged selective killing of cattle and promised the return of warrior ancestors; in 1850, he fomented war by promising to turn British bullets to water.[34]

Cattle-killing prophecies of the 1850s were the climax of this tradition. The amaXhosa suffered considerable losses of life, land, and livestock when Mlanjeni failed to liquidate bullets; he promised just before his death in 1853 that those who had died in the war would return to defeat the British.[35] Land shortages, crop failures, drought, flood, disease, and the devastation of war created a situation in which "war was impossible and peace was unviable."[36] Although the renovation of land and people and the expulsion of the British are the transformations most commonly associated with the cattle killing, Mhlakaza was also reported to have summoned the "head men of the country . . . to be washed, that they might thereby live forever, and become invulnerable to shot."[37] After the cattle killing, however, the amaXhosa sustained losses greater than those inflicted by British weapons. "Their power was broken, their strength wasted, and their counsels defeated to a greater extent than all the powder and steel of the British troops had been able to effect; proving how God by the most simple means can accomplish the most important results": so wrote missionary William Holden. Instead of Xhosa invulnerability to bullets, Holden saw "a look of subdued anguish in the countenances of the women and children, which must pierce a heart of steel."[38]

Holden's characterization of the cattle killing as more powerful than British artillery posits cultural destruction as a providential "weapon" the amaXhosa wielded against themselves; their suffering is also weaponized into steel-piercing sorrow. This description inverts two tropes in the redefinition of resistance: bulletproof claims and the rejection of conventional weapons for cultural or spiritual ones. Holden nearly makes it seem that the amaXhosa were actually "invulnerable to shot" until they turned to an alternative mode of resistance in the cattle killing. As New Africans embraced literate, reformist protest over the armed rebellion or cooperation of previous eras, the question was how to understand this history of resistance in a changing, but no less precarious, relationship to European domination. The returning Xhosa warriors heralded by Nxele in the 1810s, and by Mlanjeni, Nongqawuse, and others in the 1850s were the ultimate new (but also old) weapons.

This recurrent embrace of new weapons occurred amidst evolving understandings of the polity being fought for. New Africans worked to forge a national alliance of black South Africans, an endeavor that took institutional form in organizations associated with modern mass nationalism in South Africa: the African National Congress (ANC; founded by Pixley Seme as the South African Native National Congress in 1912) and the Industrial and Commercial Workers' Union (ICU; founded in 1919). At an ICU rally in 1928, this national project was linked to new weapons: "'I do not mean fight with guns or sticks, but . . . by constitutional methods . . . the ICU had not been formed to spill blood, but to build us into a nation.'"[39] Although the ANC's constitutional protest or the ICU's trade unionism might seem to have nothing to do with the cattle killing's millennial dreams, there are important continuities between them. As with the competing Xhosa and European millennial dreams, modernity and millennialism could be inextricably linked rather than diametrically opposed.

Most immediately, the ICU (and the Independent ICU [IICU], which split from the ICU in 1929) recognized that, for many black South Africans, "prophetic nationalism" like that in cattle killing was lived experience rather than lost history: they appealed to potential members with millenarian, Garveyite prophecies involving pig slaughter and hopes for deliverance by "aeroplanes" piloted by African Americans.[40] During a 1930 strike, one IICU speaker declaimed, "'Nongqause prophesied that the AmaXhosas should be united. Today we are carrying pick-axes, so as to dig out the Kaffir corn treasure.'" The leader of the IICU, Clements Kadalie, was described not only as David, Moses, or the son of Jesus but also as a latter-day Ntsikana.[41] These millenarian expectations were inadvertently spurred by the 1921 tour of South Africa by the Ghanaian J. E. K. Aggrey, whose survey of African education was funded by the American Phelps-Stokes Trust. Aggrey's message of interracial cooperation appealed to white liberals and the urban African elite; its nascent pan-Africanism, explicitly opposed to the black transnationalism of Marcus Garvey, linked New Africans to similar intelligentsias in West Africa and the United States (such as Alain Locke's "New Negro"). Yet some read Aggrey's visit as a sign of imminent deliverance by black liberators from overseas.[42]

These conflicting modes of black transnationalism suggest the uneasy relationship between elite and subaltern or prophetic nationalisms during this period: a broader black nation was being imagined not only through securing rights or capturing the state but also by restoring justice, social health, and *ubuntu*.[43] In good Andersonian fashion, Crais argues, participants in an early twentieth-century millenarian livestock slaughter imagined themselves as "members of a privileged and clearly supralocal community. People could imagine others whom they did not know killing their swine and chickens, entering a sacral community. . . . Their registering in a populist discourse of 'this black nation of ours' made new forms of community real: and new forms of collective action possible" (124). At the same time, the pages of the Universal Negro Improvement Association's *Negro World* in the 1920s also reflect a wide range of printed imaginings of black transnational community.[44]

Crais's description of 1920s livestock slaughter as a performative mode of imagining community and forging a black nation raises questions about the Xhosa cattle killing seventy years earlier: in what ways can we understand it as a nationalist movement? Mindful of Neil Lazarus's caution against assuming that peasant uprisings were either directed against the colonial order or the product of "*nationalist* consciousness," I also think it important to historicize, rather than reify, notions of the nation and nationalism.[45] From both Xhosa and colonial perspectives, the Xhosa *nation* was a casualty of the cattle killing. The cattle-killing movement aimed to unify clans within the Xhosa national polity through the chiefs' compliance with the prophecy. While this supralocal thinking was on a smaller scale than the New Africans' later subcontinental nationalism, adherents of cattle-killing prophecies also looked beyond the continent, imagining transnational black solidarity involving Russians, Indians, and Chinese.[46] After the cattle killing, the loss of national autonomy was remarked in an 1874 *Kaffir Express* article describing a Xhosa congregation singing Ntsikana's Great Hymn with "'a kind of national feeling, especially now that they droop their heads from the loss of national freedom.'"[47]

In colonial discourse until the late 1850s, *nation* denoted the amaXhosa (or other peoples) discretely; events in the mid-1850s eastern Cape are part of broader, crucial shifts in the conceptual relationship between empire and nation. Grey's transformation of the legal status of the amaXhosa in 1857, from "an independent 'nation' with whom treaties had to be made to a 'conquered people' with no right in the land," reflects both the global recalibration of *nation* in the wake of mid-nineteenth-century European nationalism and the rise of liberalism that underwrote high imperialism's civilizing mission.[48] In 1859, John Stuart Mill distinguished between "civilized nations and barbarians": "barbarians have no rights as a *nation*, except a right to such treatment as may, at the earliest possible period, fit them for becoming one."[49] In the long view, Grey's antinational colonialism broke the Xhosa nation, thereby enabling the rise of the New Africans' more recognizably "modern" nationalism. In invocations of the cattle killing by later nationalist projects, the content and constituency of the nation continues to vary.

Elite and subaltern nationalisms coexisted—however uneasily—in the early twentieth century; the cattle killing was not the spectacular terminus of anticolonial millenarianism but, rather, part of a living tradition. In 1920, the South African Natives' National Congress held a meeting "quite literally down the road" from the site at Bulhoek where Enoch Mgijima had settled his followers, the Israelites, in defiance of the Land Act of 1913.[50] Emboldened by Mgijima's bulletproof claims, the Israelites defied police orders to leave the site where they awaited the millennium of the "black nation"; police opened fire in May 1921 and killed nearly two hundred.[51] The spatiotemporal proximity and ideological gulf between these elite and prophetic nationalist gatherings disrupt conventional, teleological readings of black nationalism that see nationalist ideas trickling down from emergent liberal elites like the mission-educated New Africans to the unschooled masses.

The complex landscape of early twentieth-century nationalisms clarifies Dhlomo's concerns in *The Girl Who Killed to Save*. Within the critical consensus forged by Couzens's biography, Dhlomo's most important intertexts were the segregationist Hertzog Bills—introduced unsuccessfully in the 1920s and finally passed in 1936, the year *The Girl* was published. Opposition to proposed measures involving land ownership, the franchise, and political representation was sparked by the bills' reintroduction in 1935 and coalesced in the All-African Convention (AAC), chaired by D. D. T. Jabavu (son of *Imvo* editor J. T. Jabavu). At an AAC meeting in 1936, Jabavu outlined an "intermediary policy of using what can be used and fighting against all that we do not want," charting a course between the extremes of accepting segregation or militating through boycotts and reprisals to "use the fear of a bloody revolution as a weapon of propaganda."[52] Like Wauchope before him, Jabavu advocated pens over guns; nonetheless, he spoke blunt truths about "the White savage hidden beneath" the "veneer" of European enlightenment (48). The crisis surrounding the Hertzog Bills has been invoked to distinguish between *The Girl* and Dhlomo's later work: although critics disagree about whether Dhlomo's acceptance of mission apprenticeship and assimilation began to waver in *The Girl*, in the post-Hertzog plays they hear a more militant voice.

Situating Dhlomo's work within the New African context of moderate elite nationalism has become a critical commonplace; his plays on Ntsikana, Cetshwayo, Shaka, and Moshoeshoe, along with *The Girl*, contributed to the New Africans' recuperation of a heroic nineteenth-century past, reviving the memory of primary resistance for modern anticolonial nationalism. What remains mostly unremarked, however, is the currency of *The Girl*'s manifest content: less than a decade after millenarian prophecy sparked livestock slaughter throughout Natal and the Transkei in anticipation of African American deliverance, Dhlomo turned to the spectacular precursor of prophetic nationalism by dramatizing the career of Nongqawuse. In other words, *The Girl* might be not merely a work of historical recovery or a reflection of increasing segregation but also an engagement with the full range of nationalist imaginings at work in the New African era.

Before turning to the play, I want to consider another intertextual conjunction of segregationism and black nationalism. In the midst of agitation about the Hertzog Bills and the 1935 Italian invasion of Ethiopia, trade union organizer and ANC founding member Selby Msimang published *The Crisis*, a pamphlet in which he exhorted fellow Africans to rise to Hertzog's challenge. The "law of self-preservation" demands that "we can no longer loyally serve . . . a government which has . . . told us in brutal language that we can never, never be free."[53] Msimang admits:

> I am under no illusion. I know that behind this brutal injustice is the reliance of the powers-that-be on the stupendous and murderous modern weapons of war and the advantage they have thereby against us—

defenceless people. In spite of a well organised defence force, of all the deadly instruments of war and the most pagan militarism that can be given play, if my countrymen are possessed of a soul which can never perish by machine guns and artificial war devices, that soul will fight a righteous battle under the invincible captaincy of the god who made our worthy forefathers what they were. . . . If we have the soul to resist the machinations of the oppressor, I know of no power in the world and under the sun to conquer us. (59)

Msimang recombines familiar tropes of new weapons and bulletproof claims. Like Wauchope, Msimang advocates confronting a superior military force by using an alternative weapon: the soul. But like Ntsikana, Nxele, and Mlanjeni, Msimang asserts that this weapon will offer "defenceless people" invincibility against "deadly instruments of war." Msimang's combination of bulletproof claims with the advocacy of war by other means reflects his location within a dynamic tradition of resistance.

In articulating the power of the soul, Msimang makes an explicit inter-textual gesture to *Bayete! "Hail to the King!"* (1923), a novel by G. Heaton Nicholls, member of Parliament and chair of the Native Affairs Commission. "We owe an irredeemable debt of gratitude" to Nicholls, Msimang writes, for revealing the "method we should adopt to seize the reins of government and regain all the freedom we have lost since the advent of the white man in this country." *Bayete* offers a blueprint for this struggle that "calls for no machine guns, no bombs or aeroplanes. That weapon . . . is the power of the soul, the indestructible something that is in man—the Sword of God. It is the will and determination to be free . . . without which we certainly must agree to perish or be made slaves" (60).

This intertextual conversation is a strange one, indeed. In protesting the Hertzog Bills, Msimang turns to Nicholls, their "distinguished champion" (60), who stewarded their passage in 1936. In his foreword, Nicholls describes *Bayete* as a political intervention but decidedly not as a blueprint for African liberation. Nicholls sought to warn white South Africans about seemingly unrelated and even dichotomous institutions that, if drawn into concerted action, could mobilize black revolution. Imagining the cooperation of tribal chiefs, Ethiopian and other African-initiated churches,[54] trade unions, and Garveyite movements, Nicholls perceives commonalities across the dividing lines of Christianization, modernization, and class stratification that fragmented black South African polities with particular intensity after the discovery of gold and diamonds in the late nineteenth century sparked massive urbanization.[55] The novel's protagonist, Nelson (of Arab, not "Bantu" descent), becomes the charismatic successor of the Ndebele chief Lobengula. He buttresses the organizational support of Ethiopian churches and trade unions *with a stash of weapons* smuggled into South Africa by light-skinned African Americans. Passing as white, these immigrants buy farms to accumulate food in preparation for a general strike. Nelson's rival, Jacob, claims that destroying pigs, white fowl, and European kitchen implements will make his followers bulletproof; Nelson, by contrast, "had read history, and although he believed himself to be in communion with God, he could find no warrant for a belief in the non-penetration of rifle bullets" (151, 182). Like the New Africans, Nelson overcomes European weaponry not through traditional war-doctoring but by "steal[ing] from the Whites the knowledge that has made them powerful" (27). Tracing this feat of coalition building under the noses of segregationist officials, the narrator insists that Nelson's soul-power allows him to achieve what no "Bantu" could. Nelson and Jacob may represent opposing poles of elite and prophetic nationalism, yet Nelson's varied alliances also demonstrate their potential cooperation: the critical mass of mystical agitation allied with other modes of organization threatens white South Africa, but Nicholls is skeptical about the prospects for black leadership of this struggle.

Msimang, like Nicholls's protagonist Nelson, "steals" knowledge from this white supremacist novel. But in taking *Bayete* as a model, Msimang overlooks (or, following Harold Bloom, *misreads*) not only Nicholls's disqualification of African leadership but also the role played by conventional weapons in instrumentalizing the "power of the soul."[56] Msimang's invocation of *Bayete* in opposition to the Hertzog Bills complicates Van Wyk Smith's "genuine intertextuality": this textual intersection reveals not "commonality of purpose" but the ideological fault lines of the South African twentieth century. The gulf between Msimang and Nicholls only widens with this aberrant decoding of *Bayete*. Citation is a wildly unpredictable mode of textual afterlife: Msimang's willful or strategic misreading conjures a specter of the novel and turns it against its author's ideological ends. But citation also is constrained by the inertia of the text's body, the whole that resists distortion by emphasis on a single part.[57] Msimang's citation of Nicholls raises more questions about his intertextual intentions than it answers; yet this tendency toward proliferation rather than closure is precisely where (inter)textual afterlives derive their dynamism and fascination. What is at stake are not conventional ideas of textuality as authorial immortality but, rather, the unpredictable new ways in which texts revive the past—as in Xhosa visions of returning people who were both ancestral and new.

Like Msimang and Nicholls, Dhlomo draws on prophetic nationalism's "magical" resistance to comment on the predicament of black South Africans in post-Union South Africa. With the publication of his biography and collected works in the 1980s, Dhlomo was recuperated as a precursor for late-apartheid insurgencies that shifted among township street, stage, shop floor, and printed page. The reappraisal of Dhlomo as something other than a voice of submission was crucial in a milieu suffused with notions of culture as a weapon of struggle. This is not to say that Dhlomo's sometimes elitist, New African aesthetics and politics provided an ideal model for these later mass mobilizations. As with the 1980s recuperation of his own work, the cattle killing provided a suggestive, yet imperfect, conceit for Dhlomo's concerns in the 1930s.

NONGQAWUSE AND TIYO SOGA AMONG THE NEW AFRICANS

The final three scenes of Dhlomo's *The Girl Who Killed to Save* are dominated by conversations among missionaries and colonial administrators about the prospects of Xhosa desperation; this dramatic structure stages the cattle killing as a turning point in the Xhosa people's struggle to maintain their autonomy. The final scene is set a few months after the prophecy's failure, when Xhosa converts gather at the deathbed of a fellow neophyte. A white missionary enters and introduces his companion as "Tiyo Soga, the new African missionary from Scotland. Your own man."[58] Dhlomo gives his character Tiyo Soga no lines; the Xhosa missionary, newly returned to Africa, does not comment on the spectacle he finds. The crowd of new Christians, coupled with the arrival of Tiyo Soga and a doctor, seems to realize the vision articulated in the third scene:

> If these poor people carry out their scheme and starve themselves, it will
> be no national suicide at all. It will be a necessary process of metamor-
> phosis. It will be the agony of birth. . . . This great cattle-killing drama
> which we witness to-day will prepare the Xosa national soil—soul—for
> the early propagation of the message of the missionary, the blessings of

medical science, the law and order of the administrator, and the light
of education. (23)

These words are spoken by Hugh, brother-in-law of "the administrator," Mr.
Brownlee. Dhlomo includes as characters Charles Brownlee, the Ngqika
commissioner in 1856–57, and his wife Frances.

The fundamental question about *The Girl Who Killed to Save* concerns
the relationship between Hugh's rather perverse views and Dhlomo's. Published by the Lovedale mission press, the play often has been dismissed as
"apprentice literature," in Janheinz Jahn's taxonomy of mission literature:
"the literature which in its *style* follows European models, and in its *content*
adopts the ideology and social forms of colonialism . . . without argument
or reflection. Everything European is . . . assumed to be 'superior,' 'progressive' and better than the 'bad,' 'bloodthirsty,' 'savage,' 'heathen,' African
traditions."[59] The play's title might suggest that Dhlomo speaks through
Hugh.

The silent presence of Tiyo Soga, however, indicates the play's profound
ambivalence, in both form and content. Even in Chalmers's account of him
as "model Kafir," Tiyo Soga is not an *apprentice*, in Jahn's sense; within
Xhosa tradition, Soga saw the tyranny of "superstition" but also a rich
inheritance that he worked to preserve. Chalmers provides Tiyo Soga's
reaction to the aftermath of the cattle killing in an August 1857 letter (since
lost): "'My poor infatuated countrymen are now most bitterly reaping the
fruits of having been the dupes of designing impostors. The rod by which
they are now being chastised has been wielded by their own hand. They have
actually committed national suicide.'"[60] If Chalmers's transcription can be
trusted, Tiyo Soga may have coined a common epithet of the cattle killing,
the "Xhosa national suicide." In any case, Hugh implicitly challenges Tiyo
Soga's interpretation by characterizing the cattle killing as necessary, even
providential. Dhlomo and Tiyo Soga enter into a kind of conversation, but
evidence for "genuine intertextuality" in Dhlomo's inscription of "national
suicide" is scant: the phrase is so commonly associated with the cattle killing that it is doubtful that Dhlomo had Tiyo Soga in mind. Nonetheless,
the echo of the phrase gestures beyond Tiyo Soga's silence and repositions
him in opposition to European characters who see the cattle killing as
catalyzing the birth, rather than the death, of civilization.

Tiyo Soga's significance for the play is still more complex: he responded
to the cattle killing with deep sadness for his countrymen's plight but also

recognized its evangelical opportunities. He expressed doubts about "the continued existence of the Kafirs, as a nation," given their dispersal and the chiefs' diminished authority.[61] Nonetheless, he sensed a providential mechanism similar to the one Hugh identifies:

> It is by terrible things that God sometimes accomplishes his purposes. In the present calamities I think I see the future salvation of my countrymen, both in a physical and moral point of view. . . . Indeed, all things considered, the prospects of all missions in Kafirland were never better. . . . Think of poor Kafirland: pity the misery—physical and spiritual—of her sons! Pray for the speedy arrival of more auspicious times! (140–41)

The cattle killing threatened to disperse the nation while also promising salvation; what distinguishes Tiyo Soga's response from Grey's antinational colonialism or from Holden's macabre wonder at God's efficiency is that the terror of "terrible things" registers equally with, rather than being contained by, colonial or Christian teleology.[62]

As a dramatic whole, *The Girl Who Killed to Save* treats these *felix culpa* interpretations with a similar ambivalence that intensifies throughout the play.[63] In the third scene, when the cattle killing has just begun, Hugh and the missionary ruminate about its potential benefits, and Dhlomo offers no alternative view. But the fourth scene, which dramatizes the horrific aftermath, juxtaposes philosophical speculation with human suffering. The Brownlees coordinate famine relief, and Mr. Brownlee's uncharacteristic reverie on the revelatory potential of distress is interrupted by the shouts of a starving man in actual distress. Thus jolted back to his wonted pragmatism, Brownlee challenges the navel gazing of Hugh and the missionary, who debate the aesthetic value of contrasts like that between "this glory of sunset and the misery of the Xosa." Brownlee twice interrupts their "duel of wits" and asks them to help disassemble the relief camp.[64] Even critics as sensitive to the complexity of Dhlomo's stance on mission ideology as Bhekizizwe Peterson have overlooked this staging of voices by extracting from the dialogue the presumed content of Dhlomo's views while ignoring his dramatic manipulation of conflicts among characters.[65]

While Dhlomo's dramatization undermines Hugh, other textual evidence suggests the proximity of Dhlomo's and Hugh's voices. Hugh's assertion that, contrary to the opinions of "historians and writers [who] will condemn Nongqause as a fool, a traitor, a devil-possessed witch[,] . . . in the distant future someone will catch the proper spirit and get the real meaning of this incident and write about it" (26) shows Dhlomo creating a character whose prophetic vision calls his own authorial voice into being.[66] Hugh's proleptic statement anticipates the distorted colonial historiography from which Dhlomo recuperates Nongqawuse. In a 1943 essay, Dhlomo repeats what seems to be an afterthought of consonance between "soil" and "soul" in Hugh's speech: "it would be misinterpretation and insult to our very Heroes and gods, our Soul and Soil, . . . if in documenting and singing these things [the history of the tribal past], we end in mid-air, as it were, and not use these very subjects to comment on our times and aspirations."[67]

The relevance of the past for contemporary African artists was a persistent concern in Dhlomo's essays of the 1930s and '40s.[68] The syntactic "style" (following Janheinz Jahn) of these essays echoes the statements of Hugh and Mr. Brownlee, in an overfondness for oxymoron that halts thought at the recognition of paradox, rather than pursuing its unraveling. "We must go back to go forward," Dhlomo writes, "men become more of themselves by becoming transformed, when they retreat to advance"—when they kill to save, one might add.[69] Wresting salvation from the jaws of destruction is a common trope in political exhortation, as is evident in not only *The Girl*'s disturbing monologues but also Msimang's discernment of potential liberation within Hertzog's legislation. Beyond this stylistic commonality with Hugh's speech, however, the content of Dhlomo's essays rejects the "destruction" of "traditions and customs, beliefs and taboos" that Hugh glorifies as "necessary" for "progress."[70]

Instead, like Tiyo Soga, Dhlomo describes the past as a resource—a "dense forest," "reservoir," or "spiritual home"—for contemporary writers.[71] Aspects of the past that particularly interest him are African heroes and oral performance traditions. He asserts the relevance of nineteenth-century heroes, whom "the new African refuses to accept . . . as savages, murderers, and impostors of the schoolroom and the textbook. He regards and honours them as great tragic national leaders" (42). The artist, in other words, must construct a national past in opposition to the distortions of colonialist historiography and mission education, distortions on which architects of segregation drew to consign Africans to romantic and reductive versions of their respective tribal pasts: "time and again our position and future have been prejudiced and made insecure by reference to our past."[72] In the service of a national future, Dhlomo also sought to recuperate "archaic tribal artistic forms" that "reveal the common origin, the spiritual unity, the essential Oneness, the single destiny of all Bantu Tribes" at a time when segregationist notions of tribalism threatened such national unity. "This essential Oneness of the African peoples should be broadcast from the hilltops and on the most powerful 'horns'"—a metaphor revealing Dhlomo's conviction that radio and the phonograph could enhance the communicative power of traditional oral media.[73]

Reconstruction of the past for its own sake was not Dhlomo's aim; his engagement with the past, grounded in the urgencies of the present, drew on the transformative capacities of artistic representation. Poiesis is a dialectical process of "literary necromancy": "African art cannot grow and thrive by going back and digging up the bones of the past without dressing them in modern knowledge and craftsmanship."[74] In this temporal finesse, exhumation produces the skeletal frame for a future national unity recovered from the past, not created *ex nihilo.* Dhlomo's interest in the past is forward looking, envisaging an emergent, Fanonian national culture rather than a reified cultural nativism: he looks toward the "history of the future."[75] This is the characteristic tension of colonial modernity: "the evocation of figures from the past in the name of a present struggle is far more than invoking an atavistic traditionalism. . . . [M]emory is a part of modernity and the modern nation."[76] Fostering national solidarity beyond tribal identity required ambivalent and ultimately future-directed negotiations with a history of fierce, yet failed, resistance and with cultural traditions under assault.

Dhlomo's decision to write in English reflected a New African consensus that "Africans must write for Africans, but English is the medium through which Africans can be reached. It is impossible to produce a national literature through the use of a tribal language; only tribal literature will result," as the African Authors Conference resolved in 1936.[77] New Africans appropriated English in opposition to pressures like those from R. H. W. Shepherd, director of the Lovedale mission press from 1927 to 1958, to write in indigenous languages. Instilling a "thoughtful and reverent love for good literature" could give educated Africans "a substitute of a satisfactory kind to take the place of so much that has passed from them," Shepherd wrote.[78] In a 1959 address to the General Assembly of the Church of Scotland, Shepherd explained vernacular literature's capacity to compensate for colonial deracination: "'It was the Church that took away many of the African forms of recreation, because of their pagan and often obscene nature. The Church dare not leave the vacuum it has created unfilled. If she does, secular forces such as Communism will fill it.'"[79] At the height of the Cold War,

Shepherd warned that African literary production could either placate or foment political and social alienation. By contrast, Dhlomo's appropriation of both English and traditional oral forms conceives of literature not as compensation for forbidden or disavowed tribal customs but, rather, as a way to forge a viable African future amidst increasing segregation—just as D. D. T. Jabavu advocated, in his 1936 address to the AAC, the mediatory strategy of "using what can be used" and resisting the rest.[80]

"Who mines the past the future makes secure," Dhlomo wrote in his long poem *Valley of a Thousand Hills*.[81] He believed that contemporary African drama must draw on rigorous historical research, but he argued that such retrieval should be informed by literary thinking. He saw contemporary historiography as overly scientific; only narrative and dramatization could make sense of the "unique human mechanism" where "we find people doing evil that good may come."[82] His transformative metaphors—turning back to go forward, killing to save—reveal a millennial logic at work in his thinking. Relying on figuration rather than linear causation, the dramatist can look behind the "screen of exterior human behavior" to the "real human drama [that] lies deep in human fears and hopes" (20–21), as Hugh imagined someone might do for Nongqawuse.

The final moments of *The Girl Who Killed to Save* effect a "literary necromancy" that demonstrates Dhlomo's difficulties in putting his aesthetic theories into practice. After Tiyo Soga's arrival, the dying convert Daba relates a liminal vision: he sees those who died in the cattle killing gathered around Nongqause, praising her as "Liberator from Superstition, and from the rule of Ignorance," since famine drove them to the missions before they died.[83] Nongqause, last seen in a crisis of doubt in the first scene, burdened by her responsibility to the people, "laughs as she tells [the dead] she was really in earnest but was ignorant"; Daba describes her reaching out to carry him across the threshold. The ancestors have not returned, but the dead are seen (at least by Daba) to be alive or, more precisely, in their afterlife: eternal souls dressed "not in blankets and karosses . . . but in Light" (41). Nongqause's prophecy of resurrection, "earnest" yet "ignorant," is replaced by a vision of redemption predicated on Christ's resurrection. A cursory reading of the play, here abstracted as a passage from superstitious ignorance to Christian enlightenment, might suggest that Hugh was right about the cattle killing's providential impetus.

However, Nongqause's earnestness signals the ambivalence undermining such a reading. She had the right motives but the wrong methods, an important characterization given conventional portraits of the historical prophetess as a pawn of either Xhosa chiefs or Sir George Grey. Dhlomo goes some way in redressing the historiographical marginalization of Non-gqawuse. In the first two scenes, he juxtaposes her sincere concern for the people and her regret over sacrificing personal desires to public responsibilities with the self-interested machinations of Mhlakaza and other elders; at the end of the play, she gloriously reappears (in Daba's vision) without the men who promoted the prophecy. In 1933, Dhlomo wrote (in language anticipating Hugh's), "The day may come . . . when the Bantu race will produce a Bernard Shaw to dramatise the story of Nongqauza and reveal to humanity the greatness of her soul, notwithstanding the destructiveness of her dreams."[84] Such greatness of soul (echoing Nicholls and Msimang), combined with the New Africans' knowledge and modern outlook, might generate alternative dreams that could lead "the Bantu race" to glory. In language that not only echoes the Pentecostal realization of Old Testament prophecy but also anticipates Fanon's observation that nation talk "make[s] the people dream dreams" of an existence "outside the bounds of the colonial order," Msimang imagined that once people become "conscious of their fate, then we shall hope and begin to see visions and to dream the dreams of freedom."[85]

At the end of Dhlomo's play, Nongqause can promise only liberation of the soul; Daba's vision comes at a liminal moment of death rather than as a prophetic call to arms. The play concludes in neither politicized clarity nor Christian triumphalism but profound ambivalence. Daba's caretakers alternate between giving him Western medicines and herbal mixtures; the remedies are crowded on a table that becomes overburdened (or overdetermined) and falls over, interrupting a bombastic Christian prayer offered by a convert. As with the multifarious remedies, a range of poetic citations accretes in the play: the epigraph (from Browning's "Memorabilia"[86]) alternates with a praise poem in English. These alternations between Europe and Africa compete rather than cohere.

Critics have framed Tiyo Soga's silence in the play as an indication of Dhlomo's inability to reanimate the past. Ian Steadman writes that despite Dhlomo's critical interest in rehabilitating indigenous forms, *The Girl* lacks an "organic relation between Dhlomo's social consciousness and the conventions which he selects to purvey that consciousness dramatically," so that Dhlomo cannot forge "a new kind of drama, a drama which expressed for a contemporary audience a view of African history and legend, and in

A HYMN

(See: SCENE V, page 38)

KEY E♭.   Music by H. I. E. DHLOMO.

```
 m  :m  |m  :f  |f  :r  |s .f:m  ‖m  :m  |m  :f
 d  :d  |d  :t₁ |t₁ :t₁ |r .t₁:d |d  :d  |d  :t₁
 Nko-si  ka  wu-si  ke - le - le  le   I -  mfu-ndi - so
 s  :s  |s  :s  |s  :s  |s .s:s  |s  :s  |s  :s
 d  :d  |d  :r  |r  . s₁|f₁.s₁:d |d  :d  |d  :r

 f  :r  |s .f:m  ‖m  :m  |m  :m  |m  :l  |t  :d'
 t₁ :t₁ |t₁.t₁:d |d  :d  |d  :d  |d  :r  |r  :d
 ze   zwe-le - tu  U - ze  u   si  vu - se - le - le
 s  :s  |s .s:s  |s  :s  |s  :l  |s  :l  |s  :l
 r  :s₁ |s₁.s₁:d |d  :d  |d  :l₁ |s  :f  |f  :l₁

 m  :m  |m  :r  |r  :f  |t₁ :d
 d  :d  |d  :d  |d  :t₁ |s₁ :s₁
 Si - pu  tu  me  u   ku - lu - nga.
 l  :l  |l  :l  |l  :r  |f  :m
 f₁ :f₁ |f₁ :f₁ |f₁ :s₁ |s₁ :d
```

3. Hymn in the appendix of *The Girl Who Killed to Save*. Courtesy of the Lovedale Press.

dramatic discourse organically related to that view."[87] In Fredric Jameson's terms, Dhlomo had not found a form that could "disclos[e] the solidarity of [the past's] polemics and passions, its forms, structures, experiences, and struggles, with those of the present day": in other words, the dead cannot rise in Dhlomo's play.[88]

The play's music, however, more successfully yokes Christianity with Xhosa tradition to bring the past alive; Dhlomo "mines the past" by borrowing older syncretic forms. In the famine relief scene, stage directions note that the "Bell Call Song" is heard before the curtain rises. This is not among the five songs whose words and music appear in an appendix, an omission that suggests that the song is the well-known "Bell Hymn" of Ntsikana, with which he summoned followers to worship.[89] Dhlomo does provide the words and tonic sol-fa notation[90] for another hymn that the converts sing before the appearance of Tiyo Soga (see fig. 3).

Working from the play's typescript, Loren Kruger notes the similarity between the first line of this unnamed hymn, "Nkosi ka wu si kelele," and the ANC anthem "Nkosi sikelel' iAfrika" (God Bless Africa).[91] Other critics have ignored these songs, probably because the *Collected Works* does not reproduce them. Kruger believes Dhlomo wrote the hymn, but it is actually the only song in the Lovedale edition appendix whose words he does not claim to have written; he also does not attribute authorship to anyone else.

Instead, in an archival comparison of Dhlomo's play with the manuscript of a collection of Tiyo Soga's hymns, I have determined that the song is the final verse of Tiyo Soga's hymn "Lizalis' indinga lakho" (Fulfill Your Promise):

> O lord, bless
> The teachings of our land;
> Please revive us
> That we may restore goodness.[92]

In Dhlomo's appendix, it is identified only as "A Hymn":

> Nkosi ka wu si kelele
> Imfundiso ze zweletu
> Uze u si vuselele
> Sipu tu me ukulunga.[93]

Tiyo Soga does not speak in *The Girl Who Killed to Save*, but other characters sing his hymn of restoration and revive his words. Tiyo Soga is thought to have written this hymn on his return from Scotland in July 1857, around the time Dhlomo's final scene is set. The hymn's final verse is unique in invoking divine blessing on "the teachings of our land"; other verses plead for mercy in spite of the "sins" of "my fatherland" or for Christian enlightenment and amelioration of "our confusion" through which "Lands have been corrupted."[94] In the verse Dhlomo uses, by contrast, the people are not benighted and sinful but merely in need of blessing and revival. In other verses, humans are agents of sin or subjects of God's dominion; here they are eager to "restore goodness" themselves. This project of restoration and revival resonates with Xhosa prophecies whereby the ancestors aimed to "'put the country to rights'" and to renew indigenous "teaching" (rather than see their descendants acquiesce to mission Christianity) after witnessing the dislocations of colonial conquest.[95] Ntsikana yoked images of Xhosa cattle culture to Christian pastoralism in his hymns; Tiyo Soga uses diction that echoes, rather than erases, Nongqawuse's prophecy and other movements of Xhosa revival, just as his *Indaba* article metaphorized the prophecy to envision alternative paths to cultural renewal.[96]

I am arguing that this hymn is not an allusion to "Nkosi sikelel' iAfrika" (as Kruger surmised) but, rather, an inscription of an earlier text by Tiyo Soga. "Nkosi sikelel' iAfrika" closed the inaugural meeting of the South African Native National Congress (SANNC) in 1912; Tiyo Soga's hymn "Lizalis' indinga lakho" was sung at its opening.[97] Dhlomo borrows a text that links past and present and expresses Christian desires for renovation in a Xhosa prophetic idiom; he yokes the cattle killing (when his play is set and the hymn was composed) with its continuing significance in the New African context of pantribal nationalism. The imagery of revival in the verse underscores Dhlomo's assessment of the soundness of Nongqause's goals and softens his criticism of her "ignorant" methods. Taken together with the other ambivalences of the play, Dhlomo's use of Tiyo Soga's words works against reading the play as celebrating European "civilization" in the wake of destruction.

To "mine the past" requires confronting interpretations of the cattle killing as an act of providence that brought to the devastated amaXhosa the blessings of colonial stewardship. Dhlomo engages this view but not without criticism: Hugh's oblivious philosophizing in the famine relief scene reveals what Jabavu called the "White savage" lurking behind the rhetorical facade of enlightened beneficence. But the play's tensions reflect Dhlomo's situation within an elite community that embraced the missionary promise of assimilation: the New Africans' social prominence fit within such providential understandings of colonial history, yet they increasingly recognized that promises of universality would never be kept. In his play, Dhlomo stages the cattle killing as a catalyst that makes possible, and necessary, the struggle for identity, rights, and culture on a national scale: the amaXhosa, the amaZulu, and other peoples were "pacified" individually and could continue their resistance to the depredations of colonial modernity only by joining together. The destruction of the Xhosa nation was providential because it facilitated a revitalized African identity, not an uncritically colonized one. Dhlomo endorses the desire for autonomy expressed in the cattle killing, but he suggests that the magical strategies of prophetic nationalism, as they played out in Nongqawuse's prophecy, are not appropriate for the present.[98]

The Girl Who Kills to Save is poised on a fulcrum between two related but opposed views of providential history that are all too easily compressed into a simplistic notion of acquiescence to European ideology.[99] Just as Msimang appropriates *Bayete*'s soul power for the anticolonial aspirations against which Nicholls warned, the apocalyptic, providential language Dhlomo puts in the mouths of his European characters is challenged by Xhosa mourning and desires for change that both drive and survive the cattle killing. In *The Girl Who Killed to Save*, Ntsikana's and Tiyo Soga's hymns, Nongqause's soul, Christianity, and European medicine all have a place in dreams of renewal based on sound methods and goals. In Daba's vision, the assembled host is not wearing "blankets and karosses," but they are not wearing trousers and frocks either: dressed in "light that makes it impossible to see their bodies or tell their sex," they are beyond race, beyond gender, and beyond any narrowly defined mundane civilization.[100]

TEXTUAL VENTRILOQUISM: READING AND WRITING ALONGSIDE HISTORY

Because Dhlomo's reputation as a dramatist rested on *The Girl* until his *Collected Works* appeared a half century later, he left another vacuum, rather than establishing a tradition, for writers who came after him.[101] This fact is particularly ironic, given his commitment to leaving a literary legacy; in a 1941 letter, Dhlomo expressed frustration with his white patrons:

> they cannot touch my soul, my heart. It is that I fear most to lose. It is my God, my all, because out of it springs the visions and inspiration of all my creative work. . . . the greatest thing I can give to my people, to Africa. I am determined to die writing and writing and writing. . . . It will endure and speak truth even if I perish. . . . I have chosen the path to serve my people by means of literature, and nothing will deflect me from this course.[102]

Dhlomo constructs his writerly self as a prophetic medium, through which "the soul, the heart, the spirit" could "speak truth" after his death, the only limit to "writing and writing and writing" he imagines. The recovery and publication of Dhlomo's papers began a reappraisal of Dhlomo's project of salvaging an African past to meet the demands of a segregationist era.[103] Tiyo Soga advocated communal transcription of oral history; Dhlomo's historical, literary drama drew on oral genres and archival research informed by figural thinking.

Bhekizizwe Peterson identifies in Dhlomo's plays "an attempt to write *aside*, to displace, white accounts of African experiences. . . . in the presentation of precolonial African history and society without Eurocentric prejudices."[104] The results of this attempt in *The Girl* are better characterized in the intransitive sense of "writing aside," that is, writing *alongside* European historiography. Dhlomo's use of Tiyo Soga's hymn complicates the relationship between Xhosa tradition and Christian evangelism and displaces triumphalist interpretations of Xhosa catastrophe. But the historical research underwriting the play less successfully challenges "white accounts of African experiences"; rather, the play relies directly on such accounts.

One source that shaped Dhlomo's treatment of the cattle killing is Frances Brownlee, from whom Dhlomo borrows a vignette for the opening of his third scene: an incredulous Mrs. Brownlee queries her husband about rumors of the prophecy in an official letter she has been reading.[105] As with Tiyo Soga, Frances Brownlee's words are spoken in Dhlomo's play, but not always through the voice of her character. With Tiyo Soga's appearance in his final scene, Dhlomo echoes Chalmers's juxtaposition of Mhlakaza's false "new gospel" with Tiyo Soga's return "to teach his countrymen that there is a resurrection, in which all will participate, who look to Jesus."[106] Dhlomo engages with Brownlee and Chalmers, incorporating their narratives of expectation, disappointment, suffering, and Christian relief into a drama in which both Tiyo Soga and Nongqause "return" in the cattle killing's aftermath. Dhlomo's reliance upon these accounts might explain the tendency of the play to be read as embracing missionary ideology; he writes *alongside* them, dialoguing with rather than displacing them, writing in their margins or between their lines rather than erasing them.

That Dhlomo was unable to "write aside" white histories also is evident paratextually, in the historical note that prefaces the play, recounting Mhlakaza's and Nongqause's rise and the failure of their prophecies. This note is abstracted from an account of the cattle killing that Lovedale Press director Shepherd compiled (mainly from Brownlee) and published in *Lovedale, South Africa: The Story of a Century, 1841–1941.*[107] Lovedale archival records suggest that Shepherd wrote the historical note and published it with the play.[108] Regardless of what Dhlomo thought about Shepherd's inclusion of the note, its presence alongside Dhlomo's text in the published play offers evidence that is simultaneously stark and obscure (because Shepherd's editorial intervention is unmarked) with regard to the difficulty of writing aside hegemonic versions of the past. Shepherd's recension of nineteenth-century history literally replaces Dhlomo's intention to situate his play in terms of the "AmaXhosa Today."[109]

The historical note concludes with a sentence that does not appear in Brownlee or Chalmers and seems to be Shepherd's own: "For long the veld was strewn with bones bleaching in the sun." This vivid phrase and another of Shepherd's flourishes—that "the country would smile again with corn, and there would be plenty for everyone"—echo, albeit ironically, Thomas Pringle's poem "The Desolate Valley," which contrasts the emptiness of the Kat River valley in the 1820s with the time when it rang with the "Gospel's joyful sound." In 1819, the amaXhosa were expelled from the valley—the site of Joseph Williams's London Missionary Society (LMS) mission in 1816—in order to create a buffer zone for British settlement. Pringle's allotment bordered this forcibly vacated land.[110] Pringle's poem mourns the colonial destruction of "Sicána's [Ntsikana's] ancient ground," but it also looks toward a time when "The long-parched land shall laugh, with harvests crowned" and the "unburied bones / . . . withering in the blast / . . . shall awake, and shout—'Our God is nigh!'"[111] Shepherd's account of the cattle killing reverses the valence and chronology of these images: the joyous land is part of the restoration vainly promised by Nongqawuse, while the dry bones of the amaXhosa and their cattle are scattered without hope of resurrection, at least the kind imagined in the cattle killing.

The intertextual resonances among Dhlomo's play, Shepherd's embellishments, and the imagery (if not eschatology) of Pringle's poem demand a reading practice that grasps how texts engage one another in contexts of unequal power. Although Van Wyk Smith's "genuine intertextuality" emphasizes *authorial* agency, I argue that a practice of *reading* alongside is essential to grasp the relationships among these texts. Reading one text alongside another is particularly instructive in cases like Shepherd's apparent echo of Pringle's poem, where evidence of conscious borrowing is weak, yet the historical and ideological resonances construct an intertextual web far more robust than any vaguely conceived thematic convergence or geographical proximity. The notion of reading and writing alongside describes a contiguity and tension among texts that implicates writers and readers, and writers *as* readers and historical agents, within a complex network of multiform intertextuality.

Dhlomo's predicament as a dramatist was his commitment to rigorous historical research, on the one hand, and his awareness of black writers' lack of access to universities and archives, on the other.[112] So, what were the historical sources available to Dhlomo? Beyond Brownlee's *Reminiscences*, where could a dramatist looking to recover the past, to "write aside" the distortions of the colonial archive, turn? J. H. Soga's *The South-Eastern Bantu*, published as a special issue of *Bantu Studies* in 1930, is one possibility.[113] Like his father Tiyo Soga, J. H. Soga feared that "the Bantu people are losing touch with their own past." Critical of the predominance of the colonial frontier in "extant history books," Soga sought an integral African history narrated on its own terms.[114] Soga's account of the cattle killing, however, takes a stunning turn back toward the frontier perspective.

Here we begin to unravel a second intertextual web involving J. H. Soga, the missionary Mary Waterton Waters, as well as Dhlomo, Shepherd, and Pringle. Soga writes:

> The pith of the messages of Nongqause and Mhlakaza may be put in words extracted from a book by M. W. Waters . . . and although the words have been placed in the mouth of Nongqause by the writer, they may be taken as a realistic interpretation of what was intended by the original. Nongqause, speaking in her trance, said, "the spirits of our ancestors are speaking. I, Hintsa, speak. I, also, Gaika; and I, Maqoma, among others whose names are not clearly recorded to the ear. . . . Listen! they are speaking. Their words announce their sorrow. We have seen the oppression of our people by the Whites. We can no longer keep silence. We shall come to save the nation from destruction. The spirit translates me to another country: a land of death." (243)

Soga draws from the second scene of *U-Nongqause*, a play by Mary Waters, daughter of a missionary family who worked as a writer and teacher in the Cape, Natal, and Southern Rhodesia.[115] The passage Soga cites is as complex in its multivocality as Frances Brownlee's account. Soga cites Waters's words as the "pith" and "realistic interpretation" of words the ancestors "intended" for Nongqause's mouth, at the same time that he acknowledges that Waters fills Nongqause's mouth. Some of the words "placed in the mouth of Nongqause" are adapted from Mrs. Brownlee, but her mediation is not acknowledged.[116] The ancestors' names are spoken through Nongqause, although her voice (or another voice?) intercedes to note the presence of those whose names she, or we, cannot hear. These multiple layers of mediation might give a "realistic interpretation" of how chiliastic prophecies are transmitted, but within Soga's *The South-Eastern Bantu* they interweave colonial voices, rather than displacing colonial historiography with an indigenous perspective.[117] Soga writes *alongside* Waters, adding another layer of mediation to her chain of voices. Soga identifies "tradition" as his primary authority, but his citation of Waters's ventriloquism is only one way in which missionary/colonial perspectives shape his account.[118]

Soga writes that Mhlakaza's vision "translated the desires" of Kreli to "drive [the Europeans] back into the sea from whence they had come" (242). Asserting that the prophet responded to his chief's grievances, Soga offers a version of the chiefs' plot thesis, the notion that Xhosa chiefs fabricated the prophecy to provoke war against the colony: "The real object of the originators of this thing, it is said, was to drive the impis [warriors] to fight desperately in despair of any food at home" (245–46). The interposed "it is said" ascribes to commonplace, or oral tradition, a thesis that originated in the colonial archive. But Soga's description of Nongqawuse is wholly original: she was "a graduate in the school of the mystical arts" (242). This singular characterization captures Soga's own ambivalent position as a Lovedale-schooled, Edinburgh-educated historian-missionary trying to give his people a sense of their past. Soga posits Nongqawuse, conventionally the epitome of superstition associated with "red," unschooled Xhosa, as not only a "school" Xhosa but also a "graduate."[119]

Soga's *The Ama-Xosa: Life and Customs* (Lovedale, 1932) omits Waters's account and dispenses with literary flourish in its five-paragraph treatment of this "supreme instance of the folly of superstition"; I discussed the austerity of this account in chapter 1.[120] Soga qualifies his assertion of a chiefs' plot and replaces Waters's voice with Xhosa ones: "It is said, at least by historians, that the policy was to render the people so desperate as to ensure a supreme effort to drive the hated White man into the sea. It is singular that Natives can never give a reason for the perpetration of this terrible act. To a question of the motive is always given the answer *'asazi'* (We cannot tell. We do not know), and apparently in sincerity" (121–22). Soga identifies historians as the source of what "is said," and he contrasts their certainty with Xhosa refusal, or inability, to explain the Nongqawuse. Writing as a Xhosa historian, Soga mediates these perspectives rather than deploying Waters's dramatization of Nongqawuse as prophetic medium.

It is not clear whether Dhlomo consulted Soga's texts. Like Soga, however, Dhlomo accepts a version of the chiefs' plot, leaving mostly undisturbed this central tenet of colonialist historiography.[121] But Dhlomo's treatment of Nongqause is significantly more complex than Soga's in *The South-Eastern Bantu*, and it can be read alongside Waters's dramatization.[122] Dhlomo shows Nongqause manipulated by Kreli and Mhlakaza; he does not dramatize the moment she received the prophecy but, rather, what seems to be a frequent demand that she reenact that moment for curious or skeptical headmen. Whereas Soga's citation of Mary Waters emphasizes the liminal chain of voices in the prophecy's *transmission*, Dhlomo implies that its *dissemination* involves repetitive, mundane performance. In the play's first scene, Nongqause's weary performances are countered with anxious private ruminations; she recognizes that she did not understand the sounds she heard, sounds that Mhlazaka and Kreli eagerly interpreted and gave back to her as the dialogue they compel her to reenact. Dhlomo writes words for his character that suggest that Mhlakaza and Kreli, rather than the ancestors, speak through Nongqause. His characterization grants her a complex self-awareness absent in Waters's depiction of a transparent medium.[123]

Mary Waters would be a minor figure in any history of imaginative writing in southern Africa, yet the fact that she published three texts dramatizing the cattle killing between 1924 and 1928 indicates the demand of mission and educational presses for treatments of African history.[124] As with *U-Nongqause*, the mediation of voices in Waters's *Cameos from the Kraal* (Lovedale, 1927) is complex. The elaborate diegetic framework in this folktale collection purports to offer a "Kaffer" worldview—an aim fulfilled, however improbably, in its cattle-killing narrative.[125] In "The Tale of Makulu," the new cattle and grain do not appear because some refuse to jettison their cattle; consequently, "the spirits wax wroth . . . and in grief and sorrow they returned to the land of the departed . . . [A] great famine fell upon that land, and the Ama-Xosa, because of their hardness of heart, perished by their own hand. Would they had listened to the voice of Nongqause the seer."[126] Soga cites Waters putting words in Nongqawuse's mouth, but here Waters articulates, through layers of intermediary voices, the explanation for the prophecy's failure offered by the historical prophets themselves.

The contrast between this cattle-killing narrative and that in Waters's *The Light—Ukukanya: A Drama of the History of the Bantus, 1600–1924* (Lovedale, 1925) could not be more stark. In that play, which unlike *U-Nongqause* was published in English, the allegorical figure Civilization (who calls herself "Light") halfheartedly laments the "sea of blood" required to enlighten the benighted subcontinent.[127] Waters stages frontier violence as the providential unfolding of God's will: "civilization" is the watchword of colonial subjugation. Late in act I, Sareli consults with Umhlakaza for a strategy "to drive the white man in the sea," which the characters have wanted to do for nearly a century (or twelve scenes) (17). When the prophecy fails, Umhlakaza and Nongqause appear on stage "chewing bones," and, in a strange reversal, Umhlakaza laments having been deceived by Sareli (19). Governor George Grey laments his failure (another reversal), but Civilization assures him that "the land has been ploughed" by suffering and instructs him to "sow the seeds of civilization, weed out the tares, laziness, ignorance, and superstition" (20).[128]

The Light's final act is set in the present; Civilization tells despairing mine workers that fondly remembered days of precolonial autonomy were actually times of "barbarism and terror" (34). She intervenes in a debate at Fort Hare University (South Africa's first "natives' college," adjacent to Lovedale) between "graduates" and "raw Xosa" and charges the graduates with enlightening their "ignorant brethren," teaching them, among other things, that "the black and the white men were both emigrants in this land"; therefore, "the land belongs to both" (35–36). In this broad historical pageant, the cattle killing is a spectacular turning point in civilization's march across southern Africa; in the final scene, the time of preordained struggle between civilization and barbarism has passed, since the discontented are reminded of their blessings and urged to struggle no more.

This glimpse of agitating mine workers and controversies about literate education reveals contradictions that the didactic figure of Civilization is unable to resolve. Analogous contradictions are evident in the play's interpolation of poetic material: these intertextual resonances work against the play's dominant narrative of manifest destiny at any cost. Verbatim repetition of praise songs to chiefs Sareli and Dingaan deftly develops the play's implicit comparison of Xhosa and Zulu histories of futile resistance. But Waters's other poetic borrowings are less efficient, particularly those from Thomas Pringle. The humanitarianism of Pringle's ethnographic and protest poems expresses a more sympathetic view of the amaXhosa—and a more skeptical view of the civilizing mission—than does Waters's play.

Waters takes entire poems from Pringle but never acknowledges him; when she does identify a source, she attributes them to "Slater."[129] A character named "Hottentot" recites Pringle's "Song of the Wild Bushman," a poem of defiance that undercuts Hottentot's assertion that "the white man has finished [his people]" (5). This "song" is completely unattributed, unlike

Civilization's voicing of Pringle's sonnet "The Caffer," attributed to "Slater." Although Civilization believes that fate, undergirded by moral right, assures her progress, Pringle's poem (in my reading, if not Waters's) undermines colonial characterizations of the amaXhosa as savages, livestock thieves, and heathens: Pringle's speaker sees them merely responding to white banditry and evil and urges evangelization only if Europeans truly "deserv'st that name" of *Christian*.[130] In another ideologically and philologically problematic borrowing, the prophet Nxele (Makanna in Waters's text) sings "a war song," again attributed to "Slater" but actually Pringle's "Makanna's Gathering." Waters omits Pringle's third stanza, in which Makanna calls on his people to "make your choice— / To conquer or be slaves"; neither option is compatible with Waters's Civilization.[131]

These examples reveal tensions between Waters's missionary militance and Pringle's humanitarian sympathy and condemnation of colonial excesses. Her misattributions make it difficult to discern what she was doing with these poems beyond putting words in her characters' mouths; Waters's borrowings "write aside" Pringle's authorship, but the more interesting question is what happens when Pringle's poems are read alongside their intercalation into Waters's play. Their appearance in a play celebrating the fated triumph of bloody civilization over "ignorant" peoples of southern Africa a century after Pringle wrote them would confirm his worst fears about the colonial enterprise. One hundred years before Waters, Pringle brought Xhosa literary culture into English belles lettres, using five lines in isiXhosa from "Sicana's Hymn" (Ntsikana's "Great Hymn") as the epigraph to his poem "The Ghona Widow's Lullaby."[132] This poem holds out faith that true Christian values will win the hearts of not only indigenous southern Africans but also British colonial officials whose depredations and betrayals Pringle's "protest" poems denounce. Waters seems oblivious to Pringle's denunciation of the colonial violence her play posits as a bloody means justifying the ends of Civilization. When they are heard in Pringle's Romantic voice of "humane dissent,"[133] the borrowed words break through the teleology in which Civilization contains the "sea of blood." A similar tension pervades Waters's *Cameos from the Kraal*, which sympathetically offers a Xhosa perspective on the cattle killing's failure, within a diegetic framework that assumes European racial and civilizational superiority.

Reading Pringle's poems alongside Waters's dramatic *History of the Bantus* can interrupt the play's flattening of dissonant voices and discrete peoples into a single, providential, national narrative. Precisely because of its stylistic crudeness and bald didacticism, Waters's play lays bare the master narrative of settler expansionism that a decolonizing literary historiography seeks to dismantle. But the play's problematic deployment of Pringle's poems also offers a rough analogy for a new master narrative that Van Wyk Smith fears postcolonial criticism has erected in its place: a monologic, monolithic settler-colonial ideology, in which Pringle's stance is indistinguishable from Waters's.[134] Rejecting the caricatured view of Pringle as the "'archetypal white colonial'" (in Tony Voss's phrase), he argues that Pringle's writing expresses horror at recognizing "his own situation as a settler on the land of displaced people," who were "mispresented or misunderstood by the colonialists."[135] In the poems Waters uses in *The Light*, we see Pringle's representational strategy at work: his "ventriloquism" aimed to "give a voice to what he perceived to be the voiceless" in order to revise the "basic discourse available for the representation and 'voicing' of the Eastern Cape's indigenous people" (30). Yet the availability of such ventriloquism to antithetical desires is evident in Waters's placement of Pringle's words in her characters' mouths, an inscription that encompasses them within a rival discourse of unquestioning European superiority.

Waters's play offers an ideal text for the postapartheid literary historiographical project that Van Wyk Smith advocates: a return to the colonial archive to attend to its "polyphony and contradictoriness" (32). But the polyphony within Pringle's work is itself problematic for postcolonial critique. The intermediary mechanism of "ventriloquism," where authors put words in characters' mouths, becomes especially palpable when authors project their voices across a racial, ethnic, gender, or colonial divide. This practice can be an act of containment, one more scenario in which the subaltern cannot speak. In Pringle's poems, quite literally, it is the subaltern (in the broad sense of indigene, colonial subject) who is spoken through, the subaltern to whom Pringle lends his voice. Van Wyk Smith makes a compelling case that Pringle's poems (along with his other writing and activism) do more good than ill for the material and discursive status of peoples to whom he gives voice. Nonetheless, if the uneven power relations that structure Pringle's ventriloquism are not kept in mind, then his beneficent act of loaning a voice threatens instead to become predatory lending, an act of appropriation and silencing. In other words, readers have a role to play in construing acts of ventriloquism and untangling mingled voices.

Readers' roles in the politics of ventriloquism are no less urgent in intertextual relationships. The borrowed texts in Waters's and Dhlomo's plays are subordinate, if not subaltern: here the politics of intertextuality inheres less in the relative sociopolitical status of authors and characters than in the mode of incorporating one text into another. Read carefully (and perhaps even without knowledge of their authorship), Pringle's poems proleptically "write back" against the very discourse in which Waters contains them (and from which Van Wyk Smith recuperates them). By not *citing* Pringle, Waters's appropriation of his representations of Africans complicates these mediations; Waters's voice (or "Slater's") is imposed in front of Pringle's own acts of ventriloquism. Pringle's *citation* of Ntsikana's "Great Hymn" represents a more reciprocal intertextuality, complicated by the processes of transcription that captured Ntsikana's oral composition.[136] Waters actually *cites* Ntsikana's hymn when she has the Christian chief Khama recite it: it is a strange moment, because Khama "passes out" (stage directions note) when he finishes his recitation of "the poem of Ntsikana, the great Gaika [Ngqika] Christian."[137] The powerful effect of this (re)citation is not incidental in a play in which claims of inspired speech catalyze the cattle killing, the epitome and climax of devastation through which the march of civilization proceeds.

In this politics of intertextuality, readers have a role to play, by not simply tracing words back to their authors but attending to tensions among voices within a text. I am interested less in procedures of "source identification" that demand a rigorously canonical literary education than in listening for a text's full range of voices (identified or not) and attending to its internal and external contradictions. What I called earlier the inertia of the text's body means that, even if I cannot name Hottentot's tune as Pringle's "Song of the Wild Bushman," I can probably perceive its uneasy position within Waters's play. This is not to say, however, that readers can always make sense of the power that authors exercise in borrowing others' words or projecting their own words through others' voices or that authors exercise complete control over the form in which their texts circulate. Shepherd's editorial intervention in Dhlomo's play is invisible in published editions, so that his voice (ventriloquizing Mrs. Brownlee's) in the historical note appears as Dhlomo's own. We can overcome Waters's misattribution of borrowed texts and read them alongside Pringle's poems, but, in the case of *The Girl Who Killed to Save*, the borrowed hymn has disappeared from the most widely available edition of the play, in Dhlomo's *Collected Works*.[138] In neither Dhlomo's nor Waters's play are borrowed words marked textually to set authors' voices explicitly and accurately in counterpoint: these subordinate texts might be able to speak to any given audience or reader but in a vast range of possible voices and intonations.

The hymn that found its way into *The Girl* was probably familiar to Dhlomo and his audience, but its authorship might not have been.[139] Dhlomo stages Nongqause in an act of interpretation: she *knows* only that she heard "sounds," and he dramatizes her agony in wondering what they meant, at the same time that she participates in promulgating a deadly interpretation. My own practice of reading Dhlomo's play alongside other texts has been punctuated by moments of what felt like clairaudient *déjà lu*—hearing voices I sensed I had heard before. This experience of recognition in linking words heard once to words heard again emerges from a process of reading in which chronology is irrelevant: reading alongside constructs an interpretive network of texts and reader-writers rather than pursuing a unidirectional line back to origin, source, or influence.[140] It is the readerly counterpart to T. S. Eliot's notion of the retroactive effect of poetic innovation, which reconstellates relationships within the timeless-yet-temporal "living whole" of previous texts.[141] In "Tradition and the Individual Talent," Eliot "proposes to halt at the frontier of metaphysics or mysticism"—a proposal that comes too late, since Eliot describes the poet as not a "personality" but a "medium" who "surrender[s . . .] himself" and becomes an "ancestor" to other writers. The essay shifts from the overwhelming presence of the dead (mentioned six times in the opening section) and writer-ancestors to a conception of "already living" *poetic works* as a literary tradition experienced in simultaneity (1097, 1094, 1093, 1098).[142] Eliot's spectral account of intertextuality does not consider alterations that occur when authors *unwittingly* take their place among the dead: Dhlomo's occulted ventriloquization of Tiyo Soga is more interesting, not less, for the possibility that Dhlomo did not know whose words his characters sang.

Another angle from which to consider these intermediated versions of reading, writing, and ventriloquism is offered by *The Role of the Missionaries in Conquest* (1952), which argues that the cattle killing was "missionary-inspired. . . . the first fruits of the subjugation over the minds of the people": the idea of destroying precious cattle could only take hold among a demoralized people susceptible to missionaries' alien notions of resurrection.[143] Its author, Nosipho Majeke, was revealed in the 1980s to be the pseudonym of Dora Taylor, amateur white historian and member of the Non-European Unity Movement.[144] Majeke/Taylor constructs a complex voicing of affiliative identity and nonracial solidarity: although she occasionally writes of

"Non-Europeans" or "the oppressed" in the third person, more often she uses the first person to condemn "the conditions under which we live today" and to assert that "we are on the way to liberating ourselves" (131, 1).[145]

Majeke/Taylor's act of ventriloquism reflects the nonracialist aims of the Unity Movement. Rejecting "the very construct of 'race' or ethnicity itself," the Unity Movement, consisting largely of urban, middle-class, English-speaking Coloured intellectuals, developed a "half-hidden historical tradition" as much through teachers' classroom influence as through texts like Majeke/Taylor's.[146] Assessing the movement's historiographical legacy, Bill Nasson argues that Taylor's African pseudonym embodied the "ideology of unity in *ideal* form" and that her book is best understood as an artifact of its "collective historical polemic" (204–5). Taylor enjoyed access to archives that a historian whose name was Majeke (or Dhlomo) would not (206). *The Role of the Missionaries in Conquest* was republished in 1986 and has found a new black and radical readership, although some seem not to recognize that Majeke was actually Taylor, a white woman. Here again we see the interplay between acts of ventriloquism and acts of interpretation: using an African name was an act of nonracialist solidarity for Dora Taylor, but her work remains available for appropriation by a cultural politics that opposes not "herrenvolk" and "oppressed" but white and black.[147]

Like Dhlomo, Pringle, and Waters, Dora Taylor engages in an intermediary act of ventriloquism that obscures the relationship between the source of words and their apparent speaker. Her use of an African pseudonym reshapes the structure of communication characteristic of prophecy and citation, modes of supplementing the authority of one's own voice by borrowing that of others. The pseudonymous publication of *The Role of the Missionaries in Conquest* elides the intermediary function of the white female intellectual, an omission that might render the text even more suspect than Pringle's matter-of-fact, lyrical ventriloquism of indigenous southern African voices. But the mobilization of Majeke/Taylor's nonracialist polemic for black nationalism seems equally remarkable, revealing blind spots in filiative models of identity, whether they emerge from the urgencies of the antiapartheid struggle or the pieties of postcolonial theory. The anticolonial, nonracialist thrust of *The Role of the Missionaries in Conquest* posits radicalized history as a foundation and tool of struggle, a first step toward "true democracy" in which "*all* men and women [will] be able both to build civilization and to share its fruits" (140; emphasis in the original): it imagines a South African nation in which, to paraphrase Foucault's gloss of Beckett, it will not matter—at least not in the devastating and determining ways it has under colonialism and apartheid—who's speaking. This interchangeability of voices remains a utopian aspiration; as I have shown, the politics of intertextuality tell us that literary historiography, even and especially in the postapartheid era, must attend to the ways in which all voices have not been equal.

Put down the gun, pick up the pen: the tension between military and cultural modes of struggle in Wauchope's 1882 poem resonates throughout the twentieth century. Now that guns have been put down, to what use should pens be put, particularly in looking back at the relationship between guns and pens in defining, defending, and reclaiming the rights of "countrymen"?[148] This chapter has considered intertextual webs in which the cattle killing has been entangled, in order to unravel the implications of "genuine intertextuality" for postapartheid literary history. My examination of how writers in southern Africa "have actually listened and talked to one another across the cultural and linguistic rifts and abysses which till recently defined our political landscape" (in Van Wyk Smith's phrase) has produced evidence not of mutually intelligible, synchronous conversation but, rather, of the ambiguities, silences, and distortions involved in speaking with those not present and in speaking with the dead. In a disenchanted world, speaking with the absent or the dead looks a lot like talking to oneself, a physical manifestation of structural tensions that I have traced in the politics of intertextuality.

The voices of Tiyo Soga, H. I. E. Dhlomo, Frances Brownlee, Mary Waters, J. H. Soga, and Thomas Pringle meet and commingle across racial, ethnic, gender, linguistic, ideological, and temporal divides. As with Msimang's invocation of Nicholls' *Bayete*, however, these mediations only make ideological fissures more visible. The instability of meaning inherent in using others' words proliferates questions about these writers' divergent "intentional[ities]" and the products of merging voices. This indeterminacy is particularly acute in texts that revive the cattle killing. One day a young woman came home with a story about hearing voices, and the Xhosa world changed irretrievably. What happened between word and deed and what that sequence of events means has attracted so much imaginative attention precisely because of the energy released when voices meet and urge action, when revenant voices, whether textual or spectral, are heard to speak toward the future. In the afterlife of the cattle killing, Nongqawuse's vision of a renovated world becomes bulletproof precisely through its malleability, its capacity to absorb interpretive pressures in order to remain a compelling vision of both extremity and desire for transformation.

The proliferation of meanings in the afterlives of the cattle killing draws together related tropes on words and weapons: the bulletproof claim (which opposes words and actions to the brute materiality of bullets) and the appropriation of words *as* weapons by redefining the mode of struggle. An isiZulu poem by L. T. L. Mabuya, "Nkosi sikelel' iAfrika" (God Bless Africa—the title of the ANC anthem), refigures the alchemic anticolonial promise of bullets turned to water, describing the suppression of the 1976 uprisings that spread across South Africa after the student protest in Soweto as a powerful thunderstorm that strikes in Johannesburg, the Cape, Natal, and "the North," bringing "shock" and "amaze[ment]" as rain falls in each place. At the end of the poem, the raindrops revert to their literal form:

> It is a rain-storm of cannons and guns . . .
> Everything is impregnated with bullets;
> It is a scorching storm of blood and tears.[149]

In a macabre inversion of the militant optimism that drives bulletproof claims, the poem transforms bullets into water and back again; this water is as destructive as any weapon wielded by the state. We can read in it a palimpsest of the redefinition of resistance—guns, pens, hymns, schools . . . Soweto.

The spark of Soweto generates poems like Mayuba's as part of "an emergent (and insurgent) national political culture."[150] The gun/pen trope anchors Sipho Sepamla's poem "To Makana and Nongqawuse," in which the speaker is repeatedly felled by "the whizz of bullet words" as he invokes the "spirit of my ancestors" and ponders the lingering, untimely wisdom of "departed prophets." Linking the poetry disseminated at sites of struggle, including rallies, prisons, and trade union meetings, to other forms of oral and poetic performance, Jeremy Cronin shows that the transformative potential of this poetry transcends taxonomical questions of origin and influence, as he wrote in 1988 of the chanting, marching mass that is *toyi-toyi*:

> Whether the *toyi-toyi* is a song, a chant, a march, a war cry, or a poem is
> a scholastic point. Functionally, like much of the emergent culture and
> all of the poetry I have described, it serves to mobilize and unite large

groups of people. *It transforms them into a collective that is capable of facing down a viciously oppressive and well-equipped police and army.* In acting together, under the shadow of the apartheid guns, the mobilized people are forcing open space to hold proscribed meetings, to elect and mandate their own leadership, to discuss basic matters, to resolve crime in their streets, to bury their dead, to raise illegal banners, to unban their banned organizations, to discover their strength, and even to make their own poetry. In short, through it all, liberated zones are being opened up in industrial ghettos and rural locations, where the people are beginning—tenuously it is true—to govern themselves in this land of their birth. (22; emphasis added)

Cronin figures *toyi-toyi* and poetry as a kind of war doctoring, through which the people gather strength to move together even "under the shadow of the apartheid guns."[151] Attentive to what he calls elsewhere the many "voices of this land" and the varied contexts in which they speak,[152] Cronin intimates what an emergent South African literary history might look like.

In chapter 1, we saw dreams of transformation entangled within the competing modes of orality and literacy; what is implicit in this chapter, yet no less significant, is the function of language in dividing "larger narratives" of South African literary history "into diverse and discontinuous histories."[153] I have invested most of my interpretive energy into texts written in English about the amaXhosa, by no means an innocent position: having amplified resonances between prophetic and literary modes of communication that resound in the cattle killing's textual afterlives, I must acknowledge that the linguistic limitations of my project are implicated within the history of contests between isiXhosa and English and between orality and literacy.[154] Cognizant of this limitation, I nonetheless resist the suggestion that the "smaller stories" told by literary historians be strictly delimited by linguistic expertise. Because I cannot read them in the original, I have omitted from this discussion both J. J. R. Jolobe's "Ingqawule" and Vilakazi's "Inkelenkele YakwaXhoza," poems in isiXhosa and isiZulu, respectively, that offer important renditions of the cattle killing.[155] But I have made use of other texts in translation, precisely when the gulf between languages is at stake either thematically (as in Mabuya's poem on "the language war" over Afrikaans in the schools, or in Tiyo Soga's and Wauchope's negotiations with literacy and newspapers), or in the text's own trajectory of life and afterlife (as in J. H.

Soga's difficulties publishing *The South-Eastern Bantu* or in Jordan's transla-tion of Gqoba's cattle-killing narrative). The effectively invisible, inaudible presence of Tiyo Soga's isiXhosa hymn in Dhlomo's play is emblematic of the difficulty of reconstructing literary history through Malvern van Wyk Smith's "genuine intertextuality." The problem is not merely that Soga's text has disappeared from Dhlomo's play in the *Collected Works* but that it is all but absent even in the Lovedale edition for readers who do not read isiXhosa. Although I hesitate to claim interpretive authority over material for which I do not have linguistic expertise, I am compelled to call atten-tion to intertextual convergences that have gone unremarked (despite two decades of renewed attention to Dhlomo) precisely because they involve a kind of speaking in tongues, an interlinguistic intertextuality that has fallen through the cracks of the fragmented literary histories and institutions of literary scholarship in southern Africa.

Leon de Kock imagines literary historiography focused on "contestable renditions of the world and the text . . . without imagining that the world is ever amenable to textual capture in the fullest sense." He links the labor of literary historiography to a more fundamental notion of desire, the "pos-sibility that things might yet be otherwise."[156] This kind of critical desire elicits Van Wyk Smith's suspicions—a fear that the commonality that would make a national literary history viable exists only libidinally. Yet, when confronted with the empirical fact of fragments of one text within another, as in Tiyo Soga's hymn or Pringle's poems in Dhlomo's and Waters's plays, a reader's interpretive desire still remains at play. Soga's hymn and Pringle's poems have similar effects: mitigating, complicating, contradicting, even resisting the plays' seeming Christian teleology. The ultimate choice of participle in the previous sentence is a matter of desire, as is my impulse to assume that Dhlomo *at some level* recognizes the import of his intertextual gesture and Waters does not, in order to claim Dhlomo's problematic play for a tradition of resistance to the project of European civilizational supe-riority pervading Waters's texts. (I am not unaware, in other words, that *The Girl*'s contradictions may bespeak confusion as well as complexity.) I have aimed to construct a nuanced notion of resistance that, following Wauchope, encompasses not only unconventional weapons but also the ambivalence of having appropriated them from the oppressor.

Writing of the colonized artist's problematic turn from European to na-tive culture, Fanon insists, "It is to the zone of occult instability where the people dwell that we must come; and it is there that our souls are crystallized and that our perceptions and our lives are transfused with light."[157] This passage follows Fanon's argument in "On National Culture" that the alienated artist seeks in vain a reunion with the people by reclaiming a reified past. This chapter has traced conjunctions among the mediations at work in nationalism, prophecy, and intertextuality; Fanon's view of decolonizing national culture as that produced within contemporary struggles resonates with Dhlomo's literary necromancy, oriented not toward the past but toward the transfigured future limned in Fanon's luminous language. It reminds us that intertextuality is not merely a retrospective mode of ventriloquism but also an ongoing process of interpretation aptly imagined as "occult instability," shaping and shaped by the constituents of the nation, even and especially when the nation exists only aspirationally in struggles against colonialism. My practice of reading Dhlomo's and Waters's plays alongside their intertextual imbrications allows for an attentiveness to stirrings, sounds, voices whose marks on a text are not always palpable, at least not yet.

CHAPTER THREE

THE PROMISE OF FAILURE

Memory, Prophecy, and Temporal Disjunctures of

the South African Twentieth Century

Awaking on a Friday morning, June 20, 1913, the South African native found
himself, not actually a slave, but a pariah in the land of his birth.

SOL PLAATJE, *NATIVE LIFE IN SOUTH AFRICA*, 1916

The time is out of joint—O cursed spite!
That ever I was born to set it right.

WILLIAM SHAKESPEARE, *HAMLET*

African works of Art can and should reflect not only the present phase of the
National liberatory struggle but also the world of beauty that lies beyond the
conflict and turmoil of struggle.

"BASIC POLICY OF THE CONGRESS YOUTH LEAGUE," 1948[1]

The previous two chapters featured texts that posit the cattle killing's
failure as a decisive event that makes way for something new. Sir George
Grey sees an opportunity to consolidate his authority over the amaXhosa.
Missionaries see the reversal of Xhosa believers' hopes as preparing them
to embrace the gospel. Although *The Girl Who Killed to Save* has been read
in terms of these Eurocentric providential narratives, we can also see H.

I. E. Dhlomo identifying the destruction of the Xhosa nation as a catalyst for a new South African nationalism.

These varied responses share an assumption that the cattle-killing prophecy failed because it was false and could never have been realized—a medium's misreading of cosmohistorical possibility, if not a misinterpretation of the ancestors' voices. Its failure intersected with other historical processes in the eastern Cape and the British empire that shaped how the prophecy's aftermath diverged from its visionary anticipations. But the prophecy itself, historically speaking, was a rupture, a terminus, a dead end. Moreover, in some interpretations the prophecy was not merely false, but also fraudulent: willfully disseminated by decidedly uninspired human agents pursuing mundane interests, as in notions of a Xhosa chiefs' plot to spur war against the Colony or a hoax perpetrated by Grey to steal Xhosa land.

This taxonomy of reasons why prophecies are not fulfilled not only distinguishes among interpretations of the cattle killing; it also facilitates thinking about failure in terms other than falsity, fraudulence, or finality. If we can consider failed prophecy without labeling it as inadvertently or intentionally spurious, then we might be able to think through historical logics other than decisive failure as a dead end. Failure, in other words, might involve a more complex temporality, and the afterlife of prophecy might take forms other than representations of failure. Both of these aims are demonstrated in *The Role of the Missionaries in Conquest* (1952), the polemic by amateur historian and Non-European Unity Movement member Dora Taylor (writing as Nosipho Majeke) that I introduced in chapter 2.[2]

On one level, the cattle killing was for Majeke/Taylor a false prophecy, and responses to it in colonial policy and "herrenvolk history" were shaped by fraudulent duplicity.[3] She debunks Sir George Grey's reputation as an enlightened, humane advocate for native peoples. Decades before postcolonial studies or South African revisionism generated critiques of the cultural, religious, and ideological aspects of colonial conquest, Majeke/Taylor contrasted Grey's ruthless opportunism with his saintly portrait in colonial historiography. For Majeke/Taylor, the aftermath of the cattle killing illuminates the apartheid present, in which black South Africans were forced into ethnically defined territories (known first as native reserves, later as Bantustans and homelands) by prohibiting them from leasing or owning land elsewhere. As the majority population was pushed into these inadequate spaces, overpopulation and soil degradation intensified the experience of dislocation. Soil "betterment" and "rehabilitation" programs of the late 1930s and 1940s called for villagization, livestock culling, and fence construction—ostensibly to relieve problems of overstocking (rather than human overpopulation). Majeke/Taylor surmises that since "herrenvolk historians" saw Grey as the "'savior of thousands'" in the aftermath of the cattle killing, they might also "describe the Rehabilitation Scheme (the second 'Nongqause') as a scheme to 'save the Reserves.'"[4] As Majeke/Taylor argues, this "rehabilitation," which involved the destruction of wealth in livestock, intensified pressures on potential migrant laborers to seek employment outside the reserves; similarly, in the 1850s, the decimation of homesteads and kraals spurred Grey's "famine relief" policies, designed to free up Xhosa land and canalize Xhosa labor.

In labeling the Rehabilitation Scheme a "second Nongqause," Majeke/Taylor identifies a typological structure of false and fraudulent prophecy linking the British colonial past to the apartheid present. A chain of events in the nineteenth century can be traced forward on a "road" to present dislocations; conversely, contemporary oppression can be extrapolated backward to analogous situations in the past. "We who are acquainted with the dire application of the 'Rehabilitation Scheme' in the Reserves do not need to be told what devastation and exploitation" resulted from Grey's policies in British Kaffraria, particularly since they paved the road to the present (61).

On another level, Majeke/Taylor makes a more complex point about failed prophecy and its uses for liberatory historiography. It is not merely that understanding one example of colonial duplicity inoculates against others. Rather, she constructs a narrative of subjugation that generates the seeds of its own reversal: here we begin to see the promise in failure. Millennial dreams of assimilation into Christian civilization, built upon "liberty, equality, fraternity—the powerful slogans of democracy," precipitate a catalytic disillusionment:

> But while, for the White politicians, their high-sounding slogans were no more than empty promises, to the Africans they were in real earnest. They crystallised the aspirations of an oppressed people, and the very contrast between those lofty ideals and the degradations of their daily existence, was a forceful education in itself. (139)

Majeke/Taylor describes a prophecy both fraudulent and failed—fraudulent in Europeans' bad faith, but merely failed for those who embraced it—that would subsequently inspire its "earnest" African adherents to build the world its European proponents had falsely promised. As with the cattle-killing episode, she distinguishes between responses to the prophecy and motivations behind it. For New Africans, the failure of the European millennial dream enacts a "forceful education" that ultimately "heightened their consciousness of their true position, so that their very failures were from this point of view a gain" (139). Majeke/Taylor outlines a potentially liberating process of losing to gain—and gaining the very things they had been promised. New Africans who renounced tribalism and embraced the promise of a universal civilization, only to be pushed to the margins of the South African polity, would thereby come to recognize their "true position" and unite to build "a true democracy. . . . to build civilization and to share its fruits" among all South Africans (140). Her history provides the foundation for such a movement.

This example suggests a radically different temporality of failure, in which what is unrealized in one moment might yet come to pass, perhaps through a different mode than was originally expected: David Attwell calls this "an optimism of the long term,"[5] and I develop this idea in later chapters under the rubric of *unfailure*. Majeke/Taylor's example holds that the experience of interim failure creates new conditions for eventual success. She describes a millennial, dialectical logic, promising ultimate gain predicated on loss. This logic assumes an impossible economy of loss and recovery, an arithmetic that seems unlikely to add up but must if its hopes are not to be falsified. We should not forget that her description of the New Africans' egalitarian society is future projection, not fait accompli. Failed prophecies generate new prophecies.

At stake in the distinction between failure and falsity is the question of why unrealized prophecies attract historiographic or mnemonic attention. One might argue that false or fraudulent prophecies serve as a warning, as when new "Nongqawuses" are iterated in dangerously impossible or disingenuous schemes. The fundamental assumption of such monitory retrospection is that people in the present need not—indeed, must not—be as gullible as the earlier believers. Such retrospection threatens to become an exercise in comparative rationality, however deeply it might mourn sacrifices the deluded ones made in their error.

What I have in mind is not this kind of voyeuristic relationship to the past, marveling at the catastrophic lengths to which Xhosa believers went to pursue an obviously impossible dream. Such an approach would only exacerbate the shame and anger many Xhosa people continue to feel about the Nongqawuse episode: "Nobody is proud of Nongqawuse," explained a teacher from the rural Transkei in the late 1990s.[6] Steve Biko, the Black Consciousness philosopher/activist, described the historiographical and psychological problem of failure in terms of Fanon's observation about the colonization of the past:

> As one black writer says, colonialism is never satisfied with having the native in its grip but, by some strange logic, it must turn to his past and disfigure and distort it. Hence the history of the black man in this country is most disappointing to read. It is presented merely as a long succession of defeats. . . . Heroes like Makana [Nxele] who were essentially revolutionaries are painted as superstitious trouble-makers who lied to the people about bullets turning to water.[7]

For Biko, attention in colonialist historiography to Makana's bulletproof claims obscures the persistent urgency of the anticolonial desires he championed. Biko urges, "[W]e have to rewrite our history and produce in it the heroes that formed the core of our resistance to the white invaders" (95). This historiographical project demonstrates Biko's sense of the continuing potential within this vulnerable history of resistance, despite its failure in its own moment. Articulating the need for counterhistory, Bheki Peterson notes:

> The need to construct trans-historical continuities and to embark on projects of cultural retrieval is informed by the search for the causal origins of colonial conquest and the current crisis. . . . But how does one narrate in a heroic mode a "journey" that, after all, ensued with the defeat of African societies?[8]

How do writers and activists in the era of modern nationalism confront the legacy of primary resistance? How can cultural production engage histories of failure?

The cattle killing's afterlife in the twentieth-century South African imaginary consists not merely of defeatism or warnings against false hopes; memory and prophecy are temporal mechanisms for thinking beyond an untenable present and constructing vital modes of resistance. Amidst the aftermath of remembered prophecy in the cattle killing, is it possible to find a prophetic memory that shows the way beyond the present? *Remembered prophecy* and *prophetic memory* are terms that shape my examination of cultural production that combines retrospective mindfulness of past failures with expectant future projections. How might the afterlife of failure generate not only cautionary tales but also unrealized dreams that energize contemporary desires for liberation?

This chapter pursues these questions by examining key moments in the tradition of protest writing, a literary mode that aimed to ameliorate injustice by documenting oppression and making moral appeals, often to white audiences. The protest mode emerged at the turn of the twentieth century as New Africans confronted the gap between millennial dreams of assimilation and the machinery of racial exclusion. Protest dominated black South African writing through late-apartheid insurgencies that began with the Black Consciousness movement of the 1970s. The epitome of protest writing is Solomon T. Plaatje's *Native Life in South Africa* (1916), which appealed to the British to intervene against the 1913 Natives' Land Act. Plaatje was an "earnest" African (in Majeke/Taylor's phrase) who found in failed imperial promises the charge to create a nonracial society. Although his book failed in its immediate aim, Plaatje's attention to the historical rupture of the Land Act posits an aberrational present, which continues into the apartheid era. Tracing the protean life of Plaatje's text in time, I show how it accretes meaning because of—rather than despite—its failure.

The second half of the chapter traces challenges to protest writing in debates about the role of cultural production and historical imagination in the antiapartheid struggle of the 1970s and '80s. Black Consciousness challenged black South Africans to claim responsibility for their liberation rather than cultivating white allies through moral appeals. The most influential theorization of the cultural implications of Black Consciousness came from Njabulo S. Ndebele, who articulated a new vision of culture's transformative potential as a "rediscovery of the ordinary": reclaiming everyday lived experience, rather than documenting spectacular oppression as the protest mode had done. Reading Ndebele and Plaatje together, I examine the fraught temporal relationship between Ndebele's ordinary and Plaatje's aberrational present. I measure the adequacy of Ndebele's arguments by considering the work of Mtutuzeli Matshoba, an important Black Consciousness writer popular with black and white readers. His narratives combined the psychological insights and militance of Black Consciousness with the documentary aims of Plaatje's protest tradition. In his arguments for the "rediscovery of the ordinary," Ndebele singled out Matshoba as the epitome of the deleterious fiction of the spectacle that paralyzed the imagination like a false prophecy. Reading Matshoba's cattle-killing narrative, "Three Days in the Land of a Dying Illusion" (1979), I show how memory and prophecy generate the kind of defamiliarization that Ndebele advocated during the height of the struggle, and I consider how such late-apartheid debates signify today. Plaatje, Ndebele, and Matshoba ponder the difficulties of imagining life in South Africa in ordinary time.

NATIVE LIFE IN SOUTH AFRICA AND THE FAILURES OF NONRACIALISM

The 1913 Natives' Land Act heralded the legislation of the distinctive geography of apartheid, where the white minority owned nearly all the land, and black South Africans were forcibly relegated to the remaining areas, successively designated "reserves," "Bantustans," and "homelands." The Land Act constituted the reserves out of seven percent of South Africa's territory, beyond which Africans could not own or lease land. It specifically targeted sharecropping arrangements that had created a vibrant black peasantry. Sharecroppers had two options in 1913: become paid employees on farms where they lived and turn their livestock (i.e., their wealth) over to their new farmer-bosses, or leave those farms and enter the labor force.

As a lay preacher and journalist, Plaatje embraced the "weapons" of pen and petition, traveling in the Transvaal, Orange Free State, and Cape Province in 1913 to document the Land Act's effects, and to England in 1914 in a delegation of the South African Native National Congress, after they failed to persuade the South African government to suspend the act.[9] Written on the way to and during his stay in England, Plaatje's *Native Life in South Africa* appealed to British public opinion in the name of values that underwrote imperialism.

Plaatje's appeal to the British—in his book and in countless speeches to Brotherhood Societies and other groups[10]—aimed to provoke a crisis for the imperial project of spreading the blessings of Christian civilization. What is striking about reading Plaatje now, in the era of postcolonial studies, is that in the metropolis, *in the name of imperial values,* he protests injustice in a newly self-governing dominion. Imagining what would happen if men like Sir George Grey were to witness the sight of "natives . . . now debarred from tilling the soil of the Cape," Plaatje asks, "What would these Empire-builders say if they came back here and found that the hills and valleys of their old Cape Colony have ceased to be a home to many of their million brawny blacks, whose muscles helped the conqueror to secure his present hold of the country?"[11] Beyond eulogizing this muscular imperialism, Plaatje stresses the tax-paying South African natives' loyalty to the British crown—during the South African War and World War I, which erupted while Plaatje was abroad—and he contrasts this loyalty with the recent history and imminent threat of Afrikaner antagonism. The Land Act, in his account, represents the triumph of the most exploitative relationships between Afrikaners and Africans over the paternal ideals of "true Imperialism."[12] Referring to the protection of a few thousand Indians in South Africa by the viceroy of India, Plaatje warns that if the British "neglect . . . the groans of five million natives because (unlike a viceroy) the missionaries who plead for them cannot enforce their claim with a political or diplomatic blow, then there would appear to be the suggestion of more fear than justice in Imperialism" (235). Plaatje hopes the British will not find an excuse to abandon the values he accepts (at least rhetorically) as underwriting empire.[13]

Plaatje's hope was in vain: the British Parliament did not act, and the 1913 Natives' Land Act is remembered as a seminal moment in the legislation of apartheid rather than a momentary aberration. *Native Life* was, in this immediate sense, a failure: its documentary project and moral appeal failed to move its intended audience. In this outcome, the text's immediate reception reduplicates failure, since *Native Life* characterizes the Land Act as a betrayal of Africans who had embraced European promises of an egalitarian society. This catalyzing betrayal of hopes for a nonracial society is precisely what Majeke/Taylor described as a "forceful education." *Native Life* shares with *The Role of the Missionaries* a concern with failed cross-racial alliances that nonetheless retains a nonracial ideal; the author of the latter performs this conviction by writing as Nosipho Majeke rather than as Dora Taylor. She writes by turns affiliatively, about the "conditions under which we live to-day, as outcasts in the land of *our* birth," and then objectively, about the history of "the people who are to-day destitute of human rights in the land of *their* birth" (131, 166; emphasis added). Both statements draw upon the opening of *Native Life in South Africa:* "Awaking on a Friday morning, June 20, 1913, the South African native found himself, not actually a slave, but a pariah in the land of his birth" (21). Neither the 1913 Land Act nor subsequent legislation restricted Dora Taylor's status in South Africa—not even the land of *her* birth. Both Plaatje and Majeke/

Taylor perform a nonracial future imagined to emerge through appeals and alliances across (and beyond) racial lines, even while documenting the failure of such projects in the past. Their texts expose the failures of nonracialism in order to retain and realize its possibilities.

The consolidation of apartheid, its decades of crisis, and its aftermath reflect the dilated, recursive temporality of this failure of nonracialism. In exposing the falsity of colonial promises, Majeke/Taylor and Plaatje intimate the necessity of a new form of nationalism, one broader still than the New Africans' pantribal black nationalism. The nonracial ideal shaping Majeke/Taylor's history, as well as Plaatje's appeal to the British to make good their imperial promises, assumed the indispensability of white sympathy and solidarity. This assumption became increasingly untenable in the South African twentieth century, not merely because the British Parliament or white South Africa was unresponsive. In a brutally racist regime, nonracialist gestures cannot transcend racial hierarchy: the antiapartheid struggle would later confront the tension between white solidarity and white control. The nonracial ideals expressed in the Freedom Charter of 1955—that "South Africa belongs to all who live in it, black and white," and that this democratic goal would be achieved by "striv[ing] together"—were challenged by the separatist black nationalism of the Pan Africanist Congress (split from the ANC in 1959) and the Black Consciousness movement. The constituency of the nation and the means of national liberation have been crucial questions in the theory and practice of resistance, "the heterogeneous struggles and emphases which enliven any nationalism, and the struggle for prominence among such diverse forces *within* an overwhelming political nationalism."[14] Later in this chapter, I examine how these questions bear upon literary form and intended audience in late-apartheid cultural production.

REMEMBERED PROPHECY AND PROPHETIC MEMORY: PLAATJE'S ABERRATIONAL PRESENT

The tension between failed and fraudulent prophecy—between the utopian potential of unrealized dreams and the distraction and disillusionment of false hopes—deeply informs *Native Life in South Africa*. Putting some distance between failure and falsity allows us to see how writers like Majeke/Taylor and Plaatje warn against false prophecy while making their own future projections: they are prophets warning against false prophets.

For Plaatje, the most dangerous source of false hope was the promise that the Land Act's effects would be mitigated by a commission appointed to designate additional land for Africans, as stipulated by the 1913 legislation.[15] Plaatje's descriptions of families evicted from farms in the middle of winter, carrying all their possessions (including livestock, without access to water and pasture), make clear that they cannot afford to wait until the South African Lands Commission identified more land in which Africans could legally reside. To make matters worse, the commission was temporarily suspended at the outbreak of the First World War. Its always-imminent report functions as fraudulent prophecy; the forthcoming report was "naively alleged to be pregnant with fruits of the millennium, but the cruel evictions . . . are pursuing their course while the war lasts and the Union Government remains unconcerned" (246). The final section of *Native Life in South Africa* analyzes the commission's report, released in May 1916; far from offering the "fruits" of a millennial world renewed, the report confirms the consignment of Africans to a life of slavery in everything but name.[16] One difference between slavery and the report's proposal is that South African natives are to be "herd[ed] into concentration camps" and taxed to maintain them, thus "sav[ing the colonials] the expense of buying the slaves" (435–36).

Plaatje recognizes that the long-awaited report is likely to deceive "even sincere and well-informed friends of the natives": "There are pages upon pages of columns of figures running into four, five or six noughts. They will dazzle the eye until the reader imagines himself witnessing the redistribution of the whole subcontinent and its transfer to the native tribes." The magical qualities of print conjure an illusion that the commission has "'doubled' the native areas." However, Plaatje calculates, if marginalizing Africans into such a small percentage of "the land of [their] birth" amounts to "doubling it, then our teachers must have taught us the wrong arithmetic" (434). Plaatje offers what Majeke/Taylor called a "forceful education," using the tools of mission schooling to measure the characteristic gap between "lofty ideals and the degradations of . . . daily existence."[17] Plaatje intimates that literacy and numeracy, imperial gifts to natives of southern Africa,[18] have been perverted by "Colonials" ruling South Africa since 1910. Orality is susceptible to similar perversion.

Plaatje narrates the genesis of the Land Act in "gossipy rumours about somebody having met someone who said that someone else had overheard a conversation between the Baas and somebody else, to the effect that the Kaffirs were getting too rich on his property"; out of such loose talk, "floating in the wind" as Lovedale Press founder John Bennie might have written, emerged a law that dislocated millions.[19] For those made homeless by the law, experience confirms the wild improbabilities of rumor: "At first they thought the stories about a new law were inventions or exaggerations, but their own desperate straits and the prevailing native dislocation soon taught them otherwise" (93). The contest is not between orality and literacy, but rather between those with the power to turn vague lies into law, and those who must live under that law and the effects of its lies.

"Africa is a land of prophets and prophetesses," writes Plaatje (295). While he warns against the fraudulent millennialism of the Lands Commission report, he also evokes a "tone of prophetic articulation," in Es'kia Mphahlele's phrase. Mphahlele locates this prophetic tone not within the Judaeo-Christian tradition of a "singularly inspired individual," but rather the conventions of African oral poetry, where a "communal" or "public" voice "admonishes, exhorts, praises, reproaches." [20] Looking beyond a simple conception of prophecy as prediction, Mphahlele describes "the flux of life extending from a past that is reckoned in relation to one's ancestral heritage and actual events experienced by a community, through the present to some infinite time that cannot simply be equated with the western concept of 'future.' The reason I choose to call it 'prophetic' is that it has implications beyond a man's consciousness of the past and the present" (34–35). These broader implications are, I would stress, both social and temporal.

A *communal* consciousness of "infinite time" not only challenges atomizing "Western" notions of individual subjectivity; it also undermines conceptions of temporality that recognize only discrete instants in linear time like pearls knotted on a string, the "homogeneous, empty time" of secular modernity.[21] The ANC Youth League's 1944 manifesto offers a vivid, counterhegemonic comparison of these ideas about time:

> The Whiteman regards the Universe as a gigantic machine hurtling through time and space to its final destruction: individuals in it are but tiny organisms with private lives that lead to private deaths. . . . This outlook on life divides the Universe into a host of individual little entities which cannot help being in constant conflict thereby hastening the approach of the hour of their destruction.
>
> The African . . . regards the Universe as one composite whole . . . progressively driving towards greater harmony and unity whose individual parts exist merely as interdependent aspects of one whole realising their

fullest life in the corporate life where communal contentment is the absolute measure of values.[22]

These descriptions identify community and continuity as important elements in the experience of time.[23]

The prophetic aspects of *Native Life* rely upon both Africanist and Biblical notions of prophecy. Plaatje warns against fraudulent prophecies surrounding the Lands Commission report; he grounds that warning, however, not in personal experience but rather in the general dislocation he witnessed traveling throughout the country. He predicts a dire future, extrapolating from the Land Act's immediate effects. "It will only be a matter of time before we have a Natives' Urban Act enforced throughout South Africa," Plaatje writes presciently, anticipating the notorious apartheid-era influx control and "pass" laws (72). Plaatje speaks truth to power; his predictions are framed as an exhortation to forestall the future latent in the present by taking corrective action, in this case applying British parliamentary pressure to suspend the Land Act.

In order to appreciate the prophetic stance and complex temporality of *Native Life*, it is helpful to consider Plaatje's novel, *Mhudi*, written just after the publication of *Native Life* but not published by Lovedale until 1930; *Mhudi* was the first published novel in English by a black South African. The novel expands *Native Life*'s account of the nineteenth-century Boer/Barolong alliance against the Matabele. Comparing the novel's typescript against the Lovedale edition, Stephen Gray found that the novel's process of oral transmission and its temporality had been significantly revised. Plaatje wrote *Mhudi* as a "document of living oral narrative," in which the son of the main characters, in his eighties in the 1910s, relates in his own words and words others related to him, events that date back to the 1830s.[24] Gray calls Plaatje's informant/character/narrator, Half-a-Crown, "the archive of an extensive cross-section of the untold history of Southern Africa" who formed a "missing link between those who knew the history of the 1830s at first hand" and Plaatje's generation (177, 175). Just as the links between past and present, story and text, were edited out of *Mhudi*, the revised Lovedale edition reframed the novel's temporality as a linear march of progress inaugurated by the rise of British power.[25]

The typescript structures *Mhudi*'s narrative in terms of cycles of time, marked by appearances of Halley's Comet in 1835, 1910, and 1985: "Happenings on one notch of the time scale parallel those of the next, and so the future can be prescribed."[26] Rather than measuring a trajectory from bar-baric past to redeemed present, *Mhudi* offers a typological warning about contemporary imperial overreaching (in the person of Cecil Rhodes) and betrayed loyalties (nineteenth-century Boer, and twentieth-century white South African, dispossession of native peoples who had come to their aid). *Mhudi* reverses the hermeneutic thrust of historical parallels posited by Majeke/Taylor, where those who experienced disingenuous policies in the twentieth century could understand the motivations and effects of earlier policies: in *Mhudi,* the past (as told by those who experienced it) illuminates the present and future-to-come.[27]

The interpretive multivalence of past, present, and future in *Mhudi* clari-fies possible relationships between memory and prophecy. The afterlife of prophecy, whether failed, false, or fraudulent, is constituted by what I call *remembered prophecy*: the recollection of a prophecy, projection, or warning explicitly articulated in the past. *Bulletproof* traces multifarious instances of remembering the prophecies that led to the cattle killing; *Mhudi* narrates the remembrance in the 1910s of prophecies articulated in the 1830s. I am equally concerned with what I call *prophetic memory,* remembrance of a moment that, viewed retrospectively, offers a glimpse of a future that bears upon the present. This need not be a memory of literal, explicit prophecy, but rather a recognition of a relationship between moments in time: the past, viewed from the present, seems suddenly to limn a future. The "pro-phetic" agency of prophetic memory resides in a present act of memory and recognition rather than a past act of projection or premonition. In prophetic memory, retrospection generates unexpected insight about the present, offering a powerful way of imagining intertemporal relationships in contexts of rupture and dislocation.

In *Mhudi,* remembered prophecies of the nineteenth-century past are figured as prophetic memories informing the twentieth-century present. Remembered prophecy and prophetic memory help us to understand the temporality of *Native Life,* where Plaatje reads the present and future out of the past, as in *Mhudi,* but without its cyclic typology. Instead, Plaatje's periodizing statement—"Awaking on a Friday morning, June 20, 1913, the South African native found himself, not actually a slave, but a pariah in the land of his birth"—inaugurates an aberrational present in which memory becomes the warrant for future restoration.

Given his aim to document the Land Act's effects, Plaatje's investment in scenes of memory in *Native Life* is rather curious. To bring the calamity of the present into focus, Plaatje looks back to a recent rural past. He sketches an idyllic scene, where the sight of "both the natives and the landowning white farmers following to perfection the give-and-take policy of 'live and let live' ... [would lead an observer to] conclude that it would be gross sacrilege to attempt to disturb such harmonious relations"—precisely what the Land Act does (28). Elsewhere Plaatje looks back to his own experience; while traveling in 1913, he reaches the Vaal river, which evokes a vivid childhood memory of selling milk to travelers stranded by the flooded river. Since pasture, milk, food, and clothing were plentiful, young Plaatje and his friends had little use for the money they earned.

Without warning, Plaatje jolts the reader sharply away from this remembered scene of pastoral ease:

> The gods are cruel, and one of their cruelest acts of omission was that of giving us no hint that in very much less than a quarter of a century all those hundreds of heads of cattle, and sheep and horses belonging to the family would vanish like a morning mist, and that we ourselves would live to pay 30s. per month for a daily supply of this same precious fluid, and in very limited quantities. They might have warned us that Englishmen would agree with Dutchmen to make it unlawful for black men to keep milk cows of their own on the banks of that river, and gradually have prepared us for the shock. (81–82)

Plaatje's juxtaposition of past and present enacts this "shock" for the reader; the passage posits the past not as the seed of the present, but its rebuke. Nothing in the remembered scene portends the future in which Plaatje now finds himself. Plaatje continues this episode of remembrance, focusing on his response to the rupture between moments in time. Crossing into the Orange Free State, Plaatje realizes that the farm where he was born must be nearby. This nostalgic thought brings him abruptly back to his present task: "even if we had the money and the owner was willing to sell the spot upon which we first saw the light of day and breathed the pure air of heaven, the sale would be followed with a fine of one hundred pounds," as a violation of the Land Act (83). This episode literalizes the book's opening: Plaatje confronts his own alienation from the land of his birth.

The contrast between thoughts of a natal home and the fact of legislative alienation evokes a "needlelike pang" that calls forth another memory: what he felt after his father's death 18 years earlier. What is more painful than the content of these memories, however, is the contrast between those times and the present. Plaatje writes of his father's death: "but at that time our physical organs were fresh and grief was easily thrown off in tears, but then we lived in a happy South Africa that was full of pleasant anticipations, and now—what changes for the worse have we undergone!" (83). Plaatje's syntax enacts the bewilderment of temporal rupture: the two "but then" clauses, drawing Plaatje's thoughts not once but twice to the past, describe a time of individual and national good cheer, while the final "and now" clause literally breaks off in a dash. This typographical interruption, as well as the syntactic chiasmus in the final clause, disrupts the parallelism of the "but then" clauses and displaces the first-person subject in order to emphasize subjection to "changes for the worse."

Plaatje's juxtaposition of private memories with the present national predicament generates a militant nostalgia, steeped not in melancholic wistfulness but steely anger; what appear to be indulgent thoughts of his own past (his birthplace and father's death) heighten the shock of the reader when glowing reminiscence is succeeded by a chilling view of the present. The rhetorical ruthlessness of Plaatje's nostalgia is evident when he inverts this move from private past to public present, narrating an irruption of memory during his infant son's funeral in 1914. The funeral procession suddenly brings to mind, with a "sharp pang," thoughts of a wandering family he met in 1913, dislocated by the Land Act and forced to bury a child at night, in secret. This memory draws Plaatje out of his private grief: "The solemnity of the funeral procession, of which we formed the mainmast, almost entirely disappeared from our mind, to be succeeded by the spirit of revolt against this impious persecution as these thoughts came before us" (146). Plaatje's use of memory in *Native Life* has an effect similar to that of Half-a-Crown's relation of decades of "untold history" in *Mhudi:* thirty-six-year-old Plaatje's witnessing of a bygone "happy South Africa" is as temporally exotic—and yet paradoxically timely, pertinent to the present—in the 1910s described in *Native Life* as is Half-a-Crown's relation of stories his parents told him about the 1830s.[28]

Weaving his recollections into the narrative of his travels, Plaatje puts private memory to public use, approximating Mphahlele's "communal" voice. At first glance these memories might not seem to evoke the crystallized and inverted hindsight of prophetic memory: they emphasize that the present is unrecognizable from the perspective of the recollected past. But this sense of temporal disjuncture is precisely what Plaatje develops throughout *Native Life:* the rupture between happy past and alienated present is a "shock" against which the cruel gods provide no warning. An idyllic childhood in "happy South Africa" serves as an omen of future evil only if "nature, like the times, is out of joint," as Plaatje writes at the end of *Native Life* in the midst of unprecedented global warfare (431). Within this time out of joint, Plaatje's invocation of moments of past happiness functions as a prophetic memory of the rupture. Plaatje's use of prophetic memory undergirds the monitory power of his protest against the Land Act: having enacted for his readers what it felt like to have no warning of the reversal of 1913, Plaatje offers an explicit warning against condoning legislation that made it "unlawful for black men to keep milk cows of their own on the banks of that river."

Plaatje recalls his lack of interest in a story about the "last prophecy" of a "black seeress," whose warning about impending, world-historical intra-European conflict seemed so improbable when he first heard about it in 1913 that Plaatje admits (with post-1914 regret) he "did not care to listen to the whole story" (295–96). This episode involves both remembered prophecy and prophetic memory. In remembering the woman's prophecy, Plaatje recognizes that her warning is effectively inaudible until the great war throws time out of joint. The proleptic portent of prophetic memory is constituted not by the content of the memory but by its relationship to the present—in this case, by Plaatje's retrospective recognition of the relevance of her prophecy to life amidst world war.[29] Whereas remembered prophecy invites reflection on its realization or relevance in the present, with prophetic memory the lineaments of the present become visible in a remembered image, even if in negative relief. Within a time out of joint, the paradoxical exotic timeliness of a past moment in which the present is seemingly unrecognizable functions as prophetic memory of the intervening rupture.

Grasping the difference between retrospection and anticipation in remembered prophecy and prophetic memory is important not only because it illuminates Plaatje's deployment of memory in his prophetic tome. Rather, the distinction is crucial for thinking through the afterlives of failed prophecies, particularly those associated with anticolonial millenarian movements. Such movements are too often cast historiographically as backward looking, rejecting the trappings of modernity in a retrograde attempt to "turn back the clock" and recover a past state of affairs, if not an imaginary Golden Age. Given how "retro" (and unfashionably so) these movements are seen to be, how much more "retro" must be later efforts to remember them? The *remembered prophecy/prophetic memory* dyad emphasizes the ways in which acts of retrospection can be dynamic and oriented within an open-ended temporality rather than contained within the finality of realization or failure. Furthermore, prophetic memory allows us to connect moments in time without the historicist imperative to fill in the blanks between them with a neat linear narrative.

A similar commitment to open-endedness in the face of temporal dis-juncture appears in Jacques Derrida's meditation on Marx. Like Plaatje, Derrida uses Hamlet's lament—

> The time is out of joint—O cursed spite!
> That ever I was born to set it right—

to frame a consideration of broken time. He speculates that temporal dis-juncture is "the very possibility of the other. . . . the place for justice" that would arrive from a messianic future-to-come, as distinct from a "future modality of the *living present*."[30] For Plaatje, too, the out-of-joint-ness of the present implies a messianic future. Looking back to an idyllic past not only sharpens understandings of the present nightmare; this prophetic memory also suggests that the present is an aberration that might be rectified to restore transhistorical harmony, "infinite time" rather than simple futurity. Thus the past not only rebukes the present; it also implicitly guarantees restoration, in which British imperial values, God, or some combination thereof, is the providential force that transcends linear causality. The sig-nificance of Plaatje's memories of a happy past becomes fully evident only when he writes, after reading the long-heralded Lands Commission report, that "the only thing that stands between us and despair is the thought that Heaven has never yet failed us" (435). The dislocations of the present remain outside this providential history. If Plaatje can write that "Heaven has never yet failed us" while amassing scenes of a forsaken people, then the present must be an aberration. Memories are thus prophetic in another way, as they offer evidence that beyond the aberrational crux of the present, the future remains secure.

The opening of Plaatje's first chapter identifies the moment of rupture between the aberrational present and the providential time in which "Heav-en has never yet failed." He stresses the shock, of which the gods had not warned, that was the Natives' Land Act: "Awaking on a Friday morning, June

20, 1913, the South African native found himself, not actually a slave, but a pariah in the land of his birth." The concreteness of the date, the Friday morning, the individual trauma of waking to find oneself metamorphosed, much like Gregor Samsa does in Franz Kafka's tale, are equally horrifying as the abstraction of being "a pariah in the land of [one's] birth." This singular moment divides the realms of happy memory and waking nightmare; the hope that drives *Native Life* depends on the conviction that the past of happy memory was not merely a dream.[31]

The sense of temporal disjuncture characterizes what Richard Terdiman calls the "memory crisis" sparked by nineteenth-century European revolutions, in which a seemingly postmodern "logic of discontinuity" is already present as a "failure of diachronicity . . . experienced as a kind of epistemic rupture." "When time is out of joint," Terdiman writes, "nothing preoccupies the mind as much as time."[32] This salutary historicization of memory and temporality demands its own qualification: there is not a single "memory crisis" but as many "crises" as there are disruptive encounters with modernity.[33] Adapting Terdiman's notion of a memory crisis to Plaatje's South Africa is a fraught move, not least because Plaatje never loses sight of the fact that his crisis of time and memory is fundamentally a question of land, bread, and dignity.[34] Novelist Bessie Head wrote in the early 1980s that "most black South Africans suffer from a very broken sense of history [for which] *Native Life in South Africa* provides an essential, missing link."[35] Extending Terdiman's insights to consider memory as "interpretive reconstructions that bear the imprint of local narrative conventions, cultural assumptions, discursive formations and practices, and social contexts of recall and commemoration" can help us to see how Plaatje's use of memory in his depiction of the crisis of 1913 articulates the particular form of modernity that was the South African twentieth century.[36]

THE AFTERLIVES OF FAILURE

Native Life in South Africa became a foundational account of black South African experience, rather than documenting a brief detour into segregationism by way of what Plaatje called a "very strange law" (15). In its immediate failure to mitigate the Land Act, *Native Life* marked the opening of an aberrational present that extended through the South African twentieth century. Plaatje's statement of temporal rupture has an ambivalent afterlife: here I turn from memories *in* Plaatje's text to memories *of* Plaatje's text.

Majeke/Taylor's invocations of Plaatje in *The Role of the Missionaries in Conquest* are among countless echoes of his statement of Africans' alienation in the land of their birth. From Selby Msimang's 1936 protest of the Hertzog Bills, to Oliver Tambo's and Vusumzi Make's 1960 statement on behalf of the United Front, to the South African Students Organization's 1971 definition of Black Consciousness, to Archbishop Desmond Tutu's remarks before the United Nations Security Council after winning the Nobel Peace Prize in 1984, writers and speakers protest a continuing situation in which South Africans are slaves, aliens, outcastes, "pariah[s] in the land of [their] birth."[37]

The 1913 Natives' Land Act was a seminal moment in the legislative abrogation of rights, and in some cases citizenship itself, for all but a small minority of South Africans. Each law left millions even more alien than they had been at birth. The 1960s policy of separate development designated as "homelands" places where many black South Africans who were to be forcibly relocated to them had never set foot. Separate development and multinationalism (asserting the homelands' "independence" from South Africa), shared, however perversely or fraudulently, Plaatje's assumption that Africans' political rights should derive from their land of origin: influx control and forced removals (regulated through the infamous pass laws) were necessary to rectify "accidents" of birth outside the homelands.

Repeated invocations of Plaatje's statement of alienation reject the successive logics of segregation, apartheid, separate development and multinationalism, refusing to lose sight of the fundamental contradiction of being (made) an alien in the land of one's birth. Echoes of the phrase multiply to the point that it seems unnecessary to link them back to Plaatje, but this shift, from a conscious act of citation to naturalization within a lexicon of resistance, indicates *Native Life*'s complex relationship to failure. In her Foreword to the 1982 Ravan edition, Bessie Head concludes, "This book may have failed to appeal to human justice in its time, but there is in its tears, anguish and humility, an appeal to a day of retribution."[38] The continuing resonance of black alienation suggests either that Heaven did fail, breaking Plaatje's faith in providential restoration; or that these apartheid-era statements of protest remain within Plaatje's aberrational present (that Heaven has not *yet* offered deliverance).

Indeed, individual shock is all but missing from these later statements, which express a more general, moral outrage and convey what it means to live within temporal rupture. Later writers were *born in* (rather than woke to find) a land where they were always-already alien, *born into* the time of Plaatje's aberrational present. Although they inhabit different chronotopes, these writers share Plaatje's assumption that the land of one's birth is where one should expect to enjoy the right to free and full development. That fateful Friday morning inaugurates the rupture that continues into the apartheid era, still in need of emancipatory restoration.[39] Plaatje heralds a particularly South African modernity: on or about June 1913, native life changed.

What is paradoxical about the failure of *Native Life* is that Plaatje's articulation of the experience of alienation resonated so profoundly for later voices of protest against ever intensifying dislocation. Its failure to move its intended British audience made it indispensable for a later, still dispossessed black audience. But Plaatje's rhetorical strategies signify differently for these audiences. He repeatedly invites readers to imagine their experience in terms of the South African situation he describes—to imagine, for example, not being able to rent a room in London without becoming the landlord's servant (18). Instead of this sympathetic projection, a late-apartheid readership would recognize and historicize their own experience. Plaatje's rhetorical strategies in representing the experience of dislocation demand attention if we are to consider *Native Life in South Africa* not merely as a historical artifact but as a living source of succor for black life in South Africa.

Plaatje's periodizing statement expresses the wrenching into colonial modernity—the sudden economic and political alienation, the transformation by legislative stroke of people into labor units—as a trauma. We might read Plaatje's identification of the "shock" of 20 June 1913 in terms of Walter Benjamin's observation that the "shock defense" against trauma involves "assigning to an incident a precise point in time in consciousness at the cost of the integrity of its contents."[40] This precision situates the incident within *Erlebnis*, the phenomenological experience of lived-through, past time, rather than allowing it to remain active in *Erfahrung*, the continuity of "mnemonic traces of past tradition in present experience."[41] Plaatje's insistence that nothing in the idyllic past portended the catastrophe of 20 June 1913 is rhetorically effective but historically suspect. This "precise point in time" concentrates within itself every dislocation until that fateful morning; documenting the degradations of native life in South Africa, Plaatje identifies the Land Act as their sole cause.[42] In Benjaminian terms, Plaatje isolates the trauma of dislocation within *Erlebnis* in order to make the Land Act, quite literally, a thing of the past. The reverberation of the phrase throughout the South African twentieth century, however, suggests that its trauma pervades a collective, temporally layered experience of the present, equivalent to *Erfahrung*. Causes of native alienation proliferated after the Land Act of 1913; each generation faced an additional phenomenological experience of traumatic dislocation, for which Plaatje's statement continued to resonate.

In invoking trauma to analyze the Land Act's effect on what Plaatje calls "the South African native," I must acknowledge the difficulties of extrapolating from Freudian models of individual consciousness to a diachronic collective.[43] Yet Plaatje's focus on the individual is a *rhetorical* strategy that conveys the enormous scope of a legislative act that alienated millions through a racial generalization. In order to document the present state of the nation, Plaatje figures this legislative dislocation of black South Africans in terms of "the South African native['s]" individual experience of waking up one Friday morning. The afterlife of *Native Life* further complicates the traffic between individual consciousness and social experience, and between moments in time.[44] At stake in my reading of *Native Life* is not the traumatic experience of 20 June 1913 but rather the consequence of representing that experience *as* trauma.

Plaatje's description of the experience of alienation (waking to find oneself "not quite a slave, but a pariah in the land of [one's] birth") is a representation whose consumption in turn generates aesthetic experience (reading about waking to find oneself alienated). This distinction approximates that between modernity and modernism. Plaatje's description epitomizes the sense of "strangeness [*Fremdes*] and externality" that Ernst Bloch identifies as the root of both *Entfremdung* (economic alienation) and *Verfremdung* (aesthetic estrangement). While stressing their shared strangeness, Bloch distinguishes between *Entfremdung* and *Verfremdung* as "a bad contrast and a helpful one." *Entfremdung* is "bad contrast," "that exteriority wherein one is made strange even to oneself." Bloch describes Marx's account of *Entfremdung* as "self-alienation . . . [in] a system of exploitation wherein nothing remains of the human being who is forced to sell himself except the form of the disempowered worker."[45] *Verfremdung* offers a "helpful" contrast, most famously in "Brecht's instrument of estrangement, directed against estrangement [*Entfremdung*] itself" (244). Brechtian defamiliarization, the V-Effekt, "disrupts the predictability of everyday life through its heterogeneous evocation of other times and situations."[46]

Both *Entfremdung* and *Verfremdung* are at work in Plaatje's response to the Land Act. He depicts the experience of *Entfremdung*: waking to legislated alienation in which the South African native is "made strange" to himself, native no more, cast off the land with no choice but to work for others. This account of economic alienation can perform a "helpful" aesthetic estrangement for Plaatje's later readers. Plaatje describes a moment when "the predictability of everyday [native] life" in South Africa has been decidedly disrupted: for a black South African readership, *Verfremdung* derives from the historicization of their own experience. For Plaatje's immediate British audience, however, the text effects estrangement by depicting the perversion in South Africa of imperial values cherished at home. Bloch writes that *Verfremdung* "is especially likely to occur when a detour is taken into the exotic, or by means of a model that either turns the present into a historical moment or the past into a contemporary one. . . . It offers insight into what lies nearest, drawn from astonishment at what lies farthest" (245). Plaatje's juxtaposition of happy memory and present dislocation (what I have called prophetic memory) partakes in this aesthetic strategy of telescoping "near" and "far" moments in time. The continuing reverberation of Plaatje's statement recasts *Verfremdung*, Brecht's V-Effekt, as an aspect of a text's afterlife.

For later generations of South Africans, Plaatje's statement offers an arresting, illuminating, strange-making representation of waking to alienation that has *become* the everyday; its temporal dislocation becomes part of its meaning. Plaatje's text offers later readers "the memory of how the bizarre sense of disconnection, the eerie temporal flatness of [colonial] modernity arose to begin with. . . . [I]t loses its very definition and diffuses to become one of the conditions of existence of the culture for which it had arisen as a crisis. It returns to transparency by not having been resolved but by having been routinized along with the recollected experience of time upon which it inevitably depends."[47] In the moment of its enunciation in *Native Life*, Plaatje's statement stands in the same relation to later citations as his prophetic memories do to his indictment of the present condition of South African natives. Just as he lamented that he did not "care to listen" to the 1913 prophecy until its vision was realized in the first world war, Plaatje's statement becomes more audible (increasingly resonant, and repeatedly cited) as the machinery of alienation proliferates beyond what Plaatje imagined.[48] Plaatje states the legislative fact that the native was economically alienated from the land of his birth, but in the text's afterlife, it functions too as prophetic memory when South African "natives" were no longer citizens of South Africa.[49]

The efficacy of Plaatje's response to the Land Act cannot be measured solely in the immediate failure of his appeal and the consequent dilation of the aberrational present in which he wrote. Later invocations of Plaatje express dislocation in the plural, as a shared condition: from economic alienation emerges not only aesthetic estrangement but also political solidarity. The phrase also evokes a restored future, as when Nelson Mandela spoke at the 1951 ANC Youth League Conference of "the labour power of the African people [as] a force which when fully tapped is going to sweep the people to power in the land of their birth."[50] Likewise, at the UN in 1984, Desmond Tutu appealed to "white fellow South Africans to share in building a new society, for blacks are not intent on driving whites into the sea but on claiming only their rightful place in the sun in the land of their birth."[51] Setting Plaatje's reasoned appeal against centuries-old white fears of warrior-prophets inspiring cataclysmic anticolonial resistance, Tutu looks toward a new era, from the vantage point of a moment of horror.[52]

The teleology that Plaatje invokes in *Native Life* is not Bloch's or Benjamin's messianic historical materialism, but rather providential Christianity. Yet Plaatje's faith in God's protection anticipates mundane, rather than celestial, redemption: a restored native life in South Africa. Plaatje's text expresses a yearning for "concord" between "imaginatively recorded past and imaginatively predicted future, achieved on behalf of us, who remain 'in the middest,'" to adapt Frank Kermode's theorization of the relationship between apocalyptic thinking and narrative structure.[53] For Plaatje, to be "in the middest" and looking toward an "endtime" in South Africa was about exiting the aberrational present of (post)colonial alienation, rather than healing human estrangement from God. Plaatje needed to believe that the gulf between present realities and a remembered past would be bridged. Although it asserts that "Heaven has never yet failed us," *Native Life* accumulates its power not through faith in ultimate concord but rather through overwhelming documentation of a *lack* of concord between past and present. It is most powerful, as one of the narratives "by which we order our world," in the afterlife of its failure.[54]

A half-century after Plaatje, the necessary leap of faith was from the realities of the present to an imagined liberated future. In the South African twentieth century, June 20, 1913, inaugurated the aberrational present whose imminent, yet obstructed end was imagined in what Nadine Gordimer famously termed the *interregnum*. Gordimer perceived the early 1980s as a time when (borrowing from Antonio Gramsci) "the old is dying and the new cannot be born; in this interregnum a great variety of morbid symptoms appear."[55] The interregnum is a between-time—a moment "in the middest"— that assumes the imminence of a future whose lineaments and manner of emergence, Gordimer insists in "Living in the Interregnum," cannot yet be discerned.[56] As I discuss below, late-apartheid cultural production bore the burden of setting right the disjunctures of the aberrational present. To restore the disjointed time of the South African twentieth century would require not only documenting present realities, particularly as they were determined by, or marked the loss of, a remembered past, but also charting the way toward an imagined future.

THE PROTEST MODE AS FAILED PROPHECY

As I intimate in my reading of *Native Life in South Africa*, cultural production functions as a dilatory space-time in which historical failure can be understood, imagined, and re-imagined so as to realize what has been unrealized. Plaatje's achievement-in-failure was of recurrent interest to fiction writer and critic Njabulo S. Ndebele, who found in *Native Life* an observation about the effects of oppression that became central to his own late-apartheid project of reorienting the relationship between culture and the struggle. In a 1985 lecture, Ndebele cites Plaatje's analysis of the long-awaited Lands Commission report:

> While the ruling whites, on the one hand, content themselves with giving contradictory definitions of their cruelty the native sufferers, on the other hand, give no definitions of legislative phrases nor explanations of definitions. All they give expression to is their bitter suffering under the operation of what in their experience has proved to be the most ruthless law that ever disgraced the white man's rule in British South Africa.[57]

Glossing this passage, Ndebele worries that the overwhelming experience of suffering obstructs an effective, critical response. While, for Plaatje, black suffering has greater moral weight than white legalistic obfuscation, Ndebele laments oppressed people's lack of critical engagement with the forces behind their oppression. Literary resistance to apartheid, according to Ndebele, has "largely documented rather than explained"; worse, this writing constructs an image of "people completely destroyed, of passive people whose only reason for existing seemed to be to receive the sympathy of the world."[58] Ndebele's vision of transformative literary culture—his well-known project to "rediscover the ordinary"—offered a new mode of representing black South African experience.

Ndebele identifies *Native Life in South Africa* as the epitome of protest writing. He enumerates its rhetorical strategies: "one, the identification and highlighting of instances of general oppression; two, the drawing of appropriate moral conclusions from the revealed evidence and, three, the implicit belief in the inherent persuasiveness of the moral position" (63). Protest literature "appeal[ed] to the conscience of the white oppressor," even as black audiences could read it within an "aesthetics of recognition" that "does not necessarily lead to transformation" (48, 32). Ndebele sees protest continuing to dominate black South African writing even after the structural conditions that produced it ceased to exist: protest writing assumed black powerlessness even as the black working class became more powerful in 1970s industrial upheavals (66). Where Plaatje focused on the oppressors, Ndebele wants to focus contemporary thinking on the oppressed (82).

Above all, Ndebele worries about protest's effect on the self-perception of its proponents: it casts them as objects of sympathy, not agents of change. This "predominant mode of perception" obscures the actual dynamics of oppression, particularly when the mode of perception remains static while conditions of oppression change (63–64). Ndebele implies that protest has come to resemble false prophecy: "the mode of perception, by failing to transcend its own limitations, can become part of the oppression it sought to understand and undermine. . . . Easily believing an abstract moral code, they become victims of false hopes" (64). If they can only communicate the immorality of apartheid, adherents of protest believe, then they might effect its reform. This characterization—of people trapped within a structure of perception that renders them incapable of recognizing their actual situation—resonates with the concept of failed prophecy, as articulated by American sociologists Leon Festinger, Henry Riecken, and Stanley Schachter. Festinger and his colleagues argued that "disconfirmation" of a prophecy creates cognitive dissonance, yet adherents often respond with intensified commitment to their belief, "denying or rationalizing the disconfirmation," particularly if others can be persuaded to accept the prophecy.[59] The act of proselytizing can strengthen faith regardless of whether it attracts converts, so that "failed prophecy does not disprove faith but comes instead to reaffirm the very system of beliefs from which it first emerged."[60]

Festinger's notion of failed prophecy more closely resembles the irrational futility of false prophecy, as I have described it. This consolidation of belief—or rededication to the protest mode—creates "victims of false hopes" that cannot be realized because the strategy fatally misreads its context. If protest was once an appropriate strategy, as Ndebele allows, it is no longer. Festinger and his colleagues found that disconfirmation spurred evangelization; Ndebele, too, observes that the inefficacy of protest catalyzes further protest, rather than reassessment. The act of writing protest fiction spurs more writing, so that "the history of black South African writing has largely been the history of the representation of spectacle" (48–49, 41).

The resonance between false prophecy and the protest mode's hardened structure of perception is evident in Ndebele's 1984 statement about the "delusion" generated by this mindset: "We all know how, at least in the last twenty-five years of our fully conscious life, South Africa was always going to be free in the next five years: a prediction that is the very essence of the culture of spectacle. The powerful, on the other hand, have been convinced that they will rule forever."[61] This remembered prophecy's curious temporality—"always going to be free in the next five years"—echoes the tension between Plaatje's faith in restoration of the time when "Heaven has never yet failed" and his relevance for later generations of dispossessed South Africans. What does it mean to inhabit this expectant temporality for a quarter of a century (or more)? These contradictory futures are suggested in David Goldblatt's 1989 photograph, a mise-en-abyme of a First National Bank billboard that both depicts and stands amidst farmland. In the ad, a robust, young white farmer with his son on his shoulders looks out over his land; the copy declares (imperiously or assuringly, depending on one's perspective), "When this is his, we will still be here" (see fig. 4). Just after Ndebele's observation in 1984 about recurrent predictions of imminent liberation, a series of states of emergency in the late 1980s brought repressive state violence that revealed a more anxious side of the assertion of enduring white power captured in Goldblatt's photograph: whites' cataclysmic fear of "being driven into the sea," as Tutu put it.

As we saw with Plaatje and Majeke/Taylor, Ndebele exposes the protest mode as a false prophecy while offering his own vision for renewing the imagination and reclaiming the world. As opposed to a fiction of protest that documents suffering as spectacle, Ndebele calls for fiction that can

4. This billboard proclaims that "When this is his we will still be here / First National Bank / The professional people who care." The message was part of a campaign by First National Bank to win back conservative clients, many of them Afrikaner farmers, whose business had been lost as a result of the accusation by President P. W. Botha that the bank's CEO, Chris Ball, had granted an overdraft to facilitate adverts celebrating the seventy-fifth anniversary of the ANC and calling for its unbanning. Sannieshof, North-West. 19 February 1989. Silver gelatin print on fibre paper, paper size 54 x 66 cm, image size 44 x 56 cm. Photograph by David Goldblatt. Courtesy of Michael Stevenson, Cape Town, South Africa.

"rediscover the ordinary" by imagining people surviving, resisting, living.[62] "[F]reeing the imagination" to embrace the full range of everyday experience would "probe beyond the observable facts, to reveal new worlds where it was previously thought they did not exist. . . . to extend the range of personal and social experience as far as possible in order to contribute to bringing about a highly conscious, sensitive new person in a new society" (71, 73–74). This creation of a new world and new humanity echoes the millennial tones of Fanon's *The Wretched of the Earth:* for Fanon, the task of decolonization is to "change the order of the world," "to create a new man."[63] Articulating the transformative potential of the quotidian, Ndebele writes, "if it is the entire society that has to be recreated, then no aspect of that society can be deemed irrelevant to the progress of liberation" (70).

This recreative force resolves the ambiguity in the ANC Youth League manifesto cited in my epigraph—whether the "world of beauty that lies beyond . . . the struggle" is distanced in time (after the struggle) or space (outside the struggle). For Ndebele, the reconstructive force of culture has the potential to *create* (rather than merely reflect) a "world of beauty": a wholesale recreation means that no conceptual or experiential space would remain outside a struggle conceived in these millennial terms. This millennialism, oddly enough, distinguishes Ndebele's project from Plaatje's. Plaatje resolutely documents injustice and insists upon the necessity and inevitability of external deliverance. Compared with Ndebele's call to the oppressed to imagine, create, and reveal a new world within the everyday, Plaatje's writing conveys a rather Old Testament sense of expectation, as is evident in his remark that God hadn't told the Israelites to "'cheer up'" because heaven awaited them but instead rescued them from Egypt (*Native Life* 84). We might also understand the difference between Plaatje and Ndebele in terms of Paul Gilroy's discussion of the "politics of fulfillment" and the "politics of transfiguration." Plaatje's protest epitomizes "demands . . . that bourgeois civil society live up to the promises of its own rhetoric" and the conviction that "a future society will be able to realise the social and political promise that present society has left unaccomplished."[64] In contrast to this expectant politics of fulfillment, the agentive politics of transfiguration emerges through cultural production that "conjure[s] up and enacts the new modes of friendship, happiness, and solidarity that are consequent on the overcoming of the racial oppression on which modernity and its antinomy of rational, western progress as excessive barbarity relied" (38). Gilroy is more frank than Ndebele about the magic, opacity, sublimity, and impossible possibility of this utopian project undertaken "under the very nose of the overseers" whose power has yet to be overcome (37). The ordinary that Ndebele seeks to *rediscover* can only be fleetingly *anticipated* in Gilroy's account.

In essays and lectures of the 1980s advocating the redemptive power of the ordinary, Ndebele translates into cultural/aesthetic terms ideas that the Black Consciousness movement articulated in psychic/sociopolitical terms. Influenced by the militant humanism of Frantz Fanon, Steve Biko describes Black Consciousness as a project to "make the black man see himself as a complete being in himself," in order to "bestow upon South Africa the greatest gift possible—a more human face."[65] In subjective terms, Black Consciousness urged the oppressed to recognize their own participation in their oppression. Writing pseudonymously as "Frank Talk" in "I Write What I Like," a column in the South African Students' Organization (SASO) newsletter, Biko strikingly revises the complaint we have traced to Plaatje: "The first step therefore is to make the black man come to himself . . . to remind him of his complicity in the crime of allowing himself to be misused and therefore letting evil reign supreme in the country of his birth" (29). Black South Africans' alienation, Biko insists, is a predicament they have *tolerated and enabled.*

Biko rejects the fundamental assumption of protest politics: "we must realise that our situation is not a mistake on the part of whites but a deliberate act, and that no amount of moral lecturing will persuade the white man to 'correct the situation'" (91). Leaving the strategies of protest behind, particularly its deferent appeals to white audiences and benefactors, the central organizational tenet of Black Consciousness was that black South Africans should reclaim the imagination of, and movement toward, their liberation out of the hands of white liberals and white-controlled organizations, beginning with SASO's split from the National Union of South African Students in 1969. Black Consciousness exposed the failures and liabilities of nonracialism, even as it radicalized white liberals who accepted its critique and made themselves available to a liberation struggle under black leadership.[66]

Ndebele identifies the rise of Black Consciousness from the late 1960s as the end of constitutional protest politics (an end whose beginning was arguably the massacre of pass-law protestors at Sharpeville in 1960, followed by the banning of political organizations) (65). The mounting energy of Black Consciousness exploded in nationwide uprisings that began on June 16, 1976, with a student demonstration in Soweto township against Bantu Education's use of Afrikaans; police fired into the crowd, killing thirteen-year-old Hector Pietersen. The political ferment of Soweto found literary expression in a burgeoning township culture of performed poetry and a burst of writing, some published in *Staffrider,* a literary magazine launched in 1978 by the Ravan Press and Christian Institute Programmes against Apartheid (SPROCAS).[67] This creative energy spurred and was spurred by the new possibilities and hard truths of Soweto, after more than a decade of censorship, banning, and exile: children could take on the state, and the state would fight back.

For Ndebele, Soweto was "another spectacle among spectacles"—a statement that, given his indictment of the "spectacular" orientation of black

South African writing, captures his ambivalence about Black Consciousness.[68] He acknowledges that from the "tense and bitter aftermath" of Soweto emerged writing that "breaks with this tradition of spectacle" in analyzing, rather than documenting, suffering in order to foster "redemptive transformation" (50–51). Despite the movement's millennial project of creating a "new person in a new society," Ndebele deems much of the literary activity associated with Black Consciousness to be formally unequipped for this immense task (66). His seminal essay "Turkish Tales and Some Thoughts on South African Fiction," in a 1984 issue of *Staffrider,* expands a review of Turkish writer Yashar Kemal's *Anatolian Tales* into a critique of the new writing for which *Staffrider* provided an important outlet. Ndebele took to task one of the most influential of the *Staffrider* writers, Mtutuzeli Matshoba.

THE SPECTACULAR AS ORDINARY
IN 1857 AND 1976

Call Me Not a Man, Matshoba's collection of stories, was published by Ravan Press in 1979. In his foreword, Matshoba identifies Soweto as a pivotal moment. After shifting between Soweto and the eastern Cape (Matshoba studied at Lovedale in the mid-1960s, and University of Fort Hare in the early 1970s), Matshoba writes, "June 16, 1976 exploded in my face. Memories of old were revived, my life was so full that I knew that if I did not spill some of its contents out I would go berserk. I started scribbling and burning the scraps of paper on which I wrote, torn between writing or heading for the beckoning horizons, my country become my enemy." Instead of crossing the border to train as a freedom fighter, Matshoba kept writing: "I want to reflect through my works life on my side of the fence, the black side: so that whatever may happen in the future, I may not be set down as 'a bloodthirsty terrorist'. So that I may say: 'These were the events which shaped the Steve Bikos and the Solomon Mahlangus, and the many others who came before and after them.'"[69]

Like *Native Life in South Africa,* Matshoba's *Call Me Not a Man* is a book whose documentary ambition was born in the historical rupture of one day in June. But the insurgency of Soweto contrasts with the disenfranchisement and reformist protest that Plaatje's morning of metamorphosis (and its legislative erection of the "fence") engendered. Ndebele maintains that Matshoba's work succeeds only in documenting oppression; it lacks a formal strategy to convey this spirit of insurgency. He writes that Matshoba's "basic technique has been to accumulate fact after fact of oppression and suffering, so that we are in the end almost totally grounded in this reality without being offered, at the same time, an opportunity for aesthetic and critical estrangement"—what Bloch called the "helpful contrast" of *Verfremdung*.[70] This dismissal of Matshoba is seminal for Ndebele's critique of the spectacular orientation of black South African writing, trapped within the protest mode: the spectacular is concerned with surfaces and moralizing simplicity rather than sociohistorical processes and the complex characterization enabled by psychic interiority.

In a recent essay, Kelwyn Sole traces major shifts in the reception of Matshoba's writing—from its enthusiastic embrace in *Staffrider*, and by journalist and academic critics lauding Matshoba's "graphic and immediate" (often autobiographical) depictions of black experience, to the reappraisals initiated by Ndebele in 1984.[71] Ndebele's critique of Matshoba was taken up by Lewis Nkosi, who had argued against the "journalistic" orientation of black South African fiction for nearly two decades. Nkosi maintained that Matshoba's "naive realism . . . owe[s] a great deal to this frustrated desire to abolish any space between literature and the horrible reality of life under apartheid."[72] Ndebele and Nkosi see the "immediacy" of Matshoba's writing as a liability—lacking literary mediation between world and text. Michael Chapman summarized the critiques of Matshoba in 1999:

> Matshoba has retained the unsettling quality of attracting debates that have sharpened understanding of writing in a contested field. The debates also help sharpen distinctions between "elite" and "popular" expectations of the short story. According to Western, written precept Matshoba has been branded as ideologically "incorrect"; his stories do not entirely encapsulate either a race-conscious or a labour-conscious vision. . . . Matshoba has also been accused by feminist criticism of endorsing a male "public" narrative of struggle, in which men are fighters and women home-makers.[73]

In his reassessment, Sole deems previous readings all more or less reductive, having missed the productive tensions in Matshoba's narratives that draw on *manipulations* of reality, *constructions* of conflicted narrative personae, *processes* of confronting one's prejudices within a brutally racist (and, less visibly, sexist) system—precisely the *literary* techniques that critics after

Ndebele found wanting. While I do not want to overstate the satisfactions to be had in Matshoba's sometimes clunky narratives, I agree with Sole that Matshoba's work is more literarily interesting than the post-Ndebele (and now postapartheid) consensus would allow. Ndebele misses how Matshoba's narratives illustrate his own best insights about the imagination's capacity to create critical consciousness and recreate the world; they also reveal the limitations and implicit nostalgia in Ndebele's notion of the ordinary.

For Ndebele, Matshoba's work epitomized the deadening grip of spectacle over black South African writing—the counterexample against which he argued for the redemptive potential of ordinary life. In Matshoba's understanding, however, the spectacular *was* the ordinary for black South Africans: "police stations were like toilets, as they are to all blacks here, to me. Their pull is like that of the call of nature."[74] Matshoba's characters are by no means abject sufferers, vainly waiting for whites' change of heart: his narratives stage both the emergence of critical consciousness and the obstacles to such emergence. Kelwyn Sole maintains that while "[Ndebele] sees the everyday lives of black people as a source of succor, cultural expression and resistance, [Matshoba] believes that it is the very acceptance of the quotidian reality of apartheid by blacks which entrenched and naturalized its rule."[75] Yet this distinction is easily reversed: amidst the "quotidian reality" of apartheid, Matshoba finds creativity and resistance, while Ndebele too is concerned about how oppression is naturalized, reifying the psychology of spectacle and protest.

At stake is a tension between what the ordinary is and what it could be, in reality and mimesis. This tension parallels that between Plaatje's aberrational present and the "world of beauty" beyond the struggle, and it reflects broader debates about the modes of literary representation most appropriate to the struggle. Adopting what Louise Bethlehem dubs a "rhetoric of urgency," many writers agreed that realism, of one variety or another, was indispensable.[76] I will not rehearse these debates here; what interests me is how the role of temporality in mimesis can illuminate the relationship between Ndebele and Matshoba. A certain retrospection hides in plain sight in Ndebele's persistent concern to *rediscover* the ordinary. While Ndebele's ideal for cultural production is future-directed, conceiving of everyday black life as both agent and object of change, it is also implicitly nostalgic, seeking to re(dis)cover an ordinary that once was but is no longer, under the exigencies of apartheid and the struggle. Ndebele calls for renewed attention to aspects of everyday life *even under apartheid* that are overlooked in the imperative to create "relevant" art. But what does it mean to imagine apartheid as ordinary? If the ordinary must be recuperated, then perhaps the ordinary is what exists before the rupture that inaugurates Plaatje's aberrational present, before South Africans are aliens in the land of their birth.

Nostalgia, I suggested in my discussion of Plaatje, can play an important role in future-directed movements for justice.[77] The nostalgia implicit in Ndebele's project, however, seems unconsidered and problematic, particularly with regard to the rural. Ndebele observes that a "compelling and imaginative recreation of rural life" is missing from black South African writing, given its overwhelming urban orientation; he worries about the absence of an "awareness of tradition that goes back into a peasant past."[78] Plaatje documents the rupture of this tradition—the moment when black peasant existence in South Africa is outlawed. A "rediscovery of the ordinary" implies a recovery of this lost tradition and a move beyond this aberrational present.[79] Ndebele anticipates the emergence of an "urban obsession with the rural areas as genuine sources of an array of cultural symbols," and he warns against the nostalgia endemic to such pastoral reconstructions (the city-dweller's idealization of country life) (27). Yet he seems not to recognize the retrospective impulse of his own conflation of the *loss* of the ordinary with the *lack* of the rural.

In making sense of Ndebele's utopian vision of an everyday linked organically to a rural, if not explicitly precolonial, tradition, Matshoba's *Call Me not a Man* is instructive, not least because of its attention to historical geographies that shape the South African rural-urban divide. Despite Ndebele's suggestion that Matshoba's stories are immersed in an urban present, even the title of Matshoba's narrative, "A Pilgrimage to the Isle of Makana," indicates that his temporal and spatial concerns are more complex than Ndebele allows. The story "charts the country as a map of rejuvenated black history."[80] It narrates a journey to Robben Island: "the holiest of holies," the site from which twentieth-century political prisoners, as well as the nineteenth-century Xhosa prophet-warrior Makana (Nxele), pledged to return.[81] Throughout *Call Me Not a Man*, plots structured around journeys contrast country and city, or the Rand and the Cape; their spatial metaphors contextualize the present within a history of colonial dispossession and anticolonial resistance.

Matshoba uses similar geographical/historical movements in another narrative, "Three Days in the Land of a Dying Illusion." The "land" of the title is the Transkei, not only the site of the Xhosa cattle killing, but also the first homeland to become "independent," on October 26, 1976. The narrator travels from Soweto to Umtata, capital of Transkei, a few years after its purported independence. This journey transcends the urban present in two ways: the narrator gets the "chance to observe, from another angle, . . . the exodus of a landstripped peasantry from the bantustans" whose urban arrival he witnesses in Soweto; and he imagines his train as a "burning arrow searing backward through history," as he remembers earlier events in the same landscape.[82] This historical palimpsest reveals the quiescent dangers in false expectations for the future: in the nineteenth and twentieth centuries, people do not throw off exploitative regimes because "illusions" of a stake in the future prevent them from recognizing their plight. During the cattle killing, Sir George Grey described the "singular spectacle" of "whole races exerting themselves energetically to destroy all their own property, and to reduce themselves to a state of starvation."[83] Matshoba perceives a *doubled* spectacle in remembered prophecies of the cattle killing—the imagined renewal and the actual aftermath—which he links to the fraudulent inauguration of the Republic of Transkei, another spectacle of 1976.

Transkei independence, following self-government in 1963, was a culmination of the policy of separate development, which held that people in southern Africa should enjoy political representation as citizens in their own, ethnically and linguistically defined "homelands." This policy turned millions of people into "aliens in the land of their birth" more thoroughly than Plaatje could have imagined. South African statesmen appropriated the heady discourse of decolonization to posit Bantustan self-government as an advance for African freedom. However, Bantustan leaders were hard pressed to define themselves as autonomous rulers, rather than puppets of the apartheid state. In *Independence My Way* (1976), Transkei Chief Minister Kaizer Matanzima blasted his critics: "one might expect all sincere opponents of apartheid to applaud the Transkei leaders for this breakthrough. But in the world of today, people are able to argue that black is white."[84] Matanzima's autobiography, published by the Foreign Affairs Association in Pretoria, appeared simultaneously with *The Republic of Transkei* (1976), a coffee table book replete with glowing copy and glossy photographs; the book was published in Johannesburg, designed in Pretoria, and typeset in Cape Town. In other words, *The Republic of Transkei* was an all-South Africa public relations spectacle in which Bantustan "independence" was independence, black was white.[85] Matshoba's narrative exposes the fraudulent Transkei spectacle on several levels. The "exodus" *to* South African cities from the homelands, and the migrant laborers crowding the "people's class" rail and bus routes the narrator chooses for his journey, give lie to the idea that Transkei is anything but a labor reserve for South African industry (143, 144). The narrator travels without documents, having refused the "invitation" (proffered in South Africa) to apply for citizenship of a place he has never been;[86] the only visible difference between South African and Transkeian territory is a drought-ridden, eroded soil where "the maize refused to grow higher than a foot" (158–59).

Matshoba's narrative builds upon Biko's condemnation of Bantustans as "the single greatest fraud ever invented by white politicians." They are "phoney telephones" given to leaders who may believe they are securing a foothold for black freedom. "But if you want to fight your enemy," Biko warned, "you do not accept from him the unloaded of his two guns and then challenge him to a duel." Bantustans "create a false sense of hope . . . so that any further attempt by blacks to collectively enunciate their aspirations should be dampened"; they divide resistance into "eight different struggles for eight false freedoms that were prescribed long ago" in the 13 percent of land designated by the Natives' Land Acts of 1913 and 1936.[87] Matshoba's narrator also perceives Bantustans as a source of false hope. The illusion of having a stake in the "nation" buys the complicity of its mostly impoverished citizenry: "Independence, *uhuru*, had come, avowedly to break the chains of blackness and drive away poverty. Instead it had brought an ominous fog of helplessness that hung over a land marred with eroded ravines."[88] In Biko's analysis and Matshoba's narrative, Bantustans function as fraudulent spurs to false, yet fading, hope.

Given this warning about Bantustans, we might expect Matshoba to assume the mantle of prophecy and offer his own vision, as we saw with Majeke/Taylor, Plaatje, and Ndebele. Instead, Matshoba turns to the cattle-killing prophecy of the 1850s. The narrator rejects the "tale" he learned at school, which he "found hard to believe." He decides to "construct my own version of the story: the conquest, the dispossession, and the vision" (165). This remembered prophecy is only a partial analepsis in the narrative: it treats the motivation and articulation of Nongqause's vision but not its aftermath.[89] The only aftermath, or "dying illusion," narrated in the text is the disillusion of Transkei independence. By telling the hopeful beginning and middle of the 1850s story, and the disillusioned end of the 1970s story,

Matshoba finds a provisional solution to the problem of historical failure (epitomized by the horrific aftermath of the cattle killing) for those who look to the past to inspire contemporary struggles. By omitting the cattle killing's aftermath, Matshoba nearly avoids narrating the episode as even a failed prophecy, let alone a fraudulent one. Both Nongqause and Mhlakaza are concerned with their people's suffering; their plan is a sincere attempt to revive hope, unity, strength and the will to fight. Their dedicated leadership and desire to reclaim Xhosa autonomy have no twentieth-century analogue in the narrative. Far from staging past defeat or failed prophecy as a catalyst to present action, the temporal finesse of Matshoba's "Three Days" posits the defiant past as rebuke to the coopted present, just as Plaatje cites happy memories in order to condemn the alienation of 1913.

If this strategy relies to some degree on nostalgia (as it certainly does in Plaatje), the narrative makes clear that the losses mourned in the 1970s were also mourned in the 1850s. The train and bus constitute a public sphere (a "mobile meeting place," Matshoba says in an interview) for debates about the migrants' predicament and its relationship to the past.[90] The men on the bus lament that "it is no longer like when we were born"; the narrative reveals, however, that the lost state of pastoral plenty that these men recall is also mourned by the young prophetess and her father.[91] The men blame their migrant status on child-hungry women always asking for money; when a young woman chides them for forgetting their responsibilities as fathers (and asks where their own fathers were when the land and cattle of economic self-sufficiency were lost), they complain about the forwardness of contemporary women. Yet the narrative obstructs this judgment: Nongqause and the woman on the bus are parallel figures who challenge gender expectations as they move public discourse from complaint to the recognition of complicity. Nongqause too laments that "the natural course of life has changed": girls grow up too quickly because they join their mothers as "counsellors who fan the flames of resistance in the hearts of their men" (167). The young women's exhortation to would-be suitors, "*Zemk' iinkomo magwala ndini* [the cattle are being stolen, you cowards]"[92] is a reminder that courting men cannot marry without cattle for lobola, the bridewealth that fosters reciprocity between families.

Here we begin to see the import of this geographic and historical journey for Ndebele's notions of the ordinary. The journey to Transkei closes the circle of migrant labor linking cities to devastated homesteads—a circuit that, in Ndebele's depiction of a rural-urban divide, seemed an impermeable boundary. As Matshoba's narrative makes clear, it is precisely because this divide is all too permeable (in the economic necessity of migrancy and the legislated threat of forced removal) that black writers cling so fiercely to urban identities against retrograde apartheid pressures toward rural "homelands" and "tribal tradition." Likewise, the juxtaposition of nineteenth- and twentieth-century nostalgias—whether for pastoral plenty, or submissive women—pushes any sense of normalcy back in time, into an apocryphal past that, like the aftermath of the cattle killing, is not represented in the narrative. The everyday has not been ordinary for a very long time, "Three Days" maintains in its historically layered analysis of Transkei spectacles.

Matshoba's superimposition of these moments of loss ironizes nostalgia and complicates the very idea of the ordinary. Viewed together, the 1850s and the 1970s become one "state of emergency," in Walter Benjamin's sense: "The tradition of the oppressed teaches us that the 'state of emergency' in which we live is not the exception but the rule. We must attain to a conception of history that is in keeping with that insight. Then we shall realize that it is our task to bring about a real state of emergency, and this will improve our position in the struggle against Fascism."[93] Matshoba's punctuated nostalgia is diachronic, extending the lived "state of emergency" more than a century back into the past: loss of the "ordinary" cannot mark the divide between twentieth-century present and nineteenth-century past. His retrospective desire is for a committed anticolonial resistance rather than a lost precolonial world. On the other hand, Ndebele's ordinary is both nostalgic and synchronic: what has been lost is a shared awareness of the *relevance* of the ordinary to transformative cultural representation. The entire range of quotidian experience, rather than only the spectacularly political—the "rule," rather than the "exception"—must be available for the emergence of a "real state of emergency." In Ndebele's terms, only the emergence of a "new person in a new society" could realize the apocryphal future of a South Africa "always going to be free in the next five years."

My reading of Matshoba's narrative emphasizes its spatial and temporal juxtapositions, which effect estrangements (*Verfremdungen*) that Ndebele did not find in Matshoba. While Ndebele dismisses the literature of recognition, Gordimer examines its potential for bringing "black people . . . back to themselves" through a process of estrangement.[94] She adapts Walter Benjamin's account of Brechtian defamiliarization for a South African context in which characters and audience inhabit the same apartheid circumstance. Literature can educe not empathy or recognition, in Ndebele's negative sense of confirming suffering that black readers know all too well, but what Benjamin calls the "discovery (alienation)" (the German reads *Verfremdung*) of the "startling" aspects of what had been taken as the ordinary.[95] "Three Days in the Land of a Dying Illusion" stages within the narrative, and effects for the reader, this kind of estranging discovery. But what is most "startling" in the text—in terms of both Ndebele's dismissal of Matshoba and the narrative's treatment of the cattle killing—is the relationship it constructs between ordinary and spectacular in the cattle-killing prophecy itself. Given Ndebele's investment in the critical imagination, Matshoba's depiction of Nongqause as a young woman who attempts to unite and save her people "by the infinite stretching of her imagination" is significant indeed (173). She invents (rather than transmits) her prophecy, and the most spectacular aspects of the historical prophecy are transformed into figurative tropes—similes—that describe ordinary processes in magical terms. It is not at all clear, in other words, that Nongqause's "cattle-killing" prophecy calls for anything more than neighborly cooperation.

In the scene where Nongqause invents the prophecy, the "as-if" of figuration functions as a kind of prophetic memory of a world remade. Frustrated by her perception that her gender disqualifies her from accessing the ancestors' wisdom or sharing her ideas with the elders, Nongqause *imagines* an elaborate conversation with two voices that are marked as both emerging from the depths of her own mind and sounding "*as if* the voices of the great ancestors spoke to me" (173; emphasis added here and below). Warriors of old cannot return to life, but their fighting spirit can be revived among the people, who will "rise *like* a whirlwind" to reclaim what has been lost (175). Her father receives her words *as if* they were the ancestors'; he recognizes that renewing the people's fighting spirit "will be *as if* [Nxele and Mlanjeni] had risen from the dead and the spirit that will be infused in the tribes will be *like* a great hurricane that will sweep the usurpers out of the stolen heritage into the sea" (178). Mhlakaza embraces Nongqause's figurative prophecy by voicing it himself, and Matshoba's narrator, who is explicit about creating his own version of the episode, offers this story *as if* it represented what happened rather than *as* historical truth.

This vision comprises a chain of similes that translate the historical prophecy's familiar magical images into mundane (if vividly described) renewal. The transformation that Nongqause envisions, oddly enough, resembles the chiefs' plot thesis of colonial historiography: the amaXhosa will regain unity and the strength to make war on the colonial invaders and recover land and livestock—no magic cattle or resurrected ancestors required. Yet none are promised in this version, which redeems the chiefs' plot. Rather than a manipulative ploy in which the people are chiefs' pawns, this prophecy calls for leveling social inequalities, an action "*like* a great sacrifice": not killing cattle or destroying grain for its own sake, but sharing what remains, in a time of famine, "when those who still have a little share it with the destitute" (177). This renewed spirit of community will unite the people, and "with a little in their stomachs they may gain some strength to till the uncultivated soil" (178). This prophecy demands consumption and production rather than destruction: communal consumption in desperate times will surely deplete resources, but will also give the strength for cultivation that will refill cornpits and kraals, feed warriors, and put the community on the path to plenty.

This sustained figuration transforms the millennial into the metaphorical, the spectacular into the ordinary, lending paradoxical credibility to Nongqause's utterly mundane vision of renovation. The similes envision transformation through communal effort rather than external deliverance.[96] Turning magic to metaphor was also Tiyo Soga's strategy in recasting images from Nongqawuse's prophecy to "resurrect" the ancestors. Tiyo Soga sought to preserve elements of Xhosa tradition that his missionary colleagues dismissed as superstition. We can read Matshoba's metaphorization of magic similarly: he simultaneously demonstrates the visionary power of Xhosa tradition and subtly (yet thoroughly) purges its supernatural elements. Both Tiyo Soga and Matshoba confronted the shame of "superstition" in the cattle killing; Tiyo Soga did so while negotiating a position *within* a colonial machinery dedicated to sweeping away indigenous tradition, Matshoba while struggling *against* an apartheid machinery bent upon reconstituting "tribal tradition" in the Bantustans.

Although we can see Matshoba's secularization of the cattle killing as an act of resistance, such "resistance" nonetheless bears the imprint of an epistemological context that Matshoba—and we—inhabit: the hegemonic modernity that tends to deal with contemporary supernatural discourses by reading them as "metaphorical statements about something else," about "other matters of pressing social reality."[97] In Adam Ashforth's brave and troubled confrontation of the gulf between his own rationality and the lived "spiritual insecurity" of friends and neighbors in his adopted Soweto home, he warns against interpreting "statements that Africans clearly intend as literal, or factual, as if they were meant to be metaphorical or figurative" (114). When situated between Ashforth's critique of metaphorical translation and Ndebele's critique of unliterary immediacy, Matshoba's cattle-killing narrative tells us something, I think, about how millennial thinking works and about the worldliness of the literary imagination. I take Ashforth's point, but the *literary* representation of a *millenarian* prophecy in "Three Days" helps us recognize how such prophecies use figuration to capture the imagination and allegiance of prospective adherents: millenarian prophecies make comparisons with the familiar in order to envision worlds transformed beyond imagining. In this sense, prophecy presents itself as both figurative and factual, metaphorical and literal. Metaphor is inherent to the millennial imagination, even as it also serves to contain such imagining within the "common sense" of the secular.

The power of Nongqause's imagination in Matshoba's "Three Days" also tells us something about the economy of ordinary and spectacular in Ndebele's cultural project: they are imbricated rather than opposed, and one draws upon the power of the other. It is worth noting the reason why Matshoba's Nongqause turns to figuration: her gender. She knows she is a "mere maiden," that "the place of the woman was in the home": how could she claim the authority to speak publicly? Only if she claimed her message came from the ancestors.[98] What begins as a lie gathers narrative truth as the chain of similes ramifies the prophecy. Her father legitimizes this strategy by deciding that her idea "'should be seen as advice from the ancestors'" (178); the narrative demonstrates her vision's broader potential by depicting its revitalizing effect on the previously despairing Mhlakaza.[99] Given the gender-based distortions of Nongqawuse in cattle-killing historiography, Matshoba's narrative is interesting for its depiction of Nongqause seizing upon the "as-if" to project her voice into the future despite her lack of public authority. If we read Nongqause's overcoming her gendered voicelessness in terms of other forms of marginalization, "Three Days" seems to champion the literary imagination as a subaltern tool for claiming the power to speak and act in the world. Nongqause's mundane vision of revitalization also makes explicit the gender distinctions implicit in Ndebele's valorization of the (domestic, feminine) ordinary over the (public, masculine) spectacular.[100]

Yet there are several limits to reading Matshoba's narrative as an expression of Ndebele's gendered ordinary *avant la lettre*. As in the structure of metaphor itself, the narrative conflates ordinary and spectacular rather than distinguishing them: the domesticity of communal sharing in Nongqause's vision is the anticipated prelude to spectacular war. Moreover, such power-ful imaginings can be dangerous: "Three Days" elides the cattle killing's aftermath, yet also acknowledges that it was the "last nail in the coffin of the old way of life" (184). Although the narrative's gender dynamics are more complex than some feminist critiques of Matshoba might suggest, this complexity is itself problematic. The narrator uses his journey not only to historicize the Transkei (comparing past and present), but also to romanticize what he finds there as a precolonial remnant: he nostalgically imagines the women he sees as the timeless soul of the continent, "untainted by western standards" (161). His own gender thinking seems tainted by west-ern standards, however, as in the anachronism of Nongqause's observation that "the place of a woman was in the home": it was nineteenth-century missionaries, rather than Xhosa men, who were appalled by agricultural labor that took women away from the hearth. The narrator projects his own ideas about gender into the past to show Nongqause confronting her silencing as a young woman. Although critics often take Matshoba's first-person narrators as his mouthpiece, the narrator's perspective in "Three Days" is incomplete and in process, as is evident in the young woman's unanswered challenge to the male passengers' debate about the demands of women and family life. Indeed, the narrator's trajectory—from his initial critical desire to understand Transkei independence, to his concluding pledge never to return—makes him a parallel figure not to Nongqause but to Mhlakaza as we see him before hearing her vision, concerned for his people but resigned to his powerlessness. The narrative keeps space open for—and perhaps aims to create—a figure who could likewise turn the narrator's resignation to resistance.

The Nongqause of "Three Days" hatches a lie yet is decidedly not charac-terized as a liar: the imagination has a truth of its own, the story seems to suggest. Nongqause's vision is not presented as fraudulent prophecy, but the narrative does attend to the devastation caused by "illusions"—ideological gaps between appearance and reality. The "dying illusion" of the 1850s is the belief that people "can survive from the little that is left" in the wake of colonial encroachment (170); Nongqause seeks to shatter this illusion and spur her people to recover what has been lost. As Marx wrote in his critique of religion, "to call on [people] to give up their illusions about their condition is to *call on them to give up a condition that requires illusions*."[101] To rouse her people to throw off this illusory state, Nongqause turns to her imagina-tion, whose figurations trouble the relationship between appearance and reality. We might read Marx's chiasmus in terms of the narrative's gender dynamics: Nongqause's call is also a call to give up a condition that requires women to speak as if they were prophets in order to be heard. The tone of the narrative, however, valorizes the figurating exuberance of Nongqause's imagination while excoriating deceptive illusions that euphemize injustice. The difference between figuration and illusion in the narrative approximates Benedict Anderson's distinction between organic and official nationalisms: the first is a generative "myth," the second a coercive "lie."[102]

The fraudulence condemned in the narrative is the "dying illusion" of homeland independence. For the architects of the "illusion [that] was uhuru," like "vultures" feeding on carrion, "death brings sustenance / death means life" because their "shameless lies and false promises" impoverish the people while increasing their own power (143). "Three Days" unmasks the fraudulent illusions of the apartheid sign, in which the leader of "independent" Transkei complains about his critics arguing that "black was white," and "homelands" are forcibly populated by people who had never set foot in them. "The apartheid state's dislocations of signification are justly infamous," writes Louise Bethlehem about such attempts to meld sign and referent regardless of their obvious disparities. She finds that critical discourse about apartheid-era black South African writing reflects a similar "representational literalism" in its attempt "to effect a secular closure between the word and the world precisely to safeguard the ethical claims of South African literary culture."[103]

The tension between figuration and illusion in "Three Days" is thus crucial to the predicament of a literary culture inhabiting this enforced unity of the sign. On the one hand, Matshoba discloses his documentary intentions, implying a certain faith in the capacity of language to represent the world. Yet the effect of his narrative, articulated in its broadest terms, is to expose the distance between world and word, and to assess the malignant and beneficent potential of this gap. The narrator scorns the spurious "'enlightenment'" of Bantu Education (165), but he also uses "enlightenment" and tropes of knowledge-as-light to describe what Nongqause seeks from the ancestors and what Mhlakaza finds in her words (170, 173, 177). The instability of language is not unique to the apartheid era; Nongqause struggles to "elucidate the meaning she attached to sacrifice" when she explains her plan (177). The difference between the apartheid sign and Nongqause's prophecy is that meaning is imposed monologically in the first and negotiated dialogically in the second: Nongqause's prophecy develops in conversation with "spirits" and her father. In excoriating fraudulent illusions while considering the liberatory potential of a figurating imagination, Matshoba's narrative exposes the wrenching gulf between visions of change and their failure to be realized, between *independence* and Bantustan independence, and between homelands and what *home* signifies.[104] As we saw with Plaatje's description of the Land Act's genesis in "gossipy rumours," "Three Days" elicits recognition not of the arbitrariness of signification inherent in language, but rather the effects of power within discourse: the apartheid state (for whom death means life) can designate enforced ignorance and miseducation as *enlightenment* and realize that designation with the fact of Bantu Education and the force of police who shoot down its protestors.

It could be said, then, that Matshoba's narrative of remembered prophecy offers an alternative form of enlightenment that exposes the cynical gap between word and world. Such a project would seem a prerequisite for cultural production reoriented toward rediscovering the ordinary: recognition of an unjust society's distortions of reality would make way for a liberatory culture that could remake the world. Matshoba's narrative remains open to the possibility, however qualified, of the transformative potential inherent in the gaps between word and world, if troping were to be driven by dreams of freedom. We glimpse this possibility in Nongqause's *figurative* epiphany that achieving tribal unity will bring change *as if* from a millennial restoration. Eliding the historical prophecy's aftermath allows Matshoba to draw upon the purity of Nongqause's desire to restore her people, so that the reader's inevitable recognition of her historical failure exists alongside a desire for ending otherwise. Thus, remembered prophecy—the narrator's transformative meditation on the prophecy Nongqawuse voiced—can function as prophetic memory, in which her spirit of resistance and desire for liberation might be realized in the future. To entertain the possibility of thinking *as if* the prophecy had succeeded, while also recognizing the danger of accepting independence that is not *independence,* is to mobilize the transformative imagination *and* critical spirit that Ndebele hoped might generate the emergence of a new person, a new society, what Benjamin called a "real state of emergency."

Yet to what extent is my reading of Matshoba's metaphors the product of another kind of illusion, fostered by the relatively less constrained interpretive milieu that the end of apartheid—the closure of Plaatje's aberrational present—has brought? Did Ndebele charge that Matshoba's writing was ineffective because it hadn't (yet, in 1984) had an effect? How are writers to know, amidst a struggle, what modes of writing are transformative and how? And how do we evaluate their efforts now, when the "rhetoric of urgency" has given way to something else? Is it easier to perceive the utopian potential in failed prophecy from the standpoint of at least partially realized dreams? In chapter 4, I take up such questions, examining the possibilities elided by teleological, post-1994 redemptive readings of the antiapartheid struggle.

Matshoba's narrative generates space and desire for the practical imagination of a renewed world, amid the everyday indignities of apartheid. Matshoba's critique of economic, political, and semiotic illusions could help us to understand life under apartheid as a "condition that requires illusions," following Marx. The failure of millennial prophecy is an obstructed copula—an interruption of transitive desire—that can serve as an analogy for the difficulties of bridging the gap between literature and the actualization of the world it imagines. Plaatje's *Native Life in South Africa*, in its extended reception, demonstrates cultural production's potential as a generative afterlife of failure; Ndebele urges black South African writers to give up the constraining illusion of "relevant" cultural production as the warrant for future revolutionary success. Ndebele's critique of the protest mode helps us to see that the faith in causality and the future necessary to a politics of resistance requires both forgetting (or recuperative remembering of) historical rupture and imagining a kind of agency that has never yet been: Ndebele posits such a cultural-political stance as faith in a telos without the causal machinery of a teleology. "Can one remain for long in a state of cultural revolution?" Attwell asks pointedly.[105] Yet Ndebele must maintain his own illusions—about the transformative capacity of representation to generate the "helpful contrast" of *Verfremdung*, and about the immanence of a world "beyond the struggle." Plaatje, Ndebele, and Matshoba each gesture toward what Terdiman calls "an alterity potential in our present.... a time of otherness" that is not the future but "a fold in temporality that opens it up from within to the possibilities of an existence that could rectify the deficiencies of the present."[106] Here, I argue, by suspending the historicist imperative of causality as a link between past and future, prophetic memory can illuminate the productive potential of failure by pointing not to an endtime, but to an otherwise.

CHAPTER FOUR

WEAPONS OF STRUGGLE AND WEAPONS OF MEMORY

Thinking Time beyond Apartheid

A gun is a gun is a gun.

ALBIE SACHS, "PREPARING OURSELVES FOR FREEDOM," 1989

do not eat an unripe apple
its bitterness is a tingling knife.
suffer yourself to wait
and the ripeness will come
and the apple will fall down at your feet.
now is the time
pluck the apple
and feed the future with its ripeness.

NJABULO NDEBELE, "THE REVOLUTION OF THE AGED," 1981

it is not always possible even to pluck a now that has come.

ERNST BLOCH, *THE PRINCIPLE OF HOPE*, 1959[1]

In the apartheid state's final decade, a State of Emergency (from 1985–86 and 1986–90) gave way to negotiations that resulted in the transition to democratic government and the historic election of April 1994. The unconditional release of political prisoners from Robben Island began in October

1989; in February 1990, Nelson Mandela was released from twenty-seven years' imprisonment, and the African National Congress (ANC), the South African Communist Party, and the Pan Africanist Congress (PAC) were unbanned. The release of ANC leaders from Robben Island was figured as the long-awaited return of the early-nineteenth-century Xhosa warrior-prophet Nxele, in a 1992 essay, "The Return of Nxele," in the ANC magazine, *Mayibuye*. Nxele (or Makana) was imprisoned on Robben Island after leading an attack on Grahamstown in 1819; he pledged to return and save his people, inaugurating what seemed a prophetic eternity of anticipated deliverance. In the late 1850s, political prisoners (including chiefs involved in the cattle killing) were interned on Robben Island, reviving its status as a site from which deliverance might come and thus renewing the promise of Nxele's return. That this promise elicited skepticism as well as hope is evident in the isiXhosa proverb, "*Ukuza kukaNxele*," in which to speak of Nxele's return is to speak of what will never happen.[2] "The Return of Nxele" refutes this proverb by figuring the recent release of ANC leaders as a fulfillment of Nxele's promise.

"The Return of Nxele" was written by Mtutuzeli Matshoba, whose narrative, "Three Days in the Land of a Dying Illusion," I discussed in chapter 3. In "Three Days," Nongqause learns that Nxele can return only "through a medium who will be his voice and representative among the people."[3] "The Return of Nxele" marks this vision's realization: Nelson Mandela and his comrades have returned, "with the spirit of Makhanda in their hearts" (43). Makana drowned trying to make good his promises to turn British bullets to water and to lead his people in driving whites into the sea. Matshoba casts Mandela as a medium inspired by Nxele, but Mandela's words upon his return differed from those Nxele might have spoken. Two weeks after his release, Mandela appeared at a rally in Durban, the site of violent clashes between ANC supporters and supporters of the Zulu nationalist Inkatha Freedom Party that threatened to obstruct negotiations with the apartheid state. Instead of exhorting his supporters to drive white people into the sea, Mandela urged them to "take your guns, your knives, and your pangas, and throw them into the sea." He recalled the 1879 battle of Isandlwana, in which Zulu warriors armed only with "shields and spears, but filled with courage and determination, thrust back the guns and cannon of the British imperialists."[4] Guns and cannons, pangas and spears become a compound metonym in Mandela's speech for both colonial violence and the burning desire to counter it by driving whites into the sea. Mandela inverts these tropes: it was not the whites, but rather the weapons they brought, that needed to be expelled in order to achieve the unity necessary to dismantle the apartheid order. Instead of becoming bulletproof, freedom fighters needed to find a new way to fight without bullets, consigning bullets to the waters rather than turning them into water. In this sea change, the return of Nxele in the person of Mandela revised the kinds of deliverance Nxele had promised.

No less startling than Mandela's revisionary invocation of prophetic tradition was Njabulo Ndebele's response to a constellation of troubling ironies in the early 1990s. In the 1991 preface to his collected essays on the spectacular orientation of black South African literary culture, Ndebele observed that the spectacle of apartheid "seems destined to end in a comparatively nonspectacular, yet essential, process of negotiation."[5] Ndebele sensed dangers in this *lack of spectacle* analogous to those he identified in the previous decade's fascination with spectacle: the prison doors from which freedom fighters emerged were opened not by "victorious crowds pursuing a defeated enemy in flight. . . . [but] by an enemy who had declared that he was now a friend" (152). A decade earlier, Nadine Gordimer had analyzed the "'morbid symptoms'" of the interregnum, in which "'the old is dying, and the new cannot be born.'"[6] For Ndebele, talk of "the new South Africa" was a symptom not of the imminent birth of the new, but rather the changing face of old oppressions. The phrase "a new South Africa" was introduced not by the ANC in exile or the new struggle coalitions of the United Democratic Front and the Mass Democratic Movement, but rather President F.W. de Klerk in his landmark speech of February 2, 1990, announcing the unbannings and prisoner releases.[7] The interregnum's pregnant impasse gives way, in Ndebele's meditation, to a sense that too much of the old might survive in the new that was so visibly struggling to be born.

Where Matshoba saw the realization of hopes tended, disavowed, and renewed for almost two centuries, Ndebele pondered just what a returned "prophet" like Mandela could say or do within the constraints of a negotiated settlement. The "terrible choices" Ndebele saw revolved around the question of timeliness also at work in his poem, "The Revolution of the Aged": would the shift from armed struggle to negotiation bring the bitterness of unripe fruit?[8] Would the acceptance of an available settlement, as opposed to continued struggle for a more definitive liberation, mean that only a few would truly be free? What was the difference between waiting for the apple to decide it was ripe or choosing the moment to seize it, so that its imminent ripeness might "feed the future"? More than a century earlier, in a moment of military defeat, Isaac Wauchope exhorted readers of the isiXhosa newspaper *Isigidimi* to put down the gun and pick up the pen, as Ndebele reminded artists in exile at a 1987 conference in Stockholm.[9] As Mandela urged his supporters to put down their guns, Ndebele hesitated, wondering if the time for guns had really passed. His circumspection was driven by the same concern that had shaped his critique of pens aimed as weapons: instead of seizing and shaping the future, the people might resign themselves to accept terms set by their oppressors.

Matshoba's and Ndebele's responses to events of the early 1990s construe historical change in narrative terms. "The Return of Nxele" introduces a new term—fulfillment—into the taxonomy of failed, false, and fraudulent prophecy outlined in chapter 3. What does it mean to imagine late-twentieth-century events as the fulfillment of early-nineteenth-century prophecy, particularly in 1992, before the details of the negotiated settlement had been settled? In celebrating the fulfillment of prophecy, Matshoba made his own prediction of a near future in which "we shall have won."[10] Ndebele, by contrast, sensed the lack of an ending: what happens when a liberation struggle faces a transition without the definitive, catastrophic ending (in the literal and dramatic senses of *catastrophe*) that might inaugurate millennial renewal? Making sense of this strange admixture of partially realized hopes and unexpected new dilemmas, Ndebele and Matshoba confront the importance of narrative endings. In narrative, "everything is transformed by the structuring presence of the end to come," Peter Brooks writes, so that "the *anticipation of retrospection* [is] our chief tool in making sense of narrative. . . . [W]e read in a spirit of confidence, and also a state of dependence, that what remains to be read will restructure the provisional meanings of the already read."[11] Reading entails anticipating the retrospective teleological understanding offered by a completed narrative. Prophecy, in this sense, foreshadows the kind of understanding of "what remains to be read" that we have of the "already read." This view of narrative can also elucidate the temporality of the interregnum—in its very etymology a between-time that represents a suspension of plot and an anticipation of the transformative event that will enable its resumption.

This chapter examines the interpretive challenges and temporal logics (or paralogics) of the democratic transition: how do we read the end of apartheid? Reading success, I argue, is no less fraught than reading failure.

Even if Mandela's emergence from nearly three decades of spectacular obscurity could be figured as the realization of centuries-old prophecy, neither the victories nor the compromises of the years since could be divined in that event. In Ndebele's description of the Janus-faced interim of the early 1990s, the antiapartheid struggle seemed neither quite failed nor quite fulfilled. Ideas of *unfailure* and *unfulfillment*, I argue, can help us grasp the temporal complexities of reading South Africa after the interregnum: the "end" of the apartheid era is not only a culmination but also a new beginning, and this "end" hardly fulfills all the aspirations of the antiapartheid struggle, let alone earlier visions of liberation expressed by seers like Nxele or Nongqawuse.

It would be dangerous to assume, from the standpoint of 1990 or even 1994, that the negotiated transition to democracy—the avoidance of the long-predicted conflagration intimated in apocalyptic novels like Gordimer's *July's People* or Silko's *Almanac of the Dead*—was inevitable. The problem with reading historical events in narrative terms, allowing our ideas about the past to be shaped by the retrospective understanding that Brooks identifies in narrative endings, is not that we understand uncertain moments in the past as "already read," but rather that we assume eventual outcomes to be always-already written. We conflate the temporality of historical change with that of reading narrative. In June 1990, the nationwide state of emergency in effect for four years was lifted (except in Natal), marking the passage from a state of emergency to a state of emergence. "The *emergency* maneuvers to forestall or crush the *emergent*; since the *emergency* must prevent the expression of the hitherto unexpressed," Tony Voss writes, noting that in evolutionary theory, an "emergent" is what cannot be predicted in relationship to prior conditions.[12] The unpredictability of the emergent works against retrospective, teleological readings of historical events. In "Living in the Interregnum," Gordimer posited the imminence of a future without presuming to speculate about how or in what form it would arrive: a time after the interregnum was inevitable, but its content could only be a matter of faith and commitment. The end of apartheid remained as yet unwritten. This committed refusal to speculate about what lay beyond the interregnum implies an ethics of anticipation: a radical openness to an emergent, unknown, and possibly threatening future.

Mindful of "the historical responsibility of the critic—on both sides of the revolution,"[13] I propose a corollary to Gordimer's ethics of anticipation: an ethics of retrospection that maintains a radical openness to the past and its visions of the future by resisting the narrative assumption that endings make total sense of what has come before, thereby containing the emergent within teleological explanations. To read the interregnum retrospectively while assuming the inevitability of the *particular* historical form of passage beyond it not only undervalues the achievements of the antiapartheid struggle, but also obstructs attention to utopian (or dystopian) dreams that have not been realized. From the other side of the aberrational present whose inauguration Sol Plaatje marked in *Native Life in South Africa*, to mistake Plaatje's hope that "Heaven has never yet failed us" for the historical inevitability of its fulfillment is, however paradoxically, to deflate the force of his faith. An ethics of retrospection works against these tendencies.

Fictional narratives, I argue, offer alternatives to the foreclosures inherent in reading *history* as narrative, and particularly in reading the South African democratic transition in terms of a narrative closure that assumes a single, inevitable trajectory to the postapartheid present. The novels I discuss below, Sindiwe Magona's *Mother to Mother* and Zakes Mda's *The Heart of Redness*, join postrevolutionary retrospection to the unrealized vision of the cattle-killing prophecy, which offers a matrix of memory through which the anticipations, achievements, and disappointments of the antiapartheid struggle can be reconstellated without losing sight of the exigencies of the transition. That virgin births feature prominently in both plots indicates these novels' engagements with the interregnum's obstructed birth of the new and the ambivalences of a "new" South Africa. Far from offering triumphant narratives of national liberation, however, they leave the problem of passage beyond the interregnum stubbornly unresolved. The aporias of these texts obstruct a simplistic retrospective teleology that, in casting liberation as inevitable, would miss how far liberation has yet to come.

In refusing to acknowledge the momentum of the transition to democracy in the early 1990s, *Mother to Mother* serves as a limit case for my articulation of an ethics of retrospection. In the spirit of Walter Benjamin, I consider and challenge his disavowal of the historicist methods of those who "wish to relive an era" by "blot[ting] out everything they know about the later course of history."[14] Benjamin urges mindfulness of history's aftermath; I argue, however, that too much of an awareness of what comes after can blind us to the unrealized possibilities to which Benjamin's oeuvre is committed. To read Mandela's release from prison proleptically, in terms of his later status as former President of a democratic South Africa, is to lose sight of the alternative trajectories that did not play out, for better and for worse.[15] By contrast, Sindiwe Magona's *Mother to Mother* seems to epitomize an ethics of retrospection, since this 1998 novel, set in 1993, offers almost no sense that Mandela's election—or any election—is imminent or even possible. Magona's "blotting out" of the democratic transition forces us to weigh the costs of the struggle against dreams of liberation that have never yet been attained. This blinkered vision, however, elides not only the "later course of history" as it actually happened, but also any sense of a future different from the apartheid past. Taken to such an extreme, an ethics of retrospection can forsake the future rather than foster openness to unrealized possibilities in the past.

Zakes Mda's *The Heart of Redness* performs a radically different ethics of retrospection: it challenges linear understandings of temporality that assume simple relationships among past, present, and future—or memory, experience, and expectation. The novel invites us to consider prophecies as neither failed nor fulfilled, but rather as *unfailed,* alive and partially realized in the present, but also unrecognizable to their original adherents. Unfailure reveals the heterogeneity of time, a nonsynchronous multiplicity of pasts and presents in which the incompletion of the past implies the unfinishedness of the present. Mda's multitemporal narrations of the cattle killing—at once extravagantly fictional and deeply historiographical—allow us to think about narrative trajectories in terms of proliferation rather than resolution, as they reframe the problem of reading the historical end of apartheid in terms of narrative closure. These fictional narratives remind us that time can be fluid and alchemic, rather than linear and arithmetic, and that history is more complex than beginning, middle, and end. On the other hand, I suggest at the end of the chapter, the fine line between understanding time as plural and labeling Others as anachronistic should give us pause before we embrace heterotemporality as an explanatory rubric for contemporary South Africa.

ANGELS OF HISTORY

Among the symptoms of disorientation signaling a movement beyond the interregnum was the provocative proposition that ANC members "should be banned from saying that culture is a weapon of struggle." This suggestion appeared in "Preparing Ourselves for Freedom," a paper circulated at a 1989 ANC seminar in Lusaka; it was written by South African exile and legal scholar Albie Sachs, who had recently survived an assassination attempt in Mozambique. After its February 1990 publication in the Weekly Mail, many observers noted similarities between Sachs's call for an imagination unfettered enough to "grasp the full dimensions of the new country and new people that is struggling to give birth to itself" and previous interventions by critics like Ndebele, Gordimer, and Lewis Nkosi.[16] What was new about Sachs's argument was that he spoke not as a cultural worker or literary critic but as a prominent member of a political organization that had promoted the notion of culture-as-weapon.[17] This notion is often traced to poet and critic Mafika Gwala's essay "Writing as a Cultural Weapon," which argued, "Black writing cannot be divorced from the struggle for a free South Africa."[18] In this sense, Sachs's statement renewed earlier exhortations that writers reorient their attention toward the "world of beauty that lies beyond the conflict and turmoil of the struggle," in the words of the 1948 ANC Youth League manifesto.[19]

Sachs's proposal for censorship was rhetorical (he suggested "a period of, say, five years"), but his assertion of the difference between culture and a "real instrument of struggle" was in earnest: "a gun is a gun is a gun, and if it were full of contradictions, it would fire in all sorts of directions and be useless for its purpose. But the power of art lies precisely in its capacity to expose contradictions and reveal hidden tensions—hence the danger of viewing it as if it were just another kind of missile-firing apparatus" (239, 240).[20] Sachs's view of the multivalent possibilities of cultural production, and his sense of the need to forge an inclusive national culture, struck many observers as dated, Leavisite, out of touch with the way that culture was actually engaging with the struggle on the ground in South Africa, or uncognizant of postmodern theories of the relationship between culture and society. Since Sachs's concern was culture rather than guns, the strangeness of his appropriation of Gertrude Stein's modernist mantra, "Rose is a rose is a rose is a rose," went unremarked. Stein had aimed to reanimate a language deadened in the accretions of literary tradition; Sachs, too, was concerned to "make it new" (as Stein's contemporary Ezra Pound urged), his concern not with language or literary form but with the capacity of the imagination to help create a world beyond apartheid. But where Stein's repetitions focus attention on just what (a) rose is, Sachs's phrase assumes the matter-of-fact identity of its guns.[21] With the revolution not yet achieved, the hard questions of whether an MK gun is an SADF gun is an IFP gun (or spear) is a third force gun[22]—the contradictions and "hidden tensions" of an armed national liberation struggle moving closer to some kind of end—remain invisible in Sachs's formulation. Confronting these questions was the task of the Truth and Reconciliation Commission (TRC), which drew distinctions not among guns, but among the actions and motivations of those who wielded them and other weapons: those who made full disclosure to the Commission, and could establish that their actions committed between 1960 and 1994 were politically motivated, would be eligible for amnesty. Perhaps a gun is just a gun, but in the terms of the TRC, a criminal is not an uncooperative witness is not an amnestied perpetrator.

A crucial aspect of the Truth and Reconciliation Commission's mandate was to seek the whole truth as the foundation for national reconciliation: as the 1997 appearance of Winnie Madikizela Mandela before the TRC made clear, the TRC heard testimony about human rights violations committed on all sides. Among these was the August 1993 murder of US Fulbright scholar Amy Biehl, who was working on voter registration strategies at the Community Law Center of the University of the Western Cape, and was killed in Guguletu township, outside of Cape Town, a few days before she was to return to the United States. The four young men who killed Biehl were amnestied by the TRC in July 1998, as their action was connected to their membership in a student organization associated with the PAC.[23] After learning in 1996 that a childhood friend was the mother of one of Biehl's killers, Sindiwe Magona wrote *Mother to Mother*, her first novel. *Mother to Mother* is narrated by Mandisa, the fictionalized mother of the fictionalized killer, and addressed to the mother of Amy Biehl. Magona is concerned with the unpredictable directions in which "real instrument[s] of struggle" can fire; in her novel, these instruments are not guns but the ready-to-hand township weapons of stones, knives, petrol, tires, and matches. Mandisa accounts for her son's actions to the mother of his victim, and this act of accounting for the causes and costs of violence might explain the novel's unrelentingly dystopic depiction of South African townships: the only major character with any sense of an imminent democratic future is Amy Biehl, and even her thoughts of the future are more immediately focused on her return home.[24] In no way does the novel offer the mother of Amy Biehl the hollow consolation of her daughter having died for a "just cause."

Far from anticipating the future, Mandisa is transfixed by the past, particularly by what she sees as two catastrophic events: first, her unwanted and improbable pregnancy in 1973, which took her out of school before the second catastrophe, the uprisings that began in 1976, when the students of Soweto defiantly refused an inferior education. Mandisa laments, "Boycotts, strikes, and indifference have plagued the schools in the last two decades. Our children have paid the price."[25] Her pregnancy also exacted a high price, more dear because she conceived as a virgin, having refrained from vaginal intercourse. The novel accounts not only for how Mandisa's son took Biehl's life, but also how his willful conception "unreasonably and totally destroy[ed] the me I was. The me I would have become" (88). In Mandisa's view, Mxolisi stole her future; her student contemporaries and their successors robbed themselves of their own future. Children have become "monsters" (2), taking up the struggle by establishing a reign of terror in the townships and enforcing vigilante justice with rocks and matches. Mandisa's Guguletu is awash in the "morbid symptoms" of Gramsci's interregnum without any sign of a new order being born.

Mandisa's perspective approximates that of Walter Benjamin's angel of history, her "face turned toward the past" as is his. Her melancholy attachment to the alternative future foreclosed by her son's birth in the 1970s blinds her to the new possibilities being born in the 1990s. Benjamin describes the backward-looking angel of history:

> Where we perceive a chain of events, he sees one single catastrophe that keeps piling wreckage upon wreckage and hurls it in front of his feet. . . . [A] storm is blowing from Paradise. . . . This storm irresistibly propels him into the future to which his back is turned, while the pile of debris before him grows skyward. This storm is what we call progress.[26]

There is no palpable historical momentum in *Mother to Mother*. The children of the children of Soweto are still out of school; Mandisa fears that they will "end up in the kitchens and gardens of white homes . . . just like us, their mothers and fathers" (10; ellipses in original). The children's actions, their demonstrations, slogans, and demands—"all this nonsense" of the past two decades (25)—fill Mandisa with fear and revulsion. In Guguletu, "the mere gathering of so many people at the same time and place can precipitate inexplicable evil . . . unleash latent demons," and Mandisa describes collectivity in bestial or disembodied terms: millipedes, amoeba, pig intestines, ants, sausage filling (38, 11, 15, 24; ellipses in original). The only image of sociality as sustaining community, rather than menacing, mindless crowd, is a nostalgic recollection of Blouvlei, where Mandisa lived as a child until the community was scattered by the "whirlwind" of forced removal: "Guguletu killed us . . . killed the thing that held us together . . . made us human" (33;

ellipses in original). This devastating whirlwind echoes the apocalyptic tone of texts such as Sipho Sepamla's *A Ride on the Whirlwind* (1981) and Es'kia Mphahlele's *Voices in the Whirlwind* (1972); it also inverts the whirlwind of cattle-killing prophecies that was to sweep whites and unbelievers into the sea. Township life is depicted in the novel as *postapocalyptic,* in the colloquial sense of destruction without millennial recreation. Only at the novel's end, when the neighbors whom Mandisa has previously described contemptuously come to mourn with her, does she again glimpse the possibility of lifegiving collectivity.

The only "storm" blowing in *Mother to Mother* is one of three hundred years' rage "in the hearts of the people of this land" (175): even Benjamin's catastrophic notion of a storm of "progress" is scarcely palpable.[27] I do not mean to imply that South African townships were not violent in the early 1990s, nor to undermine Mandisa's denunciation of tactics like necklacing that targeted township residents (as "collaborators") rather than "the oppressors" who created and forcibly populated the townships (77). But the novel's broad demonization of mass action relies on a temporal distortion: since the momentum of political transition (however lurching and uncertain) is all but invisible in the novel, it allows no room to confront the moral ambiguities of collective struggles because their achievements appear solely as "wreckage upon wreckage," murder upon murder. Sindiwe Magona remembers having such misgivings during a township meeting before she left South Africa for the United States in 1981, but she did not speak then, knowing "that was not the revolutionary statement that was needed for this occasion."[28] Her novel, written in a postrevolutionary moment that offers the opportunity for retrospection, critiques the internally policed pressures of ideological conformity on a population already under apartheid's screws. Nkosi, Gordimer, Ndebele, Sachs, and others examined this conformity's aesthetic consequences and warned against the stifling of the imagination, the flattening out of contradictions in marshalling culture as a weapon of struggle. *Mother to Mother* depicts these pressures on everyday life—and death—in the townships.

Although the novel was written at the late edge of the transitional "cusp time,"[29] only the historical knowledge that readers bring to the text can modulate its despair into something like ambivalence. While the novel "blots out" what Magona knew in the late 1990s about South Africa since the early 1990s, many readers are likely to measure the bleakness of Magona's vision against the historical transformations of the decade. The choices at stake in an ethics of retrospection are laid bare for readers of *Mother to Mother* as they shift their focus between the novel's vision and their own historical understanding: what role should historical outcomes play in literary interpretation? What kind of reading practice can avoid being *determined* by teleological understandings of the past while also recognizing a text's historicity? I have argued that openness to the past fosters mindfulness of unrealized, suppressed possibilities; Magona's blinkered vision avoids a triumphalist sense of inevitable liberation, but in doing so it offers very little sense that change was possible, let alone likely.[30]

What complicates the novel's nihilism is remembered prophecy: Sindiwe Magona, like Mtutuzeli Matshoba, links the spectacles of 1976 with those of the cattle killing in 1856–57. Just as Matshoba substituted twentieth-century disillusionments of Transkei independence for the cattle killing's aftermath in "Three Days in the Land of a Dying Illusion," Magona concatenates discrete historical plots by positing the violence of 1993 as the aftermath of a cycle of self-destruction begun in 1976 and contextualized within a centuries-long history of resistance. In an interview, Magona identifies the fundamental similarity between the cattle killing and township insurgency: both embraced a millennial promise that "to advance we have to retreat. . . . [D]estroy everything and your lot will be improved."[31] The analogues to Xhosa cattle are the children of 1976 and after, who sacrificed their own education, and perhaps even their humanity, for the sake of liberation, without thought for how children-become-killers could be reclaimed even if their sacrifice were successful. Without the copula of a magical resurrection, how could those who had sacrificed themselves build a community even if the new world they fought for did arrive?

Mother to Mother invokes the cattle killing twice, and its role in the novel is contradictory because Mandisa's views about self-sacrifice and resistance are in flux. In the first episode, a young Mandisa hears about the cattle killing from her grandfather, whose stories provided an alternative education to her schooling; he rejects the idea that Nongqawuse was a "false prophet" deluding a "superstitious and ignorant" people. His rendering is engagingly didactic, explaining to a township child the significance of cattle and pausing with questions at moments of suspense. Mandisa's grandfather suggests that the people "allowed themselves fallacious belief," but he stresses the rationality of their actions: the prophecy may have been false, but it was not fraudulent (175).[32] "After much debate," he tells Mandisa, the "nation" decided that the "abomination" of the whites was so great that to expel it would require a "noble sacrifice" of precious cattle; "the biggest miracle, the mother reason" was that the whites would be cast by a *"great whirlwind"* into the sea (180). Mandisa's grandfather places the cattle killing within a history in which "many others tried to rid our nation of the ones without colour," including Nxele/Makana, the Zulu chief Cetshwayo, the Israelites of Bulhoek,[33] and marchers singing "One settler, one bullet!" (182–83).[34] Mandisa's grandfather concludes his litany of resistance, "But it was all to no avail. . . . The most renowned liar has not said [that the whites] are about to disappear" (183).

Mandisa's memory of her grandfather's tale appears toward the end of the novel, interposed in an account of the events of the day after Amy Biehl's murder in 1993. This analeptic episode of remembered prophecy seems not to offer the crystallized hindsight of prophetic memory, however: Mandisa makes no connection between the cattle killing and recent events. She does not link the suffering after the prophecy's failure with the violence of the interregnum. Previous visions of liberation cannot prefigure apartheid's end, since the transition is all but invisible in the novel. As a child, Mandisa reflected that her grandfather's tale made "what had seemed stupid decisions, and acts that had seemed indefensible . . . not only understandable but highly honourable" (183). This interlude implies that resistance, even that which exacts an impossibly high price, is no less honorable for having failed, an assessment that differs considerably from the adult Mandisa's exasperation. The carefully considered, consensual action in her grandfather's story echoes Mandisa's recollection of the meetings her parents attended in the face of impending forced removal; she relished these rare opportunities to play after dark while the adults discussed political matters that did not have "anything to do with me" (53). These accounts of adults debating resistance contrast starkly with Mandisa's current fear of mindless crowds and the politicized children's coercion, met with the unconsidered cheering or wary silence of adults.

At the novel's end, Mandisa invokes Nongqawuse's vision as an explicit *parallel* to Biehl's murder: the temporal distance between the events stokes the "long-simmering dark desires" of which Mxolisi is "only an agent," just as Nongqawuse "had but voiced the unconscious collective wish of the nation: rid ourselves of the scourge" (210). Where her grandfather had framed the cattle killing as a deeply considered, *rational* response to invasion, Mandisa reaches for the mechanistic fatality of Greek tragedy: Mxolisi (whose name, Mandisa notes, means *peacemaker*) was "possessed" by a "burning hatred. . . . [that] wielded the knife," transforming him into the "blind but sharpened arrow of the wrath of his race"[35] driving inexorably toward a "consummation of inevitable senseless catastrophe. . . . cruel confluence of time, place and agent" (210). Amy Biehl might have escaped this fate "but for the chance of a day, the difference of one sun's rise" (210), just as the magical sunrise anticipated in the cattle killing could have changed everything.

This penultimate statement in the novel might suggest that Biehl's death is a delayed consequence of the cattle-killing prophecy's failure, which would locate the "chance of a day" in 1857 rather than 1993: the prophecy's realization would have precipitated an alternative future without apartheid. The novel largely forecloses this possibility, however, in its treatment of the prophecy. Whereas the plot of tragedy depends upon peripety in order to sunder and restore a moral order, Xhosa believers vainly awaited a sun that would reverse course at noon. The prophecy responded to colonial disruptions of the socioeconomic order by staking the future on hopes for "the reversal of things, the natural order turned upside down," Mandisa's grandfather says (179). This fatal miscalculation perhaps explains why anticolonial millenarian movements were generally more effective in imagining an acolonial world than achieving a postcolonial state. Mandisa's grandfather implies that the prophecy's fulfillment would have been *unnatural*, would have thrown "nature . . . out of joint," in Plaatje's phrase. Similarly, the novel does not imagine how an imminent reversal of the apartheid order might amount to a restoration, rather than a reversal, of the "natural order"—a setting-right (*ukulungisa*) of colonial disjunctures, in the language of Xhosa prophecy. (In another context, Mandisa says resignedly, "*ukulunga kwenye, kukonakala kwenye,* the righting of one, is the undoing of another" [9].) Thus, Mandisa notes ominously in the novel's final words, the "chance of a day" that might have spared Biehl would have made her son "perhaps not a murderer. Perhaps, not yet" (210). Having equated the culture of violence in the townships with the inexorable mechanism of fate, Mandisa implies that while Biehl's death was a matter of chance, Mxolisi's killing was a matter of time. In this sense, the novel's "tragedy" derives from the fact that Amy Biehl, as a US citizen working for South African democracy, was an accidental and inappropriate sacrificial victim for a fated instrument of racial vengeance—Mxolisi as the "arrow" whose trajectory was both predetermined and off the mark.[36]

Mandisa offers another version of Mxolisi's fated future: "His tomorrows were his yesterday. . . . Nothing would come of the morrow. . . . He had already seen his tomorrows; in the defeated stoop of his father's shoulders. . . . Hope still-born in his heart" (203). These words, however, hardly describe the boy who seemingly willed himself into being by "jump[ing] into" his virgin mother's womb, and who grew from a four-year-old comically mouthing freedom slogans into a student leader respected by young and old in the township (112). The slogan that causes Mandisa so much concern, "LIBERATION NOW! EDUCATION LATER!" makes a hopeful (if problematic) pledge to a transformed future.[37] What Mandisa projects, then, is either her own sense that Mxolisi's future can only repeat previous generations' suffering, or bitterness about her own life. Mxolisi's birth meant that Mandisa's hopes were "still-born in [her] heart"; it led her not beyond the interregnum's "morbid symptoms," but into a nonfuture in which she is consigned to repeat her parents' drudgery.

Mother to Mother avoids a retrospective teleology that would frame the interregnum in terms of the historical facticity of passage beyond it. In 1999, Magona described returning to South Africa in 1994 to vote; far from imagining the democratic transition as the fulfillment of prophecy, Magona worried that it inspired false prophecies. Amidst the jubilation, she feared that her fellow citizens might "wake up in five years or ten years and be badly surprised and angry. . . . [P]eople will be disillusioned because they were expecting far too much, more than could be delivered."[38] Magona's lonely anxiety reverses Ndebele's apocryphal future in which South Africa was "always going to be free in five years"; both worry about the pathologies of false hope. In the novel, the upcoming election appears only in a fleeting thought of Amy Biehl. Far from associating the election with a total erasure of apartheid, or assuming its result, or even assuming that it would actually be held, *Mother to Mother* hardly acknowledges the upcoming election, nor the partial suspension of apartheid laws, nor the release of leaders and unbanning of organizations: these changes have not registered for Mandisa, and she expects less than nothing from the future.

In effect, the postrevolutionary retrospection of *Mother to Mother* denies its own possibility: Magona's narrator can imagine the future only as an extension of an entropic present. Although we may want to assume that there is some distance between author and narrator, or that Biehl's optimistic presence enables a broader view than Mandisa's,[39] Magona's own concern about the false hopes of 1994 reinforces Mandisa's pessimism, if not her melancholy ignorance (or dismissal) of current events. (Mandisa's statement, "I don't know about the government now. Whether or not it is coping with the task of ruling the country, I cannot say" (73), strains credulity in its 1993 setting; one might—at a stretch—read it in terms of a rejection of masculinist spectacular politics in favor of the domestic and the ordinary.) The novel expresses a mournful despair about the impossibility of liberation, a despair that no democratic elections, rainbow-bright flags, collated national anthems or integrated rugby matches could touch. It achieves this effect by not allowing these icons of the transition to touch the narrative except in a flicker of consciousness of a woman in the wrong place, out of joint.[40]

This bleak vision turns Mandela-as-President into a different kind of angel of history, a deus ex machina whose emergence is otherwise inexplicable and whose artifice would be inadequate to redress the cycle of self-destructive violence. Set against the novel, the historic event of the election is both miraculous and mundane: anything but inevitable, far from a panacea or even a definitive sign of the end of apartheid or what Mandisa might recognize as a different future. The novel thus depicts a historical predicament shared by TRC victim-witnesses: the conditions of possibility for their testimony represent an achievement perhaps unthinkable in Gordimer's interregnum, but the limited means of redress render devastatingly visible the unrealized promise of long-held dreams of restoration.[41] Retaining a space for such nearly forgotten hopes is central to an ethics of retrospection as I have described it. The novel's concern, however, is less to call attention to what has been left undone than to ask whether *any* struggle could be worth the sacrifice of the humanity and future of a generation of children. By refusing to succumb to the myth of the South African miracle, Magona raises difficult questions about the costs of struggle.

Yet this fictionalized act of witnessing has its own costs—not least that Mandisa's ambivalence about Mxolisi's birth leads her to present herself not so much "mother to mother" in an act of atonement, but more as the victim whose life he took before he took Biehl's. The mother of Amy Biehl is invited to mourn Mandisa's lost future as well as her own lost daughter. In this novel addressed to her bereaved mother, Amy Biehl is introduced by Mandisa in (negative) messianic terms, as a person for whom "doing good in this world is an all-consuming, fierce and burning compulsion. I wonder if it does not blinker their perception" (2). Amy Biehl is the obverse of Benjamin's angel of history, peering so far into a redeemed future that she disregards the history that informs present dangers. Far from heralding the fulfillment of prophecies of freedom, *Mother to Mother* figures the

antiapartheid struggle as one more false prophecy, a parallel and consequence of the cattle killing's futile sacrifice. The novel falsifies the vision of
liberation that drove the struggle: it "knows" what the children of the 1970s
could not, that they were fighting for nothing. Taken as a whole, the novel
constructs a prophetic memory, not out of the *vision* of the remembered
prophecy narrated by Mandisa's grandfather, but rather out of the *aftermath*
of failed prophecy whose shame he had wanted to erase. Here the apple of
revolution is only bitter or rotten, never ripe.

STORYING THE PAST: THE DEAD WILL ARISE IN
THE HEART OF REDNESS

As with Matshoba's "Three Days," Magona's narrative of remembered prophecy cannot allow both the anticipation and the devastation of the cattle
killing to resonate with the concerns of the present: while Matshoba ignores
the aftermath of the cattle killing, Magona ignores the achievements of
the antiapartheid struggle. Her treatment of the cattle killing lays bare
its vexed twentieth-century afterlife. On the one hand, the version of the
story Magona claims "we African people believe"—that Nongqawuse was
the naïve dupe of whites posing as ancestors—reflects Xhosa suspicions
that the cattle killing was a hoax orchestrated by Sir George Grey. In the
apartheid era, this view of Nongqawuse resonates strongly with condemna-
tions of "black agents of 'the system'" (informers or Bantustan leaders) who
do the bidding of the apartheid state.[42] But *Mother to Mother* itself offers
a rather different view. By situating the cattle killing in terms of cycles of
self-destructive violence, the novel echoes Bantustan leaders' attempts to
discredit the antiapartheid struggle by linking it to Nongqawuse. Prime
Minister George Matanzima of Transkei referred to Nongqawuse in con-
demning "'school unrest'" in 1980, and Chief Minister Gatsha Buthelezi of
KwaZulu blasted the international sanctions movement by warning black
South Africans against "'false prophets who urged them to destroy the
country's assets. . . . as the Xhosa prophetess Nongqawuse had done in the
last century'" (51). In a confidential memo, the South African Bantu Affairs
Department outlined a similar strategy for suppressing the PAC Poqo movement of the early 1960s: "'Full use should be made of Bantu superstition.
The disaster of Nongqawuse (1857) and the horrible results that followed
should be made to realistically indicate what will happen to the Bantu who
follow methods such as this.'"[43] Where Magona is circumspect about the

costs of struggle, Matshoba contrasts bantustan leaders' corruption with Nongqause's sincere desire to help her people.

Setting such incompatible invocations of the cattle killing against each other is the project of Zakes Mda's *The Heart of Redness*. Where Matshoba and Magona incorporate brief accounts of the cattle killing into broader narratives of apartheid and thus offer didactic assessments of the past's relationship to the present, Mda's novel depicts remembered prophecy as a process of contestation. The novel interweaves two distinct but intricately related narrative threads about conflicts between "Believers" and "Unbelievers": on the one hand, the emergence, execution, and immediate aftermath of the cattle-killing movement among the amaXhosa in the 1850s, focusing on a feud between fictional twin brothers in the coastal village of Qolorha where the prophecy was delivered; and on the other, conflicts between descendants of those brothers in the "new and democratic South Africa."

The Heart of Redness turns a century and a half of southern African history inside-out, with hardly a glance at the "Middle Generations": the years between the 1850s and the 1990s, the momentous decades of colonial and apartheid rule, as well as the epoch with which most southern African literature has been concerned.[44] The twentieth-century descendants of Believers and Unbelievers agree on almost nothing, but they both argue that "the sufferings of the Middle Generations" were the consequence of the cattle killing: the Unbelievers maintain that false prophecy misled superstitious people to destroy themselves, while the Believers lament that the prophecy failed because the original Unbelievers did not kill their cattle.[45] The leaders of the twentieth-century Believers and Unbelievers, Zim and Bhonco, trace every event in the present to either the other man or the actions of his ancestors. Their single-mindedness is the source of much humor, an odd achievement for a novel about the cattle killing.

The intricacy of the novel derives from deft shifts in setting and focalization that inventively juxtapose the 1850s and 1990s narratives and sympathetically depict both the wonders the Believers perceive as portents of an imminent resurrection and the Unbelievers' skeptical explanations of the same phenomena. The only characters presented without sympathy are those who have no use for the past, extremists—like Sir George Grey or Bhonco's daughter Xoliswa Ximiya, a haughty school principal—who see the Xhosa past as a source of barbarism or shame that must be eradicated or forgotten: a time of heathenness, or "the darkness of redness" (71). The similarity between the extreme views of Grey and Xoliswa Ximiya depends upon the novel's depiction of the dilemmas of the 1850s and 1990s in identical terms. The most visible contests between "civilization" (*ubugqobhoka*) and "backwardness" (*ubuqaba*) are sartorial and architectural (44). The twentieth-century debates about clothing styles and the shape of houses seem more petty than in the nineteenth-century missionary encounter because they have been decoupled from the imperial machinery of the civilizing mission: their metonymic associations with intangibles like "civilization" signify instead within a local interpretive community.[46] These conflicts subtly reveal that the failure of the cattle-killing prophecy, however horrific its aftermath, in no way realized Grey's vision of the "dawn of a new era" when the "ruder languages" and "antique laws and customs will molder into oblivion" (43, 206). Class and ideological divisions persist between what Xhosa historiography has termed "red people" and "school people," adherents of Xhosa tradition and the mission-educated elite, respectively. In the twentieth century, hostility to tradition comes from within the village community, most notably from Xoliswa Ximiya; the external pressure on the village is to commodify tradition to meet urban demands for "cultural tourism" and ethnic accessories. The novel frames the continuing tension between red people and school people as a love triangle involving Zim's daughter Qukezwa, Bhonco's daughter Xoliswa Ximiya, and a stranger named Camagu, a returned exile with an American Ph.D. in communications and development.[47]

As he finds himself drawn to daughters of both Believers and Unbelievers, Camagu also intervenes in the central conflict of the twentieth-century plot, which parallels the 1850s: the democratically elected central government has deemed as a project of "national importance" the commercial development of a seaside casino complex on the site where Nongqawuse received the prophecy. The twentieth-century Unbelievers "stand for" the development plan (they won't even use the word *believe*), arguing that it will bring jobs, electricity, and "civilization" to the village. Having internalized Grey's rhetoric, some nineteenth-century Christian Unbelievers also maintain that the loss of indigenous inhabitants' rights to land (and sea) is "a very small price to pay for the wonderful gift of civilization" (85). Bhonco's great-grandfather Twin-twin, however, who rejects Nongqawuse's prophecy without rejecting Xhosa tradition, identifies colonial theft as the actual motive behind this rationalization. The novel juxtaposes nineteenth- and twentieth-century projects of "civilization" (and land-grabbing) on offer from alien forces with the coercive support of the state. The prospect of tourists surfing and riding cable cars over the bay echoes the nineteenth-century prophecy's vision of armies of "new people" marching on the sea, as an increasingly disillusioned Bhonco points out. In the later conflict, it is the Unbelievers who commit to a seemingly disastrous course of action—a fraudulent prophecy.

Camagu gradually embraces the Believers' opposition to the project, and he is figured as a prophet of an alternative future for Qolorha. The beauty of Nongqawuse's valley, and his expertise in economic development, lead him to speak against the project's social and environmental costs and to point out the speciousness of its promised benefits: perhaps a few jobs and electrification, which should be a public, rather than privatized, imperative (a true project of "national importance"). In an "inspired moment," he recognizes that the history that is a source of shame and contention in the village could also secure its future: declaring the village a "national heritage site" would prohibit commercial development. The Unbelievers are predictably dismayed by Camagu's epiphany about the economic value of remembered prophecy, but Zim exclaims, "I knew that Nongqawuse would one day save this village!" (201). Camagu also recognizes that "the wonders of solar energy" could facilitate village electrification; this second epiphany—that in this "place of miracles," power can come "From the sun!"—links Camagu to the prophet Mlanjeni, described earlier in the novel as a worshipper of the sun, whose apotheosis comes when "the sun came down to touch his head, and went through his body until it was bright like the sun itself" (239–40; 15–16). This synthesis of the prophetic tradition of the red people with the epitome of school culture (Camagu's Ph.D. is explained as "the destination beyond which all knowledge ends" [97]) complements the novel's persistent analysis of the contradictions within and continuities between seeming dichotomies of past and present, Belief and Unbelief.

This terminology of "Believers" and "Unbelievers," and much more, are borrowed from *The Dead Will Arise: Nongqawuse and the Great Xhosa Cattle-Killing Movement of 1856–7*, in which J. B. Peires seeks the truth about the cattle killing behind distortions in both the colonial archive and Xhosa tradition. Mda's indebtedness to Peires, which he acknowledges in the novel's dedication, raises questions about the fictionalization of history and the fictiveness of historiography that are more diffuse, but no less important, than Magona's vicarious address to the mother of Amy Biehl. Mda borrows heavily and directly from Peires, interweaving Peires's own words with material Peires quotes from archival sources.[48] Peires's speculations about the biographies of Mhlakaza and Nongqawuse have been challenged by several historians, but Mda fleshes out these assertions.[49] To admit the extent of Mda's borrowing is not to overlook his achievement in setting this material in motion within the novel's intricate structure. Without Peires's history, however, Mda would have written a very different fiction or, perhaps, no fiction at all.[50]

Mda's indebtedness to Peires has particular significance in the context of the cattle killing and its aftermath and afterlives. We have seen earlier crossfertilizations among historical and literary texts, as in Dhlomo's use of Brownlee's *Reminiscences* or J. H. Soga's appropriation of Waters's Nongqawuse play. These intertextual relationships allegorize the structure of prophecy, raising important questions about the relationship between millennial visions and literary imagination, between inspiration and reinscription, and between endtime and narrative closure. A prophet's authority derives from what speaks through her, and Mda teases out the complexities of prophecy's reception in a colonial context. He uses identical imagery in depicting the visions and actions of Khoi, Xhosa, and Judeo-Christian prophets, thereby emphasizing resonances among them that complicate, without rejecting, the notion that cattle-killing prophecies drew on Christian ideas of resurrection promulgated by European missionaries. The suspicions that prophets tend to elicit—that they might be demonically, rather than divinely, inspired or that they shape their own interpretations of the messages they convey—are intensified in Twin-twin's growing suspicion that Grey was behind Nongqawuse's vision, and in the depiction of Mhlakaza as interested interpreter of Nongqawuse's inspired message. Ultimately, however, it is Peires's history that in large part inspires Mda's fiction, Peires's scholarship and analysis that often speak through Mda's characters.[51]

One of the problems with Mda's reliance on Peires lies in Peires's vexed relationship to his own work. In 1990, the year after the publication of *The Dead Will Arise*, Peires published an essay that weighed his book against competing versions of the past. While Peires stood by his archival work, he dismissed most of it as so much scholarly "detail" insignificant in the face of "important truths" in Xhosa versions of the past: "[T]he Xhosa don't need white academics to give them a usable past. They already have one. . . . South Africa in the 1980s cannot afford the luxury of an irrelevant history."[52] Peires's partial retraction reflects pressures of relevance similar to those at stake in late-apartheid literary-critical discourse. Mda's novel, however, ignores Peires's subjection of his scholarly authority to the prerogatives of the antiapartheid struggle. In making extensive use of Peires's version of the Xhosa past, does Mda's post-1994 fictional appropriation of this historiography give it a greater weight of truth?

The Heart of Redness has been reinscribed into official discourse, featured in enthusiastic citations by at least two South African politicians. In a May 2002 speech, Minister of Environmental Affairs and Tourism Valli Moosa read aloud the episode of the meeting with the casino development representatives, identifying in Camagu's desire for a socially and environmentally beneficial tourism "the universal challenge of sustainable development faced by humanity today."[53] The year before, at a speech in Moscow intended to assuage Russian concerns about South Africa's neoliberal economic orientation, Minister of Public Enterprises Jeff Radebe read the novel's depiction of nineteenth-century expectations for "black" Russian saviors.[54] The role of Russians in 1850s Xhosa prophecies (perhaps a surprise to the Moscow audience) was the first example of Russian contributions to antiimperialism in South Africa, according to Radebe. Mda's text thus stands ironically between a white historian's abnegation of his scholarly authority and black officials' augmentation of their political authority through citation of a polyphonic, magical-realist novel. The novel's unsparing critique of the self-servingness behind the talk of "black empowerment" and "national interest" spouted by "Aristocrats of the Revolution" and their "Club of Sycophants" ironizes such appropriations (33).[55]

Among scholars, Peires's qualification of the relevance of his work underscored, rather than resolved, methodological and ideological questions about the relationship between the protocols of academic historiography and the role of literacy in colonial conquest. Peires's critics have argued that his aim to discern "the truth" behind and between incompatible colonial and Xhosa versions of the past actually replicates the epistemological violence of nineteenth-century textualization in the eastern Cape, particularly when he challenges the Xhosa notion that Sir George Grey instigated the cattle-killing prophecy. While insisting that no version of the past is politically inviolate, Adam Ashforth considers the politics of representation, "the ambiguity of writing about domination in a context where the power to encode the past in writing is itself both a product of domination and form of domination."[56] He asks, "What would the story look like if Peires . . . constructed a text in which Xhosa ways of speaking of their past were placed in dialogue with the account produced according to Western academic conventions of research and writing premised upon equality rather than subordinating one kind of storying of the past to the truth of another?" (587).

We might be tempted to read *The Heart of Redness* as an answer to Ashforth's question: it places Xhosa ways of storying the past in dialogue with *each other*. In addition to its articulation of the central dispute between the Believers and Unbelievers, the novel depicts forms of memory outside of textuality—in Zim's joyous days under the fig tree planted by Twin's progeny, in Qukezwa's songs, and in the trance dances practiced by Bhonco's cult of Unbelievers, as I discuss below. Given the role of literacy as a technology of transformation underwriting the British civilizing mission in kwaXhosa at the time of the cattle killing, Mda's attention to nontextual memory emphasizes the incompleteness of literacy's conquest of consciousness.[57] But in representing aspects of his characters' experience that elude the processes, products, and forms of domination to which Ashforth calls our attention, the novel's reliance on *The Dead Will Arise* consolidates the authority of written scholarly history by making it an important foundation of its characters' "speaking their past." These characters are not so much in dialogue with scholarly history as they are determined by it: to a great extent, Peires's historiography constitutes their nontextual memories.

OTHERWORLDS AND UNFAILURE: THE JOYS OF BELIEF AND THE POLITICS OF MOURNING

Despite the troubling implications of Mda's use of Peires's history, the novel suggests that what can be known about the past and what it means are open to contest. In asking whether "the prophets have failed us" or "we have failed them" (254), Mda's characters deconstruct the question: which us? what does it mean to fail? what if the prophets were pawns of Sir George Grey? Understanding the novel's problematic investment in academic historiography is important not least because of its multilayered interest in the temporal assumptions underwriting colonialism and modernity. What makes *The Heart of Redness* more than a novelization of Peires's history is its engagement with questions of time; Mda's juxtaposition of competing ethics of retrospection destabilizes the common-sense understandings of temporality—the relationships among past, present, and future—that structure the act of memory.

Neither Mda's imbrication of nineteenth- and twentieth-century plots nor his staging of Believers' and Unbelievers' disputes over "redness" and "civilization" can be read as a simple dichotomy between tradition and modernity. Camagu's worldliness reveals Xoliswa Ximiya's enthusiasm for "civilization" to be based on superficial, dated notions of "what she *imagines* to be *western* civilization" (248; emphasis added).[58] Zim's daughter Qukezwa, by contrast, espouses a peculiar combination of nativism and millennial logic that is undeniably progressive. Summoned before Chief Xikixa's *inkundla* for chopping down trees, she defiantly explains that she kills invasive trees that steal water from indigenous species (216).[59] In confronting the chief's court, Qukezwa also rejects "the old law": coercive, invented, customary law that "weighed heavily on our shoulders during the sufferings of the Middle Generations. In the new South Africa where there is no discrimination, it does not work" (213).[60] Qukezwa may be the "red woman" whose "school woman" counterpart is Xoliswa Ximiya, yet she lives the most productive aspects of traditions (including tribal democracy) whose repressive appropriations she rejects as inimical to a "new South Africa." She embodies not only the living tradition of her Xhosa forefathers but also the tradition of her Khoikhoi foremother, Qukezwa, wife of the Believer, Twin, who led him and Twin-twin away from the lungsickness of the interior toward the coastal village of Qolorha. The first Qukezwa rebukes her husband when he invokes the ancestors to justify his assault on his Unbelieving brother's cattle: "You are not doing it for the dead. You are doing it for the living" (109). Both Qukezwas denounce invocations of the past that seek to disguise self-interest.

As with Xoliswa Ximiya and Qukezwa, Camagu's character blurs any reductively drawn line between tradition and modernity. He attempts to avoid aligning with Believers or Unbelievers: his ancestors are not involved in their feud. The incident that crystallizes his thinking is the appearance of a snake in his hotel room, which Camagu understands to be Majola, totem of his Mpondomise clan.[61] This auspicious visitation makes him rethink his decision to leave South Africa in search of employment—a "second exile" (27)—and he subsequently settles in Qolorha, forms cottage industry cooperatives with village women, intervenes in the tourism debate, and marries Qukezwa. When the inhabitants of Qolorha learn that Camagu is enthusiastic about Majola's visitation, they are pleasantly surprised (except Xoliswa Ximiya, who is horrified) that this cosmopolitan man has "such respect for the customs of his people" (99).[62]

What is at stake in Mda's blurring of lines between tradition and modernity is a challenge to the hegemonic notions of time and historical change that undergird the civilizing mission: the notion, for example, that literacy inevitably replaces orality. This example is particularly fraught because the novel's dialogism and attention to nontextual epistemologies and memories convey the contemporary vitality of orality, at the same time that its form (a novel in English) and content (derived from Peires's scholarly history) are implicated in the universalist aspiration of civilization-as-literacy. Sir George Grey's unfulfilled vision that Xhosa customs would be replaced by European "civilization" epitomizes what Dipesh Chakrabarty calls the "transition narrative" of "development, modernization, and capitalism," which assumes "that it is always possible to assign people, places, and objects to a naturally existing, continuous flow of historical time."[63] The act of mapping people onto time is not innocent or neutral: historicism "posited historical time as a measure of the cultural distance . . . that was assumed to exist between the West and the non-West. In the colonies, it legitimated the idea of civilization" (7). Civilization is a developmental process by which the non-West becomes (often by force) like the West; developmentalism, like narratives, is structured around "the passage of time" (23).

The historicist logic of a progress narrative holds that orality plus time equals literacy, redness plus time equals civilization. The curious narrative structure of *The Heart of Redness,* juxtaposing two chronotopes and eliding the epoch of the Middle Generations, works against this conception of time as an addend in a simple equation; the novel's temporality challenges the shared tendency of narrative, development, and historicism to fill in the blanks between moments in time, "telling the sequence of events like the beads of a rosary."[64] The reduplication of the names Qukezwa, Heitsi, Twin, Xikixa, and John Dalton for characters in the nineteenth- and twentieth-century plots makes the novel a difficult read, but this ambiguity performs the simultaneous inextricability and alterity of past and present that allow us to imagine afterlives as a protean alternative to the linearity of historicism.

In its narrative structure and attention to relationships with the past, *The Heart of Redness* depicts what Chakrabarty calls "heterotemporality," "a plurality of times existing together, a disjuncture of the present with itself" (95, 109). Both Zim and Bhonco live an ethics of retrospection; they believe that the past not only causes and makes intelligible the present but also demands commemoration. Zim spends joyous days under the fig tree planted by his great-grandfather Twin's progeny, listening to birds who speak the language of the spirits; he adopts what he calls a "new" practice among the nineteenth-century Believers as if it had just been invented (and just after we read of its invention in the nineteenth-century narrative thread). In contrast to Zim's direct access to the past, Bhonco must create rituals of mourning; although his great-grandfather Twin-twin "elevated unbelieving to the heights of a religion," he died before he could invent a ritual that would "automatically have become the cord that connected [later Unbelievers] to the world of the forebears" (260). Thus Bhonco must borrow a dance from the abaThwa (also known as the San people, or Bushmen) that induces a trance that takes the Unbelievers back "to the world of the ancestors. Not the Otherworld where the ancestors live today. Not the world that lives parallel to our world. But to this world when it still belonged to them" (73).

This distinction between the historical past—the time in which the ancestors lived their lives—and the Otherworld—where they live today—indicates the novel's particular inflection of heterotemporality. The existence of this parallel space/time from which ancestors intervene in the present implies a notion of social time and memory in which the past can never really be complete. While the novel's dialogue between Xhosa past and present is innovative, it's worth noting that Mda does not depict the thoughts and actions of ancestors in the Otherworld.[65] Rather, we see characters in the nineteenth- and twentieth-century plots trying to discern the ancestors' desires, even as the nineteenth-century characters also function as inscrutable ancestors of the twentieth-century characters. The novel's narrative structure, in other words, is not as radical as its view of time might allow.

The ancestors' vigilance can be comforting, but for Bhonco the presence of the past is also disturbing. His rituals of Unbelief become increasingly inadequate, and Camagu's alliances with Believers lead Bhonco to conclude that, rather than "coming right" (the idiom of restoration in Xhosa prophecies), the time after the Middle Generations will be a reversion to "darkness," a time out of joint. Bhonco is particularly undone when the abaThwa come to take their dance back. Cultural appropriations in the novel are doggedly literal, as are the scars on Bhonco's back, which appear in each generation after Twin-twin is whipped for defending his wife from charges of witchcraft. The scars itch when Twin-twin and Bhonco are exercised by the Believers or perplexed by the contradictions of Unbelief; Twin-twin's scars "go wild" when he sees the horrific aftermath of the cattle killing that he betrayed his brother to prevent. Previously afflicting only male descendants, the scars appear on Xoliswa Ximiya's "civilized body" just before she "leaves this heart of redness" (261).

These "scars of history" literalize and somatize the presence of the past. They function as "earlier bodies [that] emerge in the Now and send a bit of prehistoric life into it," as Ernst Bloch wrote of "nonsynchronous contradictions."[66] Bloch observed (in 1932) that "not all people exist in the same Now"; his heterotemporal notion of nonsynchronism examined the appeal of Nazism, which harnessed the "pent-up anger" of an "uncompleted past" with the promise of "nothing less than new life, despite its looking to the old" (31, 22).[67] This account of Nazism as an ambivalent, retrospective future projection bears a certain similarity to conventional analyses of millenarian movements; Bloch's analysis of the revolutionary potential of nonsynchronous and synchronous contradictions, on the other hand, helps to illuminate Mda's treatment of the cattle killing. Nonsynchronous contradictions represent an "incomplete past," while synchronous contradictions are an "impeded future." Nonsynchronous contradictions are both subjective and objective, involving both affective rage and "unsurmounted remnants of older economic being." Reactionary rather than revolutionary in tendency, they cannot themselves "precipitate a change into a new quality" (29, 33).

Such retrograde impulses erupt in *The Heart of Redness* when Bhonco suddenly exchanges mourning for vengeance: he stabs the trader John Dalton, descendant of the nineteenth-century soldier-turned-trader John Dalton, who beheaded Twin and Twin-twin's father Xikixa. When Bhonco takes up Twin-twin's vow to avenge this atrocity, he claims that the feud between the Believers and Unbelievers cannot be resolved—the past cannot be complete—while they remain under the compromised vigilance of a headless ancestor. "Only then will things come right," Bhonco concludes (273). The novel is structured around the interpenetrations of what Bloch would call different Nows. In Bhonco's attack on John Dalton, violence erupts into what had been a bloodless, often humorous conflict. This historically fraught attack represents a shift from pious mourning to aggressive melancholia, from working-through to acting-out.[68] As with the dance and the scars, Bhonco's attack is a literalization, in this case of the idea that "memory is being used to torment [whites] for the sins of their fathers. Sins committed in good faith." Characteristically, the novel juxtaposes the whites' sense of memory used as a weapon with a hegemonic "insistence" after the Middle Generations not only to forget the past but to deny it: "*It did not happen. It did not happen. It did not happen*" (137, emphasis in the original).

The Believers have a more productive relationship to heterotemporality and the nonsynchronous, as we see in Zim's vigil for the Russians. Zim stands at a seaside cliff, watching for the Russian deliverers expected by the nineteenth-century Believers; he knows they won't appear, "but he waits for them still, in memory of those who waited in vain." Zim understands that while the Russians of the 1850s (who challenged the British in the Crimean war) were "black and were the reincarnation of amaXhosa warriors. . . . [T]oday's Russians are white people" (176). Zim reads the Cold War and its pressures upon apartheid-era South Africa in terms of earlier hopes invested in "Russians":

> [T]he spirit of the ancestors continues to direct their sympathies. That is why they fought the English. That is why all those who benefited from the sufferings of the Middle Generations hated them. That is why they armed and trained those sons and daughters of the nation to bring to an end the sufferings of the Middle Generations.
>
> It is with a sense of pride that he stands on the hill. That he pines. That he waits for the Russians even though he knows they will not come. They have already come in a guise that no Believer expected. They came in the bodies of those who fought to free the Middle Generations. (176–77)

Zim sees the afterlife of the cattle-killing prophecy in the *incarnation* of Russians who aided the antiapartheid struggle. He commemorates the first Believers' disappointment, while he recognizes the prophecy's *unfailure* in this fulfillment that exceeds (temporally and substantially) its adherents' expectations. The description of Zim's vigil resonates with Jacques Derrida's account of anticipating an unknowable future: "Awaiting what one does not expect yet or any longer . . . [M]essianic opening . . . to her or to him for whom one must leave an empty place, always, in memory of the hope."[69] In the novel, Zim's vigil marks not only "messianic opening" to the future but also unrecognized fulfillment within the present.

Unfailure is not merely a matter of patience (wait long enough, and the prophecy will be fulfilled) but rather a radical patience that keeps past dreams alive as dynamic inspiration for future movements. In Bloch's terms, unfailure recognizes that the "late ripening of what is actually incomplete in the past" (i.e., the nonsynchronous) can "turn into a new quality" only by "an alliance, which liberates the still *possible future* from the *past* only by putting both in the present" (33, emphasis in the original). Unfailure realizes and confounds prophetic expectations by incorporating present (and unforeseen) circumstances into the structure of anticipation. Camagu comes to Qolorha in pursuit of a woman named NomaRussia; seeking fulfillment in the "mother of Russia," Camagu finds something else entirely.

Drawn almost inexplicably from Johannesburg to Qolorha, Camagu functions as a modest and local fulfillment of Twin's messianic desire for a prophet, like the Khoikhoi prophet Heitsi Eibib, "who will save the Xhosa people" (75).[70] His integration into Qolorha reverses the disappointment of his return from apartheid-era exile, depicted in a biting critique of the hypocritical black elite and their hollow rhetoric of "black empowerment" (33). The end of the apartheid state is no millennial restoration for Mda, but unlike Magona's dystopic view, Camagu finds utopian promise in a different kind of exile from the nation-state: within the local scale of the village, Camagu envisions a future where recalibrated dreams of liberation might be realized.[71] His village collectives exploit the appeal of failed prophecy in order to secure, at least temporarily, the village's control over its own future in the face of a fraudulent prophecy of "national" development. Zim's understanding of Russian solidarity as the unfailure of Nongqawuse's vision suggests that the remembered prophecy of the cattle killing might be realized as prophetic memory of liberation at the millennium. In Bloch's terms, Camagu and Zim recognize the value of the nonsynchronous "not in gilded pasts, but in the actual heritage of its end in the Now . . . that gains *additional revolutionary force* from the *incomplete* wealth of the past," putting to use the "still subversive and utopian contents in the relations of people to people and nature, which are not past because they were never quite attained" (38). Camagu's vision of a future for Qolorha's past would allow the community to actualize Zim's idiosyncratic understanding of unfailed prophecy. The novel ends, however, with a characteristic qualification, as Camagu's wife Qukezwa walks on the shore with their son Heitsi, who, despite his name, is not interested in "the business of saving his people" (277).[72]

The very existence of Camagu's and Qukezwa's son Heitsi, however, reflects the potential fecundity of the nonsynchronous. Heitsi is conceived—at least in narratological terms—when Qukezwa's split-toned song of "many colors" that sounds "as if a whole choir lives in her mouth" holds Camagu "spellbound" and causes him to ejaculate in his pants (152). Like Mandisa in

Mother to Mother, Qukezwa is inspected by the elders, who find that hers will be a virgin birth. Here the emphasis is on the creation rather than destruction of possibility, for her synesthetic song is a figure for and diegetic mechanism within the novel's narrative structure. Qukezwa's split-toned singing (*umngqokolo*) represents a stubborn refusal to forget that is simultaneously conservative and generative (Camagu thinks of her as the "guardian of a dying tradition"); it demonstrates the productivity of heterotemporality.

In her instructive analysis of *The Heart of Redness,* Meg Samuelson contends that the patriarchal, Christian overtones of virgin birth collapse the novel's radical temporality into nationalist teleology and displace the cattle killing's dynamic of female authorship, so that women create only through their reproductive bodies.[73] This reading, however, overlooks the importance of Qukezwa's singing (itself an important form of female authorship), which, far from undoing the novel's heterotemporality, offers its fullest expression. At the novel's end, Qukezwa walks on the shore with Heitsi, and she "fills the valley with her many voices. . . . Colors of gore. Colors of today and of yesterday" (275, 271). Her song structures this final chapter's resolution of each character's narrative trajectory; the song is a final variation on the dreams and dances that serve as diegetic links in the narrative's shifts between chronotopes. Qukezwa's final song is the most complex of these links, for it represents both chronotopes simultaneously rather than moving between them: it activates a world of memory that is immediately narrated as original experience. Qukezwa sings (of) Grey's "pacification" of Xhosaland; (of) Nongqawuse under the care of a British major's wife; (of) Twin's famished wife Qukezwa walking on the shore with her son Heitsi. She sings (of) each of these things, as if her song *creates* these lives and lifeworlds rather than merely *representing* them: "fill[ing] the valley." These two transitive modes of singing suggest that an "immaculate" (but actually rather messy) conception is a relatively simple achievement for a song that generates entire worlds.[74] The two Qukezwas—and their different Nows—merge in her/their song of many voices, itself a figure for the novel's heterotemporality. Qukezwa's song animates scenes drawn from Peires's history, yet it enacts an alchemic, rather than arithmetic, afterlife in which resuscitated histories and borrowed voices both make the past present and generate something utterly new.

Unlike other writers who invoke the cattle killing, Mda eschews a prophetic stance; his retrospective ethics maintains a radical openness not only to the content of the past, but also to its modes of conjuncture with the contested present. Beyond this formal distinction from texts like Magona's or Matshoba's is a crucial historical difference. In a reversal of postmodern versions of apocalypse, the end of apartheid, imagined for decades in apocalyptic terms, was a new beginning (however modest) without a cataclysmic end.[75] Magona's novel describes a para-apocalyptic situation in which a cycle of cataclysm recurs without renewal. Mda writes from the other side of the interregnum, beyond Plaatje's aberrational present. By no means do Believers and Unbelievers of the new millennium inhabit an *acolonial* world, but the novel stages the end of apartheid as an unfailure of some of the hopes invested in Nongqawuse's prophecy. It ends not with fulfilled prophecy or narrative closure but with tenuous solutions cognizant of their own provisionality—Camagu knows the casino development could resume any time, and both Qukezwas worry that Heitsi's aversion to the sea will mean that he will be unable to subsist if something happens to her or to save his people if something happens to them. The novel reveals how heterotemporal imaginings are both aesthetically rich and experientially fraught, following a logic of proliferation rather than resolution. Although the novel holds that pasts are abusable as well as usable, to live utterly without a past is as unthinkable as to live utterly within one; the novel's openness to the vitality of incomplete pasts leads us to imagine the present as unfinished as well.

REMEMBERING THE END

The cattle-killing prophecy in *The Heart of Redness* is at once failed and unfailed; it unites and revitalizes a community, but it also turns brother against brother in a feud that does not die with them. This ambivalence about waking up with yesterday's anger (to paraphrase Twin-twin's praise name) signals the complexity of afterlives, of thinking life after an end (212). An impassioned refusal to forget can be dangerous, as for Bhonco in a moment of violent extremity, yet it may also help, in Ndebele's words, to "free the entire social imagination of the oppressed from the laws of perception that have characterised apartheid society."[76] In 1991, Ndebele feared that the price of a premature settlement might be paid in memory (or its suppression):

> But we have to cry out when the past is being deliberately forgotten in order to ensure that what was gained by it can . . . now be enjoyed without compunction. . . . The past, no matter how horrible it has been, can

redeem us. It can be the moral foundation on which to build the pillars of the future. . . .

The past is knocking constantly on the doors of our perceptions,[77] refusing to be forgotten, because it is deeply embedded in the present. To neglect it [at] this most crucial of moments in our history is to postpone the future. (155, 158)

In order to engage the future, to "pluck the apple," the past must be confronted before it can be put to work or to rest. These questions have only become more salient since the early 1990s: what happens when not only the apartheid past, but also the struggle, is forgotten? What would Sindiwe Magona make of the kwaito generation, postmillennial youth weary of hearing their elders reminisce about the struggle?[78] Even former comrades "may no longer be able to imagine themselves symbolically united to a revolutionary ideal or action."[79] As I argued in chapter 3, Matshoba's "Three Days in the Land of a Dying Illusion" recovers a lost spirit of anticolonial resistance; the remoteness of the insurgent 1970s in turn suggests that reading Matshoba's fiction retrospectively, nearly a generation removed from the democratic transition, might induce anti-imperialist nostalgia, a longing for the incandescent hopes and luminous dreams of liberation that fueled decolonization struggles.[80]

Thinking beyond the end of the cattle killing is a productive analogue for thinking beyond the end of apartheid precisely because of the ambivalence and slipperiness of both ends: while one might readily assent to Ndebele's protest against willful forgetting, "the past" is hardly a determinate object that can be retrieved, discarded, or held closely, as Mda's novel demonstrates with such tenderness. The tensions between end and ending—*telos* and *terminus*—are at play in both events. The end that motivated the cattle killing did not come to pass in the 1857 aftermath, whether one conceives of that aim as millennial renewal, anticolonial revolt, or duplicitous conquest. Yet enormous changes did sweep kwaXhosa from 1857: the ending was a beginning—but of what? defeat? civilization? nationalism? liberation? The recuperations of the cattle killing examined in *Bulletproof* demonstrate that while ruptures between moments in time can seem self-evident, ideas about just what changed so irrevocably, why, and what it means, are wildly divergent. To imagine the cattle killing as a beginning is also complicated by its irredeemable costs in human suffering and disenfranchisement, costs both immediate and enduring.

The cattle killing's vexed temporality—its entanglement of retrospection and anticipation, and the potential for haunting by its unrealized visions of liberation—offers a timely tension for South Africa at the millennium. The vision that drove the movement, and the aftermath of its doom, are an incomplete past that can be activated in the present. In its afterlife, the cattle-killing prophecy offers a utopian surplus—a still dynamic remnant of undischarged anticipation that can be put to work. Magona's and Mda's narratives demonstrate, however, how difficult it can be to "pluck" the fruit of revolution even when its Now has arrived. The gulf between the cattle killing's vision and its aftermath makes clear that if an incomplete past is to transform the present, it must be understood as having a contradictory, doubled relationship to the present, as I explain below.

Here we return to the problem from Walter Benjamin I posed at the beginning of this chapter. Benjamin rejects the historicist method of those who "wish to relive an era": they "blot out everything they know about the later course of history."[81] Benjamin assumes that the motive for such willed forgetting is empathy with victors in the past, whose heirs are rulers in the present. I have argued, however, for an ethics of retrospection that rejects Benjamin's rejection of historical amnesia; I propose this strategic forgetting of historical aftermaths out of solidarity with Benjamin's conviction that historical materialism can grasp "a revolutionary chance in the fight for the oppressed past," "fanning the spark of hope in the past . . . [because] *even the dead* will not be safe from the enemy if he wins" (263, 255, emphasis in the original). The very impossibility of forgetting the later course of history, an impossibility that is both cognitive and ethical, necessitates a moment of hesitation, a glimpse of the past freed from anticipatory haunting by knowledge of what came after. This notion of anticipatory haunting approximates Peter Brooks's account of the temporality of reading, whose "anticipation of retrospection" in medias res looks forward to the end of the narrative as a future perfect when it will have made sense. I am arguing for the value of a "'dilatory space'—the space of suspense," in which reading has not yet reached the narrative end that makes sense of what comes before.[82] (Thus I am outlining as a *reading practice* a historical bracketing that resembles the strange suspense generated by figuration in nineteenth-century cattle-killing narratives.)[83] To isolate the past from its subsequences, while remaining aware of subsequence, not only shatters illusions that particular outcomes were inevitable but also reanimates hopes of the dead that might otherwise die with them.

It is all too easy to confuse the process of historical change for a narrative whose ending is always-already written, a historicist error that Benjamin would surely condemn. The most compelling retrospective treatments of the cattle killing imagine, however briefly or cynically, what it would be to believe that the dead would rise, temporarily suspending the burden (or relief) of the knowledge that they did not. It is the doubled perspective of this moment of hope held against knowledge of the aftermath that has made the cattle killing such a compelling repository of images for articulating later desires. A doubled relationship to the past, cognizant of but not determined by aftermaths and outcomes, can also work against the temptation to read the antiapartheid struggle within a retrospective teleology that assumes the inevitability of its democratic resolution. This retrospective inevitability differs from the inevitability asserted rhetorically *during* the struggle: Plaatje's faith in a God who has never failed, the South African equivalent of "we shall overcome." The distinction between anticipatory and retrospective inevitability is not merely the difference between faith and hindsight. Benjamin's notion of a "revolutionary chance in the fight for the oppressed past" insists on remembering hopes and fears that have not been realized; the danger of retrospective inevitability is that it has no place for things without an analogue or subsequence in the present, so that incomplete pasts are not only unrealized, but also forgotten and thus unthinkable.[84] Reading texts of the 1980s decade of emergency against the ambivalences of the 1990s decade of emergence, Anthony O'Brien argues that the earlier demand for radical democracy can work against the foreclosures of the historical settlement.[85] Such an interpretive practice takes on the gap between anticipatory and retrospective inevitability, recovering a sense of what remains undone, unrealized, and even disavowed amid the transformations since the 1980s.

An acolonial world is not on offer, and no prophecy or poem will show the way to one. How can one reconcile the antiapartheid aspirations expressed in the Freedom Charter with the fact that one cannot now, fifteen years after the election of Nelson Mandela, write "the end of apartheid" without qualification? Apartheid is (and perhaps always was) a nonsynchronous contradiction of the present; "confusing cobwebs of the past" obscure clarity about endings and beginnings.[86] This heterotemporal predicament frustrates global hopes invested in South Africa as a chance to get decolonization right. At the intersection of postcolonial and globalization studies, the ambivalence of a doubled historical perspective might inform continuing debates about whether imagining community within the nation form is a vehicle to modernity or a vestigial remnant leading only back toward the past: a postmillennial, postcolonial critique might thus reclaim the drawing of discursive lines between (and rules of engagement with) "freedom fighter" and "terrorist." Reading retrospectively while holding a sense of inevitability in abeyance—either inevitable devastation, or inevitable liberation—might recover modes of dreaming difference that would transform remembered prophecies of acolonial restoration into prophetic memories of postcolonial justice.

CODA:
NOTES ON HETEROTEMPORALITY AND THE OTHER

If one cannot yet write "the end of apartheid" without qualification, then to speak of the "postapartheid" era overlooks the continuing legacies of apartheid. Loren Kruger provocatively describes the present as a "post-antiapartheid period" in which "the consequences of the enforced poverty and displacement of the majority are pressing, while the moral conviction and commitment of antiapartheid solidarity have waned, and in their place has come postcolonial uneven development, which has created a new black elite but not eased the lives of the black majority."[87] At stake in such formulations is a heterotemporal understanding that the "apartheid past" is not so easily surmounted. Discourses of heterotemporality have proliferated in this liminal period, addressing nonsynchronous contradictions within South Africa and its place in the world: the temporality of South Africa's twentieth-century passage into and out of official racialism "does not synchronise with that of other civil communities."[88] Even if heterotemporality can elucidate the contradictions of contemporary South Africa, the role of temporality in the history of colonialism obliges us to proceed with caution.

The single, universal timescale associated with modernity—Benjamin's "homogeneous, empty time"—is itself a product of European global exploration and colonial conquest. However paradoxically, this universal time of modernity created a ground of global simultaneity from which perceived local noncontemporaneities were seen to deviate, laying the ground for Europeans' identification of lifeworlds they "discovered" as primitive and therefore anachronous.[89] The distinction between heterotemporality and anachronism is subtle, but crucial: the label of anachronism "convert[s] objects, institutions, and practices with which we have lived relationships into relics of other times" and thus "stops us from confronting the problem of the temporal heterogeneity of the 'now.'"[90] This consequence of anachronism is evident in the pervasive denial by Europeans of coevalness—recognition of existing in the same time—to Others among them; geographical distinctions and cultural differences are endlessly transformed, in colonial epistemology, into temporal distances, so that, for example, Africa becomes the past of Europe.[91]

An instructive example of the difficulty of distinguishing between heterotemporality and anachronism appears in Bloch's discussions of the nonsynchronous. In a remarkable passage in "Nonsynchronism and the Obligation to its Dialectics," Bloch writes,

> The ignorance of the white-collar worker as he searches for past levels of consciousness, transcendence in the past, increases to an orgiastic hatred of reason, to a "chthonism," in which there are berserk people and images of the cross, in which indeed—with a nonsynchronism that verges on extraterritoriality—Negro drums rumble and central Africa rises up.[92]

This description of nonsynchronism reverses the allochronic move in which geographic distance becomes temporal difference: the African heart of darkness erupts in the nonsynchronous German present, a strange textual moment and movement we might take as a symptom in Bloch's thought of the epistemological collusion between imperialism and anachronism. Elsewhere, however, Bloch denounces the conscious *deployment* of contrived notions of primitivism by reactionary European movements. In an 1932 essay on *Trader Horn*, the 1931 MGM adventure film that was the first feature film to be shot in Africa, Bloch argues that such primitivism "allows the unemployed here at home to feel thankful that they are living in an enlightened age," at the same time that the "presuppositions" that feed that "'dark-continent' archetype" also facilitate the "seductions of reaction" in Europe, offering the "new masks and fetishes. . . . [of] blood and race."[93] Moving pictures of a purportedly primeval world are a technological miracle that "carries many a changed consciousness directly away from the Enlightenment. Not simply into the lands far beyond Turkey, but into the actual barbarism here at home" (424).[94] The African "irrationalism" featured in *Trader Horn* is itself a "selected and embellished remnant" of the past—in other words, a nonsynchronous and *contrived* rendering of contemporary

Africa (425). In "Nonsynchronism," Bloch might seem to invoke Africa as an essential signifier of quintessential nonsynchronousness: eternal Africa as exotic, spatiotemporal index of European development. But Bloch's discussion in "Trader Horn in Africa" allows us to see the sudden "rising up" of the African primitive in his seminal discussion of nonsynchronism (published the same year) as part of an indictment of appropriative, reactionary primitivism rather than an uncritical deployment of it.

"Nonsynchronism," and not "Trader Horn," however, is where readers interested in the nonsynchronous will likely turn, and thus Bloch's scattered remarks about Africa offer a cautionary tale about the fine line—and the profound stakes—that distinguish anachronism from heterotemporality. Bloch writes elsewhere that *Verfremdung* (aesthetic defamiliarization) "is especially likely to occur when a detour is taken into the exotic, or . . . turns the present into a historical moment or the past into a contemporary one."[95] The "extraterritoriality" of Bloch's African examples demonstrates that the estrangements of spatiotemporal exoticism can offer either archaic visions of blood and night or the utopian glimpse of a red dawn. When power allows the privileging of one's own time as the Now, nonsynchronous thinking can be a trap.

Nonetheless, awareness of heterotemporality—a recognition of the many Nows within a Now, and the many pasts behind these presents—might be useful in thinking beyond the first versions of a "new South Africa." The potential of heterotemporality is evident in a much-cited anecdote from the cusp days of 1994, when a democratic parliament heard praises of President Mandela offered by a Xhosa *imbongi*. The response of Martha Olckers (Western Cape Minister for Education and Culture and National Party member) is telling: "'In spite of good intentions one can hurt people. I mean a praise-singer in parliament *and* dressed the way he is. And clapping and ululating. It used to be a very dignified place and this is a terrible culture shock for us.'"[96] The loss of a dignified past registers for her at the same moment that the *imbongi* hails the restoration of Xhosa democratic traditions. Her words turn against themselves, pressured by (post)colonial ironies of the politics of dress, the fall from dignity to indignity, the invasion of sacred space. One hears echoes of Sol Plaatje: the shock of having stepped into parliament and found oneself alien in the land of one's legislative berth. One aberrational present closes as another opens; Plaatje's articulation of the moment of native alienation might also be seen as a cause of Olckers's.

Benjamin reminds us that shock is a mechanism for heading off permanent trauma;[97] however ungracious and culturally insensitive the culture minister's admission may have been, perhaps tremors of "culture shock" such as these serve to ward off a national trauma such as the parliament ceasing to function. Indeed, Olckers insisted that her remarks be published; although "her manner was almost confrontational," she spoke of the need for adjustment and tolerance. Just below the profile of Olckers in *The Argus* appears a profile of Zolani Mkira, one of the *iimbongi* chosen to perform at the opening of parliament. Mkira is "a poet of the nation and not just of a tribe" who must "be found credible by the community" and "becomes [its] voice."[98] The barely veiled tension between these two profiles reveals the difficulty of reimagining a shared community: Olckers rejects the idea that Mkira speaks for her. It might be possible to write, following Benjamin, that the state of culture shock in which South Africans live is not the exception but the rule, a negative definition of the nation that captures the experience of living heterotemporality. The liberatory potential of nonsynchronousness inheres in a willingness to embrace the Now in all of its heterotemporal complexities, in order to redeem the many dreams of newness in another South Africa.

CHAPTER FIVE

ANCESTORS WITHOUT BORDERS

The Cattle Killing as Global Reimaginary

The tradition of all the dead generations weighs like a nightmare on the brains of
the living. . . . Let the dead bury their dead.

KARL MARX, *THE EIGHTEENTH BRUMAIRE OF LOUIS NAPOLEON*

We know that the dead are mighty rulers: we may be surprised to learn that they
are regarded as enemies.

SIGMUND FREUD, *TOTEM AND TABOO*

There is no forgetting how we could live if only we could find the way. We must
continue to be tormented by the idea [ideal].

NADINE GORDIMER, "LIVING IN THE INTERREGNUM"[1]

Among the reflections on South Africa's first democratic election collected
in the anthology *SA, 27 April 1994* is an epiphany by poet and critic Mazisi
Kunene: "Suddenly, like a flash of lightning, I realised that my act of voting was not simply physical; to be honest, it must represent many of those
people I knew, who would have liked to have voted, but who died in the
struggle. . . . I felt all these friends were walking with me." Kunene votes
not only *with* the dead, in their presence, but also *for* them, in their place.
His feeling of metaphysical, metonymic voting sabotages his marking the

ballot: he accidentally votes for the Pan-Africanist Congress (PAC) candidate. He is consoled, however, when he recognizes he has voted for the dead in another way, placing his mark next to invisible names and faces of "the beautiful dead, of all parties, who died for freedom" and might have liked to have run had they survived.[2]

Kunene's evocative image of voting with and for the dead is central to my concerns in this final chapter: the implications of taking seriously the desires of the dead and the limitations of the nation as a rubric for such transhistorical encounters. Voting brings to closure "earlier narratives of captivity and freedom," so that "the new nation in South Africa" becomes their teleological goal: the nation becomes the endpoint of centuries-long trajectories of suffering and struggle.[3] Kunene worries that the election is an inadequate culmination for a struggle in which "I had already voted with my life" (72). In a flash of recognition, Kunene sees the election as an opening in which past and present—or dead and living—are intertwined rather than polarized as the beginning and end of a linear narrative in the declarative mood. Recognizing that the dead "would have liked to have voted," Kunene finds a subjunctive middle ground between future perfect and past perfect, between what one *will have wanted* and what one *had wanted:* what would the dead have wanted had they survived? This grammar of desire mediates the presence of the dead, making it possible to imagine their desires in the present tense: what do the dead *want*? If voting is an act of affiliation to particular visions of the future, how do we adjudicate among competing desires of the dead? Who can be claimed as an ancestor? And how do the (sometimes unwelcome) dead claim us?[4]

This chapter untangles two forms of haunting, if we take haunting to mean spatiotemporal disruptions in which history folds and unfolds upon itself: the mobility of the past and the temporality of the transnational. These concerns range beyond the dynamics of millennial prophecy and beyond the nation. What makes the cattle killing a singular event in Xhosa history is not the idea that the ancestors are present, but the predicament of turning that knowledge into irrevocable action, interpreting the ancestors' extravagant desires in ways that had profound consequences for the living and the as yet unborn. The cattle killing offers an urgent and extreme example of a broader dilemma, not unique to millennial prophecy, of confronting the presence of the past and the desires of the dead. I have situated cattle-killing narratives in terms of various forms of South African nationalism in order to understand how the movement and its aftermath are made to speak to concerns beyond the amaXhosa. Here I examine how the cattle killing and its afterlives articulate modes of filiation and affiliation that reach beyond the borders of South Africa.

The title of this chapter, "Ancestors without Borders," refers to transgenerational affiliations imagined across national, temporal, and genealogical boundaries. My analysis of temporality and the transnational considers four modes of affiliation. First, in theorizing nonlinear intersections of past and future, I show how these temporal figurations allow us to read African diasporic solidarity constructed around a liberated future rather than a shared past. Second, I examine historical evidence that casts the cattle killing as an analogous affiliative project: some Xhosa believers, locating themselves within global resistance to British empire, imagined transgenerational *filiations* in which Russians, Indians, or Chinese in late-1850s military conflicts against the British were thought to be Xhosa ancestors who would return to the eastern Cape after victories abroad. To take seriously this "magical," transnational anti-imperialism, at odds with a dominant narrative that reads resistance to empire largely in terms of native (and sometimes metropolitan) demands that Europe fulfill the promise of the Enlightenment in the colonies, might require at least temporary affiliation with a worldview at odds with scholarly common sense.

Following this theoretical and historical discussion, I examine two literary modes of affiliation in texts that represent the history of the cattle killing in a global idiom and imagine a future perfect outside of national time. Brett Bailey's play *The Prophet* borrows from a global assortment of dramatic and spiritual traditions in staging a reenactment of the cattle killing. While Bailey's cultural appropriations raise troubling questions, we can also think about them in terms of affiliation: how do perceived affinities generate connections, whether sociopolitical or textual? The chapter concludes with a reading of John Edgar Wideman's *The Cattle Killing*, which offers an anachronistic warning about the cattle killing in its consideration of the perils of false prophecies for "Africans" in 1790s Philadelphia. Questions of transhistorical diasporic solidarity are at stake in the novel, but it also imagines affiliation in terms of narrative. The novel depicts intersubjectivity as *internarrativity*, in which stories generate relationships among the living and between the living and the dead. Bailey and Wideman treat the cattle killing as a global reimaginary, a cosmic vision in which past, present, and future are radically open. Bailey's ritual drama and Wideman's kaleidoscopic novel enact a narrative magic that, like the visions of transgenerational, transnational affiliation in 1850s Xhosa prophecy, challenges us to reimagine the desires of the dead and our relationship to them.

FIGURES OF TIME: PAST'S FUTURE, FUTURE'S PAST

To consider what the dead want is to assume that the past is not closed or finished. The concept of afterlives depends upon this assumption that the promise of failure rests in the unfinishedness of the past. Repositories of desire that things might yet be otherwise, incomplete pasts shadow the present and keep possibility alive. The uses—and perhaps even the necessity—of failure are central to Gayatri Chakravorty Spivak's reflections on the Native American ghost dance, which climaxed with the massacre of Lakota Sioux by U.S. troops at Wounded Knee, North Dakota, in 1890. The ghost dance movement emerged from a nineteenth-century millenarian prophecy that communal dances would catalyze the renovation of the world, protect dancers in the midst of the tumult, and bring back the ancestors. Spivak writes, "I would venture to say that a ghost dance cannot succeed. . . . Its uses, if there are any, are elsewhere."[5] Extrapolating from the historical phenomenon of the ghost dance, Spivak theorizes "ghostdancing" as an impossible necessity to "establish an ethical relationship with history as such, ancestors real or imagined." The "'end' of the ghost dance" is "to make a common *multinational figured* past return through the ghostly agency of haunting so that a future can dictate action *as if* already there as a 'before'" (70; emphasis added).

Spivak's account of ghostdancing has several important implications for my argument. First, Spivak's revenant "figured past" helps distinguish between two possible intersections of past and future: the past's future and the future's past. We might expect ghostdancing to be concerned with the "future in the past" (71), or the *past's future*: the past's visions of the future, which may be realized or unrealized in the present.[6] The past's future generalizes remembered prophecy: what is remembered in remembered prophecy is the past's future. But the "figured past" that ghostdancing conjures is not the historical past and its anticipations, but rather a projected past that *will have been* in the future, "as if already there as a 'before.'" In other words, ghostdancing invokes the future perfect, an "invented memory" that will have preceded an imagined future.[7] Ghostdancing's haunting by history figures a past for the future, the *future's past*.

Spivak posits ghostdancing—seemingly a retrospective revitalization—as future projection instead: a future's past rather than a past's future. The distinction between future's past and past's future is at work in the relationship between the cattle killing and its afterlives. The cattle killing can be read as an attempt to evoke a future perfect by catalyzing the unprecedented return of Xhosa ancestors and the renovation of the world. This reading of the historical event as directed toward a future's past departs significantly from the conventional historiographical treatments of primary resistance or revitalization movements as inherently regressive: instead, such anticolonial movements can be read as attempts to evoke a "past" that has never yet been. On the other hand, the *afterlives* of movements like the cattle killing and the ghost dance measure their discrepancy from what is now the past's future, the future envisioned by the movements. These doubled forms of anticipation and retrospection allow us to understand the transformation of the future's past into the past's future as the mechanism of cultural afterlives and history more broadly.[8] They point toward a palimpsestic experience of time in which desire and disappointment coexist with realized dreams and altered circumstances.

Second, Spivak's "figured past" is *multinational.* One of the uses of ghost-dancing is to haunt the nation, to channel a "continuity of insurgency" (71) against nationalist teleologies that might end, for example, at the polls in South Africa in 1994: the time of the nation is interrupted by other temporalities. Modernity inaugurates a universal timescale that allows for global simultaneity and local noncontemporaneity. The time of the world enables a stratification of temporalities that project "certain people's presents as other people's futures," so that universal time becomes "somebody's way of saying 'not yet' to someone else."[9] European imperialism construed metropolitan histories as the future perfect of so many peripheries. Instead of inaugurating history, "when imperialism arrived in Guinea it made us leave history—our history. . . . and enter another history," Amílcar Cabral maintains, revealing the epistemological violence of universal time.[10] The heterotemporality of modernity complicates Benedict Anderson's account of the secular temporality of the nation. Anderson identifies the coevalness of the "meanwhile" as the narrative mechanism that generates a national sense of simultaneity.[11] For times beyond (or within) the nation, however, we must think instead in terms of the *elsewhile* or *otherwhile.*[12] Rather than imagining fellow citizens coinhabiting national time, to think in terms of the otherwhile is to acknowledge the presence (and imagine the experience) of temporalities other than those we inhabit.

Ghostdancing expands possible relationships to the past through the border-crossing, "multinational" relationship to time I have called the *otherwhile*. Forging a relationship to "history as such, ancestors real or imagined," ghostdancing effects affiliation rather than filiation: the adoption of "imagined ancestors" and thinking through "other pasts rather referenc[ing] one's own hallucinatory heritage."[13] This kind of affiliation is at work in Paul Gilroy's argument for diaspora as an alternative to the nation as a heuristic frame for modernity, in which he imagines a mode of affiliation among diasporic subjects "constructed not so much from their African heritage as from the common orientation to the future produced by their militant struggles against slavery."[14] Such affiliation is forged out of political aspiration rather than genealogical or geographic origin: it is oriented toward an imagined future rather than a shared past.

Gilroy speculated in 1993 about the effect of South Africa's democratic transition on such transnational affiliation: he feared that "Black voices from within the overdeveloped countries may . . . turn away from the global project of black advancement once the symbolic and political, if not the material and economic, liberation of Southern Africa is completed" (35). If the universal time of modernity emerges in European exploration and colonial conquest, does the end of apartheid mark an end to global narratives of European imperialism and black transnationalism? The inauguration of a South African national narrative, rejecting apartheid's "multinational" pretensions, might involve not only a belated closing of the books of empire, but also the premature end of transnational solidarity, a shift of attention away from the otherwhile. What future remains for an aspirational transnational affiliation if its vision is realized, even partially?

This possible disjuncture between South African liberation and transnational solidarity exposes the laminate temporalities of national and global time, the tensions between meanwhile and otherwhile.[15] It is worth remembering that Nadine Gordimer's exhortation to "continue to be tormented by the idea" of a socialist utopia was delivered in 1981 as an appeal to the American Left for solidarity with Third World struggles. Her assertion that "there is no forgetting how we could live if only we could find the way" relies on a temporality of memory that assumes that what has never yet been cannot (or must not) be forgotten, a rejoinder no less timely a quarter century later, on the interregnum's other side.[16] What are the prospects for transnational remembering of what could be? Before turning to texts by Bailey and Wideman to trace answers to this question, I want to examine the cattle killing—prophecy, aftermath, and afterlives—in terms of global networks of filiation and affiliation.

INVENTED ANCESTORS AND IMAGINED LEGACIES IN THE CATTLE KILLING

The role of Russians in Xhosa prophecies of the 1850s is among the most intriguing aspects of the cattle-killing movement. When they learned of the death of former Cape Governor George Cathcart in the Crimea, the amaXhosa perceived a potential British vulnerability and possible solidarity with a fellow "black nation" against a common enemy.[17] Even before Nongqawuse, prophets in the 1850s urged noncultivation and killing cattle when they spoke of imminent deliverance by Russians arriving in ships or emerging from underground.[18] News of the Sepoy Rebellion in India revived hopes in 1858 that the Indians were on their way with new cattle.[19]

What knowledge the amaXhosa had of the Crimea, Russia, India (or China, where British imperial conflict sparked renewed hopes in 1860) is difficult to assess, given that written evidence of these transnational imaginings consists of scattered references in colonial correspondence. An informant to Commissioner Maclean reported widespread rumors in February 1858 that all British troops in the Cape had been dispatched to India. The amaXhosa "'are delighted to hear that the Indians are a black race with short hair, and very like the Kaffirs. They only regret that . . . while their race is overpowering the English in India, the Kaffirs are unable to follow up the success and fall on the English in this Country.'"[20] "'Umhlakazian agitation'" reemerged in September 1858 with reports that "'the black nations of the East have nearly extirpated the English'" (61). By 1860, rumors of British defeat "by the black tribes" everywhere but southern Africa climaxed in a story that Charles Brownlee, Commissioner of the Ngqika Xhosa, had confessed to them that "'the English were a doomed people; and that therefore he had resolved to cast himself entirely on [their] mercy . . . and trusted that . . . they would, when they became masters of the world, have pity on him, and give him a place of refuge'" (62).

The dialogic echoes in this passage, in which magistrate and former missionary J. C. Warner reports Brownlee's purported plea for mercy in anticipation of the Ngqika becoming "masters of the world," are dizzying. They offer some sense of how British imperial engagements of the late 1850s were read (and written) in the eastern Cape. Although Lupenga Mphande argues that attention to global events underplays "the authentically Xhosa origins of the Cattle Killing Movement and den[ies] them the credit they deserve for their true military and political resistance to colonial subjugation," I believe that these transnational imaginings help us to grasp more fully both how the amaXhosa understood their place in the world and the modes of anticolonial resistance available to them, as well as the historicity of these understandings.[21] Inspired by insurgencies of people they understood to be black, adherents of Xhosa prophecies had some awareness of their actions in terms of transnational resistance to British empire: they saw themselves not only as charges of transhistorical Xhosa ancestors but also as actors within a global empire and thus, at least implicitly, within the universal time of modernity inaugurated by European imperial expansion. Modernity's global temporality, in turn, inaugurates a transnational time of anti-imperialism. "Unprecedented world-historical developments brought unprecedented world-historical responses," Martin Legassick writes of the cattle killing.[22] Xhosa believers' interest in the Crimean War and the Sepoy Rebellion suggests a kind of transnational citationality.

"Pan-African" or "pan-Bantu" appeal was an innovation of nineteenth-century prophet-inspired anticolonial movements.[23] Imagining Russians and Indians as "black," however, involves a broader heuristic, not delimited by the geographic space of Africa. "Black" here denotes anti-imperial commitment rather than genetic origin or ontology: the color of resistance. On the other hand, some Xhosa prophecies contained this global solidarity within a longer trajectory by positing Russians not merely as black, but as Xhosa ancestors returned to deliver their descendants. The lieutenant governor of the eastern Cape reported in April 1856,

> They say that . . . [Nxele, Ngqika, and Mlanjeni, all deceased] are fighting against the English over the water (in the Crimea), and that it is a lie which has been told about the Russians being a white nation. Their opinion is that they are all blacks, and were formerly Kaffir warriors who have died.[24]

This global genealogy assumes magical, transnational filiation rather than mundane, anti-imperialist affiliation. In this view, it is not that the amaXhosa chose Russian "ancestors" or allies, but rather that Xhosa ancestors came to their descendants' aid by thinking (and acting) globally.

These incorporations of Russians, Indians, and Chinese within a transnational, transgenerational network of anti-imperialist solidarity anticipate early-twentieth-century hopes for deliverance by African Americans. These notions were widespread in the Transkei in the 1920s, fueled by the growing prominence of the United States and sparked by J. E. K. Aggrey's 1921 tour of Africa.[25] Aggrey aimed to combat Garveyism; nonetheless, the idea that "*Ama Melika ayeza*'—the Americans are coming," continued to spread, heralding "'an invading band of Negroes . . . who would drive the whites of South Africa into the sea.'"[26] Linking Garveyite imaginings in 1927 to "silly ideas . . . reminiscent of those that preceded the national suicide of the Xosas in 1857," W. D. Cingo lamented the "emancipation fever" in which "'the word America (*iMelika*) is a household word symbolic of nothing else but Bantu National freedom and liberty.'"[27] Prospects of African American deliverance spurred millenarian movements in the Transkei; Wellington Buthelezi told his followers to expect "aeroplanes" whose bombs would harm only white people.[28] Representatives of the Industrial and Commercial Union (ICU) sold red-and-white tickets that would gain bearers a place in the American millennium.[29] Slaughtering of pigs and fowl was associated with both movements. African Americans came to signify for many black South Africans, across class and cultural lines, the promise of empowerment and liberation, sometimes through magical means.[30]

It is difficult to miss the modernity of this millenarianism, whether its fetishization of technology (planes, automobiles, and photographs)[31] or its yoking of millenarian practices of livestock slaughter with emergent modes of organization like trade unions. Memories of the cattle killing were revived by the American excitement; while believers anticipated that aeroplanes would appear on a day when the sun reversed course, skeptics disparaged Buthelezi and ICU agents as latter-day Nongqawuses.[32] The complex appeal of prophetic nationalism was not limited to South Africa, and the transnational aspect of such movements also reveals their engagement with, rather than rejection of, modernity. Diasporic dreams of reclaiming the African continent that coalesced around the name of Marcus Garvey in turn spurred dreams of deliverance not only elsewhere in Africa (Aggrey's 1921 tour is also associated with Garveyite elements of the Simon Kimbangu movement in the Congo and Nyasaland), but also in the cargo cults of Melanesia, in which crates of modernity's treasures would be dropped from planes manned by sympathetic African Americans.[33]

Despite the misrecognitions involved in the "American dream" in South Africa,[34] it does bear some reciprocal relationship to diasporic desires to reclaim the continent, perhaps the ultimate act of transnational filiation. Examining early-twentieth-century expectations of deliverance by African Americans within the broader context of pan-Africanism allows us to understand how notions of transnational filiation and affiliation, sometimes magically inflected, circulated and shaped each other. Furthermore, they recast what might seem fanciful or even ignorant notions of Russians as Xhosa ancestors: on the contrary, Africans in the 1850s and the 1920s extrapolated from their geopolitical understandings the likelihood that a common enemy, a shared goal of African redemption, or ancestral bonds, would make indispensable allies of peoples they understood to be militarily or politically dominant. As James Scott insists in *Weapons of the Weak*, making sense of peasant resistance requires taking seriously its modes of consciousness and constructs of meaning, "however partial or imperfect their understanding of the situation."[35] We might dismiss subaltern Garveyite dreams not only because they so obviously misread Garvey's project, but also because they misread it in a particular way, replacing Garvey's black nationalist political economy with visions of magical deliverance. If we dismiss these misreadings out of hand, however, we risk our own misreading of the possibilities for black transnational imagining.[36]

Scholarly attention to Enlightenment genealogies of elite anticolonial nationalism has replaced Manichean notions of domination and resistance with more nuanced understandings of multilayered colonial interactions, gaps between intentions and outcomes, and the political efficacy of Enlightenment discourse when directed against its own failures and blind spots in the colonies.[37] Less well understood are anticolonial movements, dreams and desires that cannot be traced, through Europe or a Westernized elite, as products of rationalism and liberalism, even as the technological artifacts of modernity captured the imagination of colonized subjects. Anti-imperialism's "subaltern pasts" include movements not easily contained within Enlightenment genealogies because they invoke gods and spirits as historical agents.[38] When scholarly discourse casts such movements as nonmodern, they may be seen merely as retrograde remnants rather than dynamic epistemologies shaped by imperial encounters; in other words, we misread modernity as singular and European rather than multiple and global, and we mistake Enlightenment ideology for historical reality.

These glimpses of anticolonial prophecies' transnational aspects have a counterpart in colonial officials' responses. Governor George Grey juggled imperial priorities connected to the Crimean War, the cattle killing, the

Sepoy Rebellion, and the recently formed Boer republics. Members of the disbanded German Legion from the Crimean conflict were settled in British Kaffraria in 1857 and dispatched to India in 1858, after a misbegotten effort to recruit Xhosa men as soldiers to subdue the Sepoy Rebellion.[39] One German soldier, Gustavus Steinbart, recorded in his journal the "fact" that the cattle-killing prophet was an Irish orderly; Steinbart dismissed the "rumour" that the "Government actually prompted the prophet to mislead the Kaffirs."[40] This contemporaneous reference to a rumor of a colonial hoax anticipates interpretations widespread in Xhosa oral tradition recorded after the mid-twentieth century. Private correspondence between governors in the Cape and Bombay does not corroborate this rumor, but it does reveal that Bombay governor Lord Elphinstone hoped for advantages following the Sepoy Rebellion like those Grey secured after the cattle killing. He wrote to Grey in February 1858 about the two movements' "'strange coincidence'"; if the cattle killing "'destroy[ed] forever the influence of these false prophets,'" he hoped "'that the sanguinary revolt of the Bengal Sepoys will inflict a no less deadly blow upon the powers of the Brahmins and the prejudices of Caste.'"[41] He imagined (wrongly, it turned out) the cattle killing as precedent for the "civilizing" effect of anticolonial upheaval in India. Transimperial precedent was at work, however, when the Kaffir Relief Committee of King Williams Town took as its model the groundbreaking humanitarian response to the Crimean War. Dr. John FitzGerald of the Native Hospital longed for a Florence Nightingale: "[P]erhaps the Crimea was for her, but a preparation for South Africa."[42]

Grey met FitzGerald while serving as governor of New Zealand from 1845 to 1853 and summoned him to found the Native Hospital as part of "civilizing" the amaXhosa. When Grey returned to New Zealand as Governor in 1861, he presided over the later years of the New Zealand Wars, including the Maori King Movement's attempts to forestall land alienation. These conflicts took a millennial turn in the 1860s with the Pai Marire movement, whose militant Hauhau sect rallied warriors with bulletproof claims. Anticolonial prophecies followed Grey in the middle decades of his colonial career. In *Three Hundred Years: A History of South Africa* (1952), Non-European Unity Movement historian Mnguni (Hosea Jaffe) proposes that Grey perpetrated the cattle-killing hoax by assembling images drawn from folklore he had published in *Polynesian Mythology and Ancient Traditional History of the New Zealand Race*.[43] Like Steinbart's idea of an Irish prophet, this suggestion of Grey's transculturation of Maori cosmology into

"Xhosa" prophecy is idiosyncratic. Yet the notion of Grey grafting prophecies from farflung regions of the empire is just as suggestive as the idea of indigenous peoples around the world launching millenarian movements in response to Grey's itinerant antinational colonial policies.[44]

I have argued that we understand the events of 1856–57 in terms of the transcolonial concerns of the personnel of empire as well as the networks of transnational filiation and affiliation through which adherents of Xhosa prophecies responded to news from Europe and Asia. In the afterlives of the cattle killing, too, affinities with projects and histories beyond South Africa generate transnational invocations of Xhosa history. Perhaps the most remarkable example of the cattle killing's global afterlife is the short film *Nonquassi*, shot in 1938 by Port Elizabeth native Leon Schauder for Gaumont-British Instructional Films' *Focus on the Empire* series.[45] Schauder staged a reconstruction of the cattle killing "on the ground where this took place, and with descendants of the survivors," *Nonquassi*'s opening title tells us.[46] British imperial presence is all but invisible in this installment of *Focus on the Empire*. We hear that the "Xhosa nation" are proud, free, happy, and rich in livestock that graze in a valley "in which generations had lived and thrived": the film ignores drought, disease, a half-century of wars with the Cape Colony, shifting frontiers and expulsions, and the chiefs' cooptation. The amaXhosa seem already to inhabit the "time of ease and plenty" that bare-breasted Nonquassi promises when she brings a message from the dead chiefs; viewers might wonder why, in the words of the opening title, "a nation committed suicide."[47] (The film depicts the prophecy through Nonquassi's interpretation; we hear only muffled shouts at the river, and there is no dialogue other than voiceover narration.) Fields of corn set aflame are more visually compelling than the choppy suggestion of livestock slaughter (shots of placid cattle, goats, then a cloud of arrows)—there are no dead cattle in this film, no feasting turned to famine. There are also no chiefs or other men involved in the prophecy's dissemination, no controversy about it.

Nonquassi, along with Schauder's other Gaumont documentaries, *Twelve O.P.* [Ox power] and *Karoo*, was screened with popular feature films in London's West End.[48] *Nonquassi* caught the attention of the British Ministry of Information, which acquired world rights in 1940 for UK£1,000; in the print held by the National Film and Television Archive, the voiceover draws parallels between Xhosa patriarchal militarism—the "blind fanatical faith" with which they "followed the word of their leader" and sacrificed the "very essentials of living"—on the one hand, and Hitler's use of "propaganda" to effect collective sacrifice "in the pursuit of a mad dream of world conquest," on the other.[49] "[German] Civilization, it seems, has forced the clock back nearly one hundred years," the narrator observes in drawing parallels between "this savage race" and "the modern world"; "how ominous is this piece of history for the future," we hear as a stream of Xhosa "refugees" seek "the shelter of the Cape Colony." The enlistment of *Nonquassi* for British wartime propaganda demonstrates that primitivism could be used against fascism as well as in its service, as Ernst Bloch observed in 1932.[50]

The cattle killing also finds a place in books on topics ranging from black women's history (Simone Schwarz-Bart's *In Praise of Black Women*) to what the Library of Congress calls "Popular Errors" (the tabloid history *The World's Greatest Mistakes*).[51] The oddest example of the cattle killing's transnational afterlife that I have yet encountered is a computer program by Finnish educator Rolf Palmberg called "NONGQAWUSE," which aims to build English as a second language (ESL) reading comprehension. The program develops students' "ability to understand the plain sense of what is stated in a text and their ability to read between the lines"; students "discuss whether they believe the story [of the cattle killing] is true or not."[52] One cannot ignore the ironies of building interpretive skills by using a true story about the consequences of believing stories that seem not to be true, particularly given the role of literacy and English in cattle-killing discourse.

These transnational appropriations—in which the cattle killing finds an afterlife through incorporation into other projects and narratives—are corollaries of Xhosa incorporations of British imperial conflicts into narratives of transnational (af)filiation and black anti-imperialism. In other words, there is nothing inherently suspect in global imagining, and my use of the term *appropriation* does not imply disapprobation. Yet I cringe at *The World's Greatest Mistakes*: all appropriations are not the same. What difference does the global frame make in Brett Bailey's and John Edgar Wideman's treatments of the cattle killing's mediations of the past's future, the future's past, and the desires of the dead?

PLAYING AROUND IN A WORLD WITH WITCHES: BRETT BAILEY'S *THE PROPHET*

The global imbrications of the cattle killing and its afterlives should help us to see that nationalist invocations of the Xhosa episode are also acts of appropriation. Zakes Mda's *The Heart of Redness* identifies localism as an alternative to a coopted national project; this shift away from the nation-state reverses the tendency to imagine the cattle killing in an ever broader national frame. In the midst of the record drought year of 1999—when 60,000 cattle died in Eastern Cape Province from drought and disease—the Grahamstown National Arts Festival featured *The Prophet,* the third play commissioned from Brett Bailey by festival sponsor Standard Bank.[53] Like Bailey's previous plays *Ipi Zombi?* and *iMumbo Jumbo, The Prophet* transforms eastern Cape history into spectacular ritual theater. Set in the present, *The Prophet* stages an exorcism in its reenactment of the cattle killing. *The Prophet* retells Xhosa history in a global idiom in order to imagine a national future in which the wounds of the past will have been healed.

The pantheon of benevolent gods called the "Juju," inspired by West African masquerades, is the tip of *The Prophet*'s syncretic iceberg. The Juju perform what Bailey calls "mudras," hand gestures of Indian dance tradition. Their incantations borrow from Chinua Achebe's *Things Fall Apart* and *The Wizard of Oz*'s "Somewhere over the Rainbow." Characters sing in isiXhosa, Shona (from Zimbabwe), and buNyoro (from Uganda). Rejecting the "passive solitary watching" of contemporary theatre in the European tradition, Bailey seeks the atmosphere of a Hindu or Zen temple or a voodoo ceremony (9–10). This borrowed, New Agey spiritualism is awkward in its treatment of old-fashioned anticolonial millennialism; Bailey sketches utopian impulses in MGM Technicolor imagery.[54]

Brett Bailey is the bad boy—the *bête blanc*—of contemporary South African theater, a white playwright/director working with professional and amateur black actors in plays that stage explosive material with a heady mix of spirituality, spectacle, and showmanship.[55] In the introduction to the scripts, lyrical essays, notebook excerpts, and photographs collected in his book, *The Plays of Miracle & Wonder* (2003),[56] Bailey provides the recipe for his performance company: "[T]ake township traditions and styles, throw them in the blender with rural performance and ceremony, black evangelism, and a handful of Western avant-garde and a dash of showbiz, and flick the switch: THIRD WORLD BUNFIGHT!" (9).[57] His South Africa is less rainbow nation than chaos nation; he thrives on its "clashes of cultures, symbols, beliefs, historical eras" with an irreverence toward the politics of residual privilege and suffering that borders on dilettantish callousness (95). Bailey positions himself between alienated Europeans "who come from soils without Spirit" and alienated black "sophisticat" intellectuals and politicians whose ancestors' spirits can't penetrate their cellphone chatter

(21, 15, 97). He is flippantly contemptuous of their objections to his work; yet he can also be self-deprecating, dubbing himself a "batty whitey" and confiding, "I like my witchdoctors in skins and beads" rather than in jeans (77, 93). His rejection of Euro-American dramatic models cannot disguise his own appropriativeness—a vexed position signaled in his trope on Paul Simon's collaboration with Ladysmith Black Mambazo during the 1980s cultural boycott, "The Days of Miracle and Wonder."[58]

Only in engaging the cattle killing does Bailey confront his complicity as a "white playwright of settler stock"; Bailey finds, however, that his delight in spectacle obstructs a "dramatic offering" to the dead. Initially overwhelmed by the multifarious versions and torn between his love for the story *as story* and the horrific reality carried by the "black leather wings of history," Bailey concludes that "it really is just a story—if a tragic one—and it can be told in any way we choose" (153–57).[59] Bailey decides to tell his cattle killing story as therapeutic ritual drama. Citing Antonin Artaud's maxim that theater, like the plague, has the potential to drain ethical and social abscesses, Bailey figures the cattle killing's afterlife as a "still-festering wound" (9, 169); his global flourishes ornament a national exorcism of a revenant subnational past.[60]

The priest and priestess of *The Prophet* use the Juju as a medium to evoke "The Dead," spirits who "possess" five actors planted in the audience. Although the Dead speak through Bailey's Nongqawuse, they are not the vigilant and largely benevolent ancestors whose return was expected in the historical prophecy. Rather, they are menacing, parasitic spirits, agents of rot and decay. Their presence signifies illness rather than the cosmic harmony whose condition of possibility is the presence of Xhosa ancestors. Stage directions refer to them as "demons." The planted actors don cattle horns as they become (possessed by) the Dead; the villagers mistake these horns for those of the awaited herds, even though the Dead are the antithesis of those immortal, sustaining cattle.[61] Three times they dance around Nongqawuse, evoking expectation and disappointment for the children who play her followers; their possession of Nongqawuse is complete when she dances hysterically and roars their refrain, "We want to come out" (192). At this transhistorical climax in which "spectators" at *The Prophet* are possessed by the Dead who in turn possess the nineteenth-century prophetess, the priestess orders their exorcism, telling them to "Get out! Stay away!" after 150 years of defiling land and people (192).

As staged within *The Prophet,* the cattle killing is a fatal capitulation to what the Dead want, to "come out" and prey on the living; the play's ritual seeks to ameliorate this error and expel the Dead, not appease them. The play is less a vehicle catalyzing catharsis than the dramatization of catharsis itself: the primary target of purgation is the characters, not the audience. The cathartic thrust of *The Prophet* might seem ironic, given Bailey's desire to forge a warm-blooded African drama. Yet the figure that inspires Bailey's dramaturgy is not Aristotle, but rather the *sangoma*, the initiated healer who leads communal trance dances that channel spiritual energy and connect the community to the ancestors. The *sangoma* is called by the ancestors—"moral guardians of their society," Bailey writes—to this vocation of ghostdancing (19–20). As Helen Bradford observes in a scathing review of *The Plays of Miracle & Wonder*, "It is, above all, Bailey's transplantation of techniques rooted in the domain of African healing and religion, into showbiz, that has underpinned his rise to fame and fortune."[62] Bailey describes the *sangoma* as performance artist, and his plays offer catharsis in the key of spirit possession. Bailey himself seems a kind of aspirant *sangoma*, not only because he has spent time in residence with one, but also because of a transformative moment during a 1993 trip to Zimbabwe: an encounter with a reptilian-humanoid being—"the African Spirit, come to drink at the River of Life"—whose disappointment when he found the river dry pierced Bailey's soul. Bailey locates his vocation in this moment, a commitment to work with the African spirit to heal the figural drought (13). This "visitation" also allows Bailey to sympathize with Nongqawuse, he notes (156)—both are prophets uneasy in their own land.

One curious aspect of Bailey's syncretic method is its translation of intensely local notions of spiritual healing into the domain of dramatic performance for the national and international stage. The difficulties of this translation are evident in audience reactions. Without Bailey's "mass re-education" techniques for "engineering hysteria," Bradford contends, theater buffs might "fail to recognize his guys as their *sangomas*" (232). The situation is even dicier outside the upscale theater circuit: the possibility that rural black audiences in the Transkei might interpret the drama not as cathartic ritual, but as action to be imitated in life, led to the cancellation of performances of *Ipi Zombi?*, which dramatizes a recent witchcraft panic in which the alleged witches were killed and their corpses desecrated. The paradox of Bailey's transformation of theater into sacred space is that he seems unprepared for the responses of those who enter such spaces as believers responsive to his work's spiritual content rather than its dramatic form. Despite his interest

5. Abey Xakwe as Nongqawuse in Brett Bailey's *The Prophet*. Photograph by Elsabe van Tonder.

in indigenous spirituality, Bailey seems not to comprehend what it means "to live in a world with witches," nor to appreciate the pervasive reality of the "spiritual insecurity" of millions of South Africans.[63]

Here we see the paradox of Bailey's subnational affiliation to eastern Cape spiritual traditions: it might make least sense to those closest to the traditions he borrows, so much so that they literally run him out of town. By no means do those on the giving end of cultural appropriation always embrace such borrowing, but Bailey's delight in violent responses to his work (and his disregard for his company's distress) is troubling. *The Plays of Miracle & Wonder* reproduces a publicity photo of the actor Abey Xakwe as Nongqawuse, arms outstretched, atop a pile of human bodies and cattle bones; an ungenerous, symptomatic reading of this photo would imagine Bailey as Nongqawuse, her mantic exaltation given way to his showmanship: "Look at me!" (see fig. 5).[64]

In this light, the play's closing moments seem emblematic: the fallen bodies of the children playing the Xhosa dead are picked over by European soldiers, in the theatrical form of white child actors. On the one hand, this racialized casting seems to undermine Bailey's aspiration to heal the wound of history, "to bring the country alive. . . . sanctify the world" (156). The sight of white children pilfering from the inert bodies of black children offers neither actors nor audience a future different from their ancestors' past. On the other hand, the image may be the most honest one in the play, in terms of both South Africa's persistent racial inequities and Bailey's use of histories predicated on the deaths of Africans: this image of expropriation is as close as Bailey comes in *The Prophet* to signaling anxiety about his relationship to this material.

MOURNING, MELANCHOLY, AND MAGIC

Taken together, Bailey's self-positionings (as "batty whitey" and conduit for "African spirit"), as well as *The Prophet*'s unsettled combination of global appetite and racialized national vision, indicate the tensions between an oceanic fluidity of identity and the limits that history imposes. In identifying the troubling aspects of Bailey's appropriative gestures, I want to retain the possibility of cultural borrowing in which the perceived affinities that inspire affiliation are not overshadowed by inequities that replicate historical injustice. The cover photograph for *The Plays of Miracle & Wonder* generates mutual illumination: the photo shows three of the Dead posed after Jane Alexander's famous sculpture *Butcher Boys* (1985–86), which features three life-sized male humanoid forms on a bench, with bestial horns but without mouths or genitals (see figs. 6 and 7). *Butcher Boys* is an icon of the dehumanizing, menacing violence engendered by the violence of the apartheid state. The photograph for *The Prophet* makes an efficient and suggestive equation between extremities of late apartheid and those of the Xhosa mid-nineteenth century, in which the sinister forces Bailey associates with the Dead yearn for expression.

Bailey achieves an equally provocative telescoping of nineteenth and twentieth centuries when a Xhosa believer shouts at a skeptic, "You have a big stomach, many cattles, a nice salary, a big Mercedes Benz. Me, I have nothing. . . . This country is finished. Finished!" (183). This anachronistic characterization of the salaried, Mercedes-driving nineteenth-century unbeliever (played by a child) briefly suggests a postapartheid confronta-

6. "The Dead" in Brett Bailey's *The Prophet*. Photograph by Elsabe van Tonder.

7. *Butcher Boys*, 1985–86, plaster, bone, horn, oil paint, wood, 128.5 × 213.5 × 88.5 cm. Collection of the South African National Gallery, Iziko Museums. Copyright Jane Alexander. Photograph Cecil Kortjie.

tion between the black elite and the disillusioned masses for whom the *country* (not the Xhosa nation or people) seems "finished" rather than remade.[65]

These deft analogies between past and present compel my interest in *The Prophet*, despite the unseemly aspects of Bailey's work amply detailed by Bradford. *The Prophet* is *about* the problem of afterlives. Bailey's Dead embody the "living effects, seething and lingering, of what seems over and done with, the endings that are not over."[66] However, *The Prophet* offers little sense of the specific ways in which contemporary South Africa ails from the sickness the play aims to heal. Instead, the play's interest is in the restless past—its menacing presence in the form of the Dead, as well as the desire to undo error and defeat. The play's ceremony reverses the logic of cattle-killing prophecies; the Dead can save the living only by going away. *The Prophet* performs a strange kind of ghostdancing, inviting a haunting in order to posit a future perfect of a healed nation in which the past will have been laid to rest. The future's past, in this sense, will be a dead past.

As a sinister force in need of expiation, the Dead reveal a fundamental contradiction in the play's temporality: how can this depiction of a pathological past be reconciled with the idea of ancestors as guardians of the living? The weight of "dead generations" in *The Prophet*—as well as the Dead theatrically incarnate—are a "nightmare" from which Bailey would awaken the living. Bailey's disavowal of the Dead echoes Marx's messianic maxim, "Let the dead bury their dead."[67] The status of the dead and the past in Marxian thought can help make sense of Bailey's treatment of the desires of the Dead and the afterlife of history.

In *The Eighteenth Brumaire of Napoleon Bonaparte*, Marx claims that recycled images of a heroic past can revive "the spirit [*Geist*] of revolution" and inspire social and political movements, but are more likely to mystify with mere ghosts (*Gespenst*).[68] Skeptical about the revolutionary usefulness of glorious precursors, whose borrowed finery disguises the timidity of contemporary movements, Marx asserts: "The social revolution of the nineteenth century cannot take its poetry from the past but only from the future."[69] Yet the past can offer more than the "poetry" of revolutionary success. The utopian potential of the past's unrealized future and the afterlives of failure can revive the "spirit of revolution" as effectively as memories of victory. Hopes frustrated in the past can motivate action in the present: the spirit of resistance is more "nourished by the image of enslaved ancestors than that of liberated grandchildren," Benjamin writes.[70] Instead of leaving the dead to bury the dead, the living can be driven to action by their unmitigated suffering.

Mindfulness of past injustice enables forging ethical relationships to the past (what Spivak calls "ghostdancing"), if we imagine that "'vanishing generations'"—the dead—are somehow affected by the "'progress of history.'"[71] An understanding of history in which the past is redeemed in the future is hardly compatible with secular, linear conceptions of time. In a letter to Benjamin, Max Horkheimer objected that such a view would logically require eschatology: "'Past injustice has occurred and is completed. The slain are really slain. . . . If one takes the lack of [historical] closure entirely seriously, one must believe in the Last Judgment.'"[72] In his response, Benjamin turns this imputed logical fault into a strength, contrasting scientific conceptions of history with history as a "form of remembrance [*Eingedenken*]. What science has 'determined,' remembrance can modify. Such mindfulness can make the incomplete (happiness) into something complete, and the complete (suffering) into something incomplete. That is theology; but in remembrance we have an experience that forbids us to conceive of history as fundamentally atheological, little as it may be granted to us to try to write it with immediately theological concepts" (479). Mediated theological *concepts* are tools in the *practice* of remembrance: the "magic" of theology is a metaphor in the service of memory.

This metaphorization of magic generates additional complications. The idea that the past is not closed—that retrospection can be retroaction—obliges the living toward the dead. It compels us to imagine the Marxian project of human emancipation—the "'total recovery of man'"—not by disavowing dead generations but by recognizing "an ensemble of concrete historical beings, both living and dead."[73] An emancipated generation is indebted to the "burden of injustice borne by its predecessors" (137). But what can the living do about the fact that previous generations do not share in an emancipation that they made possible? How do the living negotiate the guilt of inhabiting the past's future? Horkheimer perceived that such obligations would demand divine intervention; for Nietzsche, they would cross "the boundary at which the past has to be forgotten if it is not to become the gravedigger of the present."[74] We have arrived nearly back where we began: the threat of the dead burying the living, staged in *The Prophet.* Even Mazisi Kunene's *friendly* dead, who walk with him to the polls, derail his electoral desires.

Kunene performs an alternative to Nietzschean forgetting in his account of voting with and for the dead: anamnestic solidarity (in Lenhardt's phrase) with those who did not survive to see freedom. Anamnestic solidarity is an act of transhistorical affiliation that confronts the imperative and impossibility of forging ethical relationships to the past, inviting a haunting that may not effect a literal redemption but works in another mode: as Spivak writes of the ghost dance, it "cannot succeed," but its "uses are elsewhere." Kunene represents the dead and their desires, both in making them figurally present once again (voting *with* the dead, or *Darstellung*) and in assuming political responsibility for realizing their desires (voting *on behalf of* the dead, or *Vertretung*). This dual task of representation faces a paradox: if remembrance is the only currency in which the debt can be repaid, but the dead cannot share in emancipation, then the living cannot hope to touch the principal of the debt. Although he walks to the ballot box in the company of his "beautiful dead," Kunene gets only one vote counted—and that for the wrong candidate. Memory is no stronger than magic: when the living assume political responsibility to represent the dead and realize their desires, the effect seems to remain metaphorical for the dead themselves. The distinction between *Vertretung* and *Darstellung* collapses, vitiating the work of *Vertretung:* for the dead, the effects of being spoken for are "merely" figurative. This redemptive project cannot succeed in the literal aim of rehabilitating the dead, but its uses are elsewhere, in the ethical imperative of memory. It is a project premised on the paradoxical inevitability and promise of failure, on the simultaneous impossibility of redeeming the dead and the necessity of acknowledging them. "Without the preservation of this wish [to awaken the dead] as a wish they would die a second time," Rolf Tiedemann writes.[75]

Although we might shrink from the idea of allowing the dead to die again, the second death of the dead is precisely the aim of mourning: loosening the affective ties that bind us to the dead in order to continue living.[76] Refusing to kill the dead again, anamnestic solidarity's orientation towards loss resembles the open-endedness of melancholia rather than the closure of mourning: "Unlike mourning, in which the past is declared resolved, finished, and dead, in melancholia the past remains steadfastly alive in the present."[77] Although conventionally understood as a pathological response to loss, melancholia can offer an ethical alternative to normative mourning or Nietzschean amnesia. This recuperation of melancholia as a potentially productive and critical relation to the past reframes the uneasy questions in Bailey's *The Prophet,* which literalizes mourning as a necessary killing of the Dead.

But just who is being mourned in the play? In *The Prophet,* the fallen believers fall prey to the Dead, who whisper in Nongqawuse's ear that they are ancestors "returned to put things right here"; these sinister forces also possess the living in the present.[78] Bailey's Dead are predators who will vacate the present only when a work of mourning is completed. In anamnestic solidarity, however, the dead are victims, locked out of the celebration but peering in through the windows, casting shadows of guilt over the emancipated living unless they can be redeemed. Their relation to the present is that which the Xhosa dead of the cattle killing would have to an audience at the Grahamstown National Arts Festival in a new and democratic South Africa, haunted by the believers who sacrificed everything to set things right.

Bailey's staging of the Dead invites us to confront the complexities of representing—speaking of and for—the dead and their extravagant desires. In this multilayered intergenerational conflict, the Dead symbolize the structural predicament of the present forming ethical relationships to its pasts: what if considering what the dead want is to forsake the future? *The Prophet* warns against the perils of hearing utopian possibility in the voice of temporal alterity, even as Bailey's "plays of miracle and wonder" draw out timely, healing spectacles from the past. By killing the Dead, the play brings an end to pathological melancholia, while its interest in the past also suggests the possibility of an ethical, therapeutic melancholic relationship to the unredeemed dead. The script's publication ensures that the Dead will be conjured and killed off in reading and performance, generating a melancholic cycle of repeated mourning.[79]

How can we distinguish between a past that is best mourned and forgotten and a past that must be remembered and its "spark of hope" kindled? The conflict at stake here is not merely intergenerational—between the dead and the living—but also historical and political—between victims and victors. "Only that historian will have the gift of fanning the spark of hope in the past who is firmly convinced that *even the dead* will not be safe from the enemy if he wins. And this enemy has not ceased to be victorious," Benjamin writes.[80] Benjamin's project is not forgiveness; not all the dead evoke solidarity from the living.[81] Historiography (or "remembrance") is a front in the war between the oppressed and the rulers, not the ground of their reconciliation: Kunene votes with and for dead friends and comrades "who died for freedom," not for fallen architects, defenders, or beneficiaries of apartheid. An ethics and politics of affiliation are at work in assuming a relation to the past. To what extent can we choose our ancestors? (or can they choose us?) And what if our biological ancestors were not the enslaved, but rather the masters? How can affiliation with the unemancipated dead be reconciled with genealogical ties to those who oppressed them?

The Prophet might offer a white South African audience the opportunity to mourn literal ancestors and their actions yet also to set this past to rest by engaging with the vanquished dead. This double movement of mourning and melancholy, putting malign specters to rest while forging solidarity with the unredeemed, might facilitate acknowledgment of racialist pasts while establishing an ongoing, future-oriented engagement with a more properly *national* past, in order to effect a nonracial future. This structure echoes Thabo Mbeki's famous "I Am an African" speech, delivered in May 1996 to mark the adoption of South Africa's new constitution.[82] Performing the role of South African citizen legislated by the constitution, Mbeki claims an impossible lineage from the southern African landscape, its flora and fauna, as well as the Khoi and the San, European migrants, Malay slaves, Zulu and Xhosa warriors, Boer concentration camp victims, miners, and indentured Asians. "I am the child of Nongqause," Mbeki says without elaboration. He confronts unflinchingly the historical role of each of these groups, "all of whom are my people"; bearing witness to the costs of injustice and the dignity of struggle, he celebrates South Africans' achievement of "the right to formulate their own definition of what it means to be African." The speech also bears witness to a textual lineage, echoing the 1955 Freedom Charter in its "firm assertion . . . that South Africa belongs to all who live in it, black and white. . . . [T]he people shall govern."[83] Mbeki's speech acknowledges a brutally divisive past at the same time that it welcomes the constitution as the foundation for new national citizenship.

Bailey's play might offer a similar promiscuous capacity for affiliation in the service of a national future, if its global repertoire of images and doubled relationship to the past are seen to demonstrate the productiveness of haunting as a refusal to be bound by temporal, geographical, or genealogical limits. Yet such a utopian reading of Bailey's appropriative shifts among region, nation-state, continent, and globe demands several qualifications. First, Bailey's relationship to eastern Cape history and his company comes uncomfortably close to replicating, rather than reimagining, expropriative and exploitative relationships between his biological ancestors and those of his company. After the 1999 production of *The Prophet*, Bailey wondered whether he had pushed too far his ghostdancing rehearsal method of putting actors in physical and emotional extremity; his actors don't have to *be* the characters, he recognized (119). This desire to collapse the actors' bodies with those of the characters—who, in *The Prophet*, are the not altogether friendly dead—demands of his company not only an imagination of an "otherwhile," but a dangerous flirtation with what Zakes Mda calls the Otherworld.[84]

In addition, Bailey's unstable taxonomy of the dead (fatalities of the cattle killing, Xhosa ancestors, and the menacing Dead) reproduces European missionaries' equations of revered ancestors in African cosmologies with malignant demons of Christian theology.[85] This demonization of the ancestors continues in some African Initiated Churches, which warn against "ancestors" as "evil spirits masquerading in the form of deceased relatives in order to seduce their descendants from the path of righteousness."[86] Despite *The Prophet*'s critique of missionary Christianity, Bailey's aspiration to decolonize the imagination, and his own ancestor work, the portrayal of the Dead posing as benevolent ancestors replicates this fear. I doubt Bailey intended his figuration of the Dead to endorse this view, but his experimental, anarchic spiritualism has unanticipated reverberations.

Finally, a transition from a racialized past to a national future perfect might describe not an ethically saturated, anamnestic process of working through historical complicities and continuing inequalities, but rather an all-too-easy *amnesiac* relationship to the past. The German *Historikerstreit* (historians' debate) of the 1980s offers a cautionary example: revisionist historians hoped to reclaim "national pride through the constitution of a refreshed, revitalized, and corrected *national* history." Those opposed to this project emphasized its ethical and empirical blindnesses, implicated in the history of Nazism.[87] The vexed valence of the nation is evident in Bailey's account of a heated exchange during the *Ipi Zombi?* tour of the Transkei. When "township fathers" outside of King William's Town attempt to shut down Third World Bunfight's zombie street performances, Bailey insists, "Yes, we can [do this], this is South Africa," and one elder retorts, "This is not South Africa, this is Ginsberg. This is our community. You don't know anything, you haven't suffered" (79). Bailey invokes the (new) nation as license for cross-cultural appropriation; the man's rejoinder is more ambiguous, emphasizing the priority of the local and experiential over shared entitlement to a national past, but also perhaps challenging Bailey's assumptions about what South Africa is. The man's stance approximates that in Mda's *Heart of Redness:* keep your national development schemes, let us tend our community's history and its future. This clash reveals a mutual unintelligibility of the "otherwhile," the heterotemporality that national narratives tend to flatten. A national future perfect for South Africa may be too easy a resolution for Bailey's play precisely because redemption of the dead and unredeemed—in all their subnational particularity—is all but impossible.

PROPHETIC VENGEANCE AND NARRATIVE MAGIC

The Prophet stages the ominous presence of the past's unrealized future, while its global appetite looks toward a future's past in which racial identities will have become irrelevant. Bailey eventually confronts the limits of the transnational imagination in grappling with vexed local histories; in the end, his syncretic vision ultimately requires the frame of the nation, so that the global becomes a vehicle for a more narrow national project. John Edgar Wideman's novel *The Cattle Killing* (1996), by contrast, envisions global affiliations that decisively refuse the nation as a temporal, political, or genealogical limit. Reading Bailey and Wideman together reveals a counterintuitive economy of appropriation and ethics: Wideman's invocation of the cattle killing in his story of the 1793 Philadelphia yellow fever epidemic is the more extreme appropriative gesture, but the novel exudes ethical concern to do justice to the dead. Readers might not notice the violence of wrenching the cattle killing out of space and time because of the care with which this act of appropriation is undertaken.

Wideman's novel offers an answer to Gilroy's question about the prospects for diasporic solidarity after the achievement—even if partial or symbolic—of a democratic South Africa. *The Cattle Killing* layers complex connections among Pittsburgh, Philadelphia, and South Africa, positing a transnational chain of "funerals and rallies and each is a story . . . different stories over and over again that are one story." "[T]he crowd that never showed up" in Philadelphia to mourn those killed in the 1985 Pennsylvania state police bombing of the MOVE house is juxtaposed with the throngs in Cape Town "welcoming Mandela back after twenty-seven years in prison."[88] Wideman's novel limns a global reimaginary: a sense of the South African struggle as a part, but not the definitive culmination, of "different stories over and over again that are one story," in which the possibility of justice is never quite fulfilled and never quite forgotten.[89]

The Dead in Bailey's *The Prophet* provoke a confrontation with pathological relationships to the past in need of the play's healing ceremony. Narrative also has a therapeutic function in *The Cattle Killing*; the pathology, however, is not the past or relationships to it, but rather millennial faith in providential destruction, faith in a *post hoc propter hoc* version of a future perfect that will have found redemption in suffering. The novel reframes the terms of debt to previous generations, where we have seen anamnestic solidarity as a tenuous alternative to eschatology or amnesia in bearing the crushing burden of the dead. In *The Cattle Killing*, the weight of dead generations demands neither belief in Last Judgment nor disavowal of the dead; instead, his awareness of profound responsibility to the dead leads Wideman's protagonist to a "second conversion" (32)—a *repudiation* of Christian eschatology. Far beyond assuming or inviting the presence of the past, Wideman's novel intimates the immanence of a nonlinear oceanic time in which no moment is lost; thus its project is not so much to "redeem" an endangered past as to recover a sense of this totality in the midst of an utterly disenchanted world.[90]

The Cattle Killing, in other words, is concerned with the desires of the dead, protean conceptions of time, and the dangerous appeal of imagined futures, particularly those sutured to racial or national collectives. Its metafictional frame narrative is set in the present and relates the thoughts and memories of the writer of a forthcoming novel called *Cattle Killing*; the writer is a middle-aged Pittsburgh native returned home for a writers' conference. We read in the frame narrative that he wants "every word of his new book to be a warning, to be saturated with the image of a devastated landscape," most immediately (but not only) the eastern Cape of southern Africa in 1857, after the Xhosa people are "seduced by false prophecy, false promises, turning away from themselves, trying to become something else, something they could never be" (7). The amaXhosa, however, are not the focus of *The Cattle Killing*'s central narrative, which seems instead to be the text of the writer's forthcoming novel, set in Philadelphia during the 1793 yellow fever epidemic. The central narrative's unnamed protagonist is a former slave who became an itinerant preacher after buying his freedom. He lives for a time in nearby Radnor with an interracial couple posing as the servant (Liam) and widow (unnamed) of British painter George Stubbs. After the couple is killed during a "night of terror" by a racist mob, the preacher arrives in Philadelphia during the epidemic. This narrative trajectory is punctuated with Liam's stories of Africa and England, and it also takes shape around the preacher's repeated encounters with a mysterious blue-clad African woman;[91] the narration is sometimes addressed to this woman as a talking cure for her unspecified illness.

The eighteenth-century preacher also has a dream of Nongqawuse: she warns him against "fall[ing] asleep in your enemy's dream" (147) on the very "night of terror" when Radnor is burned in retribution against "Africans" as the purported source of the yellow fever epidemic.[92] This dream represents a conjunction of 1850s kwaXhosa with 1790s Pennsylvania that reverses Garveyite expectations of Africans' deliverance by African Americans. That this apparent anachronism appears without comment suggests how deeply temporality is at stake in the novel: in an anticipatory "afterlife" of the Xhosa cattle killing, the "African" preacher in America mourns the dead of the cattle killing before most of them are born, if we are thinking chronologically. Here it is the future itself, rather than the future's past as in Bailey's play, that will be dead.

Thinking chronologically, however, is problematized in Wideman's novel, which is structured more around recurrent homologies than plot's cause and effect. Significance accretes to objects as they recur in the narrative: axes, blue gowns, dead and unborn children, slaughterhouses and sausages, ditches and black pools, "iron memories" and arms held like broken wings. These echoes challenge the linear temporality of both hegemonic modernity and the reading process. The weightiest homologies are false prophecies and devastated landscapes; the frame and central narratives are both palimpsests of landscapes, each one palimpsestic in its thriving and devastation. Images of slaughtered cattle and starving Xhosa believers resonate with successive razings of Pittsburgh's ethnic neighborhoods and South African townships in the twentieth century, as well as with disease-ravaged Philadelphia, the burning of an orphanage for African children, and Radnor's "night of terror" in the 1790s.

This layering of landscapes devastated by false prophecy's lies and impossible expectations has contemporary urgency because there is "[d]eadly prophecy in the air again" in the late-twentieth century, the writer warns in the frame narrative:

> I must warn you there are machines always hovering in the air, giant insects with the power to swoop down spattering death, clean out the square in a matter of instants. . . .
> And warn you there are prophecies in the air, prophecies deadlier

than machines. If you deny yourselves, transform yourselves, destroy
yourselves, the prophets say, a better world will be born. Your enemies
will be dismayed, disarmed by your sacrifice, and be your enemies no
more. From the ashes of your sacrifice a new world of peace and plenty
will arise, they say. The prophets of ghost dance, prophets of the cattle
killing, prophets of Kool-Aid, prophets of bend over and take it in your
ear, your behind, prophets of off with your head, prophets of chains and
prisons and love thy neighbor if and only if he's you, prophets of one skin
more equal than others and if the skin fits, wear it and if it doesn't, strip
it layer by layer down to the bone and then the prophets sayeth a new
and better day will dawn. (7–8, 206–7)[93]

This warning against the demands and seductions of false prophecy charts
historical millenarian movements (the North American ghost dance, the
southern African cattle killing, and the twentieth-century mass suicide of
Jim Jones's followers in Guyana) in terms of a broader logic of sacrificial
self-abnegation that consolidates the oppressive status quo. The warning
also acknowledges the nonliteral but material efficacy of bulletproof claims:
faith in magical invulnerability proves "deadlier than machines" to its
adherents. The warning invokes the novel's recurrent image of flaying—
peeling skin "layer by layer"—that aims to get beyond the "epidermalization
of inferiority" dividing the world into peoples "black" and "white."[94] The
warning reminds us that the counterpart of "funerals and rallies" in an
endless story of resistance is the machinery of state repression, figured as
monstrous helicopter-insects that perpetrate acts like the police bombing
in Philadelphia and are also a gigantized echo of the actual vector of the
yellow fever epidemic there two centuries earlier.

   This warning about deadly flying machines inverts the "undreamed possibilities for the future"—"men flying like birds"—heralded by the character
Benjamin Thrush in the 1793 launch of a hot air balloon in Philadelphia
(160–61).[95] Wideman's novel rebuts the millennial hopes associated with
the geographic revelation of the New World and the sociopolitical project
of the United States.[96] In 1793, Philadelphia was not only the U.S. capital; it
was also home to the fledgling nation's largest free black population, thanks
in part to the legislation of a gradual and limited emancipation in 1780.[97]
While Thrush (who is white) epitomizes "this new age, this new country,
and new century soon to dawn," the American hemisphere is depicted as
a devastated landscape, "This New World a graveyard for African people"

(167, 127). The self-evident truths of equality and liberty are exposed as false promises; exceptional only in its hypocrisy, America is otherwise indistinguishable from a broader hemispheric dystopia. This skeptical assessment of U.S. national liberation suggests that Wideman has no illusions about South African democracy obviating the need for black transnational solidarity.

The brute facticity of so many devastated landscapes overwhelms the imagined futures of the false prophecies depicted in the novel. The young nation's utopian promise is fatally compromised by the "madness" of its system of human property (127), but Euro-American slavery and the racism that undergirds it are implicated within a broader condemnation of false prophecy that includes Christianity itself. This critique of Christianity as false (and even fraudulent) prophecy is voiced most explicitly by "Mrs. Stubbs," who, with her West African husband Liam, left Liverpool for Pennsylvania in pursuit of New World promise; it is Liam who finds instead a genocidal "graveyard." Mrs. Stubbs rails against the Christian promise of resurrection as god's "lie of kindness": "He whispers poison in your ear. Tells you that you are different, ... exempt from the law governing all living things. He beguiles you with the false promise of a different world, different rules. . . . You forget the nature of the actual world you inhabit" (106). Mrs. Stubbs finds this "lie of kindness" incompatible with the "actual world" of cruelty, disease, and death. The preacher, however, abjures his faith because he objects to Christianity's narrative of cruelty, disease, and death *as providential.* Not limiting his indictment to New World slavery, he repudiates a "god who authors an endless chain of horror for African people" (204). The preacher can no longer view such horror as a middle passage through a narrative of ultimate redemption, in which "God sent the fever to purge us," or which promises that from the ashes of the burned orphanage *"the hopes of our people will rise again"* (194, 204: emphasis in the original). The preacher refuses the mystical rationalization in which "the seeming absence of God was God's best proof" (155). The Xhosa cattle killing is described in similar terms; the prophecy explains epidemic disease as the workings of a divine, apocalyptic plan. The "strangers" who come to Nongqawuse tell her that "the plague destroying their herds is God's curse upon those who have forsaken His ways." She concludes, however, that she heard the voices not of gods or ancestors, but rather a "spirit of despair who whispered the lies of the invaders in our ears" (146–47).

The novel layers prophetic interpretations of the 1793 Philadelphia yellow fever epidemic and the 1856 eastern Cape cattle lungsickness epizootic;

the connection between these events is not only prophecy's impossible promise of resurrecting the dead but also the implicit equation of human and bovine victims.[98] "The cattle are the people. The people are the cattle": in the frame narrative, the writer invokes this Xhosa "love song," turned "dirge" when they are persuaded to "butcher the animals that fleshed the Xhosa's intricate dreaming of themselves" (7).[99] The ennobling identification of people with cattle in the Xhosa worldview is incompatible with the dehumanizing comparison of people to cattle in capitalist slavery, where "men . . . trade in human flesh, buying and selling one another like wood, or cattle" (127). For the amaXhosa, cattle were no ordinary commodity to be bought and sold; belonging to the ancestors, cattle circulated through a complicated system of loans, exchanges, fines, and reciprocal obligations that constituted sociopolitical relationships. The warning that "the cattle are the people" assumes a metonymic relationship between Nguni people and Nguni cattle within a cosmic whole; the "madness" of New World chattel slavery is its metaphoric association of two categories that ostensibly have nothing in common—persons and property.[100]

Racial capitalism's inhuman(e) treatment of people as if they were *mere* cattle finds its logical consequence in the recurrent image of humans as sausages, dead flesh stuffed back into the organs of digestion. Liam finds in the New World "the same air thick with blood and wailing" as at the Liverpool slaughterhouse where he is apprenticed after being "panyared" to England from West Africa to become a missionary (127, 109).[101] The most striking instance of this image appears at the moment when Xhosa cosmology meets New World racism. In the dream of Nongqawuse, the earth is the body of god, nourished by water flowing down mountains into black pools that are god's throat; thunder, lightning, and rain ensure an endless cycle in which humans live and die. When the preacher wakes and finds Radnor burning in the "night of terror," we read another image of god's earthly body, this time in the register of disenchantment: "Circles within circles. Expanding and contracting at once—boundless, tight as a noose. God's throat, belly, penis, cunt, asshole, the same black ditch. The people an unbroken chain of sausages fed in one end and pulled out the other" (149). Black pools as liminal sites of generation (where creation began, and Nongqawuse received the prophecy) alternate with black ditches as disenchanted sites of death or human birth, whose sounds and smells, Liam notices, are those of the slaughterhouse.

The dream of Nongqawuse conjoins the aftermath of false prophecy for the amaXhosa with the only prophecy whose fulfillment the novel depicts. During an epileptic fit, the young preacher cries out a verse from Jeremiah: "Behold, I am making my words in your mouth a fire, and this people wood, and the fire shall devour them" (67). These fiery words are fulfilled in the burning of Radnor, however inadvertent, unrecognized, and ironic (i.e., unfailed) this realization might be: genocidal violence becomes the instrument of scriptural fulfillment. The novel's most devastating critique posits that genocide undoes the racial division inherent to Christianity: "Only fire . . . restores what God sundered when He separated light and darkness" (19). The violent racism of "white" people holding themselves above "black" people echoes this originary genesis of apartness in Christian narratives of redemption: "[T]hank Him for sundering us one from the other, black from white, rich from poor, man from woman, age from youth, so we might find ourselves, finally, so gloriously conjoined once more" (157).

If the novel disavows such gratitude for harm that creates the opportunity for redemptive redress, it is more ambivalent about the appeal of glorious conjunction, transcendent totality, and millennial renovation in themselves. For as many warnings against false prophecy that the novel delivers, it generates just as many visions of new or alternatively perceived worlds, manifold desires for resurrection. The "resurrections" include not only the resuscitation of the nearly frozen preacher by Liam and Mrs. Stubbs (82) or the mysterious African woman's ogbanje-like "serial inhabitation of mortal bodies" (15);[102] but also the "resurrectionists" of York, "body snatchers who trafficked in corpses" whom Liam encounters with George Stubbs and his fellow anatomy enthusiasts (115). The transcendent visions are equally various; one of the most remarkable is a black Christian vernacular apocalypse. Asked about his permanent grin, one of the preacher's congregants, Mr. Rowe, relates his vision of "the whole world startin again." In Rowe's future perfect, the newly created black man will have learned from history: "Black man he wake up first this time. Remember everything. Quick. Grab ax. Chop white man head." He inserts a clod of earth into the new white woman before mounting her, "her legs cocked wide open" (66). Rowe's smile is an anticipatory mimicry of this adamic black man's "smiling whilst he's ramming," not least because "she ain't never gonna push out no white babies so ain't gone to be no more white peoples cept this one woman" (66). Rowe concludes his revelation with a prayerful "Amen," but this generic convention can hardly obscure its paradoxical extremity and conventionality, within the terms of the novel: this genodical millennial vision (a new world with "no more white peoples") repeats hyperbolically the original genesis through sundering light from dark.

Relying more on ancestral memory than deliverance by ancestors, Rowe's vision exemplifies not merely *The Cattle Killing*'s critique of Christianity as a false prophecy foundational to European racism, but also the broader genocidal tendencies of millennial dreaming. "The whites would be swept from the land. . . . our enemies dead," promises Nongqawuse in her dream, echoing most historical accounts of the cattle killing (148). As we have seen throughout *Bulletproof*, images of white people swept into the sea galvanized settler attention to cattle-killing prophecies, even if the anticipated herds and returning ancestors elicited their skepticism and contempt and the mounting carcasses and famished bodies evoked pity, relief, or even greed. Cattle-killing prophecies envisioned *geographic* extermination of Europeans that also implied *physical* extermination. This exterminating impulse appears at the opening of Fanon's *The Wretched of the Earth*, where "decolonization," as "the replacing of a certain 'species' of men by another 'species' of men," describes the colonized literally "putting himself in the place of" the colonizer, who then has no place.[103] At the end of the book, Fanon offers a different millennial vision: a *humanist* project of "set[ting] afoot a new man" to be undertaken "For Europe, for ourselves, and for humanity" (316). In the opening, however, Fanon's decolonization is "tabula rasa"; it "sets out to change the order of the world"; it "is truly the creation of new men" (35–36). Its "murderous and decisive confrontation" "reeks of red-hot cannonballs and bloody knives," and thus for the colonizers its prospect is "a terrifying future."[104] In short, Fanon's apocalyptic vision of decolonization begins as genocidal, just as Revelation's account of endtime separates the saved from *les damnés*. A fundamental millennial question, then, is who will be included in the new world, and who will be destroyed?

Mr. Rowe's vision of a world "with no more white peoples" is tempered in the novel's depiction of Bishop Richard Allen in a crisis of faith after he's pledged to create a church without segregated pews. (Allen was the founder of the American Methodist Episcopal (AME) church, which fostered the "Ethiopian" strand of African Initiated Churches in late-nineteenth-century southern Africa.)[105] After considering whether he desires to be white, Allen disavows millennial genocide: "He cannot pray to God to wipe white people off the face of the earth and also keep his heart free for Christ's mercy, but if he calls on Heaven to purge whatever it is the whites fear and hate in him, must it also be a prayer for sweet annihilation." Nonetheless, he cannot help but pray "for a vision of the new world at the far end of this threatening path—the earth restored, flood receded, peace" (159).

The passion of Bishop Allen—"dead now"[106]—is narrated by the young preacher, whose rejection of Christianity is figured as a turn away from genocidal prophecies, whether those of hegemonic or African-inflected Christianity, and toward the open-endedness of storytelling. This shift is from *vengeance* to *narration,* in Paul Ricoeur's terms: "[T]here are perhaps crimes that must not be forgotten, victims whose suffering cries less for vengeance than for narration. The will not to forget alone can prevent these crimes from ever occurring again."[107] What the dead want is to have their stories told. But the preacher laments, "It was the endless parade of grieving, afflicted, injured souls . . . that had finally stopped his prayers in his throat. He could cry over them no longer, pray over them no more without forfeiting his own will to live" (199). The preacher (a preacher no longer at the moment of narration) confronts the moment when dead threaten to bury the living.

The preacher's acknowledgement of the weight of dead generations is not an amnesiac abnegation of mourning, and hardly an embrace of eschatology. "Just as I sit beside you on this bed, speaking to you, the dead speak to me. I feel them as the song says drawing me on," the preacher says (153).[108] Despite the novel's jeremiad on the devastation wrought by prophetic speech, the preacher strains to hear the dead. His statement implies not merely analogy but also causality and transmission: I speak to you *because* the dead speak to me; I tell you what they say. The "you" is the blue-clad African woman in Philadelphia, the immediate audience for the stories that constitute much of the central narrative. Hoping to heal her unspecified ailment, the preacher speaks "as if it would raise you from the dead" (78). His stories aim to heal not only the woman, but also himself, his relationship to the past, and perhaps even time itself. The novel closes with a pledge to tell "stories of my dead to keep you alive, to keep love alive. . . . [T]ell you stories so my dead are not strangers, so they walk and talk, so they will know us and welcome us. Free us. To love" (206–7). Unlike the preacher's intransitive, solipsistic act of *mourning* the dead, which breaks his faith and strains his will to live, this transitive, intersubjective act of *narrating* stories of the dead fosters relationships among the living and prevents estrangement of the dead from the living. The dead can nurture the living (and the living connect to each other) only when stories of the dead are passed among the living.

The novel imagines affiliation as *internarrativity:* transhistorical human relationship as palimpsestic narration, "each story saving the space, saving itself, saving us. *If someone is listening,*" in the novel's final words (208; emphasis added). Characters describe intersubjectivity as being written into another's story, "moving . . . through the margins of someone else's world" (197), a dynamic whose historical analogue is the cattle killing's impossible presence in the "margins" of the Philadelphia story. Affiliation and identity formation are indistinguishable and simultaneous in internarrativity: the preacher longs to share his story, "as in another's gaze I find myself. . . . [E]ach freeing the other, making the other real" (74). Although the word does not appear in the novel, this notion of mutual intersubjectivity resembles the concept of *ubuntu*—a person is a person through other people—that emerged as the prospective moral foundation of the TRC era.[109] The necessity of reception in internarrativity is manifest in the novel's opening frame, where the writer is about to read his manuscript to his father, and in the epilogue, a letter to the writer from his son, who has just finished reading the book. This frame of internarrativity, a multidirectional, intergenerational transmission among fathers and sons, is not inconsequential in a novel so achingly full of dead, unborn, and unconceived children: with the exception of the morally suspect Stubbs *père* and *fils,* these are the only extant filial relationships in the novel.

The possibility and necessity of transmission crucially distinguish the preacher's relationship to narrative from his visions of global and cosmic unity. After his epileptic fits, the preacher experiences "a startling clarity of vision" where "I glimpse a world sweet as it must have been, and still is, if we had but eyes to see it; before the Fall" (57). The only fit narrated in the novel is followed by three distinct visions. The first roars out of Revelation: a dragonlike creature "lay[s] waste this sinful land, preparing it for the Savior's coming" (67). In the others, he feels "the absolute peace of knowing the world's whole again" (74), whether in an Orientalist image of the "world, its far-flung wonders" and the universe itself shrunk to fill his gaze, or in a transgenerational throng of "More African people than I'd ever seen" at the crossroads of "a thoroughfare frequented by our ancestors, our generations yet to be born" (76). The preacher laments that these visions are so fleeting that he cannot share them. The visions that allow him to see *everything* and be *everyone* isolate him because he cannot share them with anyone.

The irony is that in telling the story of the fit and his subsequent first glimpse of the mysterious African woman, the preacher *does* communicate these brief experiences of apocatastasis to his convalescent interlocutor (who may or may not "be" this woman) and to the reader. The non-Christian visions construct cosmic unity as immanent rather than imminent: this totality "still is, if we had but eyes to see it." A disenchanted counterpart of these visions is the work of Liam's former master George Stubbs, which "exposed a bloody universe beneath the skin" (127). Wideman fictionalizes the career of painter George Stubbs (1724–1806), whose engravings in *The Anatomy of the Horse* (1766) revolutionized anatomical realism; Stubbs also made engravings of fetuses for John Burton's *Essay Towards a Complete New System of Midwifery* (1751).[110] In the novel, Stubbs seeks the "truth inside us all" by peeling layer after layer from horse carcasses that Liam carries up to his studio. Liam marvels at Stubbs's aesthetic achievement but refuses to forget its "terrible, mad price," which leaves Stubbs embarrassed by living bodies and their pain. Liam perceives a common objectifying logic that links Stubbs's flaying to his father's tannery and the "commerce in men" (128). Stubbs's penetrating vision is the cold, deadening eye of the Enlightenment; like the Christian act of creation, it sunders everything from everything else and "lift[s] nature's petticoat" (114), turning pools to ditches and living beings to specimens.

Liam and the preacher know the "soul-shriveling price" of transcendent vision, but they yearn to develop in themselves and others the capacity to see cosmic possibility immanent within the disenchanted world, the universality behind "disguises" of skin read and performed as "black" or "white" (58, 140–41). When the preacher arrives, Liam's wounded silence is broken by the company of a fellow diasporic and the catalyst of a willing audience for a flood of stories about his life in Africa and England: "I couldn't begin to talk, son, till I learned you were willing to listen" (131). He rediscovers dormant passions for his wife and for painting. In the final scene where the couple appears (long after the preacher narrates their immolation), the preacher finds Liam painting her: "Not what Liam imagined or he imagined or she imagined, but what could come next. After this time. Next and next. Always unknown. Always free" (182). Liam's painting—its openness to what is "next and next and next" (126)—suggests the distinction between genocidal prophecies of vengeance and world-healing narratives: a radically different conception of temporality. As he looks between the woman and Liam's painting, the preacher sees again what he saw in his first sight of her, a diachronic crowd of successive selves: "the room full of women. . . . Each one different. Or changing. Different women, different ages. Magically transformed by water, fire, air" (96). Liam's painting seeks access to the "different world hidden in this one. A world that couldn't be, yet there it was in all its simple glory, being what it couldn't" (133). In narrative and painting (and altered states engendered by sex and neurological disturbance), Liam and the preacher glimpse a world in which every moment is present, everything is one, and the counterfactual is.

The preacher becomes, in effect, the son that Liam never let himself have; Liam admits "fathering you in my fancy," just as he confides that he sees in his dreams children he "refused to sow" because he knew they "would not grow up in the safe world I dreamed for them" (131). Liam's painting embraces openness to future possibility that has been impossible in his embraces of his wife. This openness to what is latent, or unimagined yet possible in the future, distinguishes narrative and the aesthetic from the closed future in Christian prophecies of redemption, in which every wrong may be righted but there is nothing new under the sun.[111] Prophecy kills the future: in the dream of Nongqawuse it is a "mouth eating the people" that fatally interrupts the cosmic rhythm of life and death (147). After he admits his inability to mourn or pray over the "endless parade" of loss, the preacher simultaneously imagines and dismisses an affirmation of future possibility:

> The prayer he considered for an instant, before it too seemed futile, a prayer for souls already irretrievably lost, lost, lost, the prayer he believed for a moment he might utter, was a prayer for the unborn, the unimagined.
>
> A prayer of thanksgiving. If the new ones somehow manage to arrive, he needs to thank them. A wordless prayer of thanksgiving passing from here to there. A prayer not to any god anyone has named. A prayer thanking the ones still buried in the folds of this tainted beginning. This fallen place. Amen. (199)

This prayer—punctuated, like Mr. Rowe's vision, with an "Amen"—is what the preacher *would have* uttered, a counterfactual prayer for a future perfect that "somehow [will have] manage[d] to arrive" but is "unimagined" and unimaginable from the standpoint of "this tainted beginning." The possibility and freedom of the unknown in Liam's "next and next and next" is countered by the preacher's mournful "lost, lost, lost." The possibility of movement "from here to there," from the parade of grieving to the birth of the "new ones," remains unthinkable. The preacher can neither bear to mourn the past's unrealized future nor dare to imagine the future's impossible past, yet the transmission of his narrative leaves a trace of the counterfactual desire that he cannot himself embrace.

Narrative provides a space in which can linger traces of what is "lost, lost, lost" or what can barely be imagined—utopian shadows and haunting specters of the counterfactual contained in every life, the possibility latent in every child unborn and every book unwritten. "All stories are," the preacher tells his interlocutor, "a return. To memory, possibility, life": past, future, present (55). This narrative grammar can accommodate the desires of the dead—what they had wanted, would have wanted, and even what they want. This is not to say that the novel ignores storytelling's darker aspects—the transgressive transmission of stories "not . . . to pass on," in Toni Morrison's phrase, the contested stories that obstruct rather than foster intersubjectivity, the resemblance between authorship or vicarious narration and the ventriloqual structure of prophecy.[112] Internarrativity means that your interlocutors can call you out, hold you accountable for your stories, as "Mrs. Stubbs" did when she challenged Liam's sympathy for his former master and thereby catalyzed the wounded silence between them. Nonetheless, narrative preserves what fire destroys (29). The very mystery of the blue-clad African woman reappearing in different contexts and even different bodies (defined by narrative logic rather than a natural lifespan) enacts the narrative magic limned by the novel; like Liam's wizard father, stories can "change . . . shape or disappear instantly. . . . be many different places at once" (104). Narrative time is elastic: the preacher pursues the African woman in a journey "as long as a trek across a continent in a caravan of ox-drawn wagons" (anticipating the American and southern African nineteenth centuries), "as brief as stepping through an open door" (43). This narrative thread recalls Brett Bailey's conflation of actors, audience, and characters; for Wideman, entering another's skull to see through her eyes is an impossible necessity. The internarrativity between the preacher and the ailing woman also models for the reader an interpretive approach to the novel's temporal a-logic that accepts that "stories always go backwards . . . to go forward. Forward to go back," and yet still finds meaning in temporal rupture (54).

The central narrative performs the shape-shifting, time-bending wizardry, premised on the logic of the "otherwhile," that the writer of the metafictional frame narrative (as well as his son in the epilogue) acknowledges as technical challenge and historical limit. Whereas the central narrative posits impossible genealogies and geographies in which Nongqawuse might be Liam's half-sister or the preacher lies simultaneously under Liam's African stars and outside his Pennsylvania barn, the frame narrative must deploy cognitive association, dreams, and memory as diegetic mechanisms through which such intertemporal or transspatial links can be made. Even as the verbal echo of an offer of tea links Dan, the writer's son, to the preacher on his first morning at Liam's house (209, 79, 96), the letter from Dan in the epilogue restores the spatiotemporal parameters of commonsensical modernity by relating an archival discovery that connects the dots between the Pennsylvania preacher of the 1790s and the cattle killing of the 1850s.

The opening frame concludes with an impressive display of narrative magic, imagining a counterfactual history of Pittsburgh as past's future and future's past: *"If yesterday none of it sprawled there, if someone, traders in a canoe, Frenchmen, a Negro slave, an Iroquois guide, is drifting down a green river. . . . No city there when they reach the three rivers' magical convergence. When they arrive, will they dream towers of steel and glass rising from the wilderness. This city, this dream. Or another"* (13–14; italics in original). Wideman demonstrates how narrative can posit any point in time as a "present" with its own retrospections and anticipations, as this passage both erases and envisions (but for the first time) Pittsburgh's Golden Triangle as a contemporary urban center.[113] Yet as the passage continues, the writer in the opening frame poses a devastating question about laminate time and narrative magic: *"And if they do and die dreaming and then you find yourself here, where they once were and the kids are here in those savaged row houses bleeding where you hid when you were fifteen, plus or minus, so what"* (14).

So what. The writer demands that narrative's tricks with time be meaningful, and his plan to read to his father is an implicit answer to this question: "And will that listening, if it happens, be part of the story, the beginning of what he reads" (14). Taken together, the novel's performance of time's fluidity, and its emphasis on transmission's efficacy, construe narrative as meaningful and agentive, over revenge, genocide, and prophecy. Thematizing Peter Brooks's account of reception as "the moment of reading and understanding that [narrative] cannot itself ever know" but "seems ever to imagine in advance," Wideman's novel envisions transmission as "part of the story," whether in the father's listening or the preacher's understanding of his therapeutic stories' potential for a happy ending.[114] Taking up his interlocutor's challenge to tell a happy story for once, the preacher introduces the tale of his sojourn with Liam and Mrs. Stubbs, whose immolation he has elliptically signaled the page before.[115] "The only possible happy conclusion to any story I might recount," then, is to occur in its reception, which the preacher hopes will heal the woman so that she will "take up the telling where he must end it" (79, 179). The preacher's sense of a happy ending extends the diegetic series of tragic events to include the effect of the story's narration and continued transmission—its internarrativity. Indeed, Dan's letter in the epilogue casts the archival letters he has found, which link the preacher to his lost, southern-Africa-bound brother, as "a sort of happy ending" (210). In this sense, a happy "ending" is no ending at all, only the beginning of another tale (the son is writing his own book). The anticipation of retrospection that makes reading a teleological drive toward narrative closure, in Brooks's account, becomes instead the anticipation of narrative proliferation, "different stories over and over again that are one story." The prospects for happy endings are in the afterlives of narrative. If the afterlife of history is in narrative, the afterlife of narrative is in reception.

The narrative afterlife performed in *The Cattle Killing* has little to do with theodicy or endtime, which, as we saw earlier in this chapter, Max Horkheimer saw as logically necessary for imagining incomplete pasts. It is, rather, a notion of human intersubjectivity as internarrativity (straining to include the community of those dead and yet unborn), and of "cosmic obstinacy" (the phrase is Gordimer's) to dream of undreamt future possibility amidst the searing facts of history: the madness of racial terror, the seemingly endless superimposition of devastated landscapes and false prophecies.[116] Internarrativity effects the transformation of historical completion into incompletion and open-endedness, through the proliferation of narrative and the ramification of relationships among the dead and the living. The novel warily intimates an *unimagined* future, at once uneasy and straitened (who can bear another prophecy?) and transfigurational (who can *not* yearn to see an immanent world within this one?). Yet the glimpses of global totality scattered throughout *The Cattle Killing* never throw off the shadow of a disenchanted history that charts the African diaspora through local variations on a global theme of genocide, survival, and imagination. In this sense, *The Cattle Killing* as prose fiction, and the cattle killing as historical event that remains incomplete and available for reanimation (if not redemption), are global reimaginaries, refusing to forget what has never been and revealing a radically different map of what the world might be.

Mazisi Kunene's meditation in *SA, 27 April 1994* on voting with and for the dead introduced my consideration of what it means to open oneself to, and to represent, the dead and their desires. We have seen how Bailey and Wideman draw upon the temporal flexibility of literary representation to understand the relationship between the past's future and the future's past in the afterlives of the cattle killing: in both cases, national aspirations clash with global visions. In *The Cattle Killing*, Wideman looks beyond the traffic lines of the African diaspora and beneath the epidermalization of inequality; his affiliative genealogy of the dead offers evanescent glimpses of a world unimaginably transfigured, as opposed to the pre-scripted fulfillment of Christian providential narratives. Bailey's border-crossing affiliative gestures, on the other hand, are contained by a South African national narrative, with the exaltation and foreclosure implicit in such an end.

The recursive but ultimately future-oriented critical melancholia I have traced in the theoretical and literary texts structures a reflection in *SA, 27 April 1994* by Albie Sachs:

> I am astonished by the strain and the sadness of this our most joyous day, when we consummate and extinguish our most precious asset, our hope for the future, because we can't live for it any more, we are in it, deprived by victory of the longing for victory, destabilised by the neutered quality of the normality we have succeeded in accomplishing . . . rendered ordinary by the success of our heroism. Now we must let go of the dream so that it can transform itself and enable new chyrsalises to conceive fresh luminous fluttering creatures.[117]

Sachs describes the election neither as inaugurating a new national narrative, nor as closing the antiapartheid struggle, but as a liminal point between past and future: the uneasy and improbable predicament of having become a fulfilled prophecy, having re(dis)covered the ordinary, inhabiting both the past's future and the future's past. This insistence on relinquishing the dream for the sake of its future transformation embraces fully—if with melancholy—an openness to the future that resembles Liam's sense of narrative openness: "next and next and next." Yet Sachs's exhortation resonates too, particularly in its afterlife more than ten years on, with the preacher's lament: "lost, lost, lost."

This ambivalence is, I believe, constitutive of the problems of temporality, history, memory, and desire that I have traced in *Bulletproof.* My argument for the capacity of narrative to reimagine the history, aftermath, and contemporary legacies of the cattle killing and its unresolved tension between hope and despair has drawn on the work of a number of writers—many of them not literary critics—who valorize literature's facility with imagining temporal structures that historians find counterintuitive. The "creative arts" maintain a space outside the hegemony of historical constructions of the past, Ashis Nandy claims; fiction and film can grasp heterotemporality and nonrationalist, subaltern pasts in ways that scholarly histories cannot, Dipesh Chakrabarty suggests; visions of national liberation take refuge in postcolonial literary culture because they cannot be realized in the world, Pheng Cheah asserts.[118] Writing of the cattle killing, Sheila Boniface Davies argues that "creative accounts . . . offer new perspectives and possibilities that can enhance our understanding of history."[119]

These are utopian and dystopian versions of the same claim, which, on the one hand, hails the visionary possibilities of fictional narrative, and on the other, resignedly admits that these possibilities are "just stories." These arguments construe the literary as the sanctioned space for enchantment in an otherwise disenchanted world.[120] Throughout *Bulletproof,* I have confronted the paradox of metaphor's multivalent relationships to material realities: Tiyo Soga, Dhlomo, and Matshoba all draw on Nongqawuse's vision of the ancestors' return to generate metaphors of community, continuity, and radical change while responding to the pressures of "civilizing" missions in their respective eras. I have examined both the danger of scholarly habits of mind that translate the seemingly magical into "merely" metaphorical concepts that are "really" about the mundane, as well as the epistemological tensions between the prophecies' "magical" aspects and the rationalism of "modernity." At the same time, I have sought to understand the imaginative power and freedom inherent in thinking in terms of the "as-if." In this chapter, the paradox of metaphor and materiality concerns the impossibility of redeeming the dead: the effects of anamnestic solidarity are, for the dead themselves, "only" metaphorical, yet can we therefore disavow such relationships? At the very least, mindfulness of suffering in the past can deepen our commitment to justice in the present, so that what remains metaphorical for "dead generations" can have profound material effects in the future. This conviction is no less important for South Africans in the early decades of democracy than for scholars of "postcolonial" studies located in the U.S. imperium. In this sense, serious engagement with the seemingly magical in whatever discursive realm we find it can work against the containment and neutralization of the imagination and the literary, to help us recognize their worldliness. Although I do not believe that stories about Nongqawuse will catalyze the return of Xhosa ancestors with herds of beautiful cattle, I have sought to show how the afterlives of the cattle killing have helped to imagine—and begin to realize—a world in which things will have been set right.

NOTES

INTRODUCTION

1. Fanon, *Wretched of the Earth*, trans. Philcox, 145–46; Mbeki, speech at his inauguration, 1999.

2. Cohn, "Medieval Millenarianism," 31. See also Adas, *Prophets of Rebellion*; Wallace, "Revitalization Movements"; Linton and Hallowell, "Nativistic Movements."

3. See Spence, *God's Chinese Son*; Clark, *Hauhau*; Hittman, *Wovoka*; Singh, *Birsa Munda*; Ranger, *Revolt in Southern Rhodesia*; Cunha, *Rebellion in the Backlands*; Anderson and Johnson, *Revealing Prophets*; Martin, *Kimbangu*.

4. Joseph Kony, leader of the Lord's Resistance Army, assumed the mantle of spirit medium Alice Lakwena's 1986–87 Holy Spirit Movement; his war continues to destabilize east Africa.

5. Writing that he "began with the desire to speak with the dead," Stephen Greenblatt concedes that literature fosters not dialogue with the dead but, rather, listening to his "own voice." Greenblatt, *Shakespearean Negotiations*, 1. The vexed role of liminal and ancestral voices speaking through prophets in millenarian movements, however, makes me uneasy about collapsing the voice of the dead into a reader's own voice.

6. Devi, *Chotti Munda*, 137.

7. Birsa Munda also is commemorated in a postage stamp, a Ranchi jail and airport, army songs, and the selection of his birthday for the inauguration of the new Indian state of Jharkhand, carved from mostly tribal regions, in 2000.

8. A similar dynamic is at work in the twenty-first-century "war on terrorism," with repeated announcements of the capture or death of the "number two man in al Qaeda" or the "twentieth hijacker."

9. Silko, *Almanac*, 224–28.

10. Fanon, "Lumumba's Death," 197.

11. Marx, *Eighteenth Brumaire*, 320.

12. Gikandi, *Maps of Englishness*, 16.

13. For a fascinating investigation of North American messianic prophecies, written in the wake of Wounded Knee, see Mooney, *Ghost-Dance Religion*. For a scholarly historiographical analysis, see Hittman, *Wovoka*.

14. Attwell, *Rewriting Modernity*, 71.

15. Terence Ranger outlines and complicates this prevailing historiographical distinction between "primitive" millenarianism and secular nationalism. Ranger, "Connections." For an example, see Hobsbawm, *Primitive Rebels*, 57–65, 107.

16. This tension drives much of the (post)colonial archive, as articulated in Africa by figures like Amílcar Cabral and Frantz Fanon or in India by figures like Rabindranath Tagore and Mohandas Gandhi. On late-nineteenth- and early twentieth-century nationalism, see, for example, Korang, *Writing Ghana*; Chatterjee, *Nation and Its Fragments*.

17. Worsley, *Trumpet Shall Sound*, 245.

18. Bulletproof claims also appear outside of millenarian contexts. Bryan Wilson traces east African notions of sacred water that offered protection during warfare, beginning with the Mahdi rebellion of the 1880s. See Wilson, *Magic and the Millennium*, 240–45. Both the Maji-Maji Rebellion in Tanganyika (1905–7) and the Mai Mai rebels of the contemporary eastern Democratic Republic of the Congo take their names from *maji*, the Kiswahili word for water. In the Xhosa context, ceremonies of "national sacrifice" for making armies invulnerable in battle are described in Maclean, *Compendium*, 87–88; see also J. H. Soga, *Ama-Xosa*, 173–74.

19. Lategan, "Fire-arms"; Shineberg, "Guns," 72, 80.

20. Ranger, "Connections," 634.

21. Silko, *Almanac*, 724.

22. "Most modern third-world histories" are structured as narratives of transition from tradition to modernity, Dipesh Chakrabarty writes in *Provincializing Europe*, 31.

23. Fanon, *Wretched of the Earth*, trans. Farrington, 55–58, 109–10.

24. Chakrabarty, *Provincializing Europe*, 77. For an important critique of the oversimplifications and blindnesses of secularization narratives, see Viswanathan, "Secularism."

25. Fanon, *Wretched of the Earth*, trans. Farrington, 197.

26. Viswanathan, "Secularism," 468. Viswanathan suggests that the seeming binary of reason/religion actually represents a cooperation between secularism and mainstream religion: first because the profound influence of notions of Christian redemption on secular progress narratives is largely unrecognized; and second because neither secularism nor mainstream religion can acknowledge popular, "alternative spiritual practices," which are thereby marginalized and their historical memory repressed (472, 475).

27. Udechukwu, "Interview with Chinua Achebe," 317.

28. In Islamic contexts, the millennial expectations associated with Mahdism also have been an important source of anticolonial impulses since the late-nineteenth-century revolt of Muhammad Ahmad against Anglo-Egyptian control of the Sudan.

29. Cabral, *Revolution in Guinea*, 16–17.

30. Among the heavy ironies of the days after September 11, 2001, was the performance by Haitian-born Wyclef Jean of Bob Marley's "Redemption Song" on the fundraising marathon *America: A Tribute to Heroes*. Jean's mournful shout-outs to "New York City" and his adopted hometown of Brooklyn as he sang, in the shadow of still-smoldering towers, "How long will they kill our prophets?" and "We got to fulfill the Book" elicit profound cognitive dissonance. Jean turned Marley's millennial protest against centuries of slavery and the supression of antiracism and anti-imperialism into an elegy for those killed in the World Trade Center and the Pentagon, icons of US hegemony.

31. De Kock, "South Africa," 289.

32. Lazarus, "South African Ideology," 609.

33. Korang, *Writing Ghana*, 41–42.

34. Sekyi-Otu, *Fanon's Dialectic*, 12–14.

35. De Kock, "South Africa," 289.

36. *Toyi-toyi* was the energetic high-stepping marching dance, accompanied by song or chant, associated with the mass movements of the 1980s. *Toyi-toyi* originated in the Zimbabwean national liberation struggle in the 1970s; militants for Umkhonto we Sizwe (the armed wing of the African National Congress [ANC]) brought it back from Zimbabwean training camps.

37. In his foreword to the report of the Truth and Reconciliation Commission, Archbishop Desmond Tutu acknowledges that without the "miracle of negotiated settlement . . . we would have been overwhelmed by the bloodbath that virtually everyone predicted as the inevitable ending for South Africa." See Truth and Reconciliation Commission, *Report*, 1:5. The "bloodbath" imagined in Silko's novel (written throughout the 1980s) catalyzes a definitive expropriation of land and political power. None of these had come to pass by the time of the novel's publication in 1991, the year after Mandela's release.

38. One oral historian links the cattle killing to the Bantustan government of Transkei. In a 1967 recitation, Chief Ndumiso Bhotomane, descendant of a cattle-killing participant, claimed that in its aftermath "the Mathanzimas began to come up . . . but at the time when Sarhili was alive here, they did not dare to come near this area! . . . But now, the European government gave them that land." See Scheub, *Tongue Is Fire*, 306. Bhotomane links the British resettlement of Thembu people in lands vacated by the decimated amaXhosa to the rise of the Matanzima family; a century later, Thembu chief Kaiser Matanzima, with his brother George, ruled Transkei in collusion with the apartheid state.

39. This summary is synthesized from several sources, most importantly Peires's *The Dead Will Arise*. I untangle this history throughout *Bulletproof.*

40. Pointing to the variety of names recorded in the colonial archive, Helen Bradford argues that Nongqawuse was a name (an "alias" or ritual name) that the prophet assumed as the events of the 1850s unfolded. Bradford, "New Country." Others have suggested that Nongqawuse was a contemptuous epithet bestowed after the catastrophe.

41. Jordan, *Towards an African Literature*, 74.

42. Scheub, *Tongue Is Fire*, 308–11.

43. Crais, *White Supremacy*, 194, 212.

44. Davis, *Late Victorian Holocausts*, 12.

45. Elkins, "From Malaya to Kenya."

46. Klein, "Rise of Disaster Capitalism."

47. W. Impey to J. Maclean, letter dated April 18, 1857, GH 8/50, Cape Archives.

48. Lester, *Imperial Networks*, 159–66.

49. Williams, "Indian Mutiny," 62.

50. Stephens, *Black Empire*, 13.

51. Truth and Reconciliation Commission, *Report*, 1:25.

52. Plaatje, *Native Life*, 295.

53. Although only those who view the cattle killing as a colonial hoax have claimed that Nongqawuse had direct interaction with Europeans, there is a certain similarity with Pocahontas and La Malinche in the Americas—young indigenous women remembered (romantically and disparagingly) as playing crucial, mediating roles.

54. "Yayilishobo kwaloo nto / Ukuqalekiswa kwesizwe sikaXhosa." Yali-Manisi performed an impromptu *izibongo mbaliso* (oral narrative poem) about Nongqawuse at the instigation of Jeff Opland. See Opland, "Imbongi Nezibongo," 201.

55. Samuelson, "Historical Time," 18.

56. Mbembe, "South Africa's Second Coming." Mbembe's essay was a thinly veiled criticism of Jacob Zuma, then Thabo Mbeki's populist rival for leadership of the ANC.

57. Ibid.

58. With regard to contemporary resonances of Nongqawuse's vision, particularly sug-

gestive is the case of Golden Nonquase, a former mineworker whose home and workshop in Khayelitsha (outside Cape Town) has become a township tour destination. Golden Nonquase credits the inspiration for his cottage-industry crafting of decorative flowers out of soda cans to a visionary dream of a field of flowers that he was told could provide for his livelihood. In another version of the story, the dream told him to go to a rubbish dump and to sell the flowers he found there, "flowers" which he eventually came to recognize in the discarded cans. See Gubic, "South Africa."

59. Attwell, *Rewriting Modernity*, 8, emphasis in the original.

60. Anderson and Johnson, *Revealing Prophets*, 1; Dimock, "Planetary Time," 507, 493.

61. On Benjamin's antisystematicity, see Honneth, "Communicative Disclosure."

62. Bauman, "Walter Benjamin," 49–50, emphasis in the original.

63. Benjamin, "Task of the Translator," 71.

64. Benjamin, "Theses," 263, 255, emphasis in the original.

65. Benjamin, *Arcades Project*, 462. On the dialectical image, see Osborne, *Politics of Time*, 138–58; Buck-Morss, *Dialectics of Seeing*.

66. Pensky, "Method and Time," 179.

67. Benjamin, "Theses," 254, 261.

68. Benjamin, *Arcades Project*, 462–63.

69. Bloch, *Principle of Hope*, 1:75.

70. Tom Moylan persuasively argues that we can understand Bloch's regrettable failure to disavow Stalin as a failure to understand his own best insights about utopia as unfettered by and antithetical to teleologies, even Marxist ones. See Moylan, "Bloch against Bloch."

71. This is the "tension between experience and expectation which . . . generates historical time." See Koselleck, *Futures Past*, 275.

72. See http://keiskamma.org.

73. Gordimer, "Living in the Interregnum," 275.

74. On the "politics of literary failure" and the contingency of notions of the literary, see Barnard, *Great Depression*, 41–71.

CHAPTER ONE

1. Matshaya and Laing, "Charles Henry Matshaya," 32; Peires, *Dead Will Arise*, 237; Ong, *Orality and Literacy*, 15.

2. Jordan, *Towards an African Literature*, 70.

3. These figures come from the 1857 census and estimations of survivors entering the Cape Colony surreptitiously or through Grey's "famine relief" labor-channeling system; approximately 150,000 people were displaced by the cattle killing and subsequent attacks by the Colony. Maclean, *Compendium*, 129; Peires, *Dead Will Arise*, 267, 319–20. Approximately 85 percent of Xhosa men complied with the order to kill cattle. Peires, "Central Beliefs," 43. This calculation is complicated by the fact that many had lost their cattle to epizootic disease.

4. Gqoba titled his account "Isizatu Sokuxelwa Kwe Nkomo Ngo Nongqause," which Jordan translates as "The Cause of the Cattle-Killing at the Nongqawuse Period." See Jordan, *Towards an African Literature*.

5. Bradford, "Akukho," 220–23, 222.

6. Soga, *Ama-Xosa*, 121. Oral narratives from the 1960s and '70s are collected in Scheub, *Tongue Is Fire*. David Livingstone Phakamile Yali-Manisi's improvised *izibongo* (praise poem) on Nongqawuse appears in Opland, "Imbongi Nezibongo." Bradford notes that the hoax explanation does not appear in transcriptions of oral accounts until the mid-twentieth century; she also outlines a Xhosa periodization of the mid-nineteenth century, in which the "Nongqawuse period" of "unprecedented phenomena" extends from 1856 to 1862, rather than merely the events of 1856–57. See Bradford, "New Country," "Akukho," 216.

7. I am grateful to Jeff Peires for help with the *Isigidimi* version of Gqoba's narrative.

8. Bradford, "Women, Gender and Colonialism," 363; Gqoba quoted from Jordan, *Towards an African Literature*, 70. The relevant term in Gqoba's second installment is *imibulo nokurexeza*—incests and adulteries, although *imibulo* connotes a broader notion of sexual impurity than intrafamilial sexual relations. See Peires, afterword, 375. Bradford puts a great deal of stock in the possibility that Nongqawuse was an incest victim (perhaps by Mhlakaza), a reading I find unconvincing; it distracts from her important argument that illicit sexual practices and the difficulty of contracting legitimate relationships during a time of cattle shortage were among the forms of pollution and social unrest that provoked the cattle killing.

9. Soga, *Ama-Xosa*, 132.

10. On the importance of control over women (the means of labor reproduction) and control over the means of subsistence in agricultural societies, see Meillassoux, "From Reproduction to Production."

11. Bradford, "Women, Gender and Colonialism," 361–64. An 1856 rumor offered another sexual explanation: "it is generally believed that Krili [Sarhili] has been bewitched by a Basuto doctress for turning against his great wife," who was the sister of Umgangeni, chief of the Tembu. J. Maclean to G. Grey, letter dated December 22, 1856, GH 8/49, Cape Archives. Instead of avenging his sister through her estranged husband's death, Umgangeni was reported to have Sarhili placed "under a delusion in which he will see things that no one else sees, and which spreading thro' his tribe, will cause it to be dispersed, that they may be reduced to servitude and entirely broken up." J. Ayliff to J. Maclean, letter dated December 22, 1856, GH 8/49. As in hegemonic readings of the cattle killing, female mediums are manipulated in male rivalries; the "Basuto doctress" story, however, foregrounds the importance of marriage in Xhosa sociopolitics.

12. What the Comaroffs write of the Tswana holds true for the amaXhosa: "Cattle, in sum, were the pliable symbolic vehicles through which *men* formed and reformed their world of social and spiritual relations." See Comaroff and Comaroff, *Of Revelation and Revolution*, 1:145, emphasis added. Grey observed that for the amaXhosa "voluntarily to destroy their cattle was voluntarily to destroy their entire polity, and to sweep away all their national habits and customs." Speech before Parliament, April 7, 1857, *Imperial Blue Books* (*IBB*) 2352, p. 89. Helen Bradford notes that, in Xhosa chronicles of *iziganeko* (important events), the epizootic of the 1850s is knows as *Imofu*, the isiXhosa word for cattle of European origin. Bradford, "*Akukho*," 212.

13. Falati, "The Story of Ntsikana a Gaika Xhosa" (1895), translated by N. Falati and C. Mpaki, MS 9063, Cory Library.

14. This quarterly (published in Arabic, English, and French) was launched in 1968 and continued through the early 1990s, with funding from Egypt, the U.S.S.R., and the German Democratic Republic. Halim, "*Lotus* Project."

15. Opland, *Xhosa Poets*, 240–41.

16. De Kock, *Civilising Barbarians*, 108.

17. In his novel *The Wrath of the Ancestors*, Jordan titles one chapter "What a Fairy Tale! Nongqawuse." When a young man reveals to a fellow Lovedale student that her sweetheart is heir to the royal seat of the Mpondomise people, she interjects, "When are these fantastic Nongqawuse tales ever to end in this Africa of ours?" Jordan, *Wrath*, 18. Reverend Brownlee John Ross, descendant of nineteenth-century missionaries, wrote in 1948: "For long years after [the 1850s] any false report or baseless rumour used to be called by intelligent Natives a 'Nongqause.'" Ross and Shepherd, *Brownlee J. Ross*, 96.

18. Some cattle-killing narratives make no mention of Nongqawuse; see, for example, Laing, *Memorials of the Rev. James Laing* (1875) and Calderwood, *Caffres and Caffre Missions* (1858).

19. See the introduction, n40 on "Nongqawuse" as an alias or epithet.

20. Ashforth, "Xhosa Cattle Killing," 590.

21. Peires, *Dead Will Arise*, 179.

22. These distinctions persisted: in 1870, Tiyo Soga distinguished between the "old killing party—that say the customs of our Fathers are good enough for us—[and] the liberal party that hails light—improvement, good & orderly Govt from the whiteman." Soga, *Journal*, 42.

23. *New people* is a term that pervades colonial sources and "does not correlate directly with any phrase in the surviving Xhosa-language texts," although they do use words formed from *-tsha*, "new, young, healthy." Peires, "Central Beliefs," 53. Bradford links "new people" to Uhlanga, the creator god and the cave from which the created world emerged. Bradford, "New Country." Jan Tzatzoe, Christian chief of the amaTinde, mentioned "new people" (and a returned Adam) in a report to Commissioner Maclean. J. Tzatzoe to J. Maclean, letter dated October 15, 1856, *IBB* 2352, p. 51.

24. See Comaroff and Comaroff, *Of Revelation and Revolution*, I.75–78; Elbourne, *Blood Ground*, 43–51. For prospective African converts, "missions also brought a new view of nature . . . and a new view of history (an 'open' one, in which God and man actively create a new world)." Millennial aspects of the missionary message were particularly appealing, since converts could understand "their personal and national travail as part of global historical patterns that will culminate in the establishment of a Kingdom of God on earth." Elphick, "Africans," 305–6, 304.

25. One can be cynical about such millennial dreams as ideological cover for colonial domination; I am not suggesting that Grey led a millenarian *movement*. Yet such cynicism, like the chiefs' plot thesis that saw in the cattle killing only a pretext for war against the colony, misses the imaginative investments, on all sides of the colonial divide, in visions of a "new" Xhosa world. "The British could describe themselves to themselves as modern, and as agents of a rationalizing modernity in the world through the medium of Christianity: ironically, eighteenth-century evangelical eschatology ultimately came to sit at the feet of secular progressivism." Elbourne, *Blood Ground*, 15.

26. Quoted in Shepherd, *Lovedale, South Africa*, 67.

27. As was the case elsewhere in Africa, missions were most attractive to marginalized groups and individuals. Until the mid-nineteenth century, eastern Cape mission communities consisted mostly of the Gqunukhwebe people (of Gqonaqua and Xhosa descent) and the Mfengu (refugees of demographic upheavals to the east who settled among the amaXhosa in the 1820s and who chafed against their subordination to the Gcaleka). Williams, "Missionaries," 247–74. The Mfengu (or "Fingo") generally allied with the British against the amaXhosa; they also were fervent unbelievers in the cattle killing.

28. Keegan, *Moravians*, xxix.

29. J. Maclean to W. Liddle, letter dated August 4, 1855, *IBB* 2096, p. 18.

30. See map on page 18.

31. Mill, *On Liberty*, 11.

32. British settlers were slow to appear in what had long been either a war zone or a tense frontier. Grey supervised the settlement of German mercenaries recruited for the Crimean War effort. Magistrate John Gawler noted the ironic connection between colonial schemes and Xhosa dreams: he brought Xhosa believers to the shore to watch "'our' new people come out.'" Bradford, "New Country," emphasis added.

33. Enclosure in G. Grey to G. Grey, letter dated 17 March 1855, *IBB* 1969, p. 56.

34. Majeke, *Role of Missionaries*, 69, emphasis in the original. I discuss the pseudonymous authorship of this text in chapter 2.

35. G. Grey to H. Labouchere, letter dated March 6, 1857, *IBB* 2352, p. 67.

36. Speech before Parliament, *IBB* 2352, April 7, 1857, p. 90.

37. G. Grey to H. Labouchere, letter dated August 27, 1856, *IBB* 2352, p. 22. Maclean saw the events of late 1856 "working to a good end . . . altho' not yet broken down by conquest the nation will be humbled by famine" which "will render the Kaffir much more submissive and tractable than they have hitherto been, and an opportunity will be given of pushing toward

your Excellency's system, and will enable us to bring the natives more directly under the influence of Govt. than years of caution . . . [I]t will only remain to us to take advantage of, and hold the ground which we are now to all appearances about to gain." J. Maclean to G. Grey, letter dated November 3 and 24, 1856, GH 8/49, Cape Archives.

38. De Kock, *Civilising Barbarians*, 27.

39. Chanaiwa, "African Humanism," 34.

40. Hodgson, *God of the Xhosa*, 19; Bradford, "New Country."

41. This entanglement of new and familiar is complex, given the epistemological baggage surrounding European cultural imperialism aimed against indigenous "backwardness" and "superstition." Zimbabwe's national liberation struggle in the 1970s (second chimurenga), which drew on the authority of spirit mediums associated with primary resistance in the 1890s (first chimurenga), is apposite here: guerrillas "gained acceptance as autochthons, the warriors of the past returned in new guise. . . . The paradox is that the only reason that the guerrillas were allowed to occupy these ancient categories is that they were *not* the warriors of the past. . . . [I]f the guerrillas had *only* waved battle axes and spears and left their machine guns at home, if they had tried to revive the old techniques of resistance which had failed time and again rather than introducing new ones, their reception by the peasants would have been altogether different." Lan, *Guns and Rain*, 225, emphasis in the original. What distinguished Nongqawuse's prophecy from others in the 1850s was that she claimed that the people had *already* returned and that she had seen them. Bradford, "New Country."

42. Williams, *Umfundisi*, 4.

43. Missionary F. G. Kayser was told by a Xhosa man in 1842, "'We have for a long time resisted the Word of God, but now [that you have dug a watercourse] we will come nearer to it and lead the water out lower down from you.'" Williams, *When Races Meet*, 45. Noting that irrigation channels were among missionaries' first priorities, Williams asserts that severe droughts in kwaXhosa were crucial to their appeal. Williams, "Missionaries," 65.

44. Glasgow Missionary Society, *Report*, 27.

45. Shepherd, *Lovedale, South Africa*, 65.

46. Shepherd, *Bantu Literature*, 27.

47. Bennie knew his audience: at the top of the first sheet ever printed in isiXhosa ran the text *"Inkomo zonke zezikaTixo: ungumninizo yena,"* "All cattle belong to God: he alone is the owner." Opland, *Xhosa Oral Poetry*, 196.

48. The cattle killing drew on earlier prophecies, the first articulated between 1810 and 1820 by Nxele (or Makana), who had significant contact with European missionaries and articulated a Christian-influenced, anti-European theology: Thixo was the European god, Mdalidephu the god of black people. Nxele claimed to be a messianic son of the creator, Uhlanga, as well as the brother of Christ, for whose murder Europeans were to be punished. Nxele's insistence that his followers kill some cattle and give up witchcraft, in anticipation of the emergence of ances- tors and cattle, was a precursor to the events of the mid-1850s. As a war-doctor (*itola*), Nxele claimed that he could make his followers bulletproof. (There is no evidence that Nongqawuse had contact with missionaries.) On relationships between Xhosa prophecy and Christian theology, see Peires, *Dead Will Arise*, 134–38; Bradford, "Not a Nongqawuse Story."

49. Quoted in Beinart and Bundy, "Union," 294. This message was heard at a 1930 rally of the Independent Industrial and Commercial Workers' Union. A similar citation of Ntsikana appears in Magona's novel *Mother to Mother*.

50. Ntsikana's followers included Gqoba's grandfather. Opland, *Xhosa Poets*, 284.

51. Williams, "Missionaries," 232, emphasis in the original. Agricultural metaphors cut both ways: in an excised passage in the manuscript of his biography of Tiyo Soga, Chalmers winces at the contrast between a mature tree planted from a cutting and the diminution of converts in the intervening years: "the tree lives, 'tis still there. But where are the devout wor- shippers of three & twenty years ago?" Chalmers, "Tiyo Soga," MS PR3988, Cory Library.

246 / NOTES TO PAGES 43-45

52. Chalmers, *Tiyo Soga*, 5–6. In support of mission agriculture, Stretch donated seeds, ploughs, and half of the two hundred pounds needed to build irrigation channels at Tyhume. Williams, "Missionaries," 141.

53. Crais, *White Supremacy*, 18–22.

54. Comaroff and Comaroff, "Goodly Beasts," 210. William Kentridge's short film *Tide Table* (2003), suggests these contested regimes of value, juxtaposing images of cattle reduced to commodities with images of cattle elevated as indexes of a recreative life cycle in the era of HIV/AIDS. In an excised passage in Chalmers's manuscript, Stretch cites noneconomic value forms of cattle (and Eurocentric disdain for Xhosa gender roles) as a reason for not granting Soga's request: "'if you had oxen you would not use them to cultivate your garden, your weak and poor women are the oxen you employ to provide grain for consumption. The oxen you would only race through the country for amusement & admiration & praise the one that ran in front.' Soga assented by a very significant laugh." Chalmers, "Tiyo Soga," MS PR3988, Cory Library.

55. Marx, *Capital*, 1:163.

56. Williams, "Missionaries," 228.

57. Stewart, *Dawn in the Dark Continent*, 190. Chalmers's sketch of the Lovedale apprentice Dukwana (son of Ntsikana) implies a more favorable view of print: "because he managed the small press, and printed the school books and the leaflet newspaper . . . from which we read of the truthfulness of George Washington, [he] was looked up to as a very oracle." Chalmers, *Tiyo Soga*, 23.

58. De Kock, *Civilising Barbarians*, 30, 33–34.

59. Chalmers, *Tiyo Soga*, 37.

60. "Kuba mhla kwafik' abefundisi / Babelek' iBhayibhile ngaphambili / Kanti baxway' imfakadolo ngasemva." Opland, "*Imbongi Nezibongo*," 199, 198.

61. Opland, *Xhosa Poets*, 322. This yoking of books and guns is multivalent. Early missionaries rebuffed settler arguments that "powder and ball" were the only means of civilizing the amaXhosa; after the 1834–35 war, however, the disillusioned missionary John Ayliff wrote, "'They have rejected the Gospel which was benevolently sent unto them . . . and now they have the sword.'" The Wesleyan Missionary Society deleted Ayliff's comment from its official correspondence. Williams, "Missionaries," 366, 173. Charles Henry Matshaya recalls an encounter with a British soldier who brandished his gun and said, "'This is our book. Begone.'" Matshaya and Laing, "Charles Henry Matshaya," 34. Ngũgĩ wa Thiong'o writes that, in the scramble for Africa, "the night of the sword and the bullet was followed by the morning of the chalk and the blackboard." Ngũgĩ, *Decolonising the Mind*, 9. Reversing this trope, former freedom fighters in Umkhonto we Sizwe, the armed wing of the African National Congress, reminisce in the documentary film *Amandla!* about revising old hymns for militant ends: "changing a word here, changing a word there; put in an AK[47] there, take out a Bible there."

62. Chalmers, *Tiyo Soga*, 327. In 1868, Tiyo Soga helped to found a mission station near Sarhili at Tutura, at Sarhili's request. He worked there until his death in 1871.

63. Williams identifies this text as the first biography in southern Africa; it is a problematic source full of distortions, elisions, and editorial transformations. Chalmers's freewheeling treatment of documents yet extant casts doubts over his representations of materials (including an official journal, letters, and mission records) lost or destroyed in World War II. Williams, *Umfundisi*, xvi; Attwell, *Rewriting Modernity*, 42–44; De Kock, *Civilising Barbarians*, 175–76.

64. Hofmeyr, *Portable Bunyan*, 14.

65. Missionaries to the amaXhosa from 1818 to 1830, including Joseph Williams, John Brownlee, and W. R. Thomson, held combined offices of missionary and government agent; their dual charge was "'inculcation of civilisation'" and "'transmission of information to the Colonial Government.'" Williams, *When Races Meet*, 4, 24. Likewise, the association between literacy and colonial co-optation that Tiyo Soga reports is borne out in a reported statement by Siwani,

nephew of chief Mhala, who assured his magistrate Robert Hawkes that he had ordered his people not to kill cattle. He pledged to remain "faithful to the Government . . . having long ago 'touched the pen.'" R. Hawkes to J. Maclean, letter dated February 8, 1857, GH 8/50, Cape Archives.

66. To my knowledge, this photograph has not been published before. It was likely taken during Tiyo Soga's tenure as a missionary among Sarhili's people in the Transkei, from 1868 until his death in 1871, and perhaps at the inauguration of his new church in April 1871. Other images of Sarhili depict him in Xhosa rather than European dress. Some of the other Xhosa men in the photograph may have been among those imprisoned on Robben Island after the cattle killing, who were all released by 1869. I have noted resemblances between three of the men and extant images of the Ndlambe chief Mhala, the Ngqika chief Sandile, and the Thembu chief Fadana (cattle-killing believers all); conclusive identification of them and the remaining two men awaits further investigation.

67. Soga, *Journal*, 86–87.

68. Ong, *Orality and Literacy*, 15.

69. Hofmeyr, *Portable Bunyan*, 14, 17.

70. Peterson, *Monarchs*, 72. See also Mkhize, "Citashe's Apostrophe."

71. Ong's assertion of a gulf between oral and literate cognition has rightly been challenged, and, like Ong's critics, I see technologies of literacy not as neutral or autonomous but as deployed, contested, and appropriated ideologically. For critiques of Ong, see Finnegan, *Literacy and Orality*; Street, *Cross-cultural Approaches*. On colonial literacy, see Newell, *Literary Culture*; Barber, introduction.

72. Quoted in Peires, *Dead Will Arise*, 237, emphasis added.

73. Chalmers, "Tiyo Soga" (1871), 117.

74. Soga, *Journal*, 152.

75. I am indebted to Jeff Peires for his clarification of this passage.

76. For another contemporary account of Xhosa reactions to this eclipse, see Offenburger, "Smallpox," 363.

77. Missionaries were keen to erect watercourses not least because irrigation systems were a "useful weapon in their struggle with the rain-makers," on whom chiefs were dependent to fulfill their role as providers of rain. Williams, "Missionaries," 67. Missionaries staged rain-making contests pitting prayer services against *amagqira le-mvula* ceremonies; rainmakers blamed missionaries or their church bells for keeping rain away. Reyburn, "Missionary as Rain-maker." On rainmaking in other mission encounters in southern Africa, see Comaroff and Comaroff, *Of Revelation and Revolution*, I.203–19.

78. Defining conversion as "not a renunciation of an aspect of oneself . . . but as an intersubjective, transitional, and transactional mode of negotiation between two otherwise irreconcilable world-views," Viswanathan discusses "multiple affiliations opened up by conversion—the possibilities of occupying several positions in relation to nation and religion . . . [C]onverts may be engaged just as readily in a critique of their adopted culture and religion as in a project to reform the culture that they have renounced." Viswanathan, *Outside the Fold*, 176, 39.

79. Barber, introduction, 19.

80. Williams, "Missionaries."

81. Erlank, "Re-examining Initial Encounters."

82. Bradford, "New Country."

83. Because the uncircumcised Tiyo Soga was yet a "boy," Xhosa parents at Uniondale school in the 1840s and Mgwali mission in the 1860s strenuously objected to him teaching their children. Williams, *Umfundisi*, 19.

84. De Kock, *Civilising Barbarians*, 180.

85. Soga, *Journal*, 152.

86. "Native Press," 2. *Isigidimi* was separated from *Christian Express* (formerly *Kaffir Express*, currently *South African Outlook*) in 1876, when Elijah Makiwane became the first

Xhosa newspaper editor. Lovedale principal James Stewart edited both publications from their inauguration in 1870 until 1876. Opland, *Xhosa Poets*, 238–39.

87. Soga, *Journal*, 152; Williams, *Umfundisi*, 5.

88. Chalmers, "Tiyo Soga" (1872), 14.

89. Soga, *Journal*, 78–79.

90. For an account of Ntsikana's religious experience, see Hodgson, "Genius of Ntsikana," 28. J. C. Warner, former Wesleyan missionary and Thembu colonial agent in the 1850s, wrote that the isiXhosa word for the initiation of *amagqira* (diviners) "means 'renewal,' and is the same that is used for the first appearance of the new moon, and for the putting forth of the grass and buds at the commencement of spring. By which it is evidently intended to intimate that the man's heart is renewed, that he has become an entirely different person to what he was before, seeing with different eyes, and hearing with different ears; in short that he now holds communion and intercourse with the invisible world." Maclean, *Compendium*, 82.

91. Bokwe, *Ntsikana*, 12–13.

92. Hodgson, *Ntsikana's Great Hymn*, 9, 11.

93. Jordan, *Towards an African Literature*, 51.

94. Falati, "Story of Ntsikana," MS 9063, Cory Library. Ntsikana and Nxele were attached to rival chiefs Ndlambe and Ngqika. The conflict between Ntsikana and Nxele represented divergent modes of incorporating Christian ideas into a Xhosa worldview. See Peires, "Nxele"; Hodgson, *God of the Xhosa*; Bradford, "New Country."

95. Hofmeyr, *Portable Bunyan*, 13.

96. Bradford, "New Country."

97. See Peires, "Nxele," 53; Legassick, "State," 343n36; Peires, *Dead Will Arise*, 21. In an 1851 campaign, Governor Harry Smith captured nearly 60,000 cattle in British Kaffraria. Crais, *White Supremacy*, 197.

98. In wartime, herds would be taken to the mountains or other remote locations; immovables like grain pits and crops required additional defense closer to the homestead. This idea of destroying wealth to fight without "incumbrance" recurs throughout colonial correspondence of 1856–57; for a rare attribution of this notion to Sarhili, see *IBB* 2352, extract from information to the Chief Commissioner by a trustworthy Native, December 8, 1856, p. 81, as well as Charles Brownlee's testimony at the 1865 Commission of Native Affairs inquiry, where he recalled Sarhili's boast, "'If the Government interferes with me now, I have dogs that can bite, and they will find that instead of my men running about with cattle they will be ready to fight.'" Cape of Good Hope, *Proceedings*.

99. Bradford, "New Country."

100. Chris Andreas questions the extremely high mortality rate (more than 90 percent) claimed for lung sickness in the eastern Cape; he suggests that it may have been closer to the virulence of the disease reported elsewhere (less than 70 percent). Andreas, "Spread and Impact."

101. I owe the evocative phrase "ancestral stock exchange" to John Comaroff. The multiple notions of value that it suggests are literalized in the reported reproach by chief Sandile's nephew Oba of counselors who convinced him to kill his cattle: "by not doing so," they told him, "he had prevented his father from rising, and now that his father had not risen, he insisted that these counselors should at once make good the loss which they had counseled him to inflict on himself." C. Brownlee to J. Maclean, letter dated February 25, 1857, GH 8/50, Cape Archives.

102. "Inkomo luhlanga, zifile luyakufa uhlanga." Soga, *Ama-Xosa*, 122.

103. Chalmers, *Tiyo Soga*, 342.

104. This idea complicates the assertion that the absence of an "objective" written record allows a selective forgetting that distinguishes oral from literate societies. Goody and Watt, "Consequences of Literacy."

NOTES TO PAGES 55–58 / 249

105. Soga, *Journal*, 180.

106. De Kock, "Textual Capture," 54.

107. See chapters 2 and 3 on the "New African" elite in South Africa; for similar formations in West Africa, see Korang, *Writing Ghana*; Zachernuk, *Colonial Subjects*; Falola, *Nationalism and African Intellectuals*. On the United States and the Caribbean, see Stephens, *Black Empire*; on India, see Goswami, *Producing India*.

108. Korang, *Writing Ghana*, 34.

109. Martin Delany's *The Condition, Elevation, Emigration and Destiny of the Colored People of the United States Politically Considered* (1852) closes with what Paul Gilroy calls a "recognisably Pan-African flourish" in its voicing of the Ethiopian cry. Gilroy, *Black Atlantic*, 20. Gilroy begins his genealogy of the roots and routes of black Atlantic discourse with Delany; his identification of Delany as a pan-African figure is more convincing than Williams's claims for Tiyo Soga because Delany's concern with imagining a transnational black future drove much of his life's work and writing.

110. Attwell, "Intimate Enmity," 565.

111. Explaining his interest in Tiyo Soga, Williams wrote, "The time has come for resurrection." Soga, *Journal*, 1.

112. Chalmers, *Tiyo Soga*, 103, emphasis added. Peires surmises that Mhlakaza was a "gospel man" named Wilhelm Goliath, a servant of Nathaniel Merriman, archdeacon of Grahamstown, before he left disillusioned and became a diviner and spiritual healer in the Xhosa tradition (in colonial discourse, "witch doctor"; in isiXhosa, *igqira*). Peires, *Dead Will Arise*, 33–36. Other historians are skeptical of Peires's reading of his evidence for the identification of Mhlakaza as Wilhelm Goliath; see chapter 4, n49.

113. This lament about *dispersal* recurs throughout Tiyo Soga's writing on the cattle killing's aftermath.

114. An Englishwoman touring eastern Cape missions in 1857 drew similar conclusions: "Surely such faith in false words should put to shame some who profess to believe the truth; and, surely, when the Kafir mind is rightly directed and influenced, those traits of character which have led a deluded people to confront temporal death will lead them towards eternal life." *Recollections of a Visit*, 117.

115. A similar dynamic appears in the official correspondence of Ngqika commissioner Charles Brownlee, who recounted for chief Sandile and his councilors the Christian creation story and the eschatological promise of resurrection and judgment. Brownlee concluded, "But the time is not yet. Umhlakaza professes to have his revelations from God. God is a God of Truth, and what he has once revealed to man stands as unchangeable as himself. There will be no resurrection of men or beasts, as predicted by Umhlakaza, for his resurrection is opposed to the Word of God." Brownlee figures his own position at this meeting, where he tried to dissuade Sandile from ordering his people to kill cattle, as that of a prophet more reliable than Xhosa prophets like Mhlakaza or Mlanjeni: "Did Umlanjeni perform an iota of what he had promised, and which of my words proved false?" C. Brownlee to J. Maclean, letter dated August 5, 1856, *IBB* 2202, p. 53.

116. See White, *Tropics of Discourse*.

117. White, *Content of the Form*, 2.

118. On Theal's monumental status within South African historiography, problematic because of his racial bias, failure to cite sources, and enormous influence on history textbooks, see Thompson, *Political Mythology*; Saunders, *Making of the South African Past*.

119. Theal, *Compendium*, 51.

120. An exhaustive examination of Theal's entire body of work is beyond my scope. Theal uses the same account in *South Africa*. In *Progress of South Africa*, the account is condensed to three paragraphs.

121. Theal, *History*, 202. Commissioner Maclean claimed that anticipated atmospheric disturbances such as earthquakes and unnatural oceanic or celestial movements were "'re-

membrances of Scripture statements,'" implying that Xhosa prophecy borrowed from the Bible. Peires, "Central Beliefs," 61.

122. Brownlee, *Reminiscences*, 143–44. Unless otherwise noted, all citations of Mrs. Brownlee are taken from Saunders's 1977 edition of Charles Brownlee's *Reminiscences of Kaffir Life and History* (1896).

123. Mrs. Brownlee was the former Frances Thomson, daughter of W. R. Thomson of the Tyhume mission, established by her father-in-law, John Brownlee.

124. Holden, *Past and Future*, 289.

125. Holden's imputation of the prophecy as "jugglery" brings to mind Greenblatt's discussion of "Machiavellian anthropology," which posits "religion as a set of beliefs manipulated by the subtlety of priests to help instill obedience and respect for authority." Greenblatt traces the containment of subversive notions of *Christianity* as "confidence trick" used to exert European control over inhabitants of the New World. Greenblatt, *Shakespearean Negotiations*, 26. Holden's reading of *Xhosa* prophecy as evidence of the need for European intervention reflects similar ambivalence, yet Holden allows far less scope to the subversive thrust than do Greenblatt's early modern texts.

126. Jordan, *Towards an African Literature*, 74–75.

127. Jordan, *Towards an African Literature*, 72.

128. Chalmers, *Tiyo Soga*, 120.

129. Theal, *History*, 204.

130. Brownlee, *Reminiscences*, 148.

131. FitzGerald, letterbook, August 31, 1857, p. 95.

132. A passage by Mrs. Brownlee in the manuscript of Chalmers's biography contrasts the physical state of "weak emaciated objects" with their mental state, an "already overfed imagination." Chalmers, "Tiyo Soga," MS PR3988, Cory Library. Describing the famine's death toll, S. M. Molema writes, "The harvest of credulity was fully gathered." Molema, *Bantu Past*, 168.

133. I owe this point to John Comaroff.

134. In the manuscript of Chalmers's biography, Frances Brownlee confesses to a certain susceptibility to the prophecy: "I almost began to feel a little superstitious myself, left as I was day after day alone." She describes her husband's return from meeting with Sandile: "I fancy I see them now as they appeared on the Sunday morning, returning from that melancholy conference, 'Napakadi' [Brownlee], his followers, dragged, dispirited, wet, weary, sorrowful, & sorry company they looked, as they passed the little church at Bethel, where I had gone, uneasy and anxious, one felt it was the only place where one could be at rest." Chalmers, "Tiyo Soga," MS PR3988, Cory Library.

135. Holden, *Past and Future*, 283.

136. Chalmers, *Tiyo Soga*, 103, 106; Brownlee, *Reminiscences*, 137, 145; Theal, *Compendium*, 53; Laing, *Memorials*, 182.

137. See, for example, an anxious letter from Bryce Ross to his father and fellow GMS missionary John Ross: "Do you not see that those who at the command of Umhlakaza slaughter and sell their cattle, destroy their corn, and dispose of their ornaments, would at the command of the same individual rise and fight? . . . Did not Umlangeni do so before him?" In an unwitting reversal of the believers' expectant preparations, Bryce Ross closes the letter by suggesting "that should war break out the thatch be taken off the mission house and church." B. Ross to J. Ross, letter dated August 9, 1856, MS 7666, Lovedale Collection, Cory Library.

138. Official colonial dispatches have been regarded with historiographical suspicion, as a nineteenth-century equivalent of government press releases. Premesh Lalu offers a thoughtful discussion of the evidentiary and discursive status of official dispatches, private correspondence, and other colonial genres in "Grammar of Domination." Reading the Cape colonial archive through Ranajit Guha's notion of the "prose of counter-insurgency," Lalu

observes, "Intelligence has a way of creating a sense of intrigue even if there is none." Lalu, "Border and the Body," 116.

139. C. Brownlee to J. Maclean, letter dated August 2, 1856, *IBB* 2352, p. 13. Grey acknowledged that "the measures which the Kaffirs were taking must day by day render them less fit to embark in a war"; he told the colonial secretary that he sought to avoid provoking conflict while simultaneously increasing troop levels on the frontier. G. Grey to H. Labouchere, letter dated January 27, 1857, *IBB* 2352, p. 63.

140. Fielding to J. Maclean, letter dated October 14, 1856, BK 89, Secret Information, Cape Archives.

141. Bradford, "New Country."

142. Peires, *Dead Will Arise*, 107.

143. J. Gawler to J. Maclean, letter dated September 25, 1856, *IBB* 2352, p. 29. Other views include Stapleton's argument that the cattle killing was a "popular revolution against the weakened Xhosa upper class, which had failed miserably in its primary function to protect the nation." His central assumption is that "any call to slaughter cattle was, in essence, an attack on chiefly power and patronage." Stapleton, "They No Longer Care," 390; "Reluctant Slaughter," 356n50. Lewis argues that chiefs embraced the cattle killing in order to recover their authority and unity among the amaXhosa at a time when they were too weak to prosecute war by conventional means. Lewis, "Materialism."

144. Peires, *Dead Will Arise*, 153.

145. Theal, *Compendium*, 55. Similarly, the chiefs' plot thesis so dominates the otherwise remarkably sympathetic chapter on the cattle killing in William and Lily Rees' hagiographic *The Life and Times of Sir George Grey, K.C.B.* ([1892] 1898) that new cattle are mentioned only as a kind of bonus prize for military victory over the British, and the authors do not mention resurrected ancestors at all: the amaXhosa were to go directly from noncultivation and slaughter to attack, with no magical copula.

146. Some Xhosa survivors were literally driven into the sea, loaded on boats headed for prisons and schools in Cape Town; this fate was not insignificant, given Xhosa taboos regarding the ocean. Peires, *Dead Will Arise*, 222.

147. Chalmers, *Tiyo Soga*, 129.

148. Attwell writes, "After Ntsikana's story, the most fertile episode in nineteenth century history for telling the story of Christian emergence was the Cattle Killing." Attwell, *Rewriting Modernity*, 64. Theal describes the enduring traumatization, caused by the cattle killing, of "men living now, intelligent Christian men, then wild naked fugitives." Theal, *Compendium*, 55. An alternative ending to contemporary cattle-killing narratives describes Xhosa survivors, "hunger Africans," as ungrateful for European charity. This requital of generosity with ingratitude is a thematic reversal that nonetheless reflects historical stasis, rather than positing the cattle killing as catalyst for conversion. Van Calker, *Century*, 47; see also Moths, *Heinrich Meyer*.

149. The economy of Xhosa hostility and European charity appears in FitzGerald's letter to Maclean on August 31, 1857: "I cannot speak too highly of the exertions made by the Ladies and Gentlemen of King William's Town to save human life in the present distressing state of destitution in which the Kaffirs are placed by their own reckless folly and perverse obstinacy!" (FitzGerald, letterbook, 94). It is difficult not to read symptomatically Holden's assertion: "As, in days gone by, the English came nobly forward to save the starving population of the Emerald Isle, although the Irish had accused them of every foul deed; so also, the colonists put forth herculean efforts to keep alive these starving creatures, although their sires and friends had been engaged in desolating war, and might be so again." Holden, *Past and Future*, 294.

150. See Reverend James Laing's convoluted attributions of agency: "The country from which, by a mysterious providence, they had, through their own insane folly, been made the blind instruments of their own expulsion, is all but entirely deserted, the inhabitants having

passed in swarms into the Colony, not, as repeatedly in bygone years to spread the horrors of barbarous warfare, but to cast themselves on the compassion of those who had so lately, apparently not without good reason, been anticipating a repetition of those dread, and really dreadful invasions, to which, in recent years, they had been too much accustomed." Laing, *Memorials*, 189. Former missionary and British Kaffraria agent J. C. Warner wrote more plainly: "the way on which [the Xhosa] themselves are so obstinately bent is the one which God will make use of to bring this desirable object" of acceding to Christianity and colonial civilization. Maclean, *Compendium*, 112.

151. H. T. Waters, report dated July 7, 1857, GH 8/50, Cape Archives.

152. G. Grey to H. Labouchere, letter dated March 27, 1857, *IBB* 2352, p. 85.

153. J. Maclean to S. Douglas, letter dated August 6, 1857, FitzGerald letterbook, p. 102. Explaining why they were not operating in New Orleans after Hurricane Katrina in August 2005, the American Red Cross heeded similar logic from the Department of Homeland Security: "our presence would keep people from evacuating and encourage others to come into the city." This while tens of thousands were barred from leaving the Superdome, the convention center, and the city itself—sometimes at gunpoint. American Red Cross, Disaster FAQs.

154. I am thinking of Benjamin's famous thesis: "There is no document of civilization which is not at the same time a document of barbarism. And just as such a document is not free of barbarism, barbarism taints also the manner in which it was transmitted from one owner to another. A historical materialist therefore dissociates himself from it as far as possible. He regards it as his task to brush history against the grain." Benjamin, "Theses," 256–57. In the South African context, Ashforth identifies perils in the intersection of scholarly historiography and the cattle killing: he outlines "the problem of writing a history of a process of colonial conquest in the terms and languages of the victors, which does not simply replicate in historiographical discourse the imperial encounter by translating the colonized people's experiences into the terms of dominant discourses." Ashforth, "Xhosa Cattle Killing," 590.

155. A similar dynamic appears in secondary histories of nineteenth-century peasant rebellions in India, in which authors express sympathy for peasants' suffering under native landlords, traders, and moneylenders, while upholding the British empire as the ultimate source of law, order, and benign "civilization." Guha, "Prose of Counter-insurgency."

156. Theal, *Compendium*, 52.

157. White, *Content of the Form*, 24.

158. Kermode, *Sense of an Ending*, 83.

159. Comaroff and Comaroff, *Of Revelation and Revolution*, I.236. Attwell wonders, however, whether colonized intellectuals "merely accepted the metaphorics of the civilizing mission, or whether they appropriated them to serve their own interests. In all probability, the answer cannot simply be either-or." Attwell, *Rewriting Modernity*, 52–53.

160. The text was written by Elizabeth Harriot Hudson, who would go on to publish *Queen Bertha and Her Times* (1868), *The Life and Times of Louisa, Queen of Prussia* (1874), and *A History of the Jews in Rome* (1882).

161. *Recollections of a Visit to British Kaffraria*, 46.

162. Ishmaelites descended from Abraham's outcast son, Ishmael, from whom Muslim Arabs were thought to descend. Mid-nineteenth-century speculation that the amaXhosa were Ishmaelites was particularly ironic, since Europeans dubbed them *Kaffirs*, Arabic for infidels. Chidester, *Savage Systems*, 88–99.

163. See Erlank, "Gendered Reactions."

164. Anne McClintock writes, "the mission station became a threshold institution for transforming domesticity rooted in European gender and class roles into domesticity as controlling a colonized people. Through the rituals of domesticity . . . animals, women, and colonized peoples were wrested from their putatively 'natural' yet, ironically, 'unreasonable' state of 'savagery' and inducted through the domestic progress narrative into a hierarchical relation to white men." McClintock, *Imperial Leather*, 34.

CHAPTER TWO

1. Maclean, *Compendium*, 82; Soga, *South-Eastern Bantu*, xvii; Nicholls, *Bayete*, 128.

2. Brownlee, *Reminiscences*, 135–36. All references are to the 1977 edition unless otherwise indicated.

3. Charles Brownlee was ailing and unable to write when his *Reminiscences* were compiled. His son William transcribed stories of his career that Brownlee recounted "in a conversational manner." Brownlee, *Reminiscences*, v–vi. The chapter titled "The Cattle-Killing Delusion," by contrast, is a collocation of written sources supplemented by Charles Brownlee's recollections. An "abridgment" of Frances Brownlee's cattle-killing account, written in the 1870s for Chalmers's biography of Tiyo Soga, was among these sources; the version in *Reminiscences* contains material not in Chalmers's text. William Brownlee does not indicate whether his mother helped prepare the book. She would have been nearly seventy years old at its publication in 1896; she died in 1901.

4. Fanon, *Wretched of the Earth*, trans. Farrington, 227.

5. A broader historiography would attend to nontextual forms, both verbal and nonverbal, that, for disciplinary and practical reasons, are largely absent from my own study. For a recent study of Nongqawuse in contemporary visual culture, see Nhlangwini, "Ibali of Nongqawuse."

6. Couzens, *New African*.

7. Brooks, *American Lazarus*, 11.

8. Attwell, "Intimate Enmity," 577.

9. Revisionism began in the late 1970s among a radicalized (largely white) academic left, inspired by the Black Consciousness movement; rejecting the liberal thesis that industrialization was a progressive force that would undermine apartheid, they emphasized the continuity and cooperation among capitalism, colonialism, and apartheid. See Saunders, *Making of the South African Past*.

10. Wade, "Disclosing the Nation," 3.

11. Wade, "Disclosing the Nation," 3. "African-language literature was in fact both sponsored and censored to its present marginalised position," one critic noted at the colloquium. Swanepoel, "Merging African-Language Literature," 22.

12. Gray, "Some Problems."

13. Chapman, "Red People," 36. For a critique of Chapman, see De Kock, "Central South African Story." De Kock reassesses mid-1990s impulses toward a national narrative and traces alternatives emerging after the first decade of democracy in "Does South African Literature Still Exist?"

14. Chapman, "Writing Literary History," 42.

15. Van Wyk Smith, "White Writing," 72.

16. The difficulty of constructing South African literature as a historiographical field has a practical counterpart in the experience of writers under apartheid. Bantu Education, introduced in the 1950s to produce a subservient black underclass, severely limited opportunities for formal literary education; censorship and repression of writers and readers intensified after the 1960 Sharpeville massacre. Mtutuzeli Matshoba (chap. 3) and Sindiwe Magona (chap. 4) both mention not having had access to a South African literary tradition.

17. Kristeva, *Revolution*, 59.

18. Barthes, "Death of the Author," 160.

19. I have in mind Foucault's question borrowed from Beckett: "What matter who's speaking, someone said, what matter who's speaking." Foucault, "What Is an Author?" 141.

20. Said, *Orientalism*, 13.

21. I use "intelligentsia" in Zachernuk's sense: a small, literate group produced by colonial education. Zachernuk, *Colonial Subjects*, 13. Dhlomo was of Zulu royal lineage on his father's side and was linked to the prominent Caluza family on his mother's side;

he grew up in the assimilated community of Edendale. He enrolled in a teacher training program at the American Board's Amanzimtoti Training Institute in 1922. Couzens, *New African*, 40–50.

22. As the Comaroffs show in *Of Revelation and Revolution*, ethnic identities, no less than national ones, were produced through colonial encounters.

23. *Isigidimi* was the newspaper in which Gqoba published his cattle-killing narrative in 1888.

24. Hoho is Hohita, the Great Place (seat of power) of the Gcaleka Xhosa chief Sarhili.

25. "Zimkile! Mfo wohlanga, / Phuthuma, phuthuma; / Yishiy' imfakadolo, / Phuthuma ngosiba; / Thabath' iphepha neinki, / Likhaka lakho elo. // Ayemk' amalungelo, / Qubula usiba; / Ngxasha, ngxasha, ngeinki, / Hlala esitulweni, / Ungangeni kwaHoho; / Dubula ngosiba. // Thambeka umhlathi ke, / Bambelel' ebunzi; / Zingale iinynaniso, / Umise ngomxholo; / Bek' izitho ungalwi, / Umsindo liyilo." Opland, *Xhosa Poets*, 226–27.

26. For a recent reconsideration of the poem's original context in relationship to its later status in South African cultural history, see Mkhize, "Citashe's Apostrophe." Mkhize explains Wauchope's invocation of his grandfather, Citashe, esteemed for his bravery at the 1818 battle of Amalinde. Analyzing the consequences of A. C. Jordan's omission of the last stanza from his influential translation of "Zimkile!," Mkhize makes an argument similar to Bradford's critique of Jordan's translation of Gqoba (see chap. 1).

27. Frances Brownlee's unpublished letters from this period offer a rich account of life on a closing frontier. The letters (among the Brownlee Family correspondence held in the Cory Library), written mostly from Kokstad and King William's Town, are frank and detailed about anticipated and actual conflicts; Mrs. Brownlee does not shy from sharing opinions on policy matters (such as the 1878 Peace Preservation Act, the gun control measure that sparked rebellion when it was extended to Basutoland in 1880) with her parents, her husband (then serving as minister of native affairs), or her brother-in-law John Laing, a legislator and cabinet member.

28. *Imvo zabantsundu* was founded with financial assistance from white liberals connected to the Cape parliament. Jabavu's moderate stance and his dependence on white allies were later criticized, particularly after the South African Native Congress (with help from Cecil Rhodes) launched a rival newspaper, *Izwi Labantu* (Voice of the People) in 1897. The patronage of "friends of the natives" notwithstanding, *Imvo* was a major development in creating an autonomous space for a black reading public. Switzer, *South Africa's Alternative Press*.

29. De Kock, *Civilising Barbarians*, 132.

30. Korang, *Writing Ghana*, 12.

31. Nkosi, *Home and Exile*, 97. Such colonial intelligentsias were "medial" groups; historians of West Africa resist identifying them solely as an economic *class* because of their self-conscious *cultural* project. Zachernuk, *Colonial Subjects*, 14; Korang, *Writing Ghana*, 37; Falola, *Nationalism*.

32. Korang, *Writing Ghana*, 13.

33. Barber, introduction, 19. Crais writes, "The state in effect developed a model—a tribal model—of African society upon which it could act surgically, in the nineteenth century to destroy chiefship, in the twentieth century to reconstruct it." Under segregation and apartheid, the state buttressed "traditional" structures of chiefship in order to marginalize emergent elites and meet exploding demands for mine and industrial labor. Crais, *Politics of Evil*, 85.

34. See Peires, *Dead Will Arise*, 1–44. J. H. Soga explains that the *tola* performs *uku-kafula*, to make an army invulnerable to bullets or able to cross flooding rivers. This process requires *u-mapobe*, the capacity to "tie up" the harmful properties of people or objects. Soga, *Ama-Xosa*, 173–74.

35. Peires, *Dead Will Arise*, 30.

36. Lewis, "Materialism," 267.

37. J. Maclean to G. Grey, letter dated December 4, 1856, GH 8/49, Cape Archives. To my knowledge, historians have not noticed this report of Mhlakaza's bulletproof claims.

38. Holden, *Past and Future*, 294–95.

39. Beinart and Bundy, "Union," 283.

40. Crais, *Politics*, 141.

41. Beinart and Bundy, "Union," 313.

42. See chapter 5 and Bradford, *Taste of Freedom*.

43. Crais, *Politics of Evil*, 142, 122. *Ubuntu* is the South African concept of human intersubjectivity that holds that a person is a person through other people.

44. Garvey's Universal Negro Improvement Association (UNIA) had branches in South Africa by 1921; UNIA members also had links to the ICU and the ANC. For an invaluable archive on Garveyism in Africa, see Hill, *Marcus Garvey*.

45. Lazarus, *Nationalism*, 111.

46. Maclean described the "national feeling in which the movement had much of its support from other chiefs." J. Maclean to G. Grey, letter dated June 11, 1857, GH 8/50. Colonial intelligence reported Sarhili's "'news' that there was to be peace amongst the people . . . that all black people were one and must live in peace." The unnamed white informant surmised in this seemingly pacific news "Kreli's desire to merge all previous differences in order to combine the whole Kaffir nation against us." G. Grey to H. Labouchere, letter dated October 23, 1856, in *Imperial Blue Books* (*IBB*) 2352, encl. 2, p. 51. Maclean and Grey suspected a broader scope for the cattle killing, believing that Basuto chief Moshoeshoe thereby sought to improve his position vis-à-vis the Orange Free State.

47. Hodgson, *Ntsikana's Great Hymn*, 77.

48. Lester, *Imperial Networks*, 184; Wilson, *Origins*, 25.

49. Mill, "Few Words," 772.

50. Crais, *Politics of Evil*, 118.

51. Edgar, *Because They Chose the Plan of God*.

52. Jabavu, Presidential address, 51–52.

53. Msimang, "'Challenge,'" 58.

54. Ethiopian churches were the first African-initiated churches in South Africa, which broke from mission churches in the late nineteenth century after they mostly ceased ordaining African clergy. Keegan, *Moravians*, xxxi. Theologically, Ethiopian churches tended to remain closer to mainline Protestantism than later Zionist, messianic, and apostolic churches. Ethiopian churches often had pan-African aspirations. The classic study of African-initiated churches is Sundkler, *Bantu Prophets*; see also Chirenje, *Ethiopianism*.

55. Nicholls finished the novel in 1913 but only decided to publish it in 1921; in the intervening years, some developments anticipated in the novel were realized. He decided to publish when a prominent Afrikaner writer told him, "If it does waken the native it will, to more effectual purpose, awaken the Whites." Nicholls, *Bayete*, 5–6.

56. Another intertextual twist is Msimang's 1921 denunciation of Garveyism in *Umteteli wa Bantu*: interest in Garvey's black transnationalism could only spur false hopes and expectations of external deliverance, he warned. This article crucially misread SANNC participation in the 1921 Pan-African Conference in Paris as an alliance with Garvey, rather than with his bitter rival and the actual conference organizer, W. E. B. DuBois. Msimang, "Pan-African Congress."

57. This notion is indirectly informed by Carolyn Hamilton's argument that studies of "invented traditions" overemphasize invention while neglecting "the way in which the tradition's . . . own past shapes its present." Hamilton, *Terrific Majesty*, 26.

58. Dhlomo, *The Girl*, 40.

59. Jahn, *Neo-African Literature*, 89, emphasis added. Jahn classified *The Girl* as falling between apprentice and "protest" literature.

60. Chalmers, *Tiyo Soga*, 137.

61. Ibid., 139.

62. Assertions of the cattle killing's providential nature abound; in the Cape parliament, Grey declared that it had effected "lasting peace" and "prosperity surpassing any expectations" that "teach us to turn with thankful gratitude to that overruling Providence which has so wonderfully worked out its own designs." G. Grey to H. Labouchere, letter dated April 8, 1857, *IBB* 2352, p. 91. Missionary Henry Calderwood wrote in 1858, "It really seemed as though God had given [the amaXhosa] up to strong delusion, that they might subdue themselves. . . . God has surely interfered for us in a wonderful manner, in saving us from a savage war." Calderwood, *Caffres*, 214, 220. In *Late Victorian Holocausts*, Mike Davis shows that missionaries in China and Africa were not shy about celebrating evangelical opportunities provided by disasters like famine.

63. Martin Orkin asserts, by contrast, that Dhlomo's staging of Xhosa resistance in the first two scenes is supplanted by sympathetic articulation of missionary ideology in the final three scenes. Orkin, *Drama*, 36.

64. Dhlomo, *The Girl*, 34–36.

65. Peterson, *Monarchs*, 196–97.

66. In his reluctant foreword, Brownlee's son Frank's highest praise is for Dhlomo's characterization of his uncle Hugh, which was "done so ably that one would think he had known Hugh who actually was in life, just as he has been shown here." Hugh Thomson was a magistrate in Grey's Kaffrarian system.

67. Dhlomo, "Masses and the Artist," 62.

68. Assessing Dhlomo's theorization of African drama, Balme argues that he anticipates the syncretic innovations of Nobel Prize–winning dramatist Wole Soyinka. Balme, *Decolonizing the Stage*, 30–40.

69. Dhlomo, "Why Study," 37, 41.

70. Dhlomo, *The Girl*, 22–23.

71. Dhlomo, "Why Study," 37, 42, 38.

72. Dhlomo, "Evolution."

73. Dhlomo, "Why Study," 37. On Dhlomo's work in radio and record production, as well as print journalism and library outreach, see Couzens, *New African*, 188, 198, 208–10; see also Erlmann, *African Stars*, 164.

74. Dhlomo, "Why Study," 37, idem, "Drama," 7.

75. Dhlomo, "Evolution."

76. Gunner, "Remaking the Warrior," 54. In East Africa, Jomo Kenyatta valorized "precolonial culture as a means rather than an end, as a prerequisite for the nationalist future, rather than a return to tradition qua tradition." Gikandi, *Maps of Englishness*, 18. In West Africa, the "Gold Coast . . . was native only insofar as it had become colonial": the colonial experience necessitated the discovery of a "native" past out of which could be invented a nation. Korang, *Writing Ghana*, 106.

77. Shepherd, *Conferences on Literature*, 17. A heated debate about Zulu poetry between Dhlomo and B. W. Vilakazi demonstrates that this consensus was not absolute. Attwell, "Modernizing Tradition." The writers and scholars gathered in Eritrea in 2000 reached the opposite conclusion: African languages are "essential for the decolonization of African minds and for the African Renaissance," declares the landmark Asmara Declaration.

78. Shepherd, *Lovedale and Literature*, 26. Shepherd presents himself as a champion of African literature written, produced, and read in Africa by Africans. Shepherd's critique of metropolitan control over publishing anticipates infrastructural problems that continue to constrain literary production and distribution on the continent. However, Shepherd's patronizing view of Africans in an "adolescent period" (74) of civilizational development and his disdain for politically engaged literature exerted considerable pressure on writers

like Dhlomo. See Peires, "Lovedale Press." Discussing the contested status of literature at Lovedale, Hofmeyr notes that Lovedale's library "rivaled that of a British public school or even a university." Hofmeyr, "Reading Debating," 266.

79. Oosthuizen, *Shepherd of Lovedale*, 146.

80. In the late 1930s, Dhlomo briefly supported the development of "Union" language families (Nguni [including isiXhosa and isiZulu], Sotho, Venda, and Thonga); by the early 1940s, Dhlomo was again a decided partisan for English. Attwell, *Rewriting Modernity*, 95–96.

81. Dhlomo, *Valley*, 26.

82. Dhlomo, "African Drama," 20–21.

83. In asserting that Nongqawuse died in the 1857 famine, this scene is counterfactual: she was transported to Cape Town in 1858 and is thought to have lived into the twentieth century near Port Elizabeth. Peires, *Dead Will Arise*, 336.

84. Dhlomo, "Bantu Dramatic Society."

85. Fanon, *Wretched of the Earth*, trans. Farrington, 68; Msimang, "Challenge," 60. Msimang's allusion is itself intertextual. In Acts 2.17–21, the apostle Peter cites the Old Testament prophet Joel (Joel 2.28–32) on the pouring out of the Holy Spirit.

86. The epigraph does not appear in *Collected Works* nor does a dedication to Dhlomo's mother with a poem ("Sengiyokholwake") by Vilakazi, *Zulu Horizons*, 29.

87. Steadman, "Towards Popular Theatre," 214. For many critics, Dhlomo's later work, especially *Cetshwayo* and *Moshoeshoe*, more effectively stages the past; see Couzens, *New African*; Peterson, *Monarchs*; Kruger, *Drama*.

88. Jameson, *Political Unconscious*, 18.

89. Dhlomo uses "Ntsikana's Bell Song" in another early play, *Ntsikana*. Dhlomo's Ntsikana sets to a "tribal tune" words he receives through divine inspiration: "We shall graft the old world to the new. We shall proceed forward along the way of our songs, our language, our heritage. Why not? This thing does not say we shouldn't be ourselves, but that we should be more than ourselves." Dhlomo, *Collected Works*, 46.

90. The Curwin tonic sol-fa notation system was introduced to South Africa in 1855; it uses "letters and punctuation marks rather than notes and staffs." Although ill-suited to African music, it remained the medium for instruction at missions. Coplan, *In Township Tonight*, 33, 270.

91. Kruger, *Drama*, 57. The first verse and chorus of "Nkosi sikelel' iAfrika" were written in 1897 by Enoch Sontonga; additional verses were added by isiXhosa poet S. E. K. Mqhayi. It was sung at the closing of the 1912 inaugural meeting of the South African Native National Congress and in 1925 was adopted as the ANC closing anthem. In 1996, it became part of the South African national anthem, together with parts of the former Afrikaans anthem, "Die Stem van Suid Afrika."

92. Soga, *Journal*, 196–97.

93. Dhlomo, *The Girl*, 43. Compare the sixth verse of Tiyo Soga's "Lizalis' idinga lako": "Nkosi kausikelele / Imfundiso zezwe letu / Uze usivuselele, Siputume ukulunga." Soga, "Manuscript of Original Hymns," MS 8863, Lovedale Collection, Cory Library.

94. Soga, *Journal*, 196–97.

95. Forms of the isiXhosa root *lunga* (order, justice) recur in Nxele and Nongqawuse's prophecies; "putting [the homestead] right again is called *ukulungisa*." Peires, *Dead Will Arise*, 125–26. Tiyo Soga's hymn concludes with *ukulunga*, goodness.

96. Similarly, in the shift from war cry to new weapons in Wauchope's "Zimkile!," the poem urges "*following* an historical adjunct by *not following* its preceding historical method of engagement." Mkhize, "Citashe's Apostrophe," 108, emphasis in the original.

97. Lodge, *Black Politics*, 1. Tiyo Soga's hymn also opened the first hearing of the Truth and Reconciliation Commission. Krog, *Country*, 37.

98. In *Umteteli wa Bantu*, Dhlomo similarly distinguishes between the actual nobility

of purported "barbarity, folly, and injustice" on the part of protonationalist leaders in the nineteenth century and the susceptibility to magical thinking that "renders life unhappy" for the "rural masses" of today. Dhlomo, "Thoughts"; "Young Generation."

99. The structure of my argument resembles Jani's recent work on the shift in Karl Marx's thinking about colonialism and modernity in India. Marx's early view that the British brought to India a disruptive but necessary induction into modernity is well known and often invoked as evidence of Marxian Eurocentrism. Examining Marx's journalism on the Indian rebellion of 1857–58 (an anticolonial movement that constrained Grey's response to the cattle killing), Jani emphasizes Marx's later recognition that Indian *resistance* to colonialism was the catalyst for historical change. Jani, "Karl Marx."

100. Dhlomo, *The Girl*, 41.

101. Dhlomo attempted to publish additional plays. In 1938, he submitted to Lovedale a collection entitled *This Is Africa*. This collection presumably included *The Black Bulls*, Dhlomo's trilogy on Zulu heroes Shaka, Dingane, and Cetshwayo; the Shaka play is lost. Despite Dhlomo's assurances of demand from dramatic societies, the Carnegie Non-European Library, schools, and other groups, Shepherd (noting slow demand for *The Girl*) deemed the work "not up to publication standard." R. H. W. Shepherd to H. I. E. Dhlomo, letter dated May 19, 1938, in typescript file of "The Girl Who Killed to Save," MS 16 309(a), Lovedale Collection, Cory Library.

102. Couzens, *New African*, 211, emphasis in the original.

103. On the fate of Dhlomo's papers, lost for a time in the canteen of the library at the University of Natal, see Visser, "H. I. E. Dhlomo."

104. Peterson, *Monarchs*, 192, emphasis in the original. Writing about Anglophone West African intertextuality, Newell describes attempts to "*write over* or *write into* a contemporary text which was oppositional and radical, which was critical of the imperialist context within which it was produced." Newell, *Literary Culture*, 87, emphasis in the original.

105. Brownlee frames this episode as a literary vignette, casting herself as naive foil to her knowing husband, who predicts the consequences of Xhosa prophecy: "'Then there will either be war or you will see men, women, and children dying like dogs about your door. We must prevent either contingency.' I felt incredulous, but never was any prediction more literally fulfilled." Brownlee, *Reminiscences*, 138.

106. Chalmers, *Tiyo Soga*, 129.

107. Attwell surmises that Chalmers's biography shaped Dhlomo's interpretation of the cattle killing, but he does not note the direct borrowing in the historical note. Attwell, "Intimate Enmity," 574. Anticipating its 1941 centenary, the Governing Council of Lovedale commissioned an institutional history from Shepherd, who worked on *Lovedale, South Africa* from 1934 to 1940. Oosthuizen, *Shepherd of Lovedale*, 49. Close comparison of Chalmers's 1877 and 1878 editions and Brownlee's 1896 and 1916 editions suggests that Shepherd worked from Brownlee. Shepherd's account is reprinted in Davies and Shepherd, *South African Missions*.

108. Although the table of contents in Dhlomo's typescript mentions an introduction on "The AmaXhosa Today," neither typescript nor published play contains such an introduction. Instead, a separate document, typed in the format of Shepherd's other papers and with "Historical Note" written at the top in Shepherd's hand, is the typescript for the note in the published text. Unlike the play's typescript, the note's typescript misspells *Nongqause* (as *Nongquase*) and *kraal* (as *craal*). The typescripts and correspondence for Dhlomo's play offer no explanation for the absence of "The AmaXhosa Today" or the inclusion of the "Historical Note." Dhlomo, "The Girl Who Killed to Save," typescript MS 16 309(a), Lovedale Collection, Cory Library.

109. Although not as significant as Lovedale's editorial interventions in Sol Plaatje's novel *Mhudi* (published in 1930, during Shepherd's tenure as press director), Shepherd's intercalation of his historical note in the first play published by a black South African

adds another detail to our understanding of the mediatory role of mission presses in early twentieth-century black South African literature. I discuss Stephen Gray's scholarship on *Mhudi* in chapter 3.

110. Van Wyk Smith, "Origins Revisited," 27. Pringle emigrated from Scotland and lived in the eastern Cape from 1820 to 1826. As a settler in contested territory, Pringle was critical of policies created on his behalf, although, as Matthew Shum points out, Pringle's humanitarian stance fully emerged in his poetry only after he left Africa. Shum, "Unsettling Settler Identity." Pringle would later edit Mary Prince's 1831 slave narrative and was a member of the reconstituted Anti-Slavery Society.

111. Pringle, *Poems Illustrative of South Africa*, 70–73. Pringle's valley of bones awaiting resurrection echoes Ezekiel 37:1–15; the jubilant harvests resemble those promised to Israel in Ezekiel 36:29–35. "Ezekiel's 'dry bones' prophecy" is thought to have been the second most popular Biblical image of conversion (after the Pentecost) in the nineteenth-century eastern Cape. Wagstrom, "Daniel's Book," 169.

112. Dhlomo, "African Drama."

113. Another (unlikely) possibility is Molema's *The Bantu Past and Present* (1920), which discusses the cattle killing as the epitome of the "curse of superstition among the Bantu," without the ambivalence in J. H. Soga or Dhlomo. Molema, *Bantu Past*, 167.

114. Soga, *South-Eastern Bantu*, xvii–xviii.

115. Waters, *U-Nongqause*, 4–5. In a posthumous portrait, a former colleague at Rhodes University depicts Waters as an eccentric martinet devoted to the Coloured students at Rhodes's teacher training laboratory school, where she came in the early 1940s after retirement from mission work. Waters studied for a Lady's Licentiate in the Arts (L.L.A.) at St. Andrew's College. Late in life, she chain-smoked, took little interest in hygiene or wardrobe, and lived at the Evelyn boarding house on High Street in Grahamstown (now a Protea hotel). She was nearly ninety years old when she sailed for England in the late 1950s, stopping at St. Helena where she stayed to fill an empty teacher's post; she died soon after. When a new building for the Coloured school in Grahamstown was built in 1962, it was named (after some dispute) Mary Waters High School. Waters was the granddaughter of H. T. Waters, an Anglican who established the St. Mark's mission near Sarhili in 1855. Dan M. Morton, "Miss Mary Waters and the Mary Waters High School," typescript MS 18 814, Cory Library.

116. "She professed to have held converse with the spirits of the old Kaffir heroes—who had witnessed with sorrow the ruin of their race from the oppression of their conquerors; and as they would no longer be silent spectators of the wrongs and insults, it was their intention to come to the rescue and save their progeny from destruction." Brownlee, *Reminiscences*, 136.

117. The same passage appears in Burton's *Cauldron of Witchcraft* (1950), which interweaves historical incidents with the travails of a fictional Gcaleka family. Burton cites several sources, including Chalmers and Brownlee, but not Soga or Waters. See Burton, *Sparks*.

118. Soga's work is "the foundation on which all subsequent Xhosa history has been and will be written." He sought to give "the rising generation of the Bantu" a sense of their history and "a desire for reading and for studying their language," but he had to translate *The South-Eastern Bantu* into English in order to find a publisher. Lovedale published Soga's second historical work, *The Ama-Xosa*, which was written in English. The fate of Soga's isiXhosa and English works reverses the usual tensions between Shepherd, advocate of vernacular languages, and New Africans, who generally embraced the "national" scope of English. Peires, "Lovedale Press," 77, xvii.

119. In the conventional distinction between Xhosa "red people" and "school people," *red* refers to the ochre clay used in Xhosa hygiene and adornment; missionaries urged the amaXhosa to give up clay and blankets (as Ntsikana had done) in favor of European-style clothing.

120. Soga, *Ama-Xosa*, 121.

121. Chief Kreli asks his followers, "Are you killing your cattle? Are you ready to fight to destroy the White man? Remember our ancestors will do most of the work!" Dhlomo, *The Girl*, 15. Dhlomo does not imply, however, that Kreli merely pretends the ancestors are on their way.

122. Dhlomo would have been familiar with Waters's *U-Nongqause*, which the Bantu Dramatic Society of Johannesburg staged among its inaugural October 1933 performances, the day after their production of *She Stoops to Conquer*, in which Dhlomo acted.

123. On *U-Nongqause*, see Orkin, *Drama*. The possibility that Dhlomo was "writing aside" Waters also might account for the fact that Nongqause appears only in his first scene: in *U-Nongqause*, a missionary character is the dominant presence and privileged perspective.

124. Waters wrote several books for school use; W. G. Bennie solicited materials from her *Fairy Tales Told by Nontsomi* for Lovedale's influential Stewart Xhosa Readers. W. G. Bennie to M. W. Waters, letter dated November 22, 1929, MS 16 339(j)(5), Stewart Xhosa Reader Correspondence, Lovedale Collection, Cory Library. Bennie, descendant of Lovedale mission press founder John Bennie, served as chief inspector of native education in the Cape and editor of the Stewart readers in the 1920s and '30s. He also solicited isiXhosa poet S. E. K. Mqhayi: "I shall want some good lessons for the senior readers on famous men. Are you not disposed to give me lessons on Ntsikana, Sarili, Makanda . . . a series of biographies, written for young people, free from contentious matter. . . . And some account of Nongqawuse?" W. G. Bennie to S. E. K. Mqhayi, letter dated October 23, 1931, MS 16 339(j)(5). Men like Bennie wielded inordinate power over isiXhosa literature: his authority to demand that isiXhosa texts for educational use appear in a New Orthography allowed him to control what was published. The transition to Bantu Education in the 1950s involved similar strictures; Herbert Pahl, Cape representative to the Department of Bantu Education, promulgated a Revised Standard Orthography that further constrained African language publishing. These new orthographies were so burdensome as to "turn every literate African into a functional illiterate," in Peires's phrase, so that even J. H. Soga and Mqhayi could not use the New Orthography correctly. Opland, *Xhosa Poets*, 289.

125. This complex structure is absent in Waters's *Fairy Tales Told by Nontsomi*, which offers no account of the tales' collection; the narrative voice assumes the perspective of "we Xosa people." Waters, *Fairy Tales*, 16. Waters dedicates *Cameos* to her father, "who loved the natives as his children." She seems to share his paternalist view of "child races."

126. Waters, *Cameos*, 43.

127. Waters, *The Light*, 6. Opland and Mahlasela assert that Waters was assisted by Reverend Candlish Koti in writing *U-Nongqause* in isiXhosa. Opland, *Xhosa Poets*, 229; Mahlasela, "General Survey," 11. The published play does not mention Koti, but his collaboration would increase the text's multivocality.

128. The same "tares" are cleared in Theal's *Compendium*, which tracks colonial progress against "ignorance, superstition, and indolence." Theal, *Compendium*, 49.

129. Presumably Francis Carey Slater, poet and compiler of *The Centenary Book of South African Verse* (1925); some of Pringle's poems appear in this anthology but not those Waters uses.

130. Pringle, *Poems*, 96.

131. Pringle, *Poems*, 49. Besides Pringle's poems, Waters attributes to Slater "Tyala's Lament," written by H. M. Foot under the pseudonym "Diamond Digger" and reprinted in Brownlee's *Reminiscences*. Saunders, Commentaries, 423. When Brownlee informed the Ngqika Xhosa in 1878 that they had to move across the Kei River, Tyala, who counseled Sandile against the cattle killing and war on the colony, died before the eviction, apparently in protest or of a broken heart. Waters confuses Tyala for Tyali, an earlier Ngqika chief. Mostert, *Frontiers*, 1252–53.

132. Pringle, *Poems*, 74–77.

133. Van Wyk Smith, "Origins Revisited," 32.

134. The Christian teleology of Pringle's poems could account for their availability to such readings; both Waters and Pringle imagine a Christian future for southern Africa, yet Pringle would be appalled by Waters's rationalization of bloodshed in the service of that aim. This predicament is similar to the conflicting providential narratives that inform Dhlomo's dramatization of the cattle killing.

135. Van Wyk Smith, "Origins Revisited," 23, 25.

136. See Hodgson, *Ntsikana's Great Hymn.*

137. Waters, *The Light*, 32.

138. The Online Computer Library Center's Worldcat database indicates that *Collected Works* is held at more than three times as many libraries worldwide as the Lovedale edition of *The Girl*; in South Africa, the ratio is more than four to one.

139. Nothing in the manuscript suggests whether Dhlomo knew he used Tiyo Soga's hymn. The entry on Tiyo Soga in Skota's *The African Yearly Register* (1930) lists "the famous *Lizalis' idinga lako*" as one of his accomplishments. Skota, *African Yearly Register*, 92. Since Dhlomo also appears in Skota's "Who's Who" volume, he may well have read the entry. Correspondence from the 1950s regarding the revision of Lovedale's isiXhosa hymnbook suggests that Tiyo Soga's hymn was frequently sung at mission services; see correspondence on revision of *Incwadi Aserabe*, MS 16, 430 / II and III, Lovedale Collection, Cory Library. Hymns by Tiyo Soga were on the program for a 1938 "Grand Vaudeville" Johannesburg performance by the variety ensemble Pitch Black Follies. Coplan, *In Township Tonight*, 127.

140. Isabel Hofmeyr suggestively describes this process of recognition in terms of navigation and travel. Hofmeyr, "Reading Debating," 273.

141. Eliot, "Tradition," 1095.

142. As with Harold Bloom, I argue that we need not accept all of Eliot's assumptions about the poet's depersonalization or the constitution of tradition and value. Reading Eliot in terms of textual ancestry and prophecy is revealing, since his essay becomes an attempt to come to terms with how "the tradition of all the dead generations weighs like a nightmare on the mind of the living," as Marx wrote (*Eighteenth Brumaire*, 320). I am grateful to Patsy Yaeger for drawing my attention to Eliot's thanatopsis in this essay, published in 1919, at the close of the World War I.

143. Majeke, *Role of Missionaries*, 73–74.

144. Dora Taylor emigrated from Scotland and became an important figure in the South African left: she helped forge a critical public sphere and Marxist literary criticism in South Africa. Sandwith, "Dora Taylor." Taylor's influential critique of missionary complicity in conquest was first articulated in an analysis of Dhlomo's *The Girl Who Killed to Save*, which she sees as uncritically accepting mission ideology. Taylor also wrote a spirited, incisive analysis of Nicholls' *Bayete*. Taylor, "Africans Speak"; "They Speak of Africa."

145. Although her cattle-killing narrative is diametrically opposed to the colonial accounts discussed in chapter 1, Majeke/Taylor uses similar literary embellishments. Like earlier authors, Majeke/Taylor begins with a variation on *once upon a time*: "One day a young girl by the name of Nongqause . . . came running," bringing a message of "liberation" (rather than resurrection), in keeping with the Marxist/Leninist goal of national liberation. Majeke/Taylor develops a tropological reversal between the expected and actual aftermath of the cattle killing: "The cattle had been slaughtered and the corn-pits were empty, but [Grey's] labour bureaus were filled to the brim." Majeke, *Role of Missionaries*, 71, 74.

146. Nasson, "Unity Movement," 195. The Non-European Unity Movement (NEUM) emerged out of a crisis in the early 1940s, when the state proposed segregationist measures for the Coloured population; in 1943, the organization that opposed this policy, the anti-Coloured Affairs Department (known commonly as the Anti-CAD), joined the AAC (founded to oppose the Hertzog Bills) to form the NEUM coalition.

147. Sirayi, for example, opposes the "White perspective of the Cattle-killing movement" to the "African view which regards the White aliens as the root cause" of the events. He cites

Majeke (whom he also believes is male) as an example of the "African view" also espoused by isiXhosa poets Jolobe and Yalimanisi and isiZulu poet Vilakazi. These African writers, "the legitimate and acknowledged mouthpiece of the African nation, have advanced the African perspective of the movement." Sirayi, "African Perspective," 40, 43, 44–45.

148. Within the broader context of African literature, debates about the writer's role have been perennial. For debates on the gun/pen dilemma at the 1967 African-Scandinavian Writers' Conference, see Wästberg, *Writer in Modern Africa.*

149. Quoted in Msimang, "Status of African Literature," 62.

150. Cronin, "Even under the Rine of Terror," 12–13.

151. This phrase evokes Nkosi's story "Under the Shadow of the Guns," which depicts relationships among sexual desire, aesthetic and political expression, the post-Soweto struggle, and state surveillance and repression.

152. Cronin, "To Learn How to speak."

153. De Kock, "Pursuit," 89.

154. See Ashforth, "Xhosa Cattle Killing."

155. Excerpts from Jolobe's poem are translated in Scheub, "Xhosa Oral and Literary Traditions" and Butler and Opland, *Magic Tree*; Vilakazi's poem is translated as "The Xhosa Calamity—1856" in *Zulu Horizons.*

156. De Kock, "Pursuit," 89.

157. Fanon, *Wretched of the Earth*, trans. Farrington, 227.

CHAPTER THREE

1. Plaatje, *Native Life*, 21; Shakespeare, *Hamlet* 1.5.188–89; African National Congress Youth League, "Basic Policy," 326.

2. The publication of Majeke/Taylor's text was timed to protest the tricentennial celebration of Jan van Riebeeck's arrival at the Cape in 1652.

3. Although she does not assert a colonial hoax, Majeke/Taylor insinuates that the British so needed to break the chiefs' power that "they would therefore use any and every means to do so." Majeke, *Role of the Missionaries*, 64. She borrows the term *herrenvolk* from Nazi Germany to explain apartheid South Africa; on the Unity Movement's transnational thinking, see Lee, "Uses of the Comparative Imagination."

4. Majeke, *Role of the Missionaries*, 74.

5. Attwell, *Rewriting Modernity*, 71.

6. Renton, "What Future," 38. Also see Peires, "Suicide or Genocide?"

7. Biko, *I Write What I Like*, 95.

8. Peterson, "Apartheid," 238.

9. Voss identifies Plaatje as one of the "pilgrim creole functionaries and provincial creole printmen" whom Benedict Anderson describes as indispensable in imagining national communities. Voss, "Sol Plaatje," 72. On earlier petitions and delegations to the British Parliament and crown, see Johns, introduction.

10. The Brotherhood movement was an interdenominational organization committed to the "practical implementation of Christianity in everyday life." It provided Plaatje with audiences throughout England and helped "restore his belief in the power of Christianity to work for social and political justice." Willan, *Sol Plaatje*, 202.

11. Plaatje, *Native Life*, 188.

12. Plaatje identifies a linguistic affinity between Britain and native South Africa; he argues that English, unlike Afrikaans, has a word for *home*, which "perhaps, is the reason why [British] colonizing schemes have always allowed some tracts of country for native family life . . . in the vast South African expanses which God in His providence had created for His Children of the Sun. The Englishman, moreover, found us speaking the word *Legae* [home], and taught us how to write it. In 1910, much against our will, the British Government surrendered its immediate sovereignty over our land to Colonials and cosmopolitan aliens who know little

about a Home, because their dictionaries contain no such loving term." Plaatje, *Native Life*, 428. Interspersed throughout the book are translations of the chorus of "It's a Long Way to Tipperary" into Rolong, isiZulu, isiXhosa, Hindustani, German, Cape Dutch, and Qoranna. This wildly popular song, written in 1912 by a Londoner of Irish descent who had never been to Ireland, was adopted by British troops marching through continental Europe. Like Plaatje's book, "Tipperary" expresses nostalgia for a colonized home in a mode compatible with British imperial enthusiasm; Plaatje's translations of the song function as a kind of concrete universal, evoking a longing for home obstructed, in this instance, by the Land Act.

13. De Kock maintains that such "subversive subservience" became the New Africans' paradigmatic stance: "They had learned to use the discourse of civility and been forced to turn it against its bearers when circumstances seemed to indicate that the 'justice' of British constitutionality—for which they had forsaken war and weapons—somehow admitted inequality in the name of equality." De Kock, *Civilising Barbarians*, 136.

14. De Kock, "Pursuit," 52.

15. Plaatje, *Native Life*, 406.

16. Plaatje's text and the commission's report were published almost simultaneously; Plaatje's analysis was inserted into the second printing. Willan, *Sol Plaatje*, 200.

17. Majeke, *Role of the Missionaries*, 139.

18. Plaatje's esteem for literacy and print culture is evident in the fact that he named his son Johannes Gutenberg. Plaatje, *Native Life*, 142.

19. Plaatje, *Native Life*, 87; see chap. 1.

20. Mphahlele, "Voice of Prophecy," 34.

21. Benjamin, "Theses," 264.

22. Provision Committee, "Congress Youth League Manifesto," 301.

23. I cite distinctions between "Western" and "African" notions of time from a novelist/critic and a political manifesto rather than from anthropologists or philosophers precisely because the issue is as important as it is vexed, and I do not intend to invoke definitive, expert authority. For a critique of the essentialisms and generalizations in both European and African notions of "African time," see Adjaye, *Time in the Black Experience*. For an influential, if problematic, theorization of African time, see Mbiti, *African Religions*. Although his idea of entanglement—lived time as multilayered—has rightly received much attention, Achille Mbembe's most important temporal observation is that African time "cannot be conceptualized outside a world that is, so to speak, globalized." Mbembe, *On the Postcolony*, 9.

24. Gray, *Southern African Literature*, 175–77.

25. Rejecting Gray's speculations about a Lovedale editor who transformed Plaatje's manuscript, Michael Green opts to "respect Plaatje's decisions to go into print with the version he did, and not treat him as a purely passive victim of the mode of production available to him." The lack of diegetic and genealogical continuity in the Lovedale edition "reinforces the sense of a break, a rupture, in the continuous history of their nationhood." Green acknowledges the consequences of Gray's commitment to his argument, identifying as "one of the great acts of sacrifice in southern African literary history" Gray's insistence that Heinemann publish the 1917 typescript instead of the Lovedale edition he had just reprinted as the first (and last) book in the Quagga Press African Fiction Library. Had Heinemann picked up the Quagga/Lovedale edition, Green speculates, Gray could have used the royalties to keep the African Fiction Library going. Green, *Novel Histories*, 59–60.

26. Gray, *Southern African Literatures*, 180.

27. Peggy Kamuf translates as *future-to-come* Jacques Derrida's neologism, *l'à-venir*, which emphasizes the sense of anticipated advent merely implicit in "the ordinary word for the future, *avenir*." Derrida, *Specters*, 177n5.

28. Plaatje uses a similar strategy to historicize polygamy: elders who advised women to enter such marriages "judged present-day economics from the standard of their own happy days when there was plenty of land," rainfall, and food to sustain large households. With the

undermining of "natural hygienic and moral laws" under colonial modernity, these women turn to prostitution to earn a living, and "it is doubtful if the systematic prostitution of today is a happy substitution for the polygamy of the past." Plaatje, *Native Life*, 117, 119.

29. *Native Life* can be read as extended gloss of "the prophecy of an old Basuto [which] became increasingly believable to us," that the Boers, having assumed power after the South African War, would marginalize the British and "'make a law declaring it a crime for a native to live in South Africa, unless he is a servant in the employ of a Boer, and that from this it will be just one step to complete slavery.'" Plaatje, *Native Life*, 71.

30. Derrida, *Specters*, 22, 65.

31. Plaatje reverses Stephen Daedalus's lament in Joyce's *Portrait of the Artist:* "History is a nightmare from which I am trying to awake."

32. Terdiman, *Present Past*, 23.

33. Antze and Lambek, introduction, xiv–xv.

34. Fanon asserts, "For a colonized people the most essential value, because the most concrete, is first and foremost the land: the land which will bring them bread and, above all, dignity." Fanon, *Wretched of the Earth*, trans. Farrington, 44.

35. Head, foreword, xiii.

36. Antze and Lambek, introduction, vii.

37. Msimang, "Challenge," 57; Tambo and Make, "Statement"; South African Students Organisation, "Policy Manifesto," 482; Tutu, "Question," 51.

38. Head, foreword, xiii.

39. Under the Restitution of Land Rights Act of 1994, the earliest date of land alienation eligible for restitution claims is June 19, 1913.

40. Benjamin, "On Some Motifs," 163.

41. Ganguly, *States of Exception*, 85. Benjamin's distinction between *Erlebnis* and *Erfahrung* (and valorization of the latter) is idiosyncratic in German philosophy. Dilthey (drawing on Rousseau and Goethe) and Husserl contrasted the integrated, holistic "'inner lived experience'" of *Erlebnis* with the sensory empiricism of Kantian *Erfahrung*. For Benjamin, *Erfahrung* denotes dialectical, transmissible, communal wisdom. Jay, "Experience," 146.

42. Plaatje continued to trace dislocations of the 1920s and 1930s to the Land Act, "attribut[ing] to one piece of legislation a whole host of evils which were in reality the product of a rather broader process of industrialization." Willan, introduction, 12.

43. Freud's Lamarckianism in *Moses and Monotheism* demonstrates the perils of using analogy to bridge the individual and the social. For Benjamin, "Where there is experience [*Erfahrung*] in the strictest sense of the word, certain contents of the individual past combine with material of the collective past." Benjamin, "On Some Motifs," 159; *Illuminationen*, 189.

44. For challenges to the primacy of individual, psychic memory over social memory, see Nora, "Between Memory and History"; LaCapra, *Writing History*.

45. Bloch, "Alienation," 240.

46. Ganguly, *States of Exception*, 158.

47. Terdiman, *Present Past*, 299. Plaatje generates a "landscape of memory," in Laurence Kirmayer's phrase: a "metaphoric terrain that shapes the distance and effort required to remember affectively charged and socially defined events that initially may be vague, impressionistic, or simply absent from memory. Landscapes of memory are given shape by the personal and social significance of specific memories but also draw from *meta-memory*— implicit models of memory which influence what can be recalled and cited as veridical." Kirmayer, "Landscapes," 175.

48. Drawing upon the mechanics of aurality and acoustics, Wai Chee Dimock theorizes literary texts as "emerging phenomena, activated and to some extent constituted by the passage of time, by their continual transit through new semantic networks, modifying their tonality as they proceed." Dimock, "Theory of Resonance," 1061.

49. Apartheid policy and discourse managed this contradiction by replacing "Native"

with "Bantu" in the late 1950s. A similar recalibration of racial exclusion occurred after the cattle killing, when passes and labor contracts were used to regulate the movements of various peoples into the Colony. Several ordinances invoked the oxymoronic category of "native foreigners": "any Basuto, Barolong, Mantatee, or other native, resident in any territory adjacent to Kaffirland, and commonly regarded as and spoken of as belonging to the Kafir family." Such "natives," because they were "foreigners" to the Cape Colony, were not to enter without a pass, under threat of twelve months' hard labor. See Act 23 of 1857, "An Act for More effectually preventing Kafirs from entering the Colony without Passes," *Government Gazette*, 30 June 1857.

50. Mandela, presidential address.

51. Tutu, "Question," 52.

52. Tutu spoke just after the South African Defense Force joined police in raiding a township outside Johannesburg, an unprecedented domestic military deployment.

53. Kermode, *Sense of an Ending*, 8.

54. Kermode, *Sense of an Ending*, 67.

55. Gramsci, *Prison Notebooks*, 276.

56. Gordimer, "Living in the Interregnum." Gordimer also used Gramsci's statement as the epigraph to *July's People* (1981).

57. Plaatje, *Native Life*, 408, quoted in Ndebele, *South African Literature*, 159.

58. Ndebele, *South African Literature*, 160.

59. Festinger, Riecken, and Schachter, *When Prophecy Fails*, 12–28.

60. Stone, introduction, 6, 25.

61. Ndebele, *South African Literature*, 50. Grant Farred describes the latter view as "the apartheid state's fallacious belief in its own telos—its sense of its capacity to exist infinitely in the face of the disenfranchised majority's growing resistance." Farred, "Not-yet Counterpartisan," 592.

62. In 1992, Sowetan photographer Santu Mofokeng articulated a similar critique of international demand for spectacular images of oppression and conflict: "[N]either Sowetans nor the wider South African public were interested in such photography, recognizing the glut of these images and of the settings, events, and experiences recorded." Sowetans were more interested in Mofokeng's domestic photographs and family portraits. Cohen, *Combing of History*, 135.

63. Fanon, *Wretched*, trans. Philcox, 2, 239.

64. Gilroy, *Black Atlantic*, 37.

65. Biko, *I Write*, 92, 98. For an analysis of the psychic/subjective aspects of Black Consciousness and its indebtedness to Fanon, see Sanders, *Complicities*.

66. Sanders, *Complicities*, 168–74.

67. *Staffrider* "challenged and transformed the social image and meaning of literature in South Africa." Vaughan, "Literature and Populism," 195. Assessing *Staffrider*'s relationship to township reading publics, Vaughan worried that its race-focused populism (opposed to class-based, structural critique) was not conducive to mass mobilization. Chapman contends that Black Consciousness and *Staffrider* were "closer to the university campus than the factory floor" and that *Staffrider* existed uneasily between "literary people" and township readers, each of whom thought it came from the other. Chapman, "African Popular Fiction," 115–16.

68. Ndebele, *South African Literature*, 50.

69. Matshoba, *Call Me Not a Man*, x.

70. Ndebele, *South African Literature*, 32.

71. Sole, "Political Fiction," 62. Just as he reoriented the reception of Matshoba in the 1980s, Ndebele had earlier challenged the celebration of poet Oswald Mbuyseni Mtshali's *Songs of a Cowhide Drum* (1971) when he argued, "Poetry should not only shock us into a fresh recognition of familiar situations, but should force us to consider dismantling oppres-

sive structures." Ndebele, "Artistic and Political Mirage," 193. On Ndebele's aesthetics, with considerable attention to the South African and international contexts of their articulation and reception, see O'Brien, *Against Normalization.*

72. Nkosi, "South African Fiction," 43. Attwell identifies isiZulu poet B. W. Vilakazi as a precursor for this argument. Attwell, *Rewriting Modernity*, 211n15.

73. Chapman, "African Popular Fiction," 120. On race/class, Chapman cites Vaughan, "Can the Writer Become a Storyteller?"; on gender, Driver, "M'a-ngoana." Driver mentions Matshoba, but the object of her critique is actually Black Consciousness gender politics.

74. Matshoba, *Call Me Not a Man*, ix.

75. Sole, "Political Fiction," 69.

76. Bethlehem, "'Primary Need.'" For a recent reappraisal, see Barnard, *Apartheid and Beyond*, 119–46. Like Barnard, Attwell qualifies the realist orthodoxy, tracing the experimentalism of twentieth-century black South African writing. Attwell, *Rewriting Modernity*, 169–204. For an infamous demur to the realist imperative, see Coetzee, "The Novel Today."

77. See my "Remembering the Past's Future."

78. Ndebele, *South African Literature*, 17, 27.

79. Attwell describes Ndebele's project as an "epistemological recovery" that "links subjects as agents-of-meaning with the resistance culture that is their proper heritage." Attwell, *Rewriting* 180, 188.

80. Chapman, "African Popular Fiction," 119.

81. Matshoba, *Call Me Not a Man*, 93. Nxele was imprisoned on Robben Island in 1819, after leading an attack on Grahamstown by spurring his followers with bulletproof claims and talk of driving whites into the sea. He drowned in 1820, trying to escape. Robben Island's use as a prison resumed in 1858 with the arrival of Xhosa chiefs convicted for offenses associated with the cattle killing. Peires, *Dead*, 300–1. In a 1993 interview, Matshoba remarked, "people looked towards [Robben Island] as a place from where our liberation would come, when eventually our leaders would be released or we would release them." Munnik, "Getting Back," 126. This statement evokes the pathos of Robben Island's proximity to Cape Town: each fills the other's gaze, across miles of water.

82. Matshoba, *Call Me Not a Man*, 143, 147. The narrative invokes an additional historical parallel, the early-nineteenth-century *mfecane* or southward migration of peoples fleeing the Zulu king Shaka, and (in Matshoba's version) undertaking their own pillage and conquest in order to survive. This historical thread contributes to the meditation in "Three Days" on leadership caught between self-preservation and destruction. But Matshoba's use of the *mfecane* relies on historiography that has been challenged in recent decades. Sole, "Political Fiction," 77n65. See Hamilton, *Mfecane Aftermath.*

83. G. Grey to H. Labouchere, letter dated 27 January 1857, *Imperial Blue Book* (*IBB*) 2352, p. 63.

84. Matanzima, *Independence*, 32.

85. Another glossy publication, commemorating the first anniversary of Transkei independence, claims Tiyo Soga as "the first Transkeian Minister of Religion" and notes that his hymn "Lizalis Edinga Lakho" (Lord Fulfill your Promise) was sung at the festivities. *Transkei Independence*, 9.

86. Upon Transkei's accession to self-government in 1963, Minister of Bantu Affairs De wet Nel remarked ominously that Transkei "will be the spring from which that [Xhosa] national consciousness flows but every Xhosa, wherever he may be in South Africa, will be given the fullest opportunity to share in it." *Republic of Transkei*, preface. De wet Nel's ethnonational colonialism contrasts with Sir George Grey's antinational colonialism.

87. Biko, *I Write*, 83–85. Biko's argument about the fraudulence of Bantustan autonomy was emblematically confirmed when the flagpole fell over at the independence ceremony for the Ciskei homeland (the former British Kaffraria)—an episode that gives new meaning to critiques of "flag independence." Crais, *Politics*, 150.

88. Munnik, *Call Me Not a Man*, 159. *Uhuru*, Kiswahili for freedom, is associated with the national liberation of Kenya and Tanzania.

89. "Partial analepsis" is narrative "retrospection, which ends on an ellipsis without rejoining the first narrative." Genette, *Narrative Discourse*, 62.

90. Matshoba, "Getting Back," 129.

91. Matshoba, *Call Me Not a Man*, 154.

92. This exhortation was the title of Rubusana's 1906 anthology of isiXhosa poetry and prose.

93. Benjamin, "Theses," 257.

94. Gordimer, "Living in the Interregnum," 274.

95. Benjamin, "What Is Epic Theater," 150–51. "Diese Entdeckung (Verfremdung) von Zuständen vollzieht sich mittels der Unterbrechung von Abläufen." "Was ist das epische Theater? (2)," 535.

96. Ndebele's story "The Prophetess" similarly identifies the transformational power inherent in intersubjective human caretaking and concern, rather than spiritual ritual and faith.

97. Ashforth, *Witchcraft*, xiv, 116–17.

98. Matshoba, *Call Me Not a Man*, 167–68.

99. Matshoba repeatedly uses the term *amathongo* for the ancestors Nongqause imagines conversing with. Soga suggests the term refers primarily not to ancestors, but to dreams about "spirits of departed relatives [in which the sleeper] holds converse with them." Soga, *Ama-Xosa*, 157. In this sense, Nongqause's "prophecy" comes from an experience that approximates *amathongo*.

100. See O'Brien, *Against Normalization*, 52–55.

101. Marx, "Toward the Critique," 263.

102. Anderson, *Imagined Communities*, 161.

103. Bethlehem, "'Primary Need,'" 379, 368.

104. Nkosi discusses the perceived bifurcation between black and white writing in South Africa in terms of black writers' general lack of institutional access to formal literary education or metropolitan literary theory. Nkosi sketches a speculative reading of "Three Days" through the lens of postmodernism, casting Nongqause as a decentered subject and her encounter with the ancestors in terms of Foucauldian discourses of madness and feminist considerations of Xhosa constraints on women's speech. Nkosi's essay complicates (without invalidating) Bethlehem's charge of "nostalgia" for transparent signification in late-apartheid critical discourse by stressing material constraints that produced the "colonial status of black writing." Nkosi, "Postmodernism," 77.

105. Attwell, *Rewriting Modernity*, 163.

106. Terdiman, *Present Past*, 237–38.

CHAPTER FOUR

1. Sachs, "Preparing Ourselves," 240; Ndebele, "Revolution of the Aged"; Bloch, *Principle of Hope*, 1.179.

2. Matshoba, "Return," 42.

3. Matshoba, "Three Days," 169.

4. Mandela, "Address to Rally in Durban."

5. Ndebele, *South African Literature*, viii.

6. Gordimer, "Living in the Interregnum," 263. Stephen Gray rejects Gordimer's influential designation of the 1970s and 1980s as an "interregnum," arguing that "an actual interregnum was to occur in South Africa only in 1990–94." Gray, "Opening Southern African Studies," 207.

7. Nixon, "'An Everybody,'" 23.

8. Ndebele, *South African Literature*, 154.

9. Ndebele, "Challenges," 20.

10. Matshoba, "Return," 43.

11. Brooks, *Reading for the Plot*, 22–23.

12. Voss, "Emerging Literature," 28, 31.

13. Harlow, *After Lives*, 7.

14. Benjamin, "Theses," 256.

15. Instead, we can "conceive the past not merely as a route to the present, but as a source of alternative historical trajectories that had to be suppressed so that the present could become a possibility." Dirlik, *Postcolonial Aura*, 3.

16. Sachs, "Preparing Ourselves," 239.

17. Meintjies, "Albie Sachs," 33. For immediate responses to Sachs, see De Kok and Press, *Spring Is Rebellious*. For interviews with South African writers, critics, and cultural workers about the issues Sachs raised, see Brown and Van Dyk, *Exchanges*.

18. Gwala, "Writing," 53.

19. African National Congress Youth League, "Basic Policy," 326.

20. In the 1988 assassination attempt, Sachs lost an arm and sight in one eye to a car bomb; he could hardly not be cognizant of the effects of "real weapon[s] of struggle."

21. Speaking about designing the building that houses South Africa's Constitutional Court, Sachs rejected matter-of-fact notions that "a building is a building is a building, gravity is gravity is gravity, a structure is a structure is a structure, glass is glass is glass, a court is a court is a court." Now a Justice on the Court, Sachs speaks eloquently about the role of art, memory, history—what we might call "culture"—in designing an appropriate home for justice in the South Africa won by the anti-apartheid struggle. Sachs, "New Court." The Justices' bench is particularly striking—its façade covered with the hides of Nguni cattle in the *inkone* pattern, deep black with a streak of white running down the center of each hide. Poland, *Abundant Herds*, 113.

22. MK is the acronym for Umkhonto we Sizwe, the armed wing of the ANC; SADF is the South African Defense Force; IFP is the Inkatha Freedom Party, the Zulu nationalist party that, amidst the violence of the early 1990s, claimed the right to carry spears and other weapons as "traditional cultural weapons"; "third force" refers to counterrevolutionary elements covertly sponsored by the apartheid state.

23. The perpetrators, Mongezi Manqina, Vusumzi Ntamo, Mzikhona Nofemela, and Ntobeko Ambrose Peni were convicted in 1994 and 1995 and sentenced to eighteen years. All were amnestied on July 28, 1998. *Truth and Reconciliation Commission*, 3.510.

24. In the novel, Amy Biehl's university friends (only one of whom is named) share her excitement about the transition. As she drives them home to Guguletu, they sing jubilantly, "We have overcome! We have overcome! / . . . For deep, in our hearts, We did believe / We would overcome, one day!" Magona, *Mother to Mother*, 19.

25. Magona, *Mother to Mother*, 72.

26. Benjamin, "Theses," 257–58.

27. Ironically, however, Biehl's killers acted in the context of what APLA (the PAC's armed wing) called "Operation Great Storm." *Truth and Reconciliation Commission*, 3.511.

28. Magona came to the United States to study for a master's degree at Columbia University in 1981; she took a job at the United Nations in 1984. Magona says she left South Africa out of concern for her children's education. Magona, Attwell, and Harlow, interview, 290. For a critique of Magona's opportunistic self-positioning in her autobiographies and fiction, see Samuelson, "Reading."

29. Boehmer, "Endings," 45.

30. Rita Barnard rightly dubs the novel "a deeply troubling performance," arguing that it makes an anachronistic appeal to international, struggle-era demands for dystopic depictions of township life. Barnard, *Apartheid and Beyond*, 142–43. What is curious about *Mother to Mother*'s popularity in the United States is its seeming incompatibility with the romanticized

impressions of postapartheid South Africa that have been common here, particularly in the wake of the TRC.

31. Magona, Attwell, and Harlow, interview, 289–90.

32. The novel diverges from what Magona identifies as the "version that we African people believe," that Nongqawuse was deceived by white people claiming to be ancestors. Magona, Attwell, and Harlow, interview, 289.

33. See chapter 2.

34. "One settler, one bullet" was a late-apartheid slogan associated with APLA: a militant troping on the democratic ideal of "one man, one vote," the slogan rejects the "new weapons" advocated in Wauchope's "put down the gun, pick up the pen" in its embrace of "real instruments of struggle."

35. This phrase, "arrow of . . . his race," echoes Umkhonto we Sizwe ("spear of the nation"), the armed wing of the ANC. The difference between "nation" and "race" is at play in the novel's final movement: Nongqawuse is said to have spoken for "the nation," but Mandisa repeatedly, and rather strangely, casts her son and Amy Biehl as agent and sacrifice of their respective "race."

36. One of Biehl's killers, Ntobeko Ambrose Peni, stated to the TRC, "I feel sorry and very down-hearted especially today, realizing the contribution Amy Biehl played in the struggle . . . I took part in killing someone that we could have used to achieve our own aims. Amy was one of the people who could have, in an international sense, worked for our country so that the world knows what's going on in South Africa, so that the government of the day would not get support. I ask Amy's parents, Amy's friends and relatives, I ask them to forgive me." *Truth and Reconciliation Commission*, 3.511. Peni recognizes that Biehl was the wrong target, and he imagines an alternative history in which she would have been an instrument in the struggle. The TRC Report featured this statement, while Nofemela's more troubled testimony on the paradox of killing a white comrade is buried in the TRC's Web site; see http://www.doj.gov.za/trc/amntrans/capetown/capetown_biehl02.htm.

37. This slogan was soon replaced with "people's education for people's power," which "recognised the need for education even during the process of struggle." Ndebele, *South African Literature*, 68.

38. Magona, Attwell, and Harlow, interview, 293.

39. Mandisa is the narrator throughout, and the sections depicting Biehl's activities and thoughts on the day of her death are narratologically implausible in this realist novel, unless they are read as a rather risky and presumptuous imaginative reconstruction, given the novel's address to the murdered woman's mother. Although one might attribute such narrative slipperiness to the carelessness that allows the anachronistic suggestion that Sir George Grey sent Xhosa survivors to the mines (gold and diamonds had not yet been discovered), the novel's narrative structure means that the only place in which *Mandisa* (rather than Magona) is willing to allow for an awareness of the imminent political changes is in the consciousness of the departing white American woman and her university friends. The novel never indicates how much time elapses between the events of August 1993 and Mandisa's narration.

40. The novel insists there was no "right time" for Biehl to be in Guguletu. See Harlow, "'What Was She Doing There?'"

41. A consideration of TRC's vast archive is beyond the scope of the present discussion. One important difference between Mandisa's narrative and the testimony of a TRC witness is that Mandisa speaks in a vacuum, outside (and with no consciousness of) the institutional machinery of the TRC or the historical rupture of the Government of National Unity that created it. Beyond these institutional and historical differences, however, the daily lives of Mandisa and many victim-witnesses might be more similar than not.

42. Peires, "Suicide," 51.

43. Crais, *Politics*, 219. A similar tactic was used by Rhodesian forces in Zimbabwe's liberation struggle, when aerial broadcasts and leaflets claimed the considerable authority of spirit mediums in denouncing the guerrillas. Lan, *Guns and Rain*, 7.

44. Attwell remarks upon contemporary "amnesia" about British colonial policy from 1820 to 1857, which provided the "legal, administrative, and even epistemological basis for the 'settled system'" that became the foundation for apartheid. Attwell, "Intimate Enmity," 560. The novel's structure works against this amnesia.

45. Mda, *Heart of Redness*, 137.

46. For an incisive analysis of the novel's semiotics of clothing, see Barnard, *Apartheid and Beyond*, 164–65.

47. As with Mxolisi in *Mother to Mother*, Camagu's name connotes reconciliation. Once when Nxele was saved from being burned to death, his rescuer scolded, "'take that rope off his neck, and say *Camagu*,'" which means "'forgive and be pacified,' and is usually addressed to an ancestor or a diviner." Peires, "Nxele," 56.

48. For example, *The Dead Will Arise* combines a paraphrase of Mhlakaza and a quote from an archival source: "They [the new people] brought with them a whole new world of contentment and abundance. 'Nongqawuse said that nobody would ever lead a troubled life.'" Peires, *Dead*, 80. In Mda's novel, Mhlakaza says, "Nongqawuse has told us that when the new people come there will be a new world of contentment and no one will ever lead a troubled life again." Mda, *Heart of Redness*, 55. A cursory examination found eleven discrete (sometimes lengthy) examples of such direct borrowing; for a more extensive account of borrowed passages, see Offenburger, "Duplicity."

49. Peires asserts more forcefully his case that Mhlakaza was Wilhelm Goliath, servant of the Grahamstown Archdeacon Nathaniel James Merriman, than his suggestion that Nongqawuse was an orphan whom Goliath adopted; both claims have been challenged. See the *South African Historical Journal* 25 (1991); Bradford, "Women"; and Boniface Davies, "Raising the Dead." For a response to these critiques, see Peires, afterword and "Cry Havoc!"

50. Mda has suggested that it was Peires's interpretation of the story he had lived with since childhood that inspired him to write a novel about it.

51. I avoid labeling this borrowing "plagiarism" because I do not intend the sensational moral or legal indictment the term connotes, but I do think it important to acknowledge both the extent and directness of Mda's borrowing and the challenge it represents to the historicist notion that Chalmers, Shepherd, J. H. Soga, Waters, or other earlier authors were simply operating under a different (read *undeveloped*) understanding of propriety in intertextual relations. In a recent article, "Duplicity and Plagiarism in Zakes Mda's *The Heart of Redness*," Andrew Offenburger has made precisely such an indictment by charging Mda with plagiarism and literary critics with undue "leniency." Offenburger has invested much effort in locating borrowed passages, but his argument misses a number of important considerations, among them 1) a fully historicized and theorized understanding of literary intertextuality; 2) a reflection on Mda's staging of contested interpretations of the cattle killing, informed not only by Peires's written history (which Offenburger calls Mda's "single" source) but also by contemporary Xhosa understandings of the event—oral testimony that is unavailable to textual cross-checking and statistical analysis; and 3) a consideration of the novel as a novel rather than reading only its nineteenth-century sections as historiography. Offenburger's lack of interest in the twentieth-century narrative thread, or in the remarkably innovative ways in which Mda puts past and present into conversation, is evident in his observation that the novel opens (as Peires's history does) with Mlanjeni (169). In fact, the novel opens with Bhonco, whose itchy scars (after nearly ten pages) evoke in him thoughts of Mlanjeni; those thoughts, in turn, draw the narration into the nineteenth-century narrative thread. Offenburger's charges, in other words, might have more bite if *The Heart of Redness* purported to be a historical novel about the 1850s; he questions the novel's literary value without attending to its literary aspects.

52. Peires, "Suicide," 55–56. On the relevance of academic historiography to nationalist movements and contemporary predicaments, see Ranger, "Towards a Usable African Past."

53. Moosa, "Lend a Hand."

54. Radebe, "South African Government's Vision."

55. Mda deemed Moosa's citation of the novel a sign of "remarkable political maturity." Isaacson, "Free State Madonnas." Indeed, the embrace of *The Heart of Redness* contrasts with the hostile reaction of the ANC to Coetzee's *Disgrace*. See Attwell, "Race"; McDonald, "Disgrace Effects."

56. Ashforth, "Xhosa Cattle Killing," 590. See also Crais, "Peires."

57. On nontextual memory, see Middleton and Woods, *Literatures of Memory*; Samuel, *Theatres of Memory*.

58. Xoliswa Ximiya's reductive fondness for "civilization" resembles Lakunle in Wole Soyinka's *Lion and the Jewel*, which describes modernity in terms of indigenous cosmology by casting mechanization and electricity as domains of the Yoruba gods Ogun and Sango.

59. Qukezwa's action has a nineteenth-century parallel in the forest reserve, Manyube. In the novel, after the first failures of Nongqawuse's prophecy, King Sarhili retreats to Manyube, where the "things of nature" are preserved "for future generations," and there he issues a ban on killing cattle; this potentially momentous decision is later reversed, and the slaughter proceeds. This pivotal moment is lost on Bhonco, who denounces the conservation of "ugly" indigenous species, arguing that "we can always plant civilized trees" that grow "in straight lines"; when he is reminded of Sarhili's conservationism, Bhonco retorts that Sarhili was a "king of darkness" who "instructed his people to follow Nongqawuse." Mda, *Heart of Redness*, 132, 146, 165.

60. On colonial inventions of "customary" law, epitomized by apartheid, see Mamdani, *Citizen and Subject*.

61. For Mda's account of being twice visited by Majola, see Isaacson, "Free State Madonnas."

62. This crucial incident rewrites the plot of A. C. Jordan's landmark isiXhosa novel, *Wrath of the Ancestors* (1940), in which the wife of the Mpondomise chief kills Majola when he appears near her infant son. Her transgression confirms a prophecy that a woman born outside of the royal house of Majola would not respect its customs. The modernizing influence of the couple (who met at Lovedale) is swept away by the populist response to her action, which eventually destroys the chief and his family. Camagu, by contrast, restrains the hotel staff from killing the snake and subsequently finds a future in Qolorha.

63. Chakrabarty, *Provincializing Europe*, 31, 73–74.

64. Benjamin, "Theses," 263.

65. For such a narrative experiment, see Mpe's *Welcome to our Hillbrow* (2001), narrated by a recently deceased young resident of the vibrant and dangerous Johannesburg neighborhood of Hillbrow, where we also first meet Camagu. At the end of Mda's novel, Bhonco fears what Zim might be saying about him in the Otherworld, but it is the *inaccessibility* of this realm that generates his anxiety.

66. Bloch, "Nonsynchronism," 23.

67. I use nonsynchronism to amplify Chakrabarty's idea of heterotemporality, even though Chakrabarty rejects what he sees as Bloch's (and other Marxists') assumption of "a general historical movement from a premodern stage to that of modernity." Chakrabarty, *Provincializing Europe*, 12. Bloch's analysis of the contradictions and uses of anachronism is more supple and less normative than Chakrabarty allows, as I show at the end of this chapter.

68. "In acting-out one has a mimetic relation to the past which is regenerated or relived as if it were fully present rather than represented in memory and inscription." LaCapra, *Writing History*, 45. The narrative structure of *The Heart of Redness* makes the nineteenth-century past "fully present" as well as "represented in [twentieth-century characters'] memory and

inscription." Bhonco's attack on the descendant of the man who killed his ancestor suggests pathological mourning. See Freud, "Mourning and Melancholia."

69. Derrida, *Specters*, 65.

70. Camagu is a kind of incarnation of Twin himself. Qolorha villagers had hoped that a romance between Zim's son Twin and Bhonco's daughter Xoliswa Ximiya would repair the breach between them, but Twin left Qolorha for Johannesburg. Camagu happens upon Twin's wake in the city, where he meets NomaRussia, whom he seeks in Qolorha. Camagu effectively "returns" to Qolorha in Twin's place, but his marriage to Twin's sister Qukezwa repeats the past rather than resolving the feud between Believers and Unbelievers.

71. The rural setting of *The Heart of Redness*, or its setting several years into the transition, might account for its qualified optimism in comparison to the dehumanization of Magona's *Mother to Mother*. Mda's *Ways of Dying* (1995) also depicts an early 1990s township culture of death; its emphasis, however, is on imagination and the aesthetic as a deeply human mode of living. See Barnard, "On Laughter."

72. Cognizant of the gulf between the 1955 Freedom Charter's promised economic redistribution and the ANC's postapartheid neoliberalism, Mda hints at the limits of Camagu's vision. Camagu observes enthusiastically, "Nongqawuse really sells the holiday camp. . . . It would have been even more profitable if she had been buried there." Mda, *Heart of Redness*, 276.

73. Samuelson, *Remembering the Nation*, 51–83.

74. In my reading, the novel ironizes Christian imagery rather than privileging it; likewise, it depicts literacy as one mode of "authorship" among many (and with considerable historical and ideological baggage, to boot) rather than the privileged mode from which female characters are excluded.

75. The transition to democracy was violent and perhaps even catastrophic for some South Africans, yet the most spectacular consequences of majority rule feared during the apartheid era did not come to pass. Some white South Africans may be leaving, but they were not driven to the sea; 1994 brought not an apocalyptic whirlwind, but a "wind of change," to borrow from British Prime Minister Macmillan's 1960 speech on African decolonization. Macmillan, "Speech in the South African Parliament."

76. Ndebele, *South African Literature*, 67.

77. It is unclear whether Ndebele echoes Aldous Huxley, William Blake, or both on the need to break through constraints on human perception.

78. Kwaito is a genre of urban dance music (drawing on house and hip-hop). It emerged in the early 1990s and is associated with the generation of South Africans who came of age in the wake of the transition.

79. Chapman, "African Popular Fiction," 122.

80. See my "Remembering the Past's Future."

81. Benjamin, "Theses," 256.

82. Brooks, *Reading for the Plot*, 18.

83. See chapter 1.

84. Adorno writes, "If Benjamin said that history had hitherto been written from the standpoint of the victor, and needed to be written from that of the vanquished, we might add that knowledge must indeed present the fatally rectilinear succession of victory and defeat, but should also address itself to those things which were not embraced by this dynamic, which fell by the wayside. . . . What transcends the ruling society is not only the potentiality it develops but also all that which did not fit properly into the laws of historical movement. Theory must needs deal with cross-gained, opaque, unassimilated material, which as such admittedly has from the start an anachronistic quality, but is not wholly obsolete since it has outwitted the historical dynamic." Adorno, *Minima Moralia*, 151.

85. O'Brien, *Against Normalization*.

86. Ndebele, *South African Literature*, viii.

87. Kruger, "Black Atlantics," 113.

88. Voss, "Reading," 8. See also Farred, "Not-Yet Counterpartisan"; Pechey, "Post-Apartheid Reason."

89. I develop this idea in chapter 5. See Osborne, *Politics of Time*.

90. Chakrabarty, *Provincializing Europe*, 243.

91. See Fabian, *Time and the Other*.

92. Bloch, "Nonsynchronism," 26.

93. Bloch, "Trader Horn," 424–25.

94. This critique of primitivism continues in Bloch's denunciation of Jung, which recurs throughout *The Principle of Hope*.

95. Bloch, "Alienation," 245.

96. Verdal, "Praise-Singers."

97. See chapter 3.

98. Van Rooyen, "Poet of the Nation."

CHAPTER FIVE

1. Marx, *Eighteenth Brumaire*, 320; Freud, *Totem and Taboo*, 88; Gordimer, "Living in the Interregnum," 283.

2. Brink, *SA, 27 April 1994*, 74.

3. O'Brien, *Against Normalization*, 21.

4. The "frightening aspect of haunting" is that "powerful and material forces . . . lay claim to you whether you claim them as yours or not." Gordon, *Ghostly Matters*, 166.

5. Spivak, "Ghostwriting," 70, 79.

6. This relation is "the perspective we possess from the onetime future of past generations, or, more pithily, from a former future." Koselleck, *Futures Past*, 5.

7. Sanders, *Complicities*, 120.

8. I have noted the congruence of the past's future and remembered prophecy. Prophetic memory, a moment of crystallized hindsight, does not map so neatly onto the future's past. Prophetic memory is an act of projection that actualizes the "invented memory" of the future perfect: instead of imagining the past that will have been, the retrospection of prophetic memory recognizes the present that has become.

9. Osborne, "Modernity," 32–33; Chakrabarty, *Provincializing Europe*, 8.

10. Cabral, *Revolution*, 68.

11. Anderson, *Imagined Communities*.

12. "National chronology" has even less contemporary purchase than "national territoriality," according to Wai Chee Dimock: "For much of the world's population, time has perhaps always been subnational in one sense, supranational in another." She argues for attention to planetary time, "a duration antedating the birth of any nation and outlasting the demise of all." Dimock, "Planetary Time," 490–91.

13. Spivak, "Ghostwriting," 70.

14. Gilroy, *Black Atlantic*.

15. I borrow "laminate," the "folds and layers of production [of history] that join the past and the present," from Cohen, *Combing of History*, xxii.

16. Remembering what has never yet been is antithetical to conventional nostalgia, which may long for what has never been but confuses that invented past for a lost state of actual affairs. Awareness of the *lack* of historical realization rather than the *loss* of a better past is what gives a critical edge to afterlives.

17. British Kaffraria commissioner Maclean wrote confidentially to Governor Grey of "silly rumours . . . to the effect that the 'black nation' at war with the English is carrying everything before it and will soon come to the relief of the Kaffirs." J. Maclean to G. Grey, letter dated 30 June 1856, GH 8/49, Cape Archives.

18. Brownlee reported to Maclean in July 1856, "Umhlakaza predicts that the cause of rupture between the Kaffirs and Government will be, that the Government will dig into the

cavern in which the Russians have appeared, in order to get out the Russians, when war will ensue." C. Brownlee to J. Maclean, letter dated 30 July 1856, *Imperial Blue Book (IBB)* 2352, pp. 7–8. Frederick Reeve, magistrate with the chief Kama (later a staunch Unbeliever), reported that "[m]uch interest seems to be felt about the war with Russia. I took care to explain this matter to them, showing them that although the English had lost many men, the Russians had lost vastly more, and that in all our engagements we were victorious. . . . [T]he 'war doctors' spread false reports about the war with an evil purpose." J. Reeve to J. Maclean, letter dated 7 March 1856, *Imperial Blue Book (IBB)* 2202, p. 17.

19. Peires, *Dead*, 262.

20. Williams, "Indian Mutiny," 60.

21. Mphande, "Cattle Killing," 180.

22. Legassick, "The State," 362.

23. Ranger, "Connections."

24. Enclosure in J. Jackson to G. Grey, letter dated 15 April 1856, *Imperial Blue Book (IBB)* 2202, pp. 21–22.

25. See chapter 2. Aggrey's visit occurred five days after the massacre of the millenarian Israelites at Bulhoek. Back-to-Africa proponents had been visiting South Africa since the 1890s. Bradford, *Taste of Freedom*, 214; Shepperson, "Notes," 303–4.

26. Bradford, *Taste of Freedom*, 214–15.

27. Cingo, "Native Unrest," 407. My term "Garveyite imagining" refers to a range of ideas about diasporic deliverance not necessarily encompassed in Marcus Garvey's actual project of redeeming Africa—itself inspired by Irish nationalism, the Russian Revolution, and nascent pan-Africanism.

28. Shepperson, "Nyasaland," 145.

29. Bradford, *Taste of Freedom*, 229. On the Bunyanesque underpinnings of such "passports to heaven," see Hofmeyr, *Portable Bunyan*.

30. See Hill, *Marcus Garvey*.

31. See Crais, *Politics*, 139–40.

32. Bradford, *Taste of Freedom*, 236, 328n52; Locke, "Wellington Movement," 738.

33. See Shepperson, "Nyasaland"; Worsley, *Trumpet Shall Sound*.

34. Bradford, *Taste of Freedom*, 216.

35. Scott, *Weapons of the Weak*, 38.

36. Viswanathan writes, "The degree to which religion and secularism coincide in their inability to acknowledge alternative spiritual practices is matched only by the scholarly complicity in homogenizing religious histories to fit a composite profile of religious belief." Viswanathan, "Secularism," 475.

37. Stoler and Cooper, "Between Metropole and Colony."

38. Chakrabarty, *Provincializing Europe*, 101, 103.

39. Peires, *Dead*, 250.

40. Steinbart, *Letters*, 81. His editors speculate that Steinbart was thinking of William Fynn (W. R. D. Fynn, son of William McDowall Fynn and nephew of Henry Francis Fynn), a clerk and translator who took Nongqawuse into custody in 1858; see Burton, *Sparks*, 89–92. Additional idiosyncratic reports about Nongqawuse's fate include Kropf's claim that she was taken by Gawler to England to be trained as a domestic servant and Cory's report that she lived into the twentieth century in the eastern Cape under the name Victoria Regina. Kropf, *Die Lügenpropheten*, 14; Peires, *Dead*, 336.

41. Williams, "Indian Mutiny," 60.

42. Dowsley, "Investigation," 55.

43. Mnguni, *Three Hundred Years*, 88.

44. For an analysis of Grey's policies and indigenous responses in New Zealand and the Cape, see Gump, "Imperialism." I'm grateful to Susan Najita for reminding me of Grey's experience with millenarianism in New Zealand.

45. Gutsche, *History*, 333–34. For a fascinating discussion of the national and international contexts for the film's production, see Boniface Davies, "Cattle-Killing as Propaganda."

46. These amateur actors staged a successful wage strike during production of *Nonquassi*. Rostron, "Presenting South Africa," 77.

47. Schauder teased the *Cape Argus* film correspondent, "We are hoping that the story of the Amaxosa will not have trouble with the censor due to the lack of fashion shown by Nonquassi in her dress!" Irvin, "African Film Success." Nonquassi is the only prominently topless woman in the film.

48. Schauder was only twenty when he wrote, produced, directed, and shot these films as a "one-man production unit" (with the help of a black assistant); he also played the part of the lone white man who rescues Xhosa survivors with his ox-wagon in *Nonquassi*. Rostron, "Presenting South Africa," 77.

49. The contract indicates that ending of *Nonquassi* was altered for the Ministry of Information. Central Office of Information, "Nonquassi 1940." Whether the voiceover originally stressed the German parallel is unclear; the footage itself concerns only the amaXhosa. The film's images work against the narration's account of gender relations, in which women are said do all the work while men do nothing but wage war. This critique of patriarchal militarism is also difficult to square with the film's insistence on the absolute obedience shown to the young female prophet.

50. Besides *Nonquassi*, other links to World War II include the characterization of the expected day of resurrection as "D-day" and the claim that the cattle killing sheds light on the workings of "power psychology." Troup, *South Africa*, 137; Burton, *Sparks*, 16. Elias Canetti analyzes the cattle killing in *Masse und Macht* (Crowds and Power, 1960).

51. Blundell, *World's Greatest Mistakes*.

52. Palmberg, "NONGQAWUSE," idem, personal communication, 2004.

53. Crais, *Politics*, 220; Bailey, *Plays* 4, 9.

54. *The Prophet* recycles material from an earlier work called "Waiting for America." Bailey, *Plays*, 163.

55. Bailey thrives on controversy and hunger for "experience," as is evident in the dustup over the sacrifice of a chicken during a production of *iMumbo Jumbo* at Cape Town's Baxter Theatre, and his breathless account of being stuck in Haiti during the March 2004 ouster of Jean-Bertrand Aristide. He is "delighted" when his company is attacked in Transkei. Bailey, "My Lift"; *Plays*, 78.

56. My discussion of Bailey relies heavily on this text and is thus oriented textually rather than in terms of performance. Seeing *Orfeus*, his 2007 production at Grahamstown, did not lead me to substantially revise my view, except to acknowledge that the sensory, immersive experience of the performance must necessarily exceed what appears on the page. Nonetheless, the monumentality of *The Plays of Miracle & Wonder* demands critical attention in its own right. With its high-end design and prodigious graphics, the book resembles a coffee table volume rather than a practical collection of working scripts. The scripts are supplemented by essays and notes that show Bailey's mind at work.

57. Bailey recalls that the absence of local black performers at Grahamstown in the mid-1990s spurred him to form Third World Bunfight, with sponsorship from Standard Bank. Bailey, "Making," 4.

58. Bailey's *Ipi Zombi?* makes sly allusion to the cultural politics of South Africa's international presence. *Ipi Tombi?* (Where Are the Girls?) was a wildly successful South African musical that toured the United States in the late 1970s: the show's white producers pitched its exotic appeal to white audiences, although its affirmation of modernization and Christianity is not so far removed from Mary Waters's missionary polemic, *The Light*. A recorded performance, *Ipi Ntombi: An African Dance Celebration*, has been a staple of PBS fundraising drives in the United States.

59. Bailey's sense of the unlimited availability of Xhosa history to dramatic revision is evident in *iMumbo Jumbo*, which caricatures "Professor Peires, a prominent white historian

of the Xhosa nation." The Professor is a ridiculous, clown-faced figure, who objects to the spurious historicity of the play's central premise, that the head of the Xhosa chief Hintsa is in Scotland: "anyone who can read will know this is nonsense," he pontificates from the pulpit of literacy. Bailey, *Plays*, 117. In staging this scene of conflict between white scholarly and lived vernacular history, Bailey not only makes Peires seem arrogant and clownish; he also ignores Peires's ambivalent relationship to the Xhosa reception of his work.

60. One might compare Bailey's artistic development with Artaud's response to a Balinese performance at the 1931 Paris colonial exhibition. Artaud's theories of the differences between civilized and primitive man, his desire to liberate the spectator's subconscious, and the practice of theater in the round, are echoed in Bailey's dramaturgy. Yet where Artaud's encounter with Balinese theater is a modernist consequence of imperialism, Bailey locates himself within South African decolonization. Savarese and Fowler, "1931."

61. At least one spectator at Grahamstown interpreted the "possession" of the actors, who were "covered in white paint and given horned hoods," as their "'becoming' the cattle that are to be slaughtered." Bain, "Magical Millennium," 188.

62. Bradford, review, 231.

63. Ashforth, *Witchcraft*, xiv.

64. The striking photos in the book (tableaux that do not always appear in the productions) are as interesting as the plays themselves. See Flockemann, "Spectacles," 275. Elsabe van Tonder's photograph of the Dead emerging from the water evokes the wondrous rumors of what Nongqawuse and her followers saw and heard at the Gxarha River. In the photograph of male actor Abey Xakwe as Nongqawuse, his form captures the anguish of her predicament.

65. Bailey also introduces anachronistic technology into his reenactment: Nongqawuse and the villagers are mesmerized by singing voices emitted by a tape recorder. Voice reproduction technologies, from the phonograph to the telephone, have long been associated with spectrality. See Clinton, "Wavespeech"; Connor, *Dumbstruck*. An installation at the 2004 Democracy X exhibition at the Castle of Good Hope drew on this effect. In a dark, cramped alcove, hidden speakers projected recordings of two songs about Nongqawuse performed by Lungiswa Plaatjies and a group of girls. Visitors who stepped into the dark room were surrounded by echoing voices singing about hearing voices.

66. Gordon, *Ghostly Matters*, 195.

67. Marx borrows from Jesus' rebuke to a would-be disciple in Luke 9:59–60.

68. Marx, *Eighteenth Brumaire*, 322.

69. Given Marx's attention to the mediations among consciousness, culture, and socio-economic context, his privileging of the future as the source of revolutionary imagery is uncharacteristic. On Marxian suspicions of future projection, see Buck-Morss, *Dialectics of Seeing*, 124; Eagleton, "Marxism."

70. Benjamin, "Theses," 260.

71. Hermann Lotze quoted in Benjamin, *Arcades*, 479.

72. Benjamin, *Arcades*, 471.

73. Lenhardt, "Anamnestic Solidarity," 135. Lenhardt borrows "total recovery of man" from Marx, "Toward the Critique of Hegel's Philosophy of Right."

74. Nietzsche, "On the Uses," 62.

75. Tiedemann, "Historical Materialism," 82. Many critics concur that the power of Benjamin's work is its articulation of the imperative of mindfulness of the dead—however impossible their redemption might be. See Honneth, "Communicative Disclosure"; Bauman, "Walter Benjamin"; and Osborne, *Politics*, 147.

76. Recasting Freud's account of mourning as the detachment of cathectic attachments to the lost object, Harrison describes mourning as getting the dead to die in us, so that survivors do not "die with the dead." Harrison, *Dominion*, 50, 58.

77. Eng and Kazanjian, *Loss*, 3–4.

78. The tension in Bailey's play between the Dead and the ancestors captures the sense of

horror in some accounts of the cattle killing, that the ancestors would be resurrected among the living rather than continue their vigilant role as the "dead."

79. For an examination of reading as a practice of simultaneous mourning and melancholia, see Moynagh, "Melancholic Structure."

80. Benjamin, "Theses," 255.

81. Newman, "Suffering," 97.

82. Mbeki, statement.

83. Congress of the People, "Freedom Charter," 242.

84. On the multiple temporalities of dramatic performance created by the tensions between bodies of actors and characters, see Garner, *Bodied Spaces*.

85. Comaroff and Comaroff, *Of Revelation*, 1.218.

86. Ashforth, *Witchcraft*, 207.

87. Cohen, *Combing of History*, 67.

88. Wideman, *The Cattle Killing*, 207.

89. A similar diasporic gesture appears in the final, timebending fragment of Caryl Phillips's *Crossing the River* (1993).

90. Mbiti's analysis of "Great Time" shaped Wideman's conception of time as immersion without beginning, end, or linear progress. Baker, "Storytelling," 267. Wideman's temporality implicitly rejects Freud's designation of "oceanic" feelings (the blurring of boundaries between the ego and the external world) as primitive. Freud argues that such feelings are nonsynchronous vestiges of an early psychic state that generate the "patently infantile" "mass delusion" of religion. *Civilization and Its Discontents*, 21, 28. By contrast, Wideman's novel privileges the oceanic experience of transcendence over the false promises of religion.

91. "African" is the novel's term for people of African descent, regardless of the place of their birth.

92. Particularly suspect were Haitians recently arrived in Philadelphia in the wake of the hemisphere's first black revolution: "the contagion of freedom" is as deadly as yellow fever. Wideman, *The Cattle Killing*, 34.

93. The "cattle-killing that's going on now" in the United States is the "myth of integration" that asks African Americans to "kill their cattle, to give up what's distinctive." Wideman, interview.

94. Fanon, *Black Skin*, 13.

95. Wideman's Thrush is based on Philadelphia physician Benjamin Rush, who advocated a bleeding cure for yellow fever and coordinated black labor teams that tended to the sick and collected the dead. Rush and the balloon launch also feature in Wideman, "Ascent by Balloon."

96. See Zamora, *Apocalyptic Vision*; Bercovitch, *Rites of Assent*.

97. For a discussion of the 1793 epidemic, Rush's role therein, Bishop Richard Allen's subsequent founding of the AME church, and the importance of these events for early African American literature, see Brooks, *American Lazarus*.

98. When *The Cattle Killing* was published in 1996, the scale of the AIDS pandemic in South Africa was not yet evident, or Wideman might have included an additional layer of devastating plague and providential interpretation.

99. Wideman borrows chief Moni's warning, "'Cattle are the race, they being dead, the race dies'" (J. H. Soga, *Ama-Xosa* 122).

100. The Nguni peoples of southern Africa include the Xhosa, Zulu, Swazi, and Ndebele; traditional pastoralists, the indigenous breed of cattle they tend are known as Nguni cattle, whose cultural and cosmic significance are discussed in Poland's *Abundant Herds*, beautifully illustrated by Leigh Voigt. The *Oxford English Dictionary* traces Latin and French etymologies for *chattel* and *cattle* linked to notions of capital and property.

101. In the West African coastal slave trade, *panyar* (of Portuguese/Latinate etymol-

ogy) denotes the illicit seizure of goods, particularly enslaved human beings. This diction extends the novel's critique of Christianity, yoking the humanitarian, abolitionist strand of eighteenth-century British imperialism, which brought Liam to England to train as a missionary, with the cruder realities of the European slave trade.

102. *Ogbanje* are West African spirits repeatedly reborn as children who die as infants or in early childhood. A fragment in *The Cattle Killing* between opening frame and central narrative speaks of "certain passionate African spirits—kin to the ogbanji . . . [that] are so strong and willful they refuse to die." Wideman, *Cattle Killing*, 15.

103. Fanon, *Wretched*, trans. Farrington, 35, 52.

104. Fanon, *Wretched*, trans. Philcox, 3, 1.

105. See Shepperson, "Notes"; Chirenje, *Ethiopianism*.

106. Bishop Richard Allen died in 1831.

107. Ricoeur, *Time and Narrative*, 3.189.

108. The (presumably) anachronistic allusion is to Reverend Herbert Brewster's (1897–1987) gospel song, "Feel Something Drawing Me On." Wideman's preacher, however, is compelled by the dead rather than the Holy Spirit.

109. Sanders argues that *ubuntu* is invoked in terms of its loss and future restoration; it is the literary, he suggests, that can "render the call for *ubuntu* . . . concrete." Sanders, *Complicities*, 121.

110. Wideman depicts Stubbs's and Burton's escapades as "man-midwives" and their dealings with "resurrectionists" who procure the corpses necessary for their work. Stubbs also collaborated with Josiah Wedgwood; in the novel, his parting gift to Liam is one of Wedgwood's abolitionist plaques, with the motto "Am I not a man and a brother?"

111. Koselleck describes the eighteenth-century shift from the closed "future" of Christian eschatology to the open-ended future associated with Enlightenment progress narratives. Koselleck, *Futures Past*.

112. Morrison, *Beloved*, 275.

113. Ricoeur, *Time and Narrative*, 3.260.

114. Brooks, *Reading for the Plot*, 34.

115. "Fire on its way to do its work. Warn the people. A burning house glows orange behind dark hills." Wideman, *Cattle Killing*, 78.

116. Gordimer, "Living in the Interregnum," 283.

117. Brink, *SA, 27 April 1994*, 111–12.

118. Nandy, "History's Forgotten Doubles," 45; Chakrabarty, *Provincializing Europe*, 88; Cheah, *Spectral Nationality*, 330.

119. Boniface Davies, "Raising the Dead," 41.

120. See Viswanathan, "Secularism."

WORKS CITED

Adas, Michael. *Prophets of Rebellion: Millenarian Protest Movements against the European Colonial Order.* Chapel Hill: University of North Carolina Press, 1979.

Adjaye, Joseph K., ed. *Time in the Black Experience.* Westport, CT: Greenwood, 1994.

Adorno, Theodor W. *Minima Moralia: Reflections from Damaged Life.* London: New Left, 1974.

African National Congress Youth League National Executive Committee. "Basic Policy of the Congress Youth League." 1948. In Karis et al., vol. 2 of *From Protest to Challenge,* 323–31.

The Agronomist. DVD. Directed by Jonathan Demme. New Line Home Entertainment, 2005.

Amandla! A Revolution in Four Part Harmony. DVD. Directed by Lee Hirsch. Lionsgate/Fox/Artisan Home Entertainment, 2002.

America: A Tribute to Heroes. DVD. Directed by Joel Gallen and Beth McCarthy-Miller. Warner Brothers, 2001.

American Red Cross. Disaster FAQs. "Hurricane Katrina: Why Is the Red Cross Not in New Orleans?" September 2, 2005. Http://www.redcross.org/faq/0,1096,0_682_4524,00.html#4524.

Anderson, Benedict. *Imagined Communities: Reflections on the Origin and Spread of Nationalism.* London: Verso, 1991.

Anderson, David M., and Douglas Hamilton Johnson, eds. *Revealing Prophets: Prophecy in Eastern African History.* Athens: Ohio University Press, 1995.

Andreas, Christian B. "The Spread and Impact of the Lungsickness Epizootic of 1853–57 and the Cape Colony and the Xhosa Chiefdoms." *South African Historical Journal* 53 (2005): 50–72.

Antze, Paul, and Michael Lambek. "Introduction: Forecasting Memory." In Antze and Lambek, *Tense Past,* xi–xxxviii.

———, eds. *Tense Past: Cultural Essays in Trauma and Memory.* New York: Routledge, 1996.

Armah, Ayi Kwei. *The Beautiful Ones Are Not Yet Born.* Boston: Houghton Mifflin, 1968.

Ashforth, Adam. *Witchcraft, Violence, and Democracy in South Africa.* Chicago: University of Chicago Press, 2005.

———. "The Xhosa Cattle Killing and the Politics of Memory." *Sociological Forum* 6, no. 3 (1991): 581–92.

Asmara Declaration on African Languages and Literatures, Asmara, Eritrea, January 11–17, 2000. Delivered at "Against all odds: African Languages and Literatures in the Twenty-first Century." Http://www.outreach.psu.edu/C&I/AllOdds/declaration.html.

Attridge, Derek, and Rosemary Jane Jolly. *Writing South Africa: Literature, Apartheid, and Democracy, 1970–1995.* Cambridge: Cambridge University Press, 1998.

Attwell, David. "Intimate Enmity in the Journal of Tiyo Soga." *Critical Inquiry* 23 (1997): 557–77.

———. "Modernizing Tradition/Traditionalizing Modernity: Reflections on the Dhlomo-Vilakazi Dispute." *Research in African Literatures* 33, no. 1 (2002): 94–119.

———. "Race in *Disgrace*." *Interventions* 4, no. 3 (2002): 331–41.

———. *Rewriting Modernity: Studies in Black South African Literary History.* Scottsville: University of KwaZulu-Natal Press, 2005.

Bailey, Brett. "'My Lift to Rehearsal Made a Hasty U-Turn as Armed Mobs Closed In.'" *Guardian*, March 8, 2004. Http://www.guardian.co.uk/stage/2004/mar/08/theatre1.

———. "The Making of a Communal Bunfight: Interview with Lennox Faba, Samkelo Bunu, and Thozamile Enock Ngeju." *Artreach* (2004): 2, 4–5.

———. *The Plays of Miracle & Wonder: Bewitching Visions and Primal High-Jinx from the South African Stage.* Cape Town: Double Storey, 2003.

Bain, Keith. "Magical Millennium Dress Rehearsal: 25th Anniversary of the Standard Bank National Arts Festival." In *History and Theatre in Africa*, edited by Yvette Hutchison and Eckhard Breitinger, 179–95. Bayreuth and Breitinger/Stellenbosch: Centre for Theatre and Performance Studies, University of Stellenbosch, 2000.

Baker, Lisa. "Storytelling and Democracy (in the Radical Sense): A Conversation with John Edgar Wideman." *African American Review* 34, no. 2 (2000): 263–72.

Balme, Christopher B. *Decolonizing the Stage: Theatrical Syncretism and Post-Colonial Drama.* Oxford: Oxford University Press/Clarendon, 1999.

Barber, Karin. Introduction to *Africa's Hidden Histories: Everyday Literacy and Making the Self.* Bloomington: Indiana University Press, 2006.

Barker, Francis, Peter Hulme, and Margaret Iversen, eds. *Postmodernism and the Re-Reading of Modernity.* New York: St. Martin's, 1992.

Barnard, Rita. *Apartheid and Beyond: South African Writers and the Politics of Place.* Oxford: Oxford University Press, 2007.

———. *The Great Depression and the Culture of Abundance: Kenneth Fearing, Nathanael West, and Mass Culture in the 1930s.* Cambridge: Cambridge University Press, 1995.

———. "On Laughter, the Grotesque, and the South African Transition: Zakes Mda's *Ways of Dying*." *Novel* 37, no. 3 (2004): 277–302.

Barthes, Roland. "The Death of the Author." In *Image, Music, Text*, 155–64. New York: Hill and Wang, 1977.

Bauman, Zygmunt. "Walter Benjamin: The Intellectual." *New Formations* 20 (1993): 47–57.

Beinart, William, and Colin Bundy. "The Union, the Nation and the Talking Crow: The Ideology and Tactics of the Independent ICU in East London." In *Hidden Struggles in Rural South Africa: Politics and Popular Movements in the Transkei and Eastern Cape, 1890–1930*, edited by William Beinart and Colin Bundy, 270–320. Berkeley: University of California Press, 1987.

Benjamin, Walter. *The Arcades Project.* Translated by Howard Eiland and Kevin McLaughlin from German edition by Rolf Tiedemann. Cambridge, MA: Harvard University Press/Belknap Press, 1999.

———. *Illuminationen: Ausgewahlte Schriften.* Edited by Siegried Unseld. Frankfurt: Suhrkamp Verlag, 1977.

———. *Illuminations.* Edited by Hannah Arendt. Translated by Harry Zohn. New York: Schocken, 1969.

———. "On Some Motifs in Baudelaire." In Benjamin, *Illuminations,* 155–200.

———. "The Task of the Translator." In Benjamin, *Illuminations,* 69–82.

———. "Theses on the Philosophy of History." In Benjamin, *Illuminations,* 253–64.

———. "Was Ist Das Epische Theater? (2)." In *Gesammelte Schriften,* edited by Rolf Tiedemann and H. Schweppenhaeuser, 532–39. Frankfurt: Suhrkamp Verlag, 1974.

———. "What Is Epic Theatre?" In Benjamin, *Illuminations,* 147–54.

Bercovitch, Sacvan. *The Rites of Assent: Transformations in the Symbolic Construction of America.* New York: Routledge, 1993.

Bethlehem, Louise. "'A Primary Need as Strong as Hunger': The Rhetoric of Urgency in South African Literary Culture under Apartheid." *Poetics Today* 22, no. 2 (2001): 365–89.

Biko, Steve. *I Write What I Like: A Selection of His Writings.* Edited by A. Stubbs. London: Bowderdean, 1996.

BK 89. Secret Information, British Kaffraria. Cape Archives. Western Cape Archives and Records Service, Cape Town.

Bloch, Ernst. "Alienation, Estrangement." In *Literary Essays,* translated by Andrew Joron et al., 239–46. Stanford: Stanford University Press, 1998.

———. "Nonsynchronism and the Obligation to Its Dialectics." 1932. Reprinted in *New German Critique* 11 (1977): 22–38.

———. *The Principle of Hope.* Translated by Neville Plaice, Stephen Plaice, and Paul Knight. Cambridge, MA: MIT Press, 1986.

———. "Trader Horn in Africa." Reprinted in *Literary Essays,* translated by Andrew Joron et al., 422–26. Stanford: Stanford University Press, 1998.

Blundell, Nigel. *The World's Greatest Mistakes.* London: Octopus, 1980.

Boehmer, Elleke. "Endings and New Beginnings: South African Fiction and Transition." In Attridge and Jolly, *Writing South Africa,* 43–56.

Bokwe, John Knox. *Ntsikana: The Story of an African Convert.* Lovedale: Lovedale, 1914.

Boniface Davies, Sheila. "The Cattle-Killing as Propaganda: Leon Schauder's *Nonquassi* [1939]." *African Studies* 67, no. 2 (2008): 183–208.

———. "Raising the Dead: The Xhosa Cattle-Killing and the Mhlakaza-Goliat Delusion." *Journal of Southern African Studies* 33, no.1 (2007): 19–41.

Bradford, Helen. "*Akukho Ntaka Inokubhabha Ngephiko Elinye* (No Bird Can Fly on One Wing): The 'Cattle-killing Delusion' and Black Intellectuals, c. 1840–1910." Special issue on the Xhosa cattle-killing, *African Studies* 67, no. 2 (2008): 209–32.

———. "New Country, New Race, New Men: War, Gender, and Millenarianism in Xhosaland, 1855–57." Paper presented at the 19th International Conference on Historical Sciences: Session on Gender, Race, Xenophobia, and Nationalism, Oslo, August 2000. Http://www. oslo2000.uio.no/program/papers/r13/r13-bradford.pdf

———. "Not a Nongqawuse Story: An Anti-heroine in Historical Perspective." In *Basus'iimbokodo, bawel'imilambo/They Remove Boulders and Cross Rivers: Women in South African History,* edited by Nomboniso Gasa, 43–90. Cape Town: Human Sciences Research Council, 2007.

———. Review of *Plays of Miracle and Wonder* by Brett Bailey. *Kronos* 30 (2004): 230–34.

———. *A Taste of Freedom: The ICU Rural South Africa, 1924–1930.* New Haven, CT: Yale University Press, 1987.

———. "Women, Gender and Colonialism: Rethinking the History of the British Cape Colony and Its Frontier Zones, c. 1806–70." *Journal of African History* 37 (1996): 351–70.

Brink, André Philippus. *SA, 27 April 1994: An Authors' Diary.* Pretoria: Queillerie, 1994.

Brooks, Joanna. *American Lazarus: Religion and the Rise of African-American and Native American Literatures*. Oxford: Oxford University Press, 2003.

Brooks, Peter. *Reading for the Plot*. New York: Knopf, 1984.

Brown, Duncan, and Bruno Van Dyk. *Exchanges: South African Writing in Transition*. Pietermaritzburg: University of Natal Press, 1991.

Brownlee, Charles Pacalt. *Reminiscences of Kafir Life and History, and Other Papers*. Edited by Christopher C. Saunders. Pietermaritzburg: University of Natal Press, 1977.

———. *Reminiscences of Kafir Life and History, and Other Papers*. 2nd ed. Lovedale: Lovedale Mission, 1916.

———. *Reminiscences of Kaffir Life and History, and Other Papers*. Lovedale: Lovedale Mission, 1896.

Brownlee Family. Letters. MSS 5–67 and MSS 2321–2362. Cory Library for Historical Research, Rhodes University, Grahamstown, South Africa.

Buck-Morss, Susan. *The Dialectics of Seeing: Walter Benjamin and the Arcades Project*. Cambridge, MA: MIT Press, 1990.

Burton, Alfred W. *Sparks from the Border Anvil*. Bloemfontein: Francis, 1950.

Burton, John, and George Stubbs. *An Essay towards a Complete New System of Midwifery, Theoretical and Practical. . . .* London: Printed for James Hodges, 1751.

Butler, Guy, and Jeff Opland. *The Magic Tree: South African Stories in Verse*. Cape Town: Maskew, 1989.

Cabral, Amílcar. *Revolution in Guinea: Selected Texts*. Translated by Richard Handyside. New York: Monthly Review, 1969.

Calderwood, Henry. *Caffres and Caffre Missions: With Preliminary Chapters on the Cape Colony as a Field for Emigration, and Basis of Missionary Operation*. London: Nisbet, 1858.

Canetti, Elias. *Crowds and Power*. Translated by Carol Stewart. New York: Seabury, 1978.

Cape of Good Hope. *Proceedings of, and Evidence Taken by, the Commission on Native Affairs*. Grahamstown: Godlonton, 1865.

Central Office of Information, Records of Films. "Nonquassi 1940." INF 6/781. National Archives, Kew, London.

Chakrabarty, Dipesh. *Provincializing Europe: Postcolonial Thought and Historical Difference*. Princeton, NJ: Princeton University Press, 2000.

Chalmers, J. A. "Tiyo Soga." 1871. Reprinted in *South African Outlook*, August 1971, 116–17.

———. "Tiyo Soga." *Cape Monthly Magazine* 4 (1872): 1–24.

———. *Tiyo Soga: A Page of South African Mission Work*. Edinburgh: Elliott, 1877.

———. "Tiyo Soga: A Page of South African Mission Work." MS PR3988. Cory Library for Historical Research, Rhodes University, Grahamstown, South Africa.

Chanaiwa, David. "African Humanism in Southern Africa: The Utopian, Traditionalist, and Colonialist Worlds of Mission-Educated Elites." In *Independence without Freedom: The Political Economy of Colonial Education in Southern Africa*, edited by Agrippa T. Mugomba and Mouga Nyaggah, 9–35. Santa Barbara: ABC-CLIO, 1980.

Chapman, Michael. "African Popular Fiction: Consideration of a Category." *English in Africa* 26, no. 2 (1999): 113–23.

———. "Red People and School People from Ntsikana to Mandela: The Significance of 'Xhosa Literature' in a General History of South African Literature." *English Academy Review* 10 (1993): 36–44.

———. *Southern African Literatures*. London: Longman, 1996.

———. "Writing Literary History in Southern Africa." In Smit et al., *Rethinking South African Literary History*, 40–50.

Chatterjee, Partha. *The Nation and Its Fragments: Colonial and Postcolonial Histories*. Princeton, NJ: Princeton University Press, 1993.

Cheah, Pheng. *Spectral Nationality: Passages of Freedom from Kant to Postcolonial Literatures of Liberation.* New York: Columbia University Press, 2003.

Chidester, David. *Savage Systems: Colonialism and Comparative Religion in Southern Africa.* Charlottesville: University Press of Virginia, 1996.

Chirenje, J. Mutero. *Ethiopianism and Afro-Americans in Southern Africa, 1883–1916.* Baton Rouge: Louisiana State University Press, 1987.

Cingo, W. D. "Native Unrest." *Kokstad Advertiser,* September 30, 1927. In Hill, vol. 10 of *Marcus Garvey,* 406–8.

Clark, Paul. *Hauhau: The Pai Marire Search for Maori Identity.* Auckland: Auckland University Press, 1975.

Clinton, Alan. "Wavespeech, Tapespeech, Blipspeech." *Culture Machine* 5 (2003). Http:// culturemachine.tees.ac.uk/frm_f1.htm

Coetzee, J. M. "The Novel Today." *Upstream* 6, no. 1 (1988): 2–5.

Cohen, David William. *The Combing of History.* Chicago: University of Chicago Press, 1994.

Cohn, Norman. "Medieval Millenarianism: Its Bearing on the Comparative Study of Millenarian Movements." In *Millennial Dreams in Action: Essays in Comparative Study,* edited by Sylvia L. Thrupp, 31–43. The Hague: Mouton, 1962.

Comaroff, Jean, and John L. Comaroff. *Of Revelation and Revolution,* vol. 1, *Christianity, Colonialism, and Consciousness in South Africa.* Chicago: University of Chicago Press, 1991.

Comaroff, John L., and Jean Comaroff. "Goodly Beasts, Beastly Goods: Cattle and Commodities in a South African Context." *American Ethnologist* 17, no. 2 (1990): 195–216.

Congress of the People. "Freedom Charter." 1955. Reprinted in *Culture in Another South Africa,* edited by William Campschreur and Joos Divendal, 242–45. New York: Olive Branch, 1987.

Connor, Steven. *Dumbstruck: A Cultural History of Ventriloquism.* Oxford: Oxford University Press, 2000.

Coplan, D. B. *In Township Tonight! South Africa's Black City Music and Theatre.* London: Longman, 1985.

Couzens, Tim. *The New African: A Study of the Life and Work of H. I. E. Dhlomo.* Johannesburg: Ravan, 1985.

Crais, Clifton C. "Peires and the Past." *South African Historical Journal* 25 (1991): 236–40.

———. *The Politics of Evil: Magic, State Power, and the Political Imagination in South Africa.* New York: Cambridge University Press, 2002.

———. *White Supremacy and Black Resistance in Pre-Industrial South Africa: The Making of the Colonial Order in the Eastern Cape, 1770–1865.* Cambridge: Cambridge University Press, 1992.

Cronin, Jeremy. "'Even under the Rine of Terror . . .': Insurgent South African Poetry." *Research in African Literatures* 19, no.1 (1988): 12–24.

———. "To Learn How to Speak." In *The Lava of This Land: South African Poetry, 1960–1996,* edited by Denis Hirson, 328. Evanston, IL: Northwestern University Press, 1997.

Cunha, Euclides da. *Rebellion in the Backlands.* Translated by Samuel Putnam. 1944. Reprint, Chicago: University of Chicago Press, 1964.

Davies, Horton, and Robert H. W. Shepherd. *South African Missions, 1800–1950: An Anthology.* London: Nelson, 1954.

Davis, Mike. *Late Victorian Holocausts: El Niño Famines and the Making of the Third World.* London: Verso, 2001.

De Kock, Leon. "The Central South African Story, or Many Stories? A Response to 'Red People and School People from Ntsikana to Mandela.'" *English Academy Review* 10 (1993): 45–55.

———. *Civilising Barbarians: Missionary Narrative and African Textual Response in Nine-

teenth-Century South Africa. Johannesburg: Witwatersrand University Press and Alice: Lovedale, 1996.

——. "Does South African Literature Still Exist? Or: South African Literature Is Dead, Long Live Literature in South Africa." *English in Africa* 32, no. 2 (2005): 69–84.

——. "The Pursuit of Smaller Stories: Reconsidering the Limits of Literary History in South Africa." In Smit et al., *Rethinking South African Literary History*, 85–92.

——. "South Africa in the Global Imaginary: An Introduction." *Poetics Today* 22, no. 2 (2001): 263–98.

——. "Textual Capture in the Civilising Mission: Moffat, Livingstone, and the Case of Tiyo Soga." *English in Africa* 21, no. 1–2 (1994): 33–58.

De Kok, Ingrid, and Karen Press, eds. *Spring Is Rebellious: Arguments about Cultural Freedom*. Cape Town: Buchu, 1990.

Derrida, Jacques. *Specters of Marx: The State of the Debt, the Work of Mourning, and the New International*. Translated by Peggy Kamuf. New York: Routledge, 1994.

Devi, Mahasweta. *Chotti Munda and His Arrow*. Translated by Gayatri Chakravorty Spivak. Malden: Blackwell, 2003.

Dhlomo, H. I. E. "African Drama and Research." *English in Africa* 4, no. 2 (1977): 19–22.

[Dhlomo, H. I. E.] "Bantu Dramatic Society Stages Its First Show." *Bantu World*, April 15, 1933: 1.

——. "Drama and the African." *English in Africa* 4, no. 2 (1977): 3–11.

——. "The Evolution of the Bantu II." *Umteteli wa Bantu*, November 21, 1931.

——. *The Girl Who Killed to Save (Nongqause the Liberator)*. [Lovedale], 1936.

——. "The Girl Who Killed to Save (Nongqause the Liberator)." TS MS no. 16,309(a), Lovedale Collection. Cory Library for Historical Research, Rhodes University, Grahamstown, South Africa.

——. *H. I. E. Dhlomo Collected Works*. Edited by N. Visser and T. Couzens. Johannesburg: Ravan, 1985.

——. "Masses and the Artist." *English in Africa* 4, no. 2 (1977): 61–62.

——. "Nature and Variety of Tribal Drama." *Bantu Studies* 13 (1939): 33–48.

——. "Thoughts on the 'African Yearly Register.'" *Umteteli wa Bantu*, October 31, 1931.

——. *Valley of a Thousand Hills, A Poem*. Durban: Knox, 1962.

——. "Why Study Tribal Dramatic Forms?" *English in Africa* 4, no. 2 (1977): 37–42.

——. "The Young Generation." *Umteteli wa Bantu*, July 5, 1930.

Dimock, Wai Chee. "A Theory of Resonance." *PMLA* 112, no. 5 (1997): 1060–71.

——. "Planetary Time and Global Translation: 'Context' in Literary Studies." *Common Knowledge* 9, no. 3 (2003): 488–507.

Dirlik, Arif. *The Postcolonial Aura: Third World Criticism in the Age of Global Capitalism*. Boulder: Westview, 1997.

Dowsley, Eileen D'Altera. "An Investigation into the Circumstances Relating to the Cattle-Killing Delusion in Kaffraria, 1856–1857." M.A. thesis, University of South Africa, 1932.

Driver, Dorothy. "'M'a-Ngoana O Tsoare Thipa kaBohaleng'—The Child's Mother Grabs the Sharp End of the Knife: Women as Mothers, Women as Writers." In *Rendering Things Visible: Essays on South African Literary Culture*, edited by Martin Trump, 225–55. Athens: Ohio University Press, 1990.

Eagleton, Terry. "Marxism and the Future of Criticism." In *Writing the Future*, edited by David Wood, 177–80. London: Routledge, 1990.

Edgar, Robert. *Because They Chose the Plan of God: The Story of the Bulhoek Massacre*. Johannesburg: Ravan, 1988.

Elbourne, Elizabeth. *Blood Ground: Colonialism, Missions, and the Contest for Christianity in the Cape Colony and Britain, 1799–1853*. Montreal: McGill-Queen's University Press, 2002.

Eliot, T. S. "Tradition and the Individual Talent." 1919. Reprint in *Norton Anthology of Theory and Criticism*, edited by Vincent B. Leitch et al., 1092–98. New York: Norton, 2001.

Elkins, Caroline. "From Malaya to Kenya: An Examination of Violence in the British Empire." Paper presented at the Davis Center for Historical Studies, Princeton University, Princeton, NJ, September 2005.

Elphick, Richard. "Africans and the Christian Campaign." In *The Frontier in History: North America and Southern Africa Compared*, edited by Howard Roberts Lamar and Leonard Monteath Thompson, 270–307. New Haven, CT: Yale University Press, 1981.

Eng, David L., and David Kazanjian, eds. *Loss: The Politics of Mourning*. Berkeley: University of California Press, 2003.

Erlank, Natasha. "Gendered Reactions to Social Dislocation and Missionary Activity in Xhosaland, 1836–1847." *African Studies* 59, no. 2 (2000): 205–27.

———. "Re-Examining Initial Encounters between Christian Missionaries and the Xhosa, 1820–1850: The Scottish Case." *Kleio* 31 (1999). Http://www.unisa.ac.za/default.asp?Cmd=ViewContent&ContentID=1164.

Erlmann, Vleit. *African Stars: Studies in Black South African Performance*. Chicago: University of Chicago Press, 1991.

Fabian, Johannes. *Time and the Other: How Anthropology Makes Its Object*. New York: Columbia University Press, 1983.

Falati, N. "The Story of Ntsikana a Gaika Xhosa." Translated by N. Falati and C. Mpaki. 1895. MS 9063. Cory Library for Historical Research, Rhodes University, Grahamstown, South Africa.

Falola, Toyin. *Nationalism and African Intellectuals*. Rochester, NY: University of Rochester Press, 2001.

Fanon, Frantz. *Black Skin, White Masks*. Translated by Charles Lam Markmann. New York: Grove, 1967.

———. *Les damnés de la terre*. 2nd ed. Paris: Maspero, 1961.

———. "Lumumba's Death: Could We Do Otherwise?" In *Toward the African Revolution*, translated by Haakon Chevalier, 191–97. New York: Grove, 1969.

———. *The Wretched of the Earth*. Translated by Constance Farrington. New York: Grove, 1968.

———. *The Wretched of the Earth*. Translated by Richard Philcox. New York: Grove, 2004.

Farred, Grant. "The Not-Yet Counterpartisan: A New Politics of Oppositionality." *South Atlantic Quarterly* 103, no. 4 (2004): 589–605.

Festinger, Leon, Henry W. Riecken, and Stanley Schachter. *When Prophecy Fails: A Social and Psychological Study of a Modern Group That Predicted the Destruction of the World*. New York: Harper, 1964.

Feuer, L. S., ed. *Marx and Engels: Basic Writings on Politics and Philosophy*. New York: Anchor, 1959.

Finnegan, Ruth H. *Literacy and Orality: Studies in the Technology of Communication*. Oxford: Blackwell, 1988.

FitzGerald, J. P. Letterbook. TS no. PR3624. Cory Library for Historical Research, Rhodes University, Grahamstown, South Africa.

Flockemann, Miki. "Spectacles of Excess or Thresholds to the 'Newness'?: Brett Bailey and the Third World Bunfight Performers. *Kunapipi* 24, nos. 1–2 (2002): 275–90.

Foucault, Michel. "What Is an Author?" In *Textual Strategies: Perspectives in Post-Structuralist Criticism*, edited by Josuâe V. Harari, 141–60. Ithaca, NY: Cornell University Press, 1979.

Freud, Sigmund. *Civilization and Its Discontents*. Translated and edited by James Strachey. New York: Norton, 1962.

———. *Moses and Monotheism*. Translated by Katherine Jones. New York: Vintage, 1955.

———. "Mourning and Melancholia." 1917. Translated by James Strachey. In vol. 14 of *The Standard Edition of the Complete Psychological Works of Sigmund Freud*, 237–58. London: Hogarth, 1957.

———. *Totem and Taboo: Resemblances between the Psychic Lives of Savages and Neurotics.* Translated by A. A. Brill. London: Routledge, 1919.

Ganguly, Keya. *States of Exception: Everyday Life and Postcolonial Identity.* Minneapolis: University of Minnesota Press, 2001.

Garner, Stanton B. *Bodied Spaces: Phenomenology and Performance in Contemporary Drama.* Ithaca, NY: Cornell University Press, 1994.

Genette, Gérard. *Narrative Discourse: An Essay in Method.* Ithaca, NY: Cornell University Press, 1980.

GH 8/48–50. Correspondence, British Kaffraria. Unofficial correspondence, J. Maclean to G. Grey. Cape Archives. Western Cape Archives and Records Service, Cape Town.

Gikandi, Simon. *Maps of Englishness: Writing Identity in the Culture of Colonialism.* New York: Columbia University Press, 1996.

Gilroy, Paul. *The Black Atlantic: Modernity and Double Consciousness.* Cambridge, MA: Harvard University Press, 1993.

Glasgow Missionary Society. *Report of the Glasgow Missionary Society, for 1824.* Glasgow: Young, 1824.

Goody, Jack, and Ian Watt. "The Consequences of Literacy." 1963. Reprint in *Literacy in Traditional Societies*, edited by Jack Goody, 27–68. Cambridge: Cambridge University Press, 1968.

Gordimer, Nadine. *July's People.* New York: Viking, 1981.

———. "Living in the Interregnum." 1982. Reprint in *The Essential Gesture: Writing, Politics, and Place*, edited by Stephen Clingman, 261–84. New York: Penguin, 1989.

Gordon, Avery. *Ghostly Matters: Haunting and the Sociological Imagination.* Minneapolis: University of Minnesota Press, 1997.

Goswami, Manu. *Producing India: From Colonial Economy to National Space.* Chicago: University of Chicago Press, 2004.

Gramsci, Antonio. *Selections from the Prison Notebooks of Antonio Gramsci.* Edited by Quintin Hoare and Geoffrey Nowell-Smith. New York: International, 1971.

Gray, Stephen. "Opening Southern African Studies Post-Apartheid." *Research in African Literatures* 30, no. 1 (1999): 207–15.

———. "Some Problems of Writing Historiography in Southern Africa." *Literator* 10, no. 2 (1989): 16–24.

———. *Southern African Literature: An Introduction.* Cape Town: Philip, 1979.

Green, Michael Cawood. *Novel Histories: Past, Present and Future in South African Fiction.* Johannesburg: Witwatersrand University Press, 1997.

Greenblatt, Steven J. *Shakespearean Negotiations: The Circulation of Social Energy in Renaissance England.* Berkeley: University of California Press, 1988.

Grey, George. *Polynesian Mythology and Ancient Traditional History of the New Zealand Race, as Furnished by Their Priests and Chiefs.* London: Murray, 1855.

Gubic, Kristina. "South Africa: 10 Years of Freedom." *Travel Africa Magazine* 27 (2004). http://www.travelafricamag.com/content/view/589/56.

Guha, Ranajit. "The Prose of Counter-Insurgency." In *Selected Subaltern Studies*, edited by Ranajit Guha and Gayatri Chakravorty Spivak, 345–88. New York: Oxford University Press, 1988.

Gump, James O. "The Imperialism of Cultural Assimilation: Sir George Grey's Encounter with the Maori and the Xhosa, 1845–68." *Journal of World History* 9, no. 1 (1998): 89–106.

Gunner, Liz. "Remaking the Warrior? The Role of Orality in the Liberation Struggle and in Post-Apartheid South Africa." In *Oral Literature and Performance in Southern Africa*, edited by Duncan Brown, 50–60. Athens: Ohio University Press, 1999.

Gutsche, Thelma. *The History and Social Significance of Motion Pictures in South Africa, 1895–1940.* Cape Town: Timmins, 1972.

Gwala, Mafika. "Writing as a Cultural Weapon." In *Momentum: On Recent South African Writing,* edited by M. J. Daymond, J. U. Jacobs, and Margaret Lenta, 37–53. Pietermaritzburg: University of Natal Press, 1984.

Halim, Hala Youssef. "The *Lotus* Project, Comparative Postcoloniality, World Literature." Paper presented at the Modern Language Association Convention, Washington, D.C., December 27–30, 2005.

Hamilton, Carolyn, ed. *The Mfecane Aftermath: Reconstructive Debates in Southern African History.* Johannesburg: University of Witwatersrand Press, 1995.

———. *Terrific Majesty: The Power of Shaka Zulu and the Limits of Historical Invention.* Cambridge, MA: Harvard University Press, 1998.

Harlow, Barbara. *After Lives: Legacies of Revolutionary Writing.* London: Verso, 1996.

———. "'What Was She Doing There?' Women as 'Legitimate Targets.'" In *Women, Gender, and Human Rights: A Global Perspective,* edited by Marjorie Agosín, 267–82. New Brunswick, NJ: Rutgers University Press, 2001.

Harrison, Robert Pogue. *The Dominion of the Dead.* Chicago: University of Chicago Press, 2003.

Head, Bessie. Foreword to *Native Life in South Africa,* by Solomon T. Plaatje. Johannesburg: Ravan, 1982.

Hill, Robert A., ed. *The Marcus Garvey and Universal Negro Improvement Association Papers.* 10 vols. Berkeley: University of California Press, 1983–96.

Hittman, Michael. *Wovoka and the Ghost Dance.* Edited by Don Lynch. Lincoln: University of Nebraska Press, 1997.

Hobsbawm, E. J. *Primitive Rebels: Studies in Archaic Forms of Social Movements in the 19th and 20th Centuries.* New York: Norton, 1965.

Hodgson, Janet. "The Genius of Ntsikana: Traditional Images and the Process of Change in Early Xhosa Literature." In *Literature and Society in South Africa,* edited by Tim Couzens and Landeg White, 24–40. Harlow: Longman, 1984.

———. *Ntsikana's Great Hymn: A Xhosa Expression of Christianity in the Early 19th Century Eastern Cape.* Cape Town: Centre for African Studies, University of Cape Town, 1980.

———. *The God of the Xhosa: A Study of the Origins and Development of the Traditional Concepts of the Supreme Being.* Cape Town: Oxford University Press, 1982.

Hofmeyr, Isabel. *The Portable Bunyan: A Transnational History of* The Pilgrim's Progress. Princeton, NJ: Princeton University Press, 2004.

———. "Reading Debating/Debating Reading: The Case of the Lovedale Literary Society, or Why Mandela Quotes Shakespeare." In *Africa's Hidden Histories,* edited by Karin Barber, 258–77. Bloomington: Indiana University Press, 2006.

Holden, W. C. *The Past and Future of the Kaffir Races.* 1866. Reprint, Johannesburg: Struik, 1963.

Honneth, Axel. "A Communicative Disclosure of the Past: On the Relation between Anthropology and Philosophy of History in Walter Benjamin." *New Formations* 20 (1993): 83–94.

Imperial Blue Books. *Cape of Good Hope Further Papers Relative to the State of the Kaffir Tribes.* 1969 of 1854–55, correspondence re: Kaffir tribes; 2096 of 1856, correspondence re: Kaffir tribes; 2202 of 1857, South African correspondence, 1856; 2352 of 1857–58, correspondence re: Kaffirs, 1856–57.

Ipi Ntombi: An African Dance Celebration. DVD. Directed by Clive Morris. Clive Morris Productions, 1997.

Irvin, John. "African Film Success." *Cape Argus,* November 11, 1939.

Isaacson, Maureen. "The Free State Madonnas Prevail in Mda's New Novel." *Sunday Independent,* November 22, 2002.

Jabavu, D. D. T. "Native Unrest in South Africa." *International Review of Missions* 11 (1922): 249–59.

——. Presidential address, All Africa Convention, June 29, 1936. In Karis et al., vol. 2 of *From Protest to Challenge*, 48–52.

Jahn, Janheinz. *Neo-African Literature: A History of Black Writing.* New York: Grove, 1968.

Jameson, Fredric. *The Political Unconscious: Narrative as a Socially Symbolic Act.* Ithaca, NY: Cornell University Press, 1981.

Jani, Pranav. "Karl Marx, Eurocentrism, and the 1857 Revolt in British India." In *Marxism, Modernity and Postcolonial Studies*, edited by Crystal Bartolovich and Neil Lazarus, 81–97. Cambridge: Cambridge University Press, 2002.

Jay, Martin. "Experience without a Subject: Walter Benjamin and the Novel." *New Formations* 20 (1993): 145–55.

Johns, Sheridan. Introduction to *From Protest to Challenge.* In Karis et al., vol. 1 of *From Protest to Challenge*, 3–12.

Jordan, A. C. "FOLKTALE: The Cause of the Cattle-Killing at the Nongqause Period." *Lotus: Afro-Asian Writings* 12 (April 1972): 173–76.

——. *Towards an African Literature: The Emergence of Literary Form in Xhosa.* Berkeley: University of California Press, 1973.

——. *The Wrath of the Ancestors (A Novel).* Cape Province: Lovedale, 1980.

Karis, Thomas, Gwendolen M. Carter, Sheridan Johns, and Gail M. Gerhart, eds. *From Protest to Challenge: A Documentary History of African Politics in South Africa, 1882–1990.* 5 vols. Bloomington: Indiana University Press, 1972–97.

Keegan, Timothy, ed. *Moravians in the Eastern Cape, 1828–1928: Four Accounts of Moravian Mission Work on the Eastern Cape Frontier.* Translated by F. R. Baudert. Cape Town: Van Riebeeck Society for the Publication of South African Historical Documents, 2004.

Kentridge, William. *Tide Table.* 2003.

Kermode, Frank. *The Sense of an Ending: Studies in the Theory of Fiction.* New York: Oxford University Press, 1967.

Kirmayer, Laurence J. "Landscapes of Memory: Trauma, Narrative, and Dissociation." In Antze and Lambek, *Tense Past*, 173–98.

Klein, Naomi. "The Rise of Disaster Capitalism." *Nation*, May 2, 2005. Http://www.thenation.com/doc/20050502/klein.

Korang, Kwaku. *Writing Ghana, Imagining Africa: Nation and African Modernity.* Rochester, NY: University of Rochester Press, 2004.

Koselleck, Reinhart. *Futures Past: On the Semantics of Historical Time.* Cambridge, MA: MIT Press, 1985.

Kristeva, Julia. *Revolution in Poetic Language.* New York: Columbia University Press, 1984.

Krog, Antjie. *Country of My Skull: Guilt, Sorrow, and the Limits of Forgiveness in the New South Africa.* New York: Three Rivers, 2000.

Kropf, A. *Die Lügenpropheten des Kafferlandes.* Berlin: Berliner evangelischen Missionsgesellschaft, 1891.

Kruger, Loren. "Black Atlantics, White Indians and Jews: Locations, Locutions, and Syncretic Identities in the Fiction of Achmat Dangor and Others." *South Atlantic Quarterly* 100, no. 1 (2001): 111–43.

——. *The Drama of South Africa: Plays, Pageants and Publics since 1910.* New York: Routledge, 1999.

LaCapra, Dominick. *Writing History, Writing Trauma.* Baltimore: Johns Hopkins University Press, 2001.

Laing, James. *Memorials of the Missionary Career of the Rev. James Laing, Missionary of the Free Church of Scotland in Kaffraria.* Edited by C. William Govan. Glasgow: Bryce, 1875.

Lalu, Premesh. "The Border and the Body: Post-phenomenological Reflections." *South African Historical Journal* 55, no. 7 (2006): 106–24.

———. "The Grammar of Domination and the Subjection of Agency: Colonial Texts and Modes of Evidence." *History and Theory* 39, no. 4 (2000): 45–68.

Lan, David. *Guns and Rain: Guerrillas and Spirit Mediums in Zimbabwe.* Berkeley: University of California Press, 1985.

Lategan, Felix V. "Fire-arms, Historical." In vol. 4 of *Standard Encyclopaedia of Southern Africa*, 515–36. Cape Town: Nasou, 1976.

Lazarus, Neil. *Nationalism and Cultural Practice in the Postcolonial World.* Cambridge: Cambridge University Press, 1999.

———. "The South African Ideology: The Myth of Exceptionalism, the Idea of Renaissance." *South Atlantic Quarterly* 103, no. 4 (2004): 607–28.

Lee, Christopher Joon-Hai. "The Uses of the Comparative Imagination: South African History and World History in the Political Consciousness of the South African Left, 1943–1959." *Radical History Review* 92 (Spring 2005): 31–61.

Legassick, Martin. "The State, Racism, and the Rise of Capitalism in the Nineteenth-Century Cape Colony." *South African Historical Journal* 28 (1993): 329–68.

Lenhardt, Christian. "Anamnestic Solidarity: The Proletariat and Its Manes." *Telos* 25 (1975): 133–54.

Lester, Alan. *Imperial Networks: Creating Identities in Nineteenth-Century South Africa and Britain.* London: Routledge, 2001.

Lewis, Jack. "Materialism and Idealism in the Historiography of the Xhosa Cattle-Killing Movement 1856–7." *South African Historical Journal* 25 (1991): 244–68.

Linton, Ralph, and A. Irving Hallowell. "Nativistic Movements." *American Anthropologist* 45, no. 2 (1943): 230–40.

Locke, J. G. "The Wellington Movement." *Imvo Zabantsundu*, November 20, 1928. In Hill, vol. 10 of *Marcus Garvey*, 738–39.

Lodge, Tom. *Black Politics in South Africa since 1945.* New York: Longman, 1983.

Lovedale Collection. Cory Library for Historical Research, Rhodes University, Grahamstown, South Africa.

Lumumba. DVD. Directed by Raoul Peck. Zeitgeist Films, 2002.

Maclean, John. *A Compendium of Kafir Laws and Customs.* 1857. Reprint, Grahamstown: Slater, 1906.

Macmillan, Harold. Speech in the South African Parliament, 1960. In *Pointing the Way, 1959–1961*, 473–82. London: Macmillan, 1972.

Magona, Sindiwe, David Attwell, and Barbara Harlow. Interview with Sindiwe Magona. [Oct. 1999]. *Modern Fiction Studies* 46, no. 1 (2000): 282–95.

Magona, Sindiwe. *Mother to Mother.* Boston: Beacon Press, 1999.

Mahlasela, Benjamin Ezra Nuttall. *A General Survey of Xhosa Literature from Its Early Beginnings in the 1800s to the Present.* Vol. 2. Grahamstown: Department of African Languages, Rhodes University, 1973.

Majeke, Nosipho [Dora Taylor]. *The Role of the Missionaries in Conquest.* Alexandra Township, Johannesburg: Society of Young Africa, 1952.

Mamdani, Mahmood. *Citizen and Subject: Contemporary Africa and the Legacy of Late Colonialism.* Princeton, NJ: Princeton University Press, 1996.

Mandela, Nelson. Address to rally in Durban, February 25, 1990. Http://www.anc.org.za/ancdocs/history/mandela/1990/sp900225-1.html.

———. Presidential address at the conference of the African National Congress Youth League, December 1951. http://www.anc.org.za/ancdocs/history/mandela/1950s/sp5112.html.

Martin, Marie-Louise. *Kimbangu: An African Prophet and His Church.* Translated by D. M. Moore. Oxford: Blackwell, 1975.

Marx, Karl. *Capital: A Critique of Political Economy.* Harmondsworth: Penguin, in association with New Left Review, 1976.

———. *The Eighteenth Brumaire of Napoleon Bonaparte.* 1852. In Feuer, *Marx and Engels*, 318–48.

———. "Toward the Critique of Hegel's Philosophy of Right." In Feuer, *Marx and Engels*, 262–66.

Matanzima, Kaizer D. *Independence My Way*. Pretoria: Foreign Affairs Association, 1976.

Matshaya, Charles Henry, and John Laing. "Charles Henry Matshaya: A Follower and Convert." In *Ntsikana: The Story of an African Convert* by John Knox Bokwe, 32–35. Lovedale: Lovedale, 1914.

Matshoba, Mtutuzeli. *Call Me Not a Man*. Johannesburg: Ravan, 1979.

———. "The Return of Nxele: A Tale of How Makhanda Has at Last Come Back from Robben Island." *Mayibuye* (1992): 42–43.

Mbeki, Thabo. Speech at his inauguration as president of South Africa, June 16, 1999. Http:// www.anc.org.za/ancdocs/history/mbeki/1999/tm0616.html.

———. Statement on behalf of the African National Congress, on the occasion of the adoption by the Constitutional Assembly of the "Republic of South Africa Constitution Bill 1996," Cape Town, May 8, 1996. Http://www.anc.org.za/ancdocs/history/mbeki/1996/ sp960508.html.

Mbembe, Achille. *On the Postcolony*. Berkeley: University of California Press, 2001.

———. "South Africa's Second Coming: The Nongqawuse Syndrome." *Open Democracy*, June 15, 2006. http:www.opendemocracy.net/democracy-africa_democracy/southafrica_succession_3649.jsp.

Mbiti, John S. *African Religions and Philosophy*. Oxford: Heinemann, 1990.

McClintock, Anne. *Imperial Leather: Race, Gender, and Sexuality in the Colonial Conquest*. New York: Routledge, 1995.

McDonald, Peter D. "Disgrace Effects." *Interventions* 4, no. 3 (2002): 321–30.

Mda, Zakes. *The Heart of Redness*. New York: Farrar, 2000.

———. *Ways of Dying*. 1995. Reprint, New York: Picador, 2002.

Meintjies, Frank. "Albie Sachs and the Art of Protest." In De Kok and Press, *Spring Is Rebellious*, 30–35.

Meillassoux, Claude. "From Reproduction to Production." *Economy and Society* 1, no. 1 (1974): 93–105.

Middleton, Peter, and Tim Woods. *Literatures of Memory: History, Time, and Space in Postwar Writing*. New York: St. Martin's, 2000.

Mill, John Stuart. *On Liberty*. 1859. Edited by David Spitz. Reprint, New York: Norton, 1975.

———. "A Few Words on Non-intervention." *Fraser's Magazine*, December 1859, 766–76.

Mkhize, Khwezi. "Citashe's Apostrophe—'Zimkile! Mfo wohlanga': The Unfinished 'Preface' to an African Modernity." *Journal of Commonwealth Literature* 43, no. 1 (2008): 97–114.

Mnguni [Hosea Jaffe]. *Three Hundred Years: A History of South Africa*. 1952. Reprint, Cape Town: Lansdowne, 1982.

Molema, S. M. *The Bantu Past and Present: An Ethnographical and Historical Study of the Native Races of South Africa*. Edinburgh: Green, 1920.

Mooney, James. *The Ghost-Dance Religion and Wounded Knee*. 1896. Reprint, New York: Dover, 1973.

Moosa, Valli. "Lend a Hand for Sustainable Development, People, Planet and Prosperity: Minister of Environmental Affairs and Tourism Budget Vote Speech." May 9, 2002. Http://www.environment.gov.za.proxy.lib.umich.edu/NewsMedia/Speeches/2002may9/ BudgetVote_09052002.htm.

Morrison, Toni. *Beloved*. New York: Knopf, 1987.

Morton, Dan M. "Miss Mary Waters, and the Mary Waters High School." TS MS 18 814. Cory Library for Historical Research, Rhodes University, Grahamstown, South Africa.

Mostert, Noël. *Frontiers: The Epic of South Africa's Creation and the Tragedy of the Xhosa People*. New York: Knopf, 1992.

Moths, Paul. *Heinrich Meyer—A Stalwart of the Mission Field*. In Keegan, *Moravians*, 144–201.

Moylan, Tom. "Bloch against Bloch: The Theological Reception of *Das Prinzip Hoffnung* and the Liberation of the Utopian Function." In *Not Yet: Reconsidering Ernst Bloch*, edited by Jamie Owen Daniel and Tom Moylan, 96–121. London: Verso, 1997.

Moynagh, Maureen. "The Melancholic Structure of Memory in Dionne Brand's *At the Full and Change of the Moon*." *Journal of Commonwealth Literature* 43, no. 1 (2008): 57–75.

Mpe, Phaswane. *Welcome to Our Hillbrow*. Pietermaritzburg: University of Natal Press, 2001.

Mphahlele, Es'kia. "The Voice of Prophecy in African Poetry." *English in Africa* 6, no. 1 (1979): 33–45.

Mphahlele, Ezekiel. *Voices in the Whirlwind, and Other Essays*. New York: Hill and Wang, 1972.

Mphande, Lupenga. "The Cattle Killing as Resistance: *The Dead Will Arise* Reconsidered." *Research in African Literatures* 22, no. 3 (1991): 171–83.

Msimang, C. T. "The Status of African Literature in South African Literary History." In Smit et al., *Rethinking South African Literary History*, 51–70.

Msimang, Selby. "'The Challenge' and 'The Alternative' [Extracts from *The Crisis*, 1936]." In Karis et al., vol. 2 of *From Protest to Challenge*, 57–61.

———. "Pan-African Congress." *Umteteli wa Bantu*, August 13, 1921. In Hill, vol. 9 of *Marcus Garvey*, 146–49.

Munnik, James, and Geoffrey V. Davis. "'Getting Back to Writing': An Interview with Mtutuzeli Matshoba." In *Southern African Writing: Voyages and Explorations*, edited by Geoffrey V. Davis, 123–32. Amsterdam: Rodopi, 1994.

Nandy, Ashis. "History's Forgotten Doubles." *History and Theory* 34, no. 2 (1995): 44–66.

Nasson, Bill. "The Unity Movement: Its Legacy in Historical Consciousness." *Radical History Review* 46–47 (1990): 189–211.

"The Native Press: Lovedale Literary Society." *Christian Express* 12, no. 141 (1882): 1–4.

Ndebele, Njabulo S. "'Artistic and Political Mirage': Mtshali's *Sounds of a Cowhide Drum*." In *Soweto Poetry*, edited by Michael Chapman, 190–93. Johannesburg: McGraw-Hill, 1982.

———. "The Challenges of the Written Word." In *Culture in Another South Africa*, edited by W. Campschreur and J. Divendal, 18–31. New York: Olive Branch, 1989.

———. *Fools, and Other Stories*. Harlow: Longman, 1985.

———. "The Revolution of the Aged." *Staffrider* 3, no. 4 (1981): 2.

———. *South African Literature and Culture: Rediscovery of the Ordinary*. New York: St. Martin's, 1994.

Newell, Stephanie. *Literary Culture in Colonial Ghana: "How to Play the Game of Life."* Bloomington: Indiana University Press, 2002.

Newman, Michael. "Suffering from Reminiscences." In Barker et al., *Postmodernism*, 84–114.

Ngũgĩ wa Thiong'o. *Decolonising the Mind: The Politics of Language in African Literature*. London: Currey / Nairobi: Heinemann Kenya, 1986.

Nhlangwini, Andrew Pandheni. "The Ibali of Nongqawuse: Translating the Oral Tradition into Visual Expression." M.A. thesis, Port Elizabeth Technikon, 2004.

Nicholls, G. Heaton. *Bayete! "Hail to the King!"* London: Allen, 1923.

Nietzsche, Friedrich. "On the Uses and Disadvantage of History for Life." In *Untimely Meditations*, 57–124. Translated by R. J. Hollingdale. Cambridge: Cambridge University Press, 1997.

Nixon, Rob. "'An Everybody Claim Dem Democratic': Notes on the 'New' South Africa." *Transition* 54 (1991): 20–35.

Nkosi, Lewis. *Home and Exile*. [London]: Longman, 1965.

——. "Postmodernism and Black Writing in South Africa." In Attridge and Jolly, *Writing South Africa*, 75–90.

——. "South African Fiction Writers at the Barricades." *Third World Book Review* 2, nos. 1–2 (1986): 43–45.

——. "Under the Shadow of the Guns." In *Colors of a New Day: Writing for South Africa*, edited by Sarah Lefani and Stephen Hayward, 272–88. New York: Pantheon, 1990.

Nonquassi. Written and directed by Leon Schauder. Gaumont-British Instructional Films and the British Ministry of Information, 1940. Held at BFI National Archive, London.

Nora, Pierre. "Between Memory and History: Les Lieux de Memoire." In special issue, "Memory and Counter-Memory." *Representations* 26 (1989): 7–24.

O'Brien, Anthony. *Against Normalization: Writing Radical Democracy in South Africa.* Durham, NC: Duke University Press, 2001.

Offenburger, Andrew. "Duplicity and Plagiarism in Zakes Mda's *The Heart of Redness.*" *Research in African Literatures* 39, no. 3 (2008): 164–99.

——. "Smallpox and Epidemic Threat in Nineteenth-century Xhosaland." Special issue on the Xhosa cattle-killing, *African Studies* 67, no. 2 (2008): 159–82.

Ong, Walter J. *Orality and Literacy: The Technologizing of the Word.* London: Methuen, 1982.

Oosthuizen, G. C. *Shepherd of Lovedale: A Life for Southern Africa.* Johannesburg: Keartland, 1970.

Opland, Jeff. "Imbongi Nezibongo: The Xhosa Tribal Poet and the Contemporary Poetic Tradition." *PMLA* 90, no. 2 (1975): 185–208.

——. *Xhosa Oral Poetry: Aspects of a Black South African Tradition.* Cambridge: Cambridge University Press, 1983.

——. *Xhosa Poets and Poetry.* Cape Town: Philip, 1998.

Orkin, Martin. *Drama and the South African State.* Johannesburg: Witwatersrand University Press/New York: St. Martin's, 1991.

Osborne, Peter. "Modernity Is a Qualitative, Not a Chronological, Category: Notes on the Dialectics of Differential Historical Time." In Barker et al., *Postmodernism*, 23–45.

——. *The Politics of Time: Modernity and Avant-Garde.* London: Verso, 1995.

Palmberg, Rolf. "NONGQAWUSE: Suggestions for a CALL/Internet Lesson." *ELT Newsletter* Article 95 (2002). Http://www.eltnewsletter.com/back/April2002/art952002.htm.

Pechey, Graham. "Post-Apartheid Reason: Critical Theory in South Africa." *Current Writing* 10, no. 2 (1998): 3–18.

Peires, J. B. [Jeff]. Afterword to *The Dead Will Arise.* Johannesburg: Jonathan Ball, 2003.

——. "The Central Beliefs of the Xhosa Cattle-Killing." *Journal of African History* 28, no. 1 (1987): 43–63.

——. "Cry Havoc!: Thoughts on the Destruction of Mhlakaza." Special issue on the Xhosa cattle-killing, *African Studies* 67, no. 2 (2008): 233–56.

——. *The Dead Will Arise: Nongqawuse and the Great Xhosa Cattle-Killing Movement of 1856–7.* Johannesburg: Ravan/Bloomington: Indiana University Press, 1989.

——. "The Lovedale Press: Literature for the Bantu Revisited." *English in Africa* 7 (1980): 71–85.

——. "Nxele, Ntsikana and the Origins of the Xhosa Religious Reaction." *Journal of African History* 20, no. 1 (1979): 51–61.

——. "Suicide or Genocide? Xhosa Perceptions of the Nongqawuse Catastrophe." *Radical History Review* 46–47 (1990): 47–57.

Pensky, Max. "Method and Time: Benjamin's Dialectical Images." In *The Cambridge Companion to Walter Benjamin*, edited by David Ferris, 177–98. Cambridge: Cambridge University Press, 2004.

Peterson, Bhekizizwe. "Apartheid and the Political Imagination in Black South African Theatre." In "Performance and Popular Culture." Special issue, *Journal of Southern African Studies* 16, no. 2: (1990): 229–45.

———. *Monarchs, Missionaries and African Intellectuals: African Theatre and the Unmaking of Colonial Marginality.* Trenton: Africa World, 2000.

Phillips, Caryl. *Crossing the River.* London: Bloomsbury, 1993.

Plaatje, Solomon T. *Mhudi, an Epic of South African Native Life a Hundred Years Ago.* New York: Negro Universities Press, 1970. First published 1930 by Lovedale.

———. *Native Life in South Africa: Before and Since the European War and the Boer Rebellion.* 1916. Reprint, Johannesburg: Ravan, 1982.

Poland, Marguerite, and David Hammond-Tooke. *The Abundant Herds: A Celebration of the Cattle of the Zulu People.* Artwork by Leigh Voigt. Vlaeberg: Fernwood, 2003.

Pringle, Thomas. *Poems Illustrative of South Africa; African Sketches: Part One.* 1834. Reprint edited with an introduction by John Robert Wahl. Cape Town: Struik, 1970.

Provisional Committee of the Congress Youth League. "Congress Youth League Manifesto [1944]." In Karis et al., vol. 2 of *From Protest to Challenge,* 300–8.

Radebe, Jeff. "The South African Government's Vision for the African Renaissance and African Unity: Contextualising the Policy." Keynote address, African Unity and Revival: A Vision for the Millenium Conference, Moscow, October 2, 2001. Http://www.sacp.org. za/main.php?include=docs/sp/2001/sp1002.html.

Ranger, T. O. "Connections between 'Primary Resistance' Movements and Modern Mass Nationalism in East and Central Africa." *Journal of African History* 9, nos. 3 and 4 (1968): 437–53, 631–41.

———. *Revolt in Southern Rhodesia, 1986–97: A Study in African Resistance.* Evanston, IL: Northwestern University Press, 1967.

———. "Towards a Usable African Past." In *African Studies since 1945: A Tribute to Basil Davidson,* edited by Basil Davidson and Christopher Fyfe, 17–30. London: Longman, 1976.

Recollections of a Visit to British Kaffraria. London: Society for Promoting Christian Knowledge, Committee of General Literature and Education, 1873.

Rees, William Lee, and Lily Rees. *The Life and Times of Sir George Grey, K.C.B.* London: Hutchinson, 1898.

Renton, David. "What Future for the Past in the New South Africa?" *Soundings* 14 (2000): 31–38.

Republic of Transkei, The. Johannesburg: C. van Rensburg, 1976.

Restitution of Land Rights Act, Act 22 of 1994. November 25, 1994. http://www.info.gov.za/ restitution.

Reyburn, H. A. "The Missionary as Rain-Maker." *Critic,* 1933, 146–53.

Ricoeur, Paul. *Time and Narrative.* Vol. 3. Chicago: University of Chicago Press, 1984.

Ross, Brownlee John, and R. H. W. Shepherd. *Brownlee J. Ross: His Ancestry and Some Writings.* Lovedale: Lovedale, 1948.

Ross, Bryce. Letter to John Ross. August 9, 1856. MS 7666, Lovedale Collection. Cory Library for Historical Research, Rhodes University, Grahamstown.

Rostron, Frank. "Presenting South Africa to the World's Cinema Audiences: The Story of Leon Schauder, Port Elizabeth's Young Producer-Prodigy." *Outspan,* June 28, 1940, 13, 15, 77.

Rubusana, W. B. *Zemk'inkomo magwalandini.* 2nd ed. London: Frome Somerset; printed for the author by Butler & Tanner, 1911.

Sachs, Albie. "A New Court for a New Democracy: Art, Memory, and Human Rights Come Together in Building South Africa's Constitutional Court." Marc and Constance Jacobson Lecture, University of Michigan Institute for the Humanities, Ann Arbor, January 29, 2004.

———. "Preparing Ourselves for Freedom." In Attridge and Jolly, *Writing South Africa,* 239–48.

Said, Edward W. *Orientalism.* New York: Vintage, 1979.

Samuel, Raphael. *Theatres of Memory.* London: Verso, 1994.

Samuelson, Meg. "Historical Time, Gender, and the 'New' South Africa in Zakes Mda's *The Heart of Redness.*" *Sephis e-magazine* 2, no. 2 (2006): 15–18. Http://www.sephis.org/pdf/ezine5.pdf

———. "Reading the Maternal Voice in Sindiwe Magona's *To My Children's Children* and *Mother to Mother.*" *Modern Fiction Studies* 46, no. 1 (2000): 227–45.

———. *Remembering the Nation, Dismembering Women? Stories of the South African Transition.* Durban: University of KwaZuluN Natal Press, 2007.

Sanders, Mark. *Complicities: The Intellectual and Apartheid.* Durham, NC: Duke University Press, 2002.

Sandwith, Corinne. "Dora Taylor: South African Marxist." *English in Africa* 29, no. 2 (2002): 5–29.

Saunders, Christopher C. *The Making of the South African Past: Major Historians on Race and Class.* Totowa: Barnes & Noble, 1988.

———. Commentaries and Notes in *Reminiscences of Kaffir Life and History, and Other Papers,* by Charles Pacalt Brownlee, edited by Christopher C. Saunders, 385–428. Pietermaritzburg: University of Natal Press, 1977.

Saverese, Nicole, and Richard Fowler. "1931: Antonin Artaud Sees Balinese Theater at the Paris Colonial Exhibition." *Drama Review* 45, no. 3 (2001): 51–77.

Scheub, Harold. *The Tongue Is Fire: South African Storytellers and Apartheid.* Madison: University of Wisconsin Press, 1996.

———. "Xhosa Oral and Literary Traditions." In *Literatures in African Languages: Theoretical Issues and Sample Surveys,* edited by B. W. Andrzejewski, Stanisław Piłaszewicz, and Witold Tyloch, 529–608. Cambridge: Cambridge University Press, 1985.

Schwarz-Bart, Simone, and Andre Schwarz-Bart. *In Praise of Black Women.* Madison: University of Wisconsin Press, 2001.

Scott, James C. *Weapons of the Weak: Everyday Forms of Peasant Resistance.* New Haven, CT: Yale University Press, 1985.

Sekyi-Otu, Ato. *Fanon's Dialectic of Experience.* Cambridge, MA: Harvard University Press, 1996.

Sepamla, Sydney Sipho. *A Ride on the Whirlwind: A Novel.* London: Heinemann / London: Readers International, 1986.

———. "To Makana and Nongqawuse." *The Blues Is You in Me.* Johannesburg: Ad. Donker, 1976.

Shepherd, R. H. W. *Bantu Literature and Life.* Lovedale: Lovedale, 1955.

———, ed. *Conferences on Literature for the Southern African Bantu.* Alice: Lovedale, 1936.

———. Letter to H. I. E. Dhlomo. May 19, 1938. In MS file of "The Girl Who Killed to Save" by H. I. E. Dhlomo. Vol. PR16,309a, Lovedale Collection. Cory Library for Historical Research, Rhodes University, Grahamstown, South Africa.

———. *Lovedale and Literature for the Bantu: A Brief History and a Forecast.* 1945. Reprint, New York: Negro Universities Press, 1970.

———. *Lovedale, South Africa: The Story of a Century, 1841–1941.* Lovedale: Lovedale, 1940.

Shepperson, George. "Notes on Negro American Influences on the Emergence of African Nationalism." *Journal of African History* 1, no. 2 (1960): 299–312.

———. "Nyasaland and the Millennium." In *Millennial Dreams in Action; Essays in Comparative Study,* edited by Sylvia L. Thrupp, 144–59. The Hague: Mouton, 1962.

Shineberg, Dorothy. "Guns and Men in Melanesia." *Journal of Pacific History* 6 (1971): 61–82.

Shum, Matthew. "Unsettling Settler Identity: Thomas Pringle's Troubled Landscapes." *English in Africa* 33, no. 2 (2006): 21–44.

Silko, Leslie Marmon. *Almanac of the Dead: A Novel.* New York: Simon & Schuster, 1991.

Singh, K. S. *Birsa Munda and His Movement, 1874–1901: A Study of a Millenarian Movement in Chotanagpur.* Calcutta: Oxford University Press, 1983.

Sirayi, G. T. "The African Perspective of the 1856/1857 Cattle-Killing Movement." *South African Literature in African Languages* 11, no. 1 (1991): 40–45.

Skota, T. D. Mweli. *The African Yearly Register: Being an Illustrated National Biographical Dictionary (Who's Who) of Black Folks in Africa.* Johannesburg: Esson, 1930.

Slater, Francis Carey. *The Centenary Book of South African Verse (1820–1925).* New York: Green, 1925.

Smit, Johannes A., Johan van Wyk, and Jean-Philippe Wade. *Rethinking South African Literary History.* Durban: Y Press, 1996.

Soga, J. H. *The Ama-Xosa: Life and Customs.* Lovedale: Lovedale, 1932.

———. *The South-Eastern Bantu (Abe-Nguni, Aba-Mbo, Ama-Lala).* Special issue of *Bantu Studies.* Supplement, 4. Johannesburg: Witwatersrand University Press, 1930.

Soga, Tiyo. *The Journal and Selected Writings of the Reverend Tiyo Soga,* edited by Donovan Williams. Cape Town: published for Rhodes University Grahamstown by A. A. Balkema, 1983.

———. "Manuscript of Original Hymns." MS 8863, Lovedale Collection. Cory Library for Historical Research, Rhodes University, Grahamstown, South Africa.

Sole, Kelwyn. "Political Fiction, Representation and the Canon: The Case of Mtutuzeli Matshoba." In *Apartheid Narratives,* edited by N. Yousaf, 61–80. Amsterdam: Rodopi, 2001.

South African Students Organisation (SASO). SASO Policy Manifesto (July 1971). In Karis et al., vol. 5 of *From Protest to Challenge,* 481–82.

Soyinka, Wole. *The Lion and the Jewel.* London: Oxford University Press, 1963.

Spence, Jonathan D. *God's Chinese Son: The Taiping Heavenly Kingdom of Hong Xiuquan.* New York: Norton, 1996.

Spivak, Gayatri Chakravorty. "Ghostwriting." *Diacritics* 25, no. 2 (1995): 64–84.

Stapleton, Timothy J. "'They No Longer Care for Their Chiefs': Another Look at the Xhosa Cattle-Killing of 1856–1857." *International Journal of African Historical Studies* 24, no. 2 (1991): 383–92.

———. "Reluctant Slaughter: Rethinking Maqoma's Role in the Xhosa Cattle-Killing (1853–1857)." *International Journal of African Historical Studies* 26 no. 2 (1993): 345–69.

Steadman, Ian. "Towards Popular Theatre in South Africa." *Journal of Southern African Studies* 16, no. 2 (1990): 208–28.

Steinbart, Gustav. *The Letters and Journal of Gustav Steinbart.* Vol. 2, *The Journal.* Port Elizabeth: University of Port Elizabeth Press, 1987.

Stephens, Michelle Ann. *Black Empire: The Masculine Global Imaginary of Caribbean Intellectuals in the United States, 1914–1962.* Durham, NC: Duke University Press, 2005.

Stewart, James. *Dawn in the Dark Continent: Or Africa and Its Missions.* Edinburgh: Oliphant, 1903.

Stoler, Ann Laura, and Fred Cooper. "Between Metropole and Colony: Rethinking a Research Agenda." In *Tensions of Empire: Colonial Culture in a Bourgeois World,* edited by Ann Laura Cooper and Fred Stoler, 1–56. Berkeley: University of California Press, 1997.

Stone, Jon R. Introduction to *Expecting Armageddon: Essential Readings in Failed Prophecy,* edited by Jon R. Stone, 1–29. New York: Routledge, 2000.

Street, Brian V. *Cross-Cultural Approaches to Literacy.* Cambridge: Cambridge University Press, 1993.

Stubbs, George. *Anatomy of the Horse.* 1766. Reprint, London: Bracken, 1996.

Sundkler, Bengt. *Bantu Prophets in South Africa.* 2nd ed. London: published for the International African Institute by Oxford University Press, 1961.

Swanepoel, C. F. "Merging African-Language Literature into South African Literary History." In Smit et al., *Rethinking South African Literary History,* 20–30.

Switzer, Les. *South Africa's Alternative Press: Voices of Protest and Resistance, 1880s–1960s.* Cambridge: Cambridge University Press, 1997.

Tambo, Oliver, and Vusumzi L. Make. Statement on behalf of the South Africa United Front. New York: 1960. Http://www.anc.org.za/ancdocs/pr/1960s/pr600000.html.

Taylor, Dora. "Africans Speak." *Trek*, August 28, 1942. Reprinted in *English in Africa* 29, no. 2 (2002): 66–69.

———. "They Speak of Africa III" *Trek*, June 19, 1942. Reprinted in *English in Africa* 29, no. 2 (2002): 50–54.

Terdiman, Richard. *Present Past: Modernity and the Memory Crisis.* Ithaca, NY: Cornell University Press, 1993.

Theal, George McCall. *Compendium of the History and Geography of South Africa.* Alice: Lovedale, 1878.

———. *History of South Africa, from 1795–1872.* London: Allen, 1915.

———. *Progress of South Africa in the Century.* Toronto: Linscott / London: Chambers, 1902.

———. *South Africa: The Union of South Africa, Rhodesia, and All Other Territories South of the Zambesi.* 8th ed. Vol. 38. London: Unwin, 1917.

Thompson, Leonard M. *The Political Mythology of Apartheid.* New Haven, CT: Yale University Press, 1985.

Tiedemann, Rolf. "Historical Materialism or Political Messianism? An Interpretation of the Theses 'On the Concept of History.'" *Philosophical Forum* 15, no. 1–2 (1984): 71–104.

Transkei Independence. Durban: Black Community Programmes, 1976.

Transkei Independence Anniversary Souvenir. Umtata: Clark, 1977.

Troup, Freda. *South Africa: An Historical Introduction.* London: Eyre Methuen, 1972.

Truth and Reconciliation Commission. *Truth and Reconciliation Commission of South Africa Report.* Cape Town: The Commission / New York: Macmillan Reference, Grove's Dictionaries, 1999.

Tutu, Desmond. "The Question of South Africa." *Africa Report* 30 (1985): 50–52.

Udechukwu, Obiora. "Interview with Chinua Achebe." In *The Short Century: Independence and Liberation Movements in Africa, 1945–1994,* edited by Okwui Enwezor, Chinua Achebe, and Museum Villa Stuck, 314–19. Munich: Prestel, 2001.

Van Calker, Ernst. *A Century of Moravian Mission Work in the Eastern Cape Colony and Transkei, 1828–1928.* In Keegan, *Moravians,* 1–143.

Van Rooyen, Francesca. "A Poet of the Nation." *Argus,* May 26, 1994, 14.

Van Wyk, Johan. "Towards a South African Literary History." In Smit et al., *Rethinking South African Literary History,* 31–39.

Van Wyk Smith, Malvern. "Origins Revisited: Dissent and Dialectic in Early South African Writing." In *Constructing South African Literary History,* edited by Elmar Lehmann, Erhard Reckwitz, and Lucia Vennarini, 11–32. Essen, Germany: Verlag die Blaue Eule, 2000.

———. "White Writing/Writing Black: The Anxiety of Non-Influence." In Smit et al., *Rethinking South African Literary History,* 71–84.

Vaughan, Michael. "Can the Writer Become a Storyteller? A Critique of the Stories of Mtutuzeli Matshoba." *Staffrider* 4, no. 3 (1981): 45–47.

———. "Literature and Populism in South Africa: Reflections on the Ideology of Staffrider." In *Marxism and African Literature,* edited by Georg M. Gugelberger, 195–220. London: Currey, 1985.

———. "Storytelling and Politics in Fiction." In *Rendering Things Visible: Essays on South African Literary Culture,* edited by Martin Trump, 186–204. Athens: Ohio University Press, 1990.

Verdal, Garth. "Praise-Singers in Parliament a 'Culture Shock' to New Minister." *Argus,* May 26, 1994, 14.

Vilakazi, B. Wallet. *Zulu Horizons*. Translated by Florence Louie Friedman, D. Mck. Malcolm, and J. Mandlenkosi Sikakana. Johannesburg: Witwatersrand University Press, 1973.

Visser, N. W. "H. I. E. Dhlomo (1903–1956): The Re-Emergence of an African Writer." *English in Africa* 1, no. 2 (1974): 1–10.

Viswanathan, Gauri. *Outside the Fold: Conversion, Modernity, and Belief*. Princeton, NJ: Princeton University Press, 1998.

———. "Secularism in the Framework of Heterodoxy." *PMLA* 123, no. 2 (2008): 466–76.

Voss, A. E. "Reading and Writing in the New South Africa." *Current Writing* 4 (1992): 1–9.

———. "Sol Plaatje, the Eighteenth Century, and South African Cultural Memory." *English in Africa* 21, nos. 1 and 2 (1994): 59–75.

Voss, Tony. "Emerging Literature: The Literature of Emergency." *Jo-Fo* 1 (1990): 25–34.

Wade, Jean-Philippe. "Disclosing the Nation." In Smit et al., *Rethinking South African Literary History*, 1–9.

Wagstrom, Thor A. "Daniel's Book Unsealed: Protestant Missionaries and Indigenous Prophecies in Nineteenth Century New Zealand and South Africa." PhD diss., University of Nebraska, 1999.

Wallace, Anthony F. C. "Revitalization Movements." *American Anthropologist* 58, no. 2 (1956): 264–81.

Wästberg, Per, ed. *The Writer in Modern Africa*. Uppsala, Nord. Afrikainst / Stockholm, Almqvist and Wiksell, 1968.

Waters, M. W. *Cameos from the Kraal, with Illustrations by a Raw Native*. Lovedale: Lovedale, 1927.

———. *Fairy Tales Told by Nontsomi*. London: Longman, 1927.

———. *The Light—Ukukanya: A Drama of the History of the Bantus, 1600–1924*. Lovedale: Lovedale Institution Press, 1925.

———. *U-Nongqause: Isiganeko so Ku Xelwa Kwe Nkomo 1857*. Cape Town: Maskew Miller, 1924.

Wenzel, Jennifer. "The Pastoral Promise and the Political Imperative: The Plaasroman Tradition in an Era of Land Reform." In "South African Fiction after Apartheid." Special issue, *Modern Fiction Studies* 46, no. 1 (2000): 90–113.

———. "Remembering the Past's Future: Anti-Imperialist Nostalgia and Some Versions of the Third World." *Cultural Critique* 62 (Winter 2006): 1–29.

When We Were Kings. DVD. Directed by Leon Gast. Polygram Video, 2002.

White, Hayden V. *The Content of the Form: Narrative Discourse and Historical Representation*. Baltimore: John Hopkins University Press, 1987.

———. *Tropics of Discourse: Essays in Cultural Criticism*. Baltimore: Johns Hopkins University Press, 1985.

Wideman, John Edgar. "Ascent by Balloon from the Yard of Walnut Street Jail." *Callaloo* 19, no. 1 (1996): 1–5.

———. *The Cattle Killing*. Boston: Houghton, 1996.

———. "Interview with Laura Miller." *Salon*, 1996. Http://www.salon.com/nov96/interview961111.html.

Willan, Brian. Introduction to *Native Life in South Africa: Before and Since the European War and the Boer Rebellion*, by Sol T. Plaatje, edited by Brian Willan, 1–14. Athens: Ohio University Press, 1991.

———. *Sol Plaatje, South African Nationalist, 1876–1932*. Berkeley: University of California Press, 1984.

Williams, Donovan. "The Indian Mutiny of 1857 and the Cape Colony." *Historia* 32, nos. 1 and 2 (1987): 55–69, 56–67.

———. "The Missionaries on the Eastern Frontier of the Cape Colony, 1799–1853." PhD diss., University of the Witwatersrand, 1959.

———. *Umfundisi: A Biography of Tiyo Soga, 1829–1871*. Lovedale: Lovedale, 1978.

———. *When Races Meet: The Life and Times of William Ritchie Thomson, Glasgow Society Missionary, Government Agent and Dutch Reformed Church Minister, 1794–1891*. Johannesburg: A. P. B., 1967.

Wilson, Bryan R. *Magic and the Millennium: A Sociological Study of Religious Movements of Protest among Tribal and Third-World Peoples*. New York: Harper, 1973.

Wilson, Henry S. *Origins of West African Nationalism*. New York: Macmillan, 1969.

Worsley, Peter. *The Trumpet Shall Sound: A Study of "Cargo" Cults in Melanesia*. New York: Schocken, 1968.

Zachernuk, Philip S. *Colonial Subjects: An African Intelligentsia and Atlantic Ideas*. Charlottesville: University Press of Virginia, 2000.

Zamora, Lois Parkinson. *The Apocalyptic Vision in America: Interdisciplinary Essays on Myth and Culture*. Bowling Green, Ohio: Bowling Green University Popular Press, 1982.

INDEX

Page numbers for figures are in italic.